THE THERAPEUTIC RELATIONSHIP IN COGNITIVE BEHAVIOURAL THERAPY

Sara Miller McCune founded SAGE Publishing in 1965 to support the dissemination of usable knowledge and educate a global community. SAGE publishes more than 1000 journals and over 800 new books each year, spanning a wide range of subject areas. Our growing selection of library products includes archives, data, case studies and video. SAGE remains majority owned by our founder and after her lifetime will become owned by a charitable trust that secures the company's continued independence.

Los Angeles | London | New Delhi | Singapore | Washington DC | Melbourne

THE THERAPEUTIC RELATIONSHIP IN COGNITIVE BEHAVIOURAL THERAPY

EDITED BY
STIRLING MOOREY &
ANNA LAVENDER

SAGE

Los Angeles | London | New Delhi
Singapore | Washington DC | Melbourne

SAGE

Los Angeles | London | New Delhi
Singapore | Washington DC | Melbourne

SAGE Publications Ltd
1 Oliver's Yard
55 City Road
London EC1Y 1SP

SAGE Publications Inc.
2455 Teller Road
Thousand Oaks, California 91320

SAGE Publications India Pvt Ltd
B 1/I 1 Mohan Cooperative Industrial Area
Mathura Road
New Delhi 110 044

SAGE Publications Asia-Pacific Pte Ltd
3 Church Street
#10-04 Samsung Hub
Singapore 049483

Editor: Susannah Trefgarne
Editorial Assistant: Talulah Hall
Production Editor: Rudrani Mukherjee
Copyeditor: Sunrise Setting
Proofreader: Derek Markham
Indexer: Cathryn Pritchard
Marketing Manager: Camille Richmond
Cover Design: Sheila Tong
Typeset by: C&M Digitals (P) Ltd, Chennai, India

First published in 2019

Library of Congress Control Number: 2018941253

British Library Cataloguing in Publication data

A catalogue record for this book is available from the British Library

ISBN 978-1-5264-1949-1 (HC)
ISBN 978-1-5264-1950-7 (PBK)

CONTENTS

LIST OF FIGURES AND TABLES

NOTES ON THE EDITORS AND CONTRIBUTORS

THE EDITORS

Dr Stirling Moorey is a Consultant Psychiatrist in CBT at the South London and Maudsley NHS Foundation Trust and Visiting Senior Lecturer in Psychiatry at the Institute of Psychiatry, Psychology & Neuroscience. He was formerly Professional Head of Psychotherapy for SLaM. He has trained in Cognitive Analytic Therapy and Schema Therapy and is also a Mindfulness Based Cognitive Therapy teacher. He has been training mental health professionals in CBT for 30 years and regularly gives workshops on managing complexity, adversity and interpersonal process in CBT. His research interests are in the application of CBT to cancer and physical illness.

Dr Anna Lavender is a Principal Clinical Psychologist at South London and Maudsley NHS Foundation Trust. She has 20 years' experience in CBT treatment and supervision and is also a qualified Schema Therapist and supervisor. She teaches training psychologists on interpersonal processes in therapy and has worked extensively with individuals with personality disorders. She is joint UK lead on an international trial of the use of Group Schema Therapy with individuals with Borderline Personality Disorder.

THE CONTRIBUTORS

Dr Patricia d'Ardenne is a Consultant Clinical Psychologist who has established and directed NHS services as well as working across Europe, the USA and East Africa. She has researched and published widely in transcultural practice. She currently works in a Health Partnership between the East London NHS Foundation Trust and Butabika Hospital in Kampala, Uganda.

Kathy Burn is a Clinical Nurse Specialist in Palliative Care who then trained as a Cognitive Behavioural Therapist at The Institute of Psychiatry. She set up and leads the CBT clinical and educational services at St Christopher's Hospice, seeing patients, supervising staff and delivering accredited courses in CBT 'first aid' for physical health professionals. She is also a CBT supervisor on the Pg Dip in CBT at the Institute of Psychiatry. She sees patients with long-term, life-limiting conditions and at the end of life.

Suzanne Byrne is a Course Co-Director in CBT, at the Institute of Psychiatry, Psychology and Neuroscience (IoPPN), Kings College London. She has worked as a CBT therapist for the past 17 years and been involved in teaching and supervising CBT therapists for the past 13 years. Alongside her teaching role Suzanne sees patients for CBT in the Centre for Anxiety Disorders and Trauma (CADAT), South London and Maudsley NHS Foundation Trust London.

Professor Trudie Chalder is Professor of Cognitive Behavioural Psychotherapy at King's College London. She has worked as a clinician and a researcher in the area of long-term conditions and medically unexplained symptoms for about 30 years. She develops specific cognitive behavioural models for understanding and treating these conditions and evaluates the approaches within the context of randomised controlled trials in primary and secondary care. Her research involves investigating not only whether treatment works in the context of gold standard randomised controlled trials but how, and for whom, it works. Her work spans adolescents and adults.

Dr Annis Cohen is a Principal Clinical Psychologist at the Psychological Interventions Clinic for Outpatients with Psychosis, where she provides specialist CBT for individuals with psychosis. She is also the joint course lead on the Post Graduate Diploma in CBT for Psychosis programme at the Institute of Psychiatry, Psychology & Neuroscience, King's College London.

Dr Marion Cuddy is a Clinical Psychologist specialising in cognitive behavioural interventions for individuals and couples. She currently works at the Maudsley Hospital and King's College London. She supervises on CBT and behavioural couple therapy postgraduate training programmes and is also conducting research into couple-based interventions for people with physical health problems.

Professor Mark Freeston is a career clinical academic who has been developing, testing and disseminating cognitive behavioural treatments for anxiety and related disorders. He was a member of the team that developed the Intolerance of Uncertainty model and treatment of GAD and worry at Université Laval in Québec, Canada in the early 1990s. In the last ten years, Mark has led a research programme at Newcastle University that promotes the idea that intolerance of uncertainty is both specific to GAD, where it finds its strongest expression, as well as a transdiagnostic issue across anxiety disorders and beyond.

Dr Charlotte Gardner is a Clinical Psychologist at the South London & Maudsley NHS Foundation Trust. She offers specialist Older Adult placements and teaches CBT with older people to trainee psychologists studying at the IoPPN. She has worked within the older adult speciality for 8 years.

Dr Nick Grey is a Consultant Clinical Psychologist and Clinical Research and Training Fellow at Sussex Partnership NHS Foundation Trust (SPFT) and University of Sussex. He has worked clinically across primary, secondary and tertiary care. He is a member of the Wellcome Trust Anxiety Disorders Group led by David Clark and Anke Ehlers. He is a Fellow of the British Association of Behavioural and Cognitive Psychotherapies and is an accredited CBT practitioner, supervisor and trainer.

Susan Harrison trained as a Psychological Wellbeing Practitioner following careers in advocacy in the third sector and a pastoral role in secondary schools. With three years' experience in North Tyneside Talking Therapies, an IAPT service with a very diverse clientele, she is very familiar with worry and GAD, alongside a range of other problems. Susan recognises the difficulties of working with these problems in the context of time-limited low intensity interventions.

Dr Jennifer House is a Clinical Psychologist and CBT Therapist who has a special interest in working with people with PTSD. She has worked in specialist PTSD services in Berkshire and London, delivering assessments and trauma-focused CBT.

Dr Rebecca Kelly is a Principal Clinical Psychologist working at the Psychological Interventions Clinic for Outpatients with Psychosis, where she provides therapy and expert training and supervision in CBT for psychosis and bipolar disorder. She is also a visiting researcher at the Institute of Psychiatry, Psychology & Neuroscience, King's College London, where she supervises research into psychological therapy approaches to psychosis, bipolar disorder and trauma, and an honorary teaching fellow at University College London.

Dr David McCormack is a Clinical Psychologist at the Maudsley Hospital, London and a lecturer and clinical tutor on the Doctorate in Clinical Psychology programme at Queen's University Belfast. He has an interest in CBT, trauma and unexplained and persistent symptoms. For the past three years, he has been working on randomised controlled trials examining the effectiveness of CBT for persistent physical symptoms.

Dr Kevin Meares, although recognised for his expertise in the treatment of complex trauma, has a long standing interest in understanding and treating GAD, both as the main problem but also as a comorbid difficulty across a range of presenting problems. He has co-authored a self-help book and a therapist manual for the treatment of GAD and worry. Kevin works in the NHS at the Newcastle Centre for Behavioural and Cognitive Therapies, where he provides therapy and supervision. He is recognised for his training in CBT, generally, and for trauma and GAD, in particular.

Dr Emmanuelle Peters is Reader in Clinical Psychology at the Institute of Psychiatry, Psychology & Neuroscience (IOPPN), King's College London, and an Honorary Consultant Clinical Psychologist for the South London and Maudsley NHS Foundation Trust (SLaM), where she is the director of an award-winning specialist outpatients psychological therapies service for psychosis (PICuP). She has specialised in psychosis for the past 25 years as a clinician, researcher and trainer. Her research interests include the continuum view of psychosis, cognitive models of psychotic symptoms and CBT for psychosis.

Professor Ulrike Schmidt is Professor of Eating Disorders at King's College London and a Consultant Psychiatrist at the Maudsley Hospital. Her research focuses on the development of new treatments, including psychotherapies, those using new technologies and a range of targeted brain-directed treatments.

Dr Michael Scott is a Consultant Psychologist, working in Liverpool and author of 12 books including *Simply Effective Group CBT*, published in 2011 by Routledge and *Brief Group Counselling* published by Wiley in 1998. He regularly gives workshops on group CBT and is Chair of a proposed BABCP Special Interest Group on Group CBT. His other main interest is post *Traumatic Stress* disorder and in 2015 he edited Traumatic Stress a 4-Volume work published by Sage.

Dr Helen Startup is a Consultant Clinical Psychologist and Senior Research Fellow with Sussex Partnership NHS Foundation Trust. She is an accredited advanced level Schema Therapist and Cognitive Behavioural Therapist. She is co-Director of Schema Therapy School, which is a training organisation offering schema therapy trainings and events in London and along the South Coast.

Dr Richard Stott is a Clinical Psychologist with particular expertise in anxiety disorders and the use of technology-based interventions. He has contributed to the development, evaluation and dissemination of evidence-based psychological treatments for anxiety disorders and trauma, including novel online treatments. He is currently Senior Lecturer in e-Mental Health at King's College London.

Dr Lorna Taylor, PhD, DClinPsy, is a highly specialist Clinical Psychologist working with adolescents displaying high-risk behaviours and neurodevelopmental difficulties. She works clinically within South London and Maudsley NHS Foundation Trust and is affiliated with the Institute of Psychiatry, Psychology & Neuroscience, King's College London.

Dr Troy Tranah BSc, MSc, PhD, is Head of Child and Adolescent Psychology and Psychological Therapies for The South London and Maudsley NHS Foundation Trust. Dr Tranah is a Consultant Psychologist and an Honorary Lecturer at King's College London. Dr Tranah has worked with children and adolescents for over 20 years.

Professor David Veale is a Consultant Psychiatrist in Cognitive Behaviour Therapies at the South London and Maudsley NHS Trust (SLaM) and Institute of Psychiatry, Psychology & Neuroscience, King's College London. He leads a national outpatient and inpatient service for people with severe treatment refractory OCD and BDD at the SLaM and the Priory Hospital North London. He is a member of the group revising the diagnostic guidelines for ICD11 for Obsessive Compulsive and Related Disorders for the World Health Organization. He was a member of the group that wrote the NICE guidelines on OCD and BDD in 2006 and chaired the NICE Evidence Update on OCD in 2013. He is a Past President of the British Association of Behavioural and Cognitive Psychotherapies. He is a current Trustee of the charities OCD Action and the BDD Foundation.

Deborah Walker is a Consultant Psychotherapist (CBT) at the South London & Maudsley NHS Foundation Trust and is clinical lead of the older adult Psychology & Psychotherapy Service. She also lectures on CBT with older people to trainee psychologists studying at the IoPPN. She has worked within the older adult speciality for 28 years and has BABCP accreditation.

Graeme Whitfield, MB ChB, MSC, MRCPsych, is a Consultant Psychiatrist in Psychotherapy (CBT). He trained in Leeds and worked until recently in the secondary care CBT department in Leicester, which provides the majority of its CBT in a group format. He has published in the areas of self-help and group CBT and has written a textbook on the basics of CBT targeted at psychiatrists in training (Cognitive Behavioural Therapy Explained). He is a past governing board member of the British Association for Behavioural and Cognitive Psychotherapies (BABCP).

Lisa Williams is the Deputy Manager at the Anxiety Disorder Residential Unit, Bethlem Royal Hospital, South London and Maudsley NHS Trust. In her clinical work, she uses both CBT and Compassion Focused Therapy with people suffering anxiety disorders, especially OCD, BDD, emetaphobia and PTSD. Lisa is an honorary lecturer on the Post Graduate Diploma in CBT at Salomons, Canterbury Christ Church University. Lisa is the chair of the BABCP Branch Liaison committee and regularly presents to audiences on Compassion Focused Therapy and CBT.

Kerry Young is a Consultant Clinical Psychologist and Clinical Lead of the Woodfield Trauma Service in London (Central and Northwest London NHS Foundation Trust). This is an innovative service offering evidence-based cognitive behavioural treatment to refugees and asylum seekers suffering from PTSD. Kerry also works at the Oxford Rose Clinic, a centre for the medical and psychological treatment of women who have experienced female genital mutilation (FGM). She has worked for 21 years in trauma and has written and lectured widely on how to treat simple and Complex PTSD, working with mental imagery, and how to help traumatised asylum seekers and refugees.

ACKNOWLEDGEMENTS

In compiling an edited volume on the current status of the therapeutic relationship in CBT, we recognise our debt to our teachers and supervisors in CBT and Schema Therapy who have shaped our practice. AT Beck's innovation of 'collaborative empiricism' is the foundation of the whole cognitive approach. In our consideration of 'transference' and 'countertransference' in CBT, we are indebted to the work of Robert Leahy but also to insights from Anthony Ryle, whose Cognitive Analytic Therapy has informed the particular view of interpersonal schemas presented in some of the chapters. We would also like to thank the colleagues who have contributed to this book. Reading their chapters has been a fascinating experience, which has enriched our understanding of areas less familiar to us and given us much to think about.

The team at Sage, Talulah Hall and Susannah Trefgarne, have been supportive, flexible and encouraging throughout, and for this we thank them too. And, of course, our long-enduring families, who perhaps recognised before us that 'It's only an edited book' does not quite do justice to the time and effort this enterprise entails.

Above all, we would like to thank our patients, who have taught us so much about the therapeutic relationship over the years. We feel privileged to have had the opportunity to work therapeutically with individuals from whom we have learned so much.

Stirling Moorey and Anna Lavender

FOREWORD

Did you know that the original 'bible' of CBT, *Cognitive Therapy of Depression,* devoted an *entire chapter* to the therapeutic relationship? Published by Aaron Beck and colleagues in 1979, the chapter asserts that a strong therapeutic alliance is an essential part of treatment. Therefore, it is mystifying to me when I learn that some professionals in the mental health field believe that CBT does not consider the relationship to be important.

Fortunately, this first-rate volume, edited by Stirling Moorey and Anna Lavender, provides practical, specific and clinically useful knowledge. Both new and experienced therapists will appreciate the skills and tips from leading expert practitioners in their fields. Their recommendations are firmly based on the latest research on the therapeutic relationship, including the efficacy of basic counselling skills and the effect of the alliance on treatment outcome.

A number of chapters focus on specific disorders. A hallmark of CBT is the underlying cognitive formulation for each disorder, including mechanisms of action, central beliefs and coping behaviours. This formulation becomes the basis of treatment. Another hallmark is the individual conceptualisation for each patient, identifying the specific cognitions and coping strategies that are most important for that person. The disorder-focused chapters in this book use the same approach, as it applies to the therapeutic relationship. While there are some commonalities of conceptualisation and principles of treatment to develop and maintain a strong alliance across disorders, populations and settings, there are also important differences. The conceptualisation becomes even more important when there is a therapeutic rupture. Repairing ruptures often requires that therapists reflect on their own beliefs and use creativity to get the relationship back on track.

In the final sections of the book, various authors cover the therapeutic relationship when working with children and adolescents, older adults and minority ethnic groups. Group CBT and couples CBT are also included, along with a final chapter on supervision.

It is relatively easy to develop the relationship with 'easy' patients. As I describe in our training programmes, it is important to be a nice human being in the room, to treat the patient the way you would like to be treated if *you* were a patient, to remember that (many) patients are supposed to be difficult (that's why they're patients) and to create an atmosphere that patients perceive as safe. These guidelines apply to every patient at every session.

Some patients pose unique challenges to the therapeutic relationship. There is much to be learned from studying the relationship in therapy and from reading about how experienced clinicians conceptualise and work with relationship issues in their particular area of expertise. I predict that reading this book will deepen your understanding of the therapeutic process and assist you in building stronger and more effective relationships with your patients.

Judith S Beck, PhD
President, Beck Institute for Cognitive Behavior Therapy
Clinical Professor of Psychology in Psychiatry, University of Pennsylvania

INTRODUCTION

STIRLING MOOREY AND ANNA LAVENDER

Why should the cognitive behaviour therapist be interested in the therapeutic relationship? Isn't it enough to competently deliver an evidence-based protocol? Establishing rapport and collaboration is important, but don't we run the risk of deviating from the clear problem-focused goals of CBT if we spend time exploring the therapist–client interaction? These may be some of the concerns that have led to the therapeutic relationship receiving far less attention than many other aspects of CBT.

Historically, behaviour therapists and cognitive therapists like Beck and Ellis wanted to emphasise how their approach was fundamentally different from the dominant schools of the day. Person-centred and Psychodynamic psychotherapies both put the relationship at the heart of their enterprise. The new boys in town wanted to show that it was possible to bring about change without focusing exclusively on what was going on between therapist and client. Beck (personal communication) talks about how there was a fundamental shift in emphasis when therapists found that attending to presenting problems could effect improvement without attention to the underlying personality.

So, CBT progressed very successfully without paying too much attention to the therapeutic relationship, other than recognising that therapist characteristics such as warmth, genuineness and empathy were necessary but not sufficient conditions for good outcomes. This is an oversimplification because there has always been a recognition of the need to build rapport and establish a collaborative partnership for CBT to work. In texts on CBT, reference to the relationship is generally addressed in a single chapter or can be found scattered through discussions of managing difficulties in CBT. Books that have been dedicated to the therapeutic relationship in CBT have looked at the relationship across disorders but have not addressed the particular issues that arise in different disorders.

Perhaps the main impetus for an interest in what goes on between therapist and client in the therapy session has been the increased complexity of the clients we treat: texts on CBT for personality disorders will always have to pay attention to relationship factors and relationship ruptures. One of the most striking features of CBT as it has developed has been its tendency to devise disorder specific models and manuals which adapt the basic principles for different client groups. We would argue that, just as different disorders and settings require different adaptations of therapy, they also pose unique challenges to the therapeutic relationship. We hope that this book demonstrates that there is much to be learned from spending time thinking about the relationship in therapy and from reading about how experienced clinicians conceptualise and work with relationship issues in their particular areas of expertise.

THE AIM OF THE BOOK

This is a book for clinicians, from the novice therapist in the initial stages of learning CBT to the seasoned CBT therapist seeking to deepen their understanding of the therapeutic relationship in their work. It will also be of interest to clinicians from orientations where the interpersonal focus is central, who may be curious about the relationship in CBT. Our aim has not been to offer an academic text on the subject, although there are reviews of relevant research throughout the book. Our aim has, instead, been to provide a source of practical, specific and clinically useful knowledge, with skills and tips from some of the leading expert practitioners in their fields, on this potentially rich and complex aspect of CBT.

BOOK OUTLINE

The book is divided into four sections. Section One addresses broad issues in the therapeutic relationship in CBT which are relevant for work across disorders, client groups and delivery situations. The concept of the therapeutic relationship is broad and covers various aspects of the therapist-client interaction. Chapter 1 considers the core conditions that some have felt are essential for effective therapy: these include therapist characteristics of warmth, genuineness, empathy and positive regard. It reviews the evidence and looks in more detail at the place of empathy in CBT. Chapter 2 addresses the collaborative aspect of the relationship, referred to by some as the working alliance and known as 'collaborative empiricism' in CBT. How do we build collaborative relationships and manage alliance ruptures, and what is the evidence for the effect of alliance on therapy outcome? Chapter 3 then investigates the interaction between the beliefs of therapists and their clients in the therapy setting, using the concept of interpersonal schemas to demystify 'transference' and 'countertransference' in CBT.

Clients with different disorders present specific needs and challenges within the therapeutic relationship, and this is addressed in Section Two. Common conditions seen in psychiatric and psychological therapy settings each have their own chapter: depression (Stirling Moorey), generalised anxiety disorder (Kevin Meares, Susan Harrison and Mark Freeston), panic, specific phobias, agoraphobia and social anxiety disorder (Richard Stott), obsessive compulsive disorder and body dysmorphic disorder (Lisa Williams and David Veale), posttraumatic stress disorder (Nick Grey, Jennifer House and Kerry Young), psychosis (Rebecca Kelly, Annis Cohen and Emanuelle Peters) and personality disorders (Anna Lavender and Helen Startup). Therapists working in health psychology and psychological medicine settings will find chapters on medically unexplained symptoms (David McCormick and Trudie Chalder), physical illness and palliative care (Stirling Moorey and Kathy Burn) and eating disorders (Ulrike Schmidt).

Section Three looks at the therapeutic relationship with different client groups, including children and adolescents (Lorna Taylor and Troy Tranah), older adults (Deborah Walker and Charlotte Gardner), and transcultural issues in the therapeutic relationship (Patricia d'Ardenne). The book is completed by Section Four, which covers group CBT (Graeme Whitfield and Michael Scott), work with couples (Marion Cuddy) and supervision (Stirling Moorey and Suzanne Byrne).

In each chapter, an overview of the model underpinning treatment is outlined and the role of the therapeutic relationship in this context explored, along with potential challenges within the relationship for each group. Chapters describe how to build a collaborative relationship, how to predict and prevent alliance ruptures and how to manage these when they arise. Negotiating the ending of therapy is also addressed. Case illustrations are used throughout the book, with sample dialogue to show how conversations may play out in therapy. Therapists are encouraged to think about how they would manage some of these scenarios, and there are reflective questions to help them with this practice. Handy 'Therapist tips' summarise good practice.

We are confident that this book will show you that there is more to CBT than simply delivering a protocol: in fact, the therapeutic relationship is at the heart of effective therapy. We also believe that you will find it is possible to attend to relationship issues alongside the more technical aspects of therapy without being drawn away from problems and goals. Helping people with CBT requires us to be sensitive to their needs and to work in partnership. Building and maintaining that partnership involves respect, curiosity and reflection on the therapeutic relationship. Attention to this in therapy can lead to increased effectiveness as therapists and greater fulfilment in our work. We hope this book helps you to deepen your understanding of the therapeutic process and build even more fruitful partnerships with your patients.

PART I

THE THERAPEUTIC RELATIONSHIP IN CBT

1

THE FOUNDATIONS OF THE THERAPEUTIC RELATIONSHIP: THERAPIST CHARACTERISTICS AND CHANGE

STIRLING MOOREY AND ANNA LAVENDER

CHAPTER OVERVIEW

Carl Rogers identified what he thought were the essential characteristics a therapist should embody to promote growth and change - genuineness, positive regard, empathy and unconditional acceptance. Cognitive behaviour therapists have generally accepted that these therapist characteristics form the foundations of the therapeutic relationship. But what is the evidence for an association between these factors and therapy outcome? This chapter reviews the evidence and focuses on empathy, a key requirement for building a collaborative relationship, formulating problems and employing effective change methods. Some of the pitfalls that arise from being too empathic or insufficiently empathic are considered together with ways to help therapists empathise with challenging clients.

CORE CONDITIONS OF PSYCHOLOGICAL THERAPY

In the seminal text on the cognitive therapy of depression, Beck cites warmth, accurate empathy and genuineness as therapist characteristics which facilitate the application of cognitive therapy (Beck et al., 1979: 45): a therapist 'who carefully utilizes these qualities can substantially increase his effectiveness'. The core therapist conditions were identified by Carl Rogers over 60 years ago and the theory remains highly influential. Person-centred therapists believe that these elements are *essential* for change, while therapists from other backgrounds generally see them as *necessary but not sufficient* for therapeutic benefit. According to Rogers, *genuineness* entails the therapist expressing their true feelings, not hiding behind a false professional façade; *positive regard* involves valuing the client and behaving warmly towards them; *empathy* requires the therapist to understand what the client's emotions feel like to them and show that they understand them; and *unconditional regard* means accepting the client regardless of what they say or who they are (Rogers, 1957; Rogers, 1961). Although the primary goal of CBT is to change cognitions and behaviour, these factors may facilitate the process. By acting in a genuine way, the therapist models the normalising rationale of therapy. Valuing the client encourages them to engage in CBT tasks, while the therapist needs *empathy* to understand and support the client in exploring alternative thoughts and strategies. Finally, all therapists would consider it a sine qua non that they do not pass moral judgement on their clients. Keijsers' review of the evidence (Keijsers et al., 2000) found that, while cognitive behavioural therapists were more active and directive and gave higher levels of emotional support than insight-oriented therapists, they were not more superficial, cold or mechanical: they showed as much empathy and unconditional regard as therapists from other traditions. Rogers' core conditions may be part of therapeutic conventional wisdom, but are they really *necessary* even if not sufficient?

HOW IMPORTANT ARE THE CORE CONDITIONS?

Numerous studies have been conducted since Rogers suggested the importance of these therapist behaviours, and there is general consensus that clients with better outcomes rate their clinicians more highly on them (Bozarth et al., 2002; Elliott et al., 2011; Klein et al., 2001). In 2010, a task force commissioned by the American Psychological Association's Divisions of Psychotherapy and Psychology published a review of evidence-based therapy relationships (Norcross and Lambert, 2011). Eminent researchers conducted meta-analyses of studies which had explored the link between the therapeutic relationship and outcome. These studies consistently found an association between Rogers' core characteristics and treatment outcome. Positive regard or non-possessive warmth had a moderate association with outcome (effect size $r = 0.27$ from 18 studies); the only moderator identified was ethnicity: as the percentage of racial/ethnic minority groups in the study increases, the overall effect size also increases. Therapist empathy also showed a moderate association (effect size $r = 0.30$ from 57 studies), which was strongest for client rated empathy. Therapist genuineness/congruence refers to the combination of the therapist's self-awareness and communication of his or her experience to the client: 'the feelings and attitudes which are at the moment flowing within him' (Rogers et al., 1967: 100). The effect size was 0.24 (from 16 studies). Thus, there seems to be a small, but significant, association between these factors and therapy outcome – each factor explaining between 6 and 9% of the variance – which is common across different therapies. One of the main methodological criticisms of these studies, however, is that the evaluation of the therapeutic relationship was often obtained retrospectively, so it is possible that, if your therapist gets you better, you perceive him or her to be more warm, genuine and empathic. This interpretation is reinforced by the finding that it is the client's rating of these factors, rather than therapist or observer rating, that is most strongly correlated with outcome (see Chapters 2 and 4 for evidence that symptom change predates positive rating of alliance in CBT for depression). It has been observed that it is unlikely that 'patient and therapist evaluations of Rogerian therapist variables are directly reflective of the *actual therapist behavior* [our italics] during the treatment' (Keijsers et al., 2000: 270). Although the empirical evidence that Rogerian factors mediate change in CBT is contested, from a clinical and theoretical perspective a case can be made that they enhance the collaborative relationship and encourage the client to participate in therapy. Manipulating how warm therapists are when implementing systematic desensitisation has been shown to improve outcome with snake phobics (Morris and Magrath, 1979), though this does not seem to apply to therapist aided exposure for height phobia (Morris and Suckerman, 1974). Generally, it is felt that if the client perceives the therapist as warm, genuine and understanding, they will be more likely to engage in the tasks of therapy and consequently be more appreciative of the therapist's positive qualities if they recover. In this sense, the core characteristics act to enhance the working alliance. The therapy alliance, and in particular CBT's unique version of it which is termed *collaborative empiricism*, will be covered in depth in Chapter 2. In the rest of this chapter, we will focus on the role of empathy in CBT, because the therapist needs to have an accurate understanding of what the patient is thinking and feeling in order to help them discover alternative perspectives.

EMPATHY

The psychologist Hoffman defines empathy as 'an emotional state triggered by another's emotional state or situation, in which one feels what the other feels or would normally be expected to feel in his situation' (Hoffman, 2008: 440). He identifies five empathy-arousing modes: mimicry, conditioning, direct association, verbally mediated association and perspective taking. The first three are automatic: passive, involuntary and triggered by stimuli. They operate preverbally and are found in infants and primates. The final two modes require language and cognitive processing. Multiple modes can be activated together:

> Facial, vocal, and postural cues are picked up through *mimicry*; situational cues through *conditioning* and *association*; distress expressed orally, in writing, or by someone else can arouse empathy through the cognitive modes. (Hoffman, 2008: 442)

For clinical convenience, we collapse these modes into the categories of emotional and cognitive empathy. *Emotional empathy* (sometimes termed *sympathy*: see, for instance, Gilbert, 1989) refers to the automatic response to another's distress where we feel similar emotions to those experienced by the sufferer. This type of empathy can be evoked without the subject being aware of the goal of the experiments (Blakemore et al., 2005; Singer et al., 2004). It is preverbal and may be associated with so-called *mirror neurones*, which fire when the individual feels an emotion and also when they witness the emotion in someone else (Botvinik et al., 2005; Cheng et al., 2008; Iacoboni and Lenzi, 2002; Iacoboni et al., 2005; Morrison et al., 2004). *Cognitive empathy*, on the other hand, requires a conscious engagement with another's suffering where we put ourselves in their shoes and imagine what it might be like to be experiencing the same emotions. It is therefore effortful and requires a developed theory of mind. The left anterior insula is associated with both types of empathy, while the right anterior insula may be more active in emotional empathy and the left anterior medial cingulate cortex in cognitive empathy (Fan et al., 2010). Roger's concept of empathy is closer to cognitive empathy than emotional empathy:

> the therapist's sensitive ability and willingness to understand the client's thoughts, feelings and struggles from the client's point of view.... to see completely through the client's eyes, to adopt his frame of reference.... It means entering the private perceptual world of the other ... (Rogers, 1980: 85)

> *Emotional empathy* is an automatic response where we feel similar emotions to another person.
>
> *Cognitive empathy* is the conscious engagement with another's suffering where we imagine what it is like to be experiencing the thoughts and feelings of the other person.

Mercer and Reynolds (2002) identify three functions of empathy in a clinical setting: (i) to understand the patient's situation, perspective and feelings, (ii) to communicate this and check its accuracy, and (iii) to act on that understanding with the patient in a helpful way. For the CBT therapist to help the client explore and change their unhelpful beliefs, it is first necessary to understand their cognitive world. During a panic attack, for instance, the patient will often fear they are in imminent danger of dying, but the catastrophic thoughts will be specific for the individual. They may fear they will have a heart attack, a stroke or suffocate, usually based upon a misinterpretation of bodily symptoms (e.g. palpitations, dizziness and headache, or breathlessness respectively). Demonstrating that the therapist understands how frightening the situation is and how real it feels at the time is an important part of establishing rapport and ensuring that the therapist has accurately identified the relevant thoughts. Understanding the personal meaning of the symptoms is essential in order to set up effective behavioural experiments to test the catastrophic fears. Each of the Mercer and Reynolds' three stages of clinical empathy contributes to effective therapy: asking questions to understand the client's view of the world, summarising and reflecting back this understanding and demonstrating how this understanding can make a difference.

ESTABLISHING EMPATHY IN CBT

1. UNDERSTANDING THE CLIENT'S PERSPECTIVE

The secret to empathy in CBT practice is curiosity. Can I make sense of how the person before me is caught up in their problems? The therapist must suspend judgement to listen carefully for the explicit and implicit meanings in the client's communications, asking the key question: If I saw the situation in this way, would I feel the same way? If the answer is No, then the therapist has not yet grasped the full personal meaning of the situation for the client, and further exploration is needed. The general cognitive model (appraisals drive emotions and behaviour) and disorder specific models (e.g. catastrophic misinterpretations of bodily symptoms in panic) guide us in the questions we might ask to clarify our understanding. So, if a client with panic disorder reports they had an overwhelming sense of dread but no cognitions, we need to inquire further about what they felt in their body at the time and what was the worst thing they thought might happen? Showing the client that you really want to understand what it was about the experience that made it so dreadful helps build the relationship, and finding that their experience fits the cognitive model of panic makes their symptoms more comprehensible. The therapist should not, however, hold on too strongly to a model if the patient does not feel it fits their experience. A patient described anxiety attacks which were overwhelming and filled him with dread but he was unable to identify any specific cognitions beyond a felt sense of impending doom. When the therapist attempted to elicit catastrophic thoughts about death, he got nowhere and the patient felt he was not getting the point. Reframing the problem as one of intolerance of the feeling of doom allowed them to discuss cognitions such as 'I can't stand this' and 'it's not going to stop' and set up appropriate experiments to test these beliefs.

2. CHECKING YOU HAVE UNDERSTOOD AND SHOWING YOU UNDERSTAND

The therapist often feels more closely connected with the client when they have understood their appraisal of the upsetting situation. Putting oneself in the client's position and allowing a felt sense to arise can help us get in touch with how they are feeling. This allows the therapist to genuinely say, 'I can see how that must have been very upsetting for you.' Paraphrasing what the client has said, and using verbatim their hot thoughts alongside these empathic comments, helps the patient see the therapist is on track. For instance, a client with anger control problems may have described an incident of road rage. The therapist might summarise:

> So when the other driver cut you up, the first thought that went through your mind was, 'What a ****! He's not looking where he's going. He needs to be taught a lesson!' You thought he was being selfish and inconsiderate and that made you want to get back at him. Have I got that right?

Here, the therapist is exploring the belief that a person who breaks the social rule of courtesy needs to be punished. The therapist might then say, 'Most of us who drive have been in this sort of situation, but it seems to have been particularly upsetting for you. I'd like to understand what it was that made your anger go into the red zone.' This might lead the client to describe how his life is full of people who treat him disrespectfully: this is just another example of the self-centredness around him. The therapist might then empathically respond:

> I understand now that although in some ways this was a minor incident, it symbolised all those occasions when people disrespect you. You felt incredibly angry that here was a complete stranger doing it again.

Further exploration might elicit thoughts and feelings of helplessness and impotence, allowing the therapist to empathise with the vulnerable emotions beneath the angry compensatory response:

> Although you felt so angry, you say that underneath was a feeling of powerlessness.

3. DEVELOPING EFFECTIVE CHANGE METHODS

Accurate cognitive empathy allows the therapist to devise appropriate interventions, while emotional empathy allows the client to feel heard so they engage and contribute to these interventions. With our angry client, the identification of the sequence:

'I'm being dissed. I'm nothing. I'm powerless.'

|

VULNERABLE

|

'What a ****! He's not looking where he's going. He needs to be taught a lesson!'

|

ANGRY

|

DRIVING FAST TO OVERTAKE AND GESTICULATE AT OTHER DRIVER

can give him a perspective on his angry reaction. Empathising with the underlying feeling of vulnerability and recognising how the angry reaction is a compensatory strategy to manage the helplessness may allow the client to begin to look at the validity and usefulness of his response. This can generate some in-session interventions:

1. Examining the pros and cons of responding in the way he did.
2. Devising alternative strategies to manage anger in a similar situation.
3. Examining the initial appraisal - is there evidence the driver did this deliberately?

and between-session work:

1. Monitoring angry reactions.
2. Using alternative strategies - count to ten before doing anything; leave at least ten minutes before answering an email that makes him angry.
3. Noticing the underlying hurt and learning strategies for self-soothing.
4. Empathy exercises to understand the other person's perspective.

PROBLEMS IN EMPATHISING

Some problems in empathising too much

Emotional overidentification – through emotional contagion, the therapist mirrors the client's emotional response and becomes overwhelmed by feelings of hopelessness. Assumptions may be made about what the client *must* be thinking if they are feeling this way.

Cognitive overidentification – the therapist 'buys into' the client's world view and is unable to establish sufficient distance to help them find alternative ways of thinking or acting.

Joan is a 28-year-old single parent with a two-year-old daughter. She has been depressed for the last year following the ending of a relationship and receiving a diagnosis of breast cancer. She has been successfully treated with a lumpectomy and chemotherapy but remains depressed. She is socially isolated and has very little that gives her any pleasure in life. She has not responded to a variety of antidepressants and feels pessimistic that CBT can help.

Her automatic thoughts are:

> 'There's no point in doing anything, my life's over.'
>
> 'I've got nothing to look forward to.'
>
> 'I'm not a fit mother.'
>
> 'I'm damaging my daughter.'

She had a stable but strict family upbringing. Her father was highly critical of any mistakes. Her mother was 'a doormat' who seems to have been crushed by her husband's dominant control. Joan has a younger sister who she feels was the favourite, who was not scrutinised as much by the father as Joan. She has not worked since having the baby. When the child was a year old, she was diagnosed with breast cancer, and her partner could not cope. He left, and she has been berating herself for getting involved with him in the first place, since her father had warned her he was no good from the start.

Reflective question

Read through the brief description of Joan's case. What would be your emotional reactions if you were Joan's therapist? What empathic traps might a therapist fall into when treating her?

1. EMOTIONAL OVERIDENTIFICATION

In the presence of great distress, we naturally feel similar emotions to the person before us. This form of emotional empathy may lead us to feel tense with an anxious patient or sad with a depressed patient. Confronted by Joan's deep sadness, it is understandable that the therapist will feel sad and his or her emotions and body language will mirror hers. Feeling the client's sadness is an important part of the therapist's emotional response, but there are dangers in becoming too identified with the client's suffering. One possibility is that what might be termed our *empathic countertransference* (Moorey, 2014; our reaction generated by our identification with the client's emotional state) might lower our mood to such an extent that we feel hopeless ourselves. As our mood drops, we naturally think in a more negative way, and this may make it harder to find alternatives to what seems a realistically negative situation. A second danger is that our emotional empathy may trick us into thinking we have accurate cognitive empathy with Joan. This is a common problem when working with life-threatening illness. Our own thoughts and feelings about death may lead us to believe that we know why the patient is distressed without checking out the idiosyncratic meaning for them. We will discuss this further in Chapter 12. Finally, the strength of our own empathic suffering can be difficult to bear. Hoffman (1978) coined the term *empathic overarousal* for the tendency to feel overwhelmed in the presence of another person's suffering. This can lead us to shut off emotionally and use distancing tactics, such as intellectualisation, to manage our emotions. This can be a challenging balance between approach and distancing: we need the courage to genuinely explore the meaning of difficult situations for the patient while being able to stand back enough not to be totally absorbed by negative feelings. Supervision can be very useful in helping the therapist achieve this balance.

2. COGNITIVE OVERIDENTIFICATION

When we truly understand the thoughts and feelings of someone who is in great distress, we can lose our objectivity, in effect 'buying into' their world view. This is particularly an issue in depression (see Chapter 4) but can occur with any disorder. We begin to believe the client really is a failure, or that they are too damaged to ever get better, or too lacking in coping skills to successfully engage in behavioural experiments. The challenge for the therapist is to empathise sufficiently to have emotional contact with the client while holding onto the possibility that there may be alternative, more constructive, ways to view and manage the situation. A therapist working with Joan may be influenced by the external difficulties she faces (serious illness, abandonment by her partner, social isolation) and start to agree with her hopeless construction. This may lead the therapist to conclude that CBT is not the right treatment and that another therapy, like supportive counselling, may be more appropriate. It is important to stand back from the situation and balance empathy with a rational assessment of the client's thoughts. A few methods include:

1. Examining the client's thoughts for cognitive biases.
2. Doing our own thought record to look at our reactions to the client's beliefs.
3. Bringing the case to supervision.

Reflective question

Imagine the ways in which the therapist might 'buy into' Joan's view. What are the distortions in Joan's thinking? How might the therapist address these while remaining empathic?

3. FAILURE TO EMPATHISE

Difficulties in empathising

We may find it hard to empathise because we are frightened of empathising too much. The threat of empathic overarousal makes us shut down and distance ourselves from the client.

Or we may find the client's world view so different or unpalatable that we cannot imagine ourselves in their situation.

We cannot empathise with all our patients. While it is easy to identify with some patients, others seem very alien to us. Their ethnic or cultural background may be very different from ours. Their values, priorities or ethics may be so far away from our own that it is very hard to walk in their shoes. Nonetheless, an inquiring, curious approach to building a conceptualisation of the person's beliefs and their origins can help to bridge these divides. Devising not only a maintenance conceptualisation of the problems but also a fuller developmental conceptualisation may be important here. What are the cultural, family and personal experiences that shaped this person's beliefs? Can I create a story that explains how these beliefs came about? Can I see how I might have come to similar conclusions about the world if I had had these experiences? Getting a deeper understanding of culture and religion may be important with clients from different backgrounds to our own (see Chapter 16). Feeding back our understanding and showing positive regard (Norcross and Lambert, 2011) may be especially important when working with clients from different cultures. These gaps can usually be bridged, because it is possible to empathise with the form of the person's suffering even if the context and content are different. There is a universality about loss, grief, fear which we can usually empathise with, even if the person's background is very different from our own. Empathy becomes more difficult when the client's beliefs elicit a negative response from the therapist. This is often the case with people with a diagnosis of personality disorder. Piers was a successful 30-year-old entrepreneur who came to therapy because of lifelong feelings of dissatisfaction and self-hatred. He spent much of the therapy session either talking about the amount of money he was making, describing angry ruminations about the people who had put him down in his work and private life or subtly undermining the therapist's competence. Piers coped with his painful feelings through alcohol and cocaine use and compulsive use of prostitutes. The therapist's emotional reaction was to feel angry, defensive and repulsed by Piers' narcisisstic lifestyle. He used a number of approaches to feel more empathy towards his patient:

1. Enquire about Piers' childhood to understand where his feelings of emptiness and self-hatred originated.
    i. He discovered Piers was an only child. His parents were cold and distant, gave him lots of material gifts but little love and sent him to boarding school from an early age. His father was a high flyer in the City who expected him to succeed, and so the only positive rewards he received were for success.
2. Try to imagine Piers as a child experiencing coldness and withholding of affection and how this might have felt.
3. Empathise with the vulnerability beneath the compensatory strategies of being dismissive and self-aggrandising, or escaping into maladaptive self-soothing.
4. Recognise that, while his strategies for achieving his goals were unhelpful and put others off, his underlying goals to feel worthwhile and to be loved were legitimate.

We will return to Piers' story in Chapter 3, where we will explore the therapist–patient relationship in the context of interpersonal schemas.

You may find the following empathy exercise helpful if you have a client with whom you find it difficult to empathise.

This exercise often produces a shift in affect and some insights into what the patient may be experiencing in the session. Occasionally, the new insight leads to a sense of overwhelming identification with the client with empathic overload. One therapist mentioned how empathising with the client's hopelessness changed their affect from irritation and resentment to hopelessness. If this occurs in the imagery exercise, it can be helpful to review the evidence for the client's beliefs and hold in mind that, as therapists, we can be responsible for doing our best for the client but, ultimately, they are on their own life journey and we cannot live it for them.

CHAPTER SUMMARY

This chapter has reviewed the evidence for the small, but consistent, association between the 'core conditions' (genuineness, positive regard, empathy and unconditional acceptance) and outcome which is found across all therapies. Limitations of the research studies mean that it is not possible to conclude that these factors are necessary preconditions for effective CBT, but clinicians would generally agree that a therapist who did not possess these qualities might struggle to deliver good treatment. Empathy has a particularly important place in CBT, because without an understanding of the client's cognitive world it is not possible to formulate, identify relevant beliefs or explore adaptive alternatives, and the therapist needs to demonstrate that

Empathy Exercise

Step One

1. Choose a client who evokes strong negative emotions in you.
2. Sit comfortably in a chair, close your eyes and allow yourself to rest in the present moment. Notice the sensations of your feet on the floor, your bottom on the chair, your hands resting on the arms of the chair or on your body. Let go as best you can of thoughts about the future and past and be present.
3. Imagine your client sitting opposite you. How do they look? What are their body movements? Are they saying anything to you? What emotions and body sensations do you feel as you picture them in front of you?
4. Open your eyes and reflect on the exercise.

Step Two

1. Revisit your formulation for your client. Can you create a narrative linking their life experiences, beliefs and behaviours that helps you understand how they are approaching therapy?
2. Now close your eyes again and focus on the present moment, spending a few seconds grounding yourself.
3. Imagine you are your client, sitting opposite the therapist. What emotions do you feel; what body sensations? What thoughts are going through your mind?
4. Open your eyes and reflect on the exercise.

Step Three

1. Close your eyes and ground yourself.
2. Imagine your client sitting in front of you. What does this evoke now? What thoughts, feelings and body sensations arise as you picture your client?
3. Has anything changed? Do you have different understanding of their experience and attitude towards you? Can you empathise with their situation?

understanding in order to engage the client in the therapeutic journey. Some tips for establishing empathy are suggested and the traps of emotional overidentification, cognitive overidentification and failure to empathise are described, together with ways to manage them. Finally, an experiential exercise is introduced which can be used when empathy seems to fail.

FURTHER READING

Beck AT, Rush AJ, Shaw BF and Emery G (1979) The therapeutic relationship: application to cognitive therapy. In: *Cognitive Therapy of Depression*. New York: Guilford Press.

REFERENCES

Beck AT, Rush AJ, Shaw BF and Emery G (1979) *Cognitive therapy of depression*. New York: Guilford Press.

Blakemore SJ, Bristow D, Bird G, Frith C and Ward J (2005) Somatosensory activations during the observation of touch and a case of vision-touch synaesthesia. *Brain 128*: 1571–1583.

Botvinick M, Jha AP, Bylsma LM, Fabian SA, Solomon PE and Prkachin KM (2005) Viewing facial expressions of pain engages cortical areas involved in the direct experience of pain. *NeuroImage, 25*, 312–319.

Bozarth JD, Zimring FM and Tausch R (2002) Client-centred therapy: the evolution of a revolution. In: Cain DJ and Seeman J (eds) *Humanistic Psychotherapies: Handbook of Research and Practice*. Washington DC: American Psychological Association, pp. 147–188.

Cheng Y, Yang CY, Lin CP, Lee PR and Decety J (2008) The perception of pain in others suppresses somatosensory oscillations: a magnetoencephalography study. *NeuroImage 40*: 1833–1840.

Elliott R, Bohart AC, Watson JC and Greenberg LS (2011) Empathy. *Psychotherapy 48*: 43–49.

Fan Y, Duncan NW, de Greck M and Northoff G (2010) Is there a core neural network in empathy? An fMRI based quantitative meta-analysis. *Neuroscience and Biobehavioral Reviews 35*: 903–911.

Gilbert P (1989) *Human Nature and Suffering*. Hove: Psychology Press.

Hoffman ML (1978) Empathy: Its development and prosocial implications. In: Keasey CB (ed) *Nebraska Symposium on Motivation*. Vol. *25*. Lincoln: University of Nebraska Press, pp. 169–218.

Hoffman ML (2008) Empathy and Prosocial Behaviour. In: Haviland-Jones JM, Lewis M and Feldman Barrett L (eds.) *Handbook of Emotions, Third Edition*. New York: Guilford Publications, pp. 440–455.

Iacoboni M and Lenzi GL (2002) Mirror neurons, the insula, and empathy. *Behavioral and Brain Sciences 25*: 39–40.

Iacoboni M, Molnar-Szakacs I, Gallese V, Buccino G, Mazziotta JC and Rizzolatti G (2005) Grasping the intentions of others with one's own mirror neuron system. *Public Library of Science Biology 3*: 529–535.

Keijsers GPJ, Schaap CPDR and Hoogduin CAL (2000) The impact of interpersonal patient and therapist behavior on outcome in cognitive-behavior therapy a review of empirical studies. *Behavior Modification 24*: 264–297.

Klein MH, Michels JL, Kolden GG and Chisolm-Stockard S (2001) Congruence or genuineness. *Psychotherapy: Theory, Research, Practice, Training 38*: 396–400.

Mercer SW and Reynolds WJ (2002) Empathy and quality of care. *British Journal of General Practice 52*: 9–13.

Moorey S (2014) 'Is it them or is it me?' Transference and countertransference in CBT: In: Whittington A and Grey N (eds) *How to Become a More Effective CBT: Therapist: Mastering Metacompetence in Clinical Practice*. Chichester: Wiley.

Morris RJ and Magrath KH (1979) Contribution of therapist warmth to the contact desensitization treatment of acrophobia. *Journal of Consulting and Clinical Psychology 47*: 786–788.

Morris RJ and Suckerman KR (1974) The importance of the therapeutic relationship in systematic desensitization. *Journal of Consulting and Clinical Psychology 42*: 148.

Morrison I, Lloyd D, Di Pellegrino G and Roberts N (2004) Vicarious responses to pain in anterior cingulate cortex: Is empathy a multisensory issue? *Cognitive, Affective, & Behavioral Neuroscience 4*: 270–278.

Norcross JC and Lambert MJ (2011) Psychotherapy relationships that work II [Special Issue]. *Psychotherapy 48*(1): 4–8.
Rogers CR (1957) The necessary and sufficient conditions of therapeutic personality change. *Journal of Consulting Psychology*, *21*(2): 95–103.
Rogers CR (1961) The Process Equation of Psychotherapy. *American Journal of Psychotherapy*, *15*(1): 27–45.
Rogers CR (1980) *A way of being*. Boston: Houghton Mifflin.
Rogers CR, Gendlin ET, Kiesler DJ and Truax CB (eds) (1967) *The therapeutic relationship and its impact: A study of psychotherapy with schizophrenics*. Madison, WI: University of Wisconsin Press.
Singer T, Seymour B, O'Doherty J, Kaube H, Dolan RJ and Frith CD (2004) Empathy for pain involves the affective but not sensory components of pain. *Science 3*: 1157–1162.

2

THE THERAPEUTIC ALLIANCE: BUILDING A COLLABORATIVE RELATIONSHIP AND MANAGING CHALLENGES

STIRLING MOOREY AND ANNA LAVENDER

CHAPTER OVERVIEW

All talking therapies need collaboration between client and therapist, and there has been substantial research on the relationship between alliance and outcome. This chapter examines alliance-outcome associations and considers the interaction between change methods and the therapy alliance. The focus is on individual CBT, where most research has been carried out: Chapters 17 and 18 address the therapy alliance in group and couple work. The central role of collaborative empiricism in CBT is discussed and some suggestions made about how to build the collaborative relationship and manage when collaboration breaks down.

THE WORKING ALLIANCE IN PSYCHOTHERAPY

All psychotherapies depend upon a partnership between therapist and client. Freud himself recognised that analysis was not possible without collaboration between analyst and patient (Freud, 1912/1966), and the concept of the *working alliance* was first developed by other writers in analytic tradition (see Wiseman et al., 2012 for a review). Bordin (1979) extended this thinking with his pan-theoretical model of the therapeutic alliance. He suggested that the alliance relates to three areas: the *tasks* and *goals* of therapy, and the emotional *bond* between therapist and client. CBT involves many tasks, which all need to be negotiated with the client, such as identifying goals, engaging in experiments and carrying out homework assignments. Therapy cannot begin unless the client is prepared to attempt some of these activities. Box 2.1 lists some of the commitments we expect of the patient in CBT.

Box 2.1 Tasks in CBT

1. Attend regularly.
2. Establish and work towards specific goals.
3. Collaborate on agenda setting.
4. Comply with structure and focus of the session.
5. Collaborate on various tasks, including homework assignments and various behavioural experiments.
6. Be honest about internal experiences.

Effective CBT also requires agreement on the goals of treatment. These need to be described in clear, operational terms (improve my depressed mood so I can get up by 9 am regularly in preparation for returning to work), as opposed to broad and diffuse ones (understand why I am not motivated). Clients may come with very different expectations about what they will get from therapy, especially if they have previously received more insight-based treatments, so engagement often involves clarifying misperceptions of CBT. The primary aim of CBT is problem resolution rather than insight; alongside this, the therapist also aims to help the client learn effective strategies for managing their condition and methods to prevent relapse (Box 2.2).

Box 2.2 Goals in CBT

1. Solve problems and resolve symptoms.
2. Learn strategies for coping.
3. Prevent relapse and change underlying cognitive structures.

Finally, although the affective bond is not singled out for special attention in CBT, clients need to feel understood and respected and to be able to trust their therapist so they can enter into a therapeutic partnership. The relational contract requires the client to be honest about their experiences and to adopt an active, problem-solving approach, while the therapist must, in return, compassionately understand and validate the client's experience to create a safe, trusting environment (Box 2.3).

Research has consistently shown a correlation between the therapeutic alliance and outcome across psychological therapies and disorders, including CBT (Horvath and Symonds, 1991; Martin et al., 2000). This is one of the most robust factors associated with successful therapy (Wampold, 2001). Horvath and colleagues identified

Box 2.3 The relational contract or bond in CBT

Therapist:

1. understands client's cognitive world (compassionate conceptualisation) and
2. validates client's experience.

Client:

1. takes on here and now adult responsibility (unlike some dynamic therapies which may require regression and work at primitive levels) and
2. actively participates in becoming own therapist.

201 studies (14,000 patients between 1973 and 2009) that investigated the relationship between alliance and outcome. The overall effect size was $r = 0.275$, accounting for 8% of the variance in therapy outcomes. This was free from publication bias, and effect sizes were similar across types of treatments (Horvath et al., 2011). Client rating of alliance is the best predictor of outcome, and alliance-outcome associations seem to relate more to the clinician's rather than the client's ability to establish an alliance (Baldwin et al., 2007; Del Re et al., 2012). Horvath's meta-analysis found that the correlation between alliance and outcome increases as treatment progresses, but the alliance early in therapy (sessions 3–5) seemed to provide reliable prognosis for both outcome and treatment completion. Similar results ($r = 0.33$) have been found for studies which examined the correlation between goal consensus or collaboration and outcome (Tryon and Winograd, 2011).

ALLIANCE–OUTCOME CORRELATIONS IN CBT

In 1990, DeRubeis and Feeley presented data that challenged the conventional wisdom that the working alliance influenced symptom change. They observed that previous studies had often taken average ratings of the alliance across all treatment sessions rather than looking at alliance and symptom change over time (e.g. Krupnick et al., 1996). DeRubeis and Feeley asked raters to listen blind to audiotape samples taken from session 2, sessions 4–6, 7–9 and 10–12 of a 12 week cognitive therapy (CT) for depression. Ratings were made of core facilitative conditions (empathy, warmth etc.), working alliance, 'concrete', symptom-focused CBT methods (e.g. examining evidence concerning beliefs) and 'abstract' methods (e.g. exploring the personal meaning of thoughts). They found that neither core conditions nor working alliance predicted symptom reduction in subsequent sessions, but the presence of concrete symptom-focused methods in session 2 predicted outcome. Later in treatment, the therapeutic alliance was predicted by *prior* symptom reduction (DeRubeis and Feeley, 1990). They concluded that therapists who achieved better outcomes encouraged their patients to scrutinise their problems and beliefs in precise terms, encouraged them to undertake straightforward, focused tasks between sessions, integrated discussions of completed tasks in the session and conducted simple, direct tests of beliefs. The therapists' goals in these sessions were to 'promote symptom relief and to teach the patients skills they could use on their own to combat depressive mood states' (DeRubeis and Feeley, 1990: 478). The finding that the problem-focused rather than more abstract components of CBT predicted outcome was replicated in a later study, though the influence of symptom change on therapeutic alliance was less robust (Feeley et al., 1999). These results were based on small samples (25 and 32, respectively). In a larger trial of 367 depressed patients treated with the cognitive behavioural analysis system of psychotherapy (CBASP), Klein et al. (2003) found that early alliance *did* predict symptom change. Klein et al. used patient ratings of alliance whereas the previous studies had used observer ratings. Another difference between the studies was the patient group. CBASP is designed to treat people with chronic depression, and it is conceivable that the relationship is a more important factor in this group than in acute depression. McEvoy et al. (2014) found that, in patients with anxiety and depression treated with individual CBT, higher patient-rated alliance predicted completion of treatment but was not associated with symptom change. Many studies have taken the working alliance (as measured by the Working Alliance Inventory: WAI, Horvath and Greenberg 1986, 1989) as a single construct, despite Bordin's view of it as multidimensional, but in fact it seems to consist of two factors: (a) agreement on tasks and goals, and (b) the relational bond (Andrusyna et al., 2001). Gelso and Hayes (1998) referred to this as the difference between the 'working bond' and the 'liking bond'. Webb et al. (2011) reanalysed data from two randomised controlled trials (RCT) of cognitive therapy for depression ($n = 105$) and found that symptom change subsequent to an early session was significantly related to the WAI factor that assessed therapist-patient agreement on the goals and tasks of therapy but not to the factor assessing the affective bond. Both factors, when assessed in a late session, were predicted by prior symptom change. A study by Ramnerö and Öst (2007) supports this idea: agoraphobic clients who therapists assessed as showing active participation and goal direction had better outcome at posttreatment and follow-up.

While getting agreement on tasks and goals seems central to collaboration in CBT, the emotional bond may be more important in certain subtypes of depression. For instance, Weck et al. (2013) found that alliance was a predictor of time to relapse in people with recurrent depression receiving maintenance CT. The alliance-outcome relationship was particularly important in patients with five or more previous depressive episodes. Contrary to this finding, Lorenzo-Luaces et al. (2014) reported that alliance predicted outcome in clients with zero to two prior episodes ($r = 0.52$) but not in those with three or more prior episodes ($r = -0.02$). Gaston et al. (1991) found a strong effect of alliance on outcome in CBT for depression in older adults. They concluded that

> a sense of being in an intimate collaborative relationship with another person may be particularly important for older depressed adults who have lost significant persons, capacities, or occupations. (Gaston et al., 1991: 111)

Research in other conditions has also produced mixed findings. Turner et al. (2015) found that, in a group of 94 adults with eating disorders treated with CBT, greater early symptom reduction predicted a strong early therapeutic alliance. Cloitre et al.

(2004) investigated a two stage CBT for complex post traumatic stress disorder (PTSD): stabilisation followed by imaginal exposure. The therapeutic alliance established early in treatment predicted improvement; this was mediated by patients' improved capacity to regulate emotions in the exposure phase of the treatment. Goldsmith et al. (2015) found that, in both CBT and supportive counselling for psychosis, a good therapeutic alliance was associated with a positive outcome while a poor alliance was associated with poor outcome; and, with a poor alliance, more sessions actually made the patient worse! The association between specific techniques, symptom change and alliance is likely to be a complex one. As McAleavey and Castonguay (2015) point out:

> the distinction between 'common' and 'unique' factors may be a false dichotomy when comparing many face-to-face psychotherapies, because neither common factors nor unique factors can exist without the other. (McAleavey and Castonguay, 2015: 293)

Because CBT is such a technical therapy, agreement on the tasks and goals of therapy is the foundation of the alliance. This is also the area where 'resistance' is most often encountered. Evidence suggests that, if agreement is obtained on the goals and tasks of therapy, the affective bond often takes care of itself; but it is possible that certain groups, such as older people and survivors of childhood abuse, may require more attention to the emotional elements of the therapeutic relationship for effective therapy to take place.

BUILDING THE ALLIANCE

Terry was a 40-year-old mental health worker who had been suffering from depression for six months following the end of a relationship. Although he was still able to hold down his job, he struggled to do much else when he was not at work and described pervasive feelings of loss, hopelessness and lack of energy. He had little motivation and avoided tasks but then ruminated about his failure to do things like get his telephone mended, saying to himself, 'I can't keep my life together; I'm letting it all fall apart; I'm an idiot.' He described a pattern of giving up and withdrawing when things got difficult and leaving others to 'pick up the pieces' for him. This pattern worsened when he became depressed: this was his third episode of depression, though he had never before sought treatment. Terry's parents had divorced when he was eight years old. When he was 13, his mother found a new partner, who often complained that Terry was allowed to 'get away with murder' (she moaned about his adolescent laziness, but still tidied up after him). He seemed contemptuous of Terry, who in return never respected him. Terry was assessed in the local NHS talking therapies service and allocated to CBT. He scored 20 on the Patient Health Questionnaire (PHQ 9; Spitzer et al., 1999) and 11 on the General Anxiety Disorder scale (GAD 7; Spitzer et al., 2006).

In the first session, the therapist clarified that Terry wanted depression to be the main focus of treatment and explained that they would be meeting for 12 sessions of CBT. Terry agreed that he needed to get rid of his depression but was concerned 12 sessions would not be enough. Exploring his expectations further revealed that he believed that his problems were deep rooted and needed much longer attention.

He had received some training in psychodynamic counselling and felt that, unless he revisited his reaction to the divorce and his relationship with his mother and stepfather, he would never fully resolve his depression. The therapist recognised this potential mismatch of goals and described the rationale for treatment: the focus would initially be on practical ways to help him out of his depression and to give him tools he could use to manage his mood, while it might also be possible to look at some of the factors that had made him vulnerable to depression. The goal of therapy was symptom change rather than insight. She began to build collaboration by asking him what would indicate his depression had improved - he wanted to be more motivated, enjoy being with his friends and to live rather than just exist. When asked what he might be doing differently when his motivation returned, he identified going regularly to the gym, meeting friends, not procrastinating so much and having the confidence to look for a girlfriend. The therapist said:

> You have some clear goals for what you would like to do when you feel better. The interesting question is whether you need to understand where your problems came from in order to get out of this depression. What helped you out of your previous depressive episodes?

When therapist and patient discussed this, it became clear that one episode resolved gradually and apparently spontaneously, while the other quickly ended when he found a girlfriend.

> So this change in your confidence, and how you saw yourself – valuing yourself because someone else wanted and valued you – dissolved the feelings of worthlessness. This fits very much with how we see depression: when we are depressed we see ourselves as worthless and inadequate. You didn't suddenly become worthwhile; it seems that someone recognising the good in you allowed you to see that in yourself. What if we could help you to find that self-worth yourself?

The therapist then went on to explore how Terry's social withdrawal and procrastination might be feeding into this sense of worthlessness.

> We have lots of evidence that when we are depressed we become demotivated. If we wait for motivation it never comes. We can restore our motivation by gradually building up what we do, step by step.

Following a discussion of behavioural activation, Terry agreed to monitor his activity over the next week and rate his levels of motivation, achievement and pleasure when engaged in various tasks. He identified two tasks to try - contacting the phone company and making one trip to the gym.

This example illustrates the importance of asking about the client's expectations of therapy and tailoring the rationale for therapy to the client's situation. Terry's belief that he needed a depth therapy to solve his problems might also lead him to see some of the techniques of CBT as superficial, so it would be important for the therapist to be clear about the rationale for activity scheduling, to check Terry's understanding of it and his willingness to engage in homework. Coming from a more insight-focused background, he might find the structure of CBT sessions unpalateable, so the therapist would again need to discuss the reasoning behind setting an agenda and homework etc. Socialising the patient to the model is a key component of the early stage of therapy. *Socialisation* includes helping the patient to understand the basic CBT model (thoughts, influences, feelings and behaviour), how this is applied to the condition and how it applies to the client. It also involves an understanding that CBT is time-limited, structured, focused and requires the client to work both in and between sessions. In this sense, better socialisation is likely to be associated with better therapy alliance. While direct psychoeducation and the use of information handouts can be helpful, socialisation is more than simply explaining the model and what will be happening in therapy. It is an interplay between explanation, problem identification, formulation and testing whether the model works. Throughout this early phase, each homework task was a test of the two hypotheses:

- A. insight and motivation were needed to resolve his depression, or
- B. becoming more active and thinking differently would increase his motivation and self-esteem.

Therapist Tips for building collaboration

- Empathise and validate.
- Use collaborative language: We, Let's, Our job is to ... together.
- Adopt a curious, inquiring approach.
- Imagine placing the problems on the table, and share the task of problem-solving.
- Explain the rationale for interventions and check the client understands and agrees.
- Use data from self-monitoring, results of experiments etc. to reinforce shared understanding.
- Always be 'empirical' – let's find out together.

COLLABORATIVE EMPIRICISM

The work that Terry and his therapist did together to test his beliefs about insight and motivation is a good example of what Beck termed *collaborative empiricism*. While all therapies recognise the importance of the therapeutic alliance, the nature of this relationship differs across therapies. In CBT, collaboration refers to the *active shared work* between client and therapist (Dattilio and Hanna, 2012). This is a problem-solving partnership where old ways of thinking and acting are compared and weighed against alternative, new ways. Beliefs are turned into testable hypotheses about the world. Beck and Emery (1985) succinctly summarised this:

> The cognitive therapist implies that there is a team approach to the solution of the patient's problem: that is, a therapeutic alliance where the patient supplies raw data (reports on thought and behavior ...) while the therapist provides structure and expertise on how to solve the problems. The emphasis is on working on problems rather

> than on correcting deficits or changing personality. The therapist fosters the attitude 'two heads are better than one' in approaching personal difficulties. (Beck and Emery, 1985: 175)

As Tee and Kazantzis (2011) have observed, despite agreement on the central importance of collaborative empiricism (CE) in CBT, there is a lack of agreed definitions, measures or empirical investigations of the construct. They questioned whether CBT trials could have been more effective if they had included more systematic training and evaluation of collaborative empiricism. Kazantzis (Kazantzis et al., 2013) has edited a special edition of *Cognitive and Behavioural Practice* dedicated to Collaborative Empiricism. This includes theoretically and clinically useful articles on collaboratively developing case formulations, structuring sessions, encouraging self-monitoring and facilitating exposure. Much more research is needed before we can be confident the techniques we use for forming and maintaining a collaborative relationship in CBT are strongly evidence-based.

It can be argued that this empirical approach enhances the therapeutic alliance, because nothing is taken for granted. Although therapy may be guided by a disorder specific formulation or a developmental formulation based on the patient's history, the therapist does not make assumptions. Ideas are always formulated as hypotheses and, wherever possible, shared explicitly with the client. Similarly, the client's beliefs are formulated as hypotheses. The collaborative work involves testing these hypotheses. Terry's model of his depression was centred on the idea that because its origins were in his childhood he needed long term insight focused therapy to feel better; he also had an implicit belief, common to many people with depression, that he needed to feel motivated before he could do anything. As we have seen, his therapist proposed two alternative hypotheses:

1. It is possible to overcome depression by understanding the cognitive and behavioural processes maintaining it, and then changing thoughts and behaviour.
2. Becoming more active can generate motivation.

Terry found that doing more made him feel confident to do even more. Setting up experiments goes a long way to prevent resistance: the therapist's stance is 'We don't know if this is the case or not. Let's find out.' Sometimes it is helpful to juxtapose the two alternative hypotheses, as in the use of Theory A and Theory B in anxiety disorders e.g. a patient with OCD who fears he may be a paedophile is helped to construct two alternative hypotheses:

- Theory A. The problem is that I am a dangerous person who could abuse children.
- Theory B. The problem is that I have obsessional worries that I might abuse children.

In depression, it can be helpful to compare Plan A (behaving in line with depressive thinking) with Plan B (behaving in line with more adaptive, positive thinking). For Terry, this might be:

- Plan A. Continue to avoid, procrastinate and wait for motivation.
- Plan B. Work to overcome avoidance and return to previous activities in a graded way.

'Collaboration empiricism' may not always involve a 50:50 contribution from therapist and client. Early on, the therapist may have to do more of the work. This is particularly the case in depression, where the therapist may have to provide much of the energy, in perhaps a 70:30 ratio, or even 90:10 with severely depressed patients (Freeman and McCloskey, 2003). As clients become less symptomatic and more familiar with CBT, they take more responsibility for setting the agenda, creating homework tasks etc.

Reflective questions

- What problems have you encountered in forming and maintaining a therapeutic alliance with your clients?
- Did this arise from disagreements about the goals of CBT (e.g. problem-focus rather than insight)?
- Did this arise from disagreements about the tasks of CBT (e.g. structure, homework)?
- Did this arise from disagreements about your relationship with the patient?
- Did it arise from something else, not covered in Bordin's working alliance triad?

DISRUPTION TO THE THERAPEUTIC ALLIANCE

Occasional breakdowns in collaboration are inevitable. Safran and Muran (2000) identified two broad categories of alliance rupture: confrontation and withdrawal ruptures. *Confrontation ruptures* are overt disagreements over the tasks and goals of therapy (structure of sessions, homework etc.) and the relationship (attacking the therapist's competence or personality). *Withdrawal ruptures* are more subtle ways of avoiding the emotional activation necessary for effective therapy, such as shifting topic, intellectualising or talking in the third person. In anxiety disorders, these strategies are ways to escape talking about feared topics (e.g. a health anxious patient who cannot say the word cancer) or carrying out behavioural experiments. Withdrawal ruptures are familiar to therapists working with PTSD who recognise how patients avoid engaging emotionally with trauma memories. Paradoxically, confrontation ruptures commonly arise in reaction to the components of CBT that make it most collaborative. CBT is problem-focused, structured and requires active participation by the client. It gives the client an opportunity to contribute to therapy in a way that most traditional psychotherapies do not: as an equal partner in problem-solving. But the problem-focused approach can be misunderstood to be trivial, 'just a sticking plaster', the structure of therapy can be seen as too restricting and the client can perceive homework as an imposition. Paying attention to socialisation and getting early results goes a long way to preventing these difficulties. A good formulation can also help to predict and prevent alliance ruptures. For instance, knowing that a client with dyslexia had a really hard time at school might lead the therapist to be wary of using the term 'homework.' Understanding that a client has experienced multiple rejections in their life might lead the therapist to predict they would have difficulty in trusting them. Recognising and naming these potential roadblocks allows client and therapist to work together to prevent them happening. If they do occur, it is easier to manage them. There is evidence that there may be an association between repair processes and positive treatment outcome. Safran et al. (2011) conducted two sets of meta-analyses of alliance ruptures. The first examined the relation between rupture-repair episodes and outcome. The overall effect size was 0.24 (though there were only three studies; n = 148 patients) suggesting that managing alliance ruptures well may have an effect on outcome. The second set of meta-analyses (eight studies; n = 188) examined the effect of rupture resolution training on outcome. The overall pre-post r for the rupture resolution training was 0.65. However, in the seven of these studies that used controls (n = 155), the comparison between therapists trained in rupture resolution and the control group yielded an effect size of only 0.15 - small but statistically significant.

MANAGING ALLIANCE RUPTURES

Terry initially found that activity scheduling and a graded approach to returning to previous activities worked well. His mood improved and he no longer worried about needing exploratory therapy. Between session 4 and 5, however, he had a bad experience at work. His boss, who was not known for his diplomacy, criticised him in front of his colleagues. He became more depressed and again questioned whether CBT was right for him. He complained that the homework assignments were no longer working: he recently went out with his friends but felt he was just going through the motions and was putting on a mask. He also now believed homework was too trivial and didn't get to the heart of his problems.

> **Reflective question**
>
> How might you work with Terry to manage the alliance rupture and return to effective collaboration?

STEP ONE: EXPLORE AND FORMULATE THE PROBLEM

The check-in at the beginning of the session showed that Terry's scores had increased: the therapist asked if anything had happened to cause this setback. Terry did not immediately link the mood drop to his difficulties at work, so some careful exploration of the events of the week was necessary. Feedback from the homework helped identify the point at which Terry's mood dropped. The therapist summarised what they had learned so far.

> If we look at your scores over the last few weeks they have been coming down until this week. Then you had the incident at work. What do you make of that?

Terry agreed that this was what had set him back. Clarifying the trigger allowed him to get a little distance from his resentment but was not enough to re-establish collaboration. He was still sure that the therapy wasn't addressing the real problems. He believed 80% that the therapy wasn't going deep enough. His therapist asked what evidence he had for this belief, and he said his main evidence was the fact that he had put on a mask in front of his friends and had no enjoyment the whole evening. He wasn't being his real self, and he needed to understand this split between his false self (i.e. acting more positively) and his real self (which is depressed and worthless).

STEP TWO: CHECK THAT YOU HAVEN'T CAUSED THE ALLIANCE RUPTURE!

There are many ways in which we can contribute to alliance ruptures. For instance, we may not have been clear about the rationale for an intervention, so the client failed to do it. Or we may have chosen the wrong intervention - perhaps the patient was too depressed to carry out the assignments. In this case, the therapist felt that Terry had been enthusiastic about meeting his friends at the last session and, given his improved depression scores, this seemed an appropriate homework task. It looked like it was the drop in his mood that had led him to become hopeless about therapy. If the problem had been a result of poor technique, it would have been important to acknowledge this and explore together how a more effective assignment could be planned.

STEP THREE: CHOOSE A STRATEGY TO REPAIR THE RUPTURE

Terry had, until recently, benefited from therapy and accepted the CBT rationale, so his therapist decided to find a way to gently remind him of this.

Therapist: If we had been talking about the usefulness of this behavioural work last week, what would you have said?

Terry: I would have said it was helping, but I was just fooling myself.

Therapist: That's interesting. What makes you sure that your 'real self' is the depressed one? Was there something about the incident with your boss that pushed some buttons?

Terry was angry with his boss for humiliating him, but he also believed that it confirmed his inadequacy. Alongside the thoughts, 'Who does he think he is!' he reported the thoughts, 'I'm useless. He's right.' Examining the evidence for his beliefs uncovered the fact that Terry had not done the particular job very well, but his performance was not significantly worse than any of his colleagues. The boss criticised them just as much as Terry. As well as challenging these depressive cognitions, the therapist linked these to Terry's secret fears about himself: 'I am worthless and inadequate' and 'Others will criticise and treat me with contempt.' By discussing how the boss's behaviour reminded him of his stepfather and activated his core negative beliefs, Terry was able to see that this is what triggered the drop in his mood. He also learned that CBT can address early experiences.

Therapist: What do you make of that?

Terry: I can see that it set off something deep about how I feel about myself.

Therapist: Yes, and once that happens and we start to believe our negative thoughts the depression can spiral.

Terry: It certainly has done this week. But don't we need to look at how I'm playing out the same pattern I had with my stepfather?

Therapist: You've said your boss puts down everyone else in the team. Have they all had problems with their fathers? Is it that you're re-enacting a pattern, or is it that criticism triggers these memories and negative beliefs about yourself?

Terry: I suppose it's the second.

Therapist: If we can help you to challenge these thoughts that you're inadequate and worthless, perhaps you can withstand his criticism. Would you be willing to try?

They then discussed the meeting with his friends, and Terry quickly remembered that he had been ruminating about the incident at work all evening. He decided that this could have been a factor in his failure to engage and enjoy their night out. Returning to the activity schedule, the therapist noted that Terry had been doing less and had given lower ratings for pleasure, mastery and motivation for the second half of the week - after his run in with the boss. He recognised that his mood had dropped and he had fallen back into withdrawal and rumination. The therapist asked Terry to remind her of the rationale for activity scheduling and what he had been finding helpful up to now. By the end of the session, his belief that the therapy wasn't deep enough had reduced to 30% and his belief that it might help him had increased to 70%. Terry resumed scheduling activities and made a commitment to look out for temptations to avoid and procrastinate. He also agreed to an experiment: to monitor his automatic thoughts in various situations over the subsequent week, to see if there was a correlation between berating himself for being inadequate, his mood and his sense that he was putting on a mask.

The strategy was:

1. to evaluate Terry's belief that his setback occurred because therapy wasn't addressing the important issues, and to demonstrate that CBT does not ignore early experiences (clarifying a misunderstanding of the model)
2. then to return to the benefits he had been getting from behavioural work (repeating the therapeutic rationale)
3. but also to move on to monitoring some of the thoughts and beliefs that had originated in childhood to evaluate their effect in the present (changing tasks to make them relevant to client's concerns).

CHAPTER SUMMARY

There is a wealth of evidence that the therapeutic alliance is associated with better outcome across all psychotherapies, but in CBT this correlation may be a result of effective change strategies creating a better alliance rather than the alliance being the driver for change. Agreements on the tasks and goals of therapy are probably of more significance in CBT than the affective bond, but in some conditions, such as depression in the elderly, a supportive relationship may be an important factor in itself. Socialisation to the model is therefore a key part of establishing a therapeutic relationship in CBT, as is the use of collaborative empiricism throughout treatment. A case is used to illustrate how a collaborative relationship can be built and how to manage an alliance rupture when there is a disagreement over the goals of therapy.

FURTHER READING

Dattilio FM and Hanna MA (2012) Collaboration in cognitive-behavior therapy. *Journal of Clinical Psychology: In Session* 68: 146–158.

REFERENCES

Andrusyna TP, Tang TZ, DeRubeis RJ and Luborsky L (2001) The factor structure of the Working Alliance Inventory in cognitive-behavioral therapy. *Journal of Psychotherapy Practice and Research 10*: 173–178.

Baldwin SA, Wampold BE and Imel ZE (2007) Untangling the alliance-outcome correlation: Exploring the relative importance of therapist and patient variability in the alliance. *Journal of Consulting and Clinical Psychology 75*: 842.

Beck AT, Emery G with Greenberg R (1985) *Anxiety disorders and phobias: A cognitive perspective*. New York, NY: Basic Books.

Bordin ES (1979) The generalizability of the psychoanalytic concept of the working alliance. *Psychotherapy: Theory, Research, Practice 16*: 252-260.

Cloitre M, Chase SK, Miranda R and Chemtob CM (2004) Therapeutic alliance, negative mood regulation, and treatment outcome in child abuse-related posttraumatic stress disorder. *Journal of Consulting and Clinical Psychology 72*: 411–416.

Dattilio FM and Hanna MA (2012) Collaboration in cognitive-behavior therapy. *Journal of Clinical Psychology: In Session 68*: 146–158.

Del Re AC, Flückiger C, Horvath AO, Symonds D and Wampold BE (2012) Therapist effects in the therapeutic alliance-outcome relationship: A restricted-maximum likelihood meta-analysis. *Clinical Psychology Review 32*: 642–649.

DeRubeis RJ and Feeley M (1990) Determinants of change in cognitive therapy for depression. *Cognitive Therapy and Research 14*: 469–482.

Feeley M, DeRubeis RJ and Gelfand LA (1999) The temporal relation of adherence and alliance to symptom change in cognitive therapy for depression. *Journal of Consulting and Clinical Psychology 67*: 578–582.

Freeman A and McCloskey RD (2003) Impediments to effective psychotherapy. In: Leahy RL (ed) *Roadblocks in cognitive-behavioral therapy: Transforming challenges into opportunities for change*. New York: Guilford Press, pp. 24-48.

Freud S (1912/1966). *The Dynamics of Transference*. Standard Edition, *12*, 97–108.

Gaston L, Marmar CR, Gallagher D and Thompson LW (1991) Alliance prediction of outcome beyond in-treatment symptomatic change as psychotherapy processes. *Psychotherapy Research 1*: 104–113.

Gelso CJ and Hayes JA (1998) *The psychotherapy relationship: Theory, research, and practice*. New York: Wiley.

Goldsmith LP, Lewis SW, Dunn G and Bentall RP (2015) Psychological treatments for early psychosis can be beneficial or harmful, depending on the therapeutic alliance: an instrumental variable analysis. *Psychological Medicine 45*(11): 2365–2373.

Horvath AO and Greenberg LS (1986) The development of the Working Alliance Inventory. In: Greenberg LS and Pinsoff WM (eds) *The Psychotherapeutic Process: A Research Handbook*. New York, NY: Guilford Press, pp. 529–556.

Horvath AO and Greenberg LS (1989) Development and validation of the Working Alliance Inventory. *Journal of Counseling Psychology 36*: 223–233.

Horvath AO and Symonds BD (1991) Relation between working alliance and outcome in psychotherapy: a meta-analysis. *Journal of Counselling Psychology 38*, 139–149.

Horvath AO, Del Re AC, Flückiger C and Symonds D (2011) Alliance in individual psychotherapy. *Psychotherapy 48*: 9–16.

Kazantzis N, Tee JM, Dattilio FM and Dobson KS (2013) How to develop collaborative empiricism in cognitive behavior therapy: Conclusions from the C&BP special series. *Cognitive and Behavioral Practice 20*: 455–460.

Klein DN, Schwartz JE, Santiago NJ, Vivian D, Vocisano C, Castonguay LG, Arnow B, Blalock JA, Manber R, Markowitz JC, Riso LP, Rothbaum BO, McCullough JP, Thase ME, Borian FE, Miller IW and Keller MB (2003) Therapeutic alliance in depression treatment: controlling for prior change and patient characteristics. *Journal of Consulting and Clinical Psychology 71*(6): 997–1006.

Krupnick JL, Sotsky SM, Simmens S, Moyer J, Elkin I, Watkins J and Pilkonis PA (1996) The role of the therapeutic alliance in psychotherapy and pharmacotherapy outcome: findings in the National Institute of Mental Health Treatment of Depression Collaborative Research Program. *Journal of Consulting and Clinical Psychology 64*: 532–539.

Lorenzo-Luaces L, DeRubeis RJ and Webb CA (2014) Client characteristics as moderators of the relation between the therapeutic alliance and outcome in cognitive therapy for depression. *Journal of Consulting and Clinical Psychology 82*: 368.

Martin DJ, Garske JP and Davis MK (2000) Relation of the therapeutic alliance with outcome and other variables: a meta-analytic review. *Journal of Consulting and Clinical Psychology 68*: 438–450.

McAleavey AA and Castonguay LG (2015) The process of change in psychotherapy: Common and unique factors. In: Gelo, OCG, Pritz, A, and Rieken, B. (eds.) *Psychotherapy Research*. Vienna: Springer, pp. 293–310.

McEvoy PM, Burgess MM and Nathan P (2014) The relationship between interpersonal problems, therapeutic alliance, and outcomes following group and individual cognitive behaviour therapy. *Journal of Affective Disorders 157*: 25–32.

Ramnerö J and Öst LG (2007) Therapists' and clients' perception of each other and working alliance in the behavioral treatment of panic disorder and agoraphobia. *Psychotherapy Research 17*(3): 320–328.

Safran JD and Muran JC (2000) *Negotiating the therapeutic alliance: A relational treatment guide*. New York, NY: Guilford Press.

Safran JD, Muran JC and Eubanks-Carter C (2011) Repairing alliance ruptures. In: Norcross JC (ed), *Psychotherapy relationships that work: Evidence-based responsiveness* (2nd ed.,). New York, NY: Oxford University Press, pp. 224–238.

Spitzer RL, Kroenke K, Williams JB and Löwe B (2006) A brief measure for assessing generalized anxiety disorder: the GAD-7. *Archives of Internal Medicine 166*: 1092–1097.

Spitzer RL, Kroenke K, Williams JB and Patient Health Questionnaire Primary Care Study Group (1999) Validation and utility of a self-report version of PRIME-MD: the PHQ primary care study. *Journal of the American Medical Association 282*: 1737–1744.

Tee J and Kazantzis N (2011) Collaborative empiricism in cognitive therapy: A definition and theory for the relationship construct. *Clinical Psychology: Science and Practice 18*: 47–61.

Tryon GS and Winograd G (2011) Goal consensus and collaboration. In: Norcross JC (ed), *Psychotherapy Relationships That Work: Evidence-based Responsiveness* (2nd ed.). New York, NY: Oxford University Press, pp. 153–167.

Turner H, Bryant-Waugh R and Marshall E (2015) The impact of early symptom change and therapeutic alliance on treatment outcome in cognitive-behavioural therapy for eating disorders. *Behaviour Research and Therapy 73*: 165–169.

Wampold BE (2001) *The great psychotherapy debate: Models, methods, and findings*. Mahwah, NJ: Erlbaum.

Webb CA, DeRubeis RJ, Amsterdam JD, Shelton RC, Hollon SD and Dimidjian S (2011) Two aspects of the therapeutic alliance: differential relations with depressive symptom change. *Journal of Consulting and Clinical Psychology 79*: 279.

Weck F, Rudari V, Hilling C, Hautzinger M, Heidenreich T, Schermelleh-Engel K and Stangier U (2013) Relapses in recurrent depression 1 year after maintenance cognitive-behavioral therapy: The role of therapist adherence, competence, and the therapeutic alliance. *Psychiatry Research 210*: 140–145.

Wiseman H, Tishby O and Barber JP (2012) Collaboration in Psychodynamic Psychotherapy, *Journal of Clinical Psychology: In Session 68*: 136–145.

3

INTERPERSONAL SCHEMAS: UNDERSTANDING TRANSFERENCE AND COUNTERTRANSFERENCE IN CBT

STIRLING MOOREY AND ANNA LAVENDER

CHAPTER OVERVIEW

This chapter will review the concept of the interpersonal schema: a template for perception, prediction and performance of our interactions with other people. It will examine how the therapy relationship in CBT differs from that in more interpersonally based therapies and why transference and countertransference do not require close attention in CBT for Axis I disorders. It suggests that, as the degree of personality difficulty increases, it becomes more likely that the relationship becomes a focus for therapy. The contributions of writers like Robert Leahy to the CBT understanding of transference and countertransference are considered, and the Interpersonal Schema Worksheet is introduced as a method for conceptualising the therapeutic interaction.

THE THERAPEUTIC RELATIONSHIP IN CBT

In the first chapter, we examined the role of common factors in CBT, noting how empathy can facilitate effective alliance building, formulation and treatment. In Chapter 2, we explored the therapeutic alliance itself and considered how CBT manages alliance ruptures. For many patients, the core conditions of warmth, genuineness and empathy, combined with sensitive attention to the alliance, are sufficient to keep the process of collaborative empiricism on track. The relationship is not singled out for special attention beyond the need to establish and maintain a therapeutic partnership. Past experiences are addressed when it is helpful to understand how particular beliefs may have been formed, but this exploration is always in the service of solving here-and-now problems. Figure 3.1 illustrates the relative place of the problem, past experiences and the therapy relationship in CBT.

Psychodynamic psychotherapy works very differently. The therapeutic relationship is itself the vehicle for change, so the collaboration (working alliance) from the 'healthy' part of the patient is focused on gaining insight into the maladaptive patterns of relating with the therapist in the session. Classically, psychodynamic psychotherapy looks at how past relationship patterns are played out in the patient's current relationships outside and inside the therapy consultation. This transfer of feelings from significant attachment figures from the past to the therapist in the present is termed transference. Through recognition and exploration of these patterns as they are repeated in the therapy relationship, the patient gains insight and can find new ways to think, feel and behave. Figure 3.2 illustrates the place of current problems, past experience and patient–therapist relationship in psychodynamic psychotherapy.

Psychodynamic therapists were initially surprised that cognitive and behaviour therapists achieved results without attending to the transference. But there are a number of aspects of CBT that discourage the development of a negative regressive transference. By focusing openly and explicitly on problems 'out there,' the relationship is kept on a more business-like level: the therapist does not give it the exquisite attention seen in other therapies. The structure of therapy - agenda setting, summaries and feedback - helps to maintain the problem focus and gives less room for the development of transference. The more open, more active role of the therapist, together with appropriate personal disclosure, means that the patient achieves an impression of a real person. The building of a collaborative problem-solving partnership brings the patient's healthy rational side to the foreground

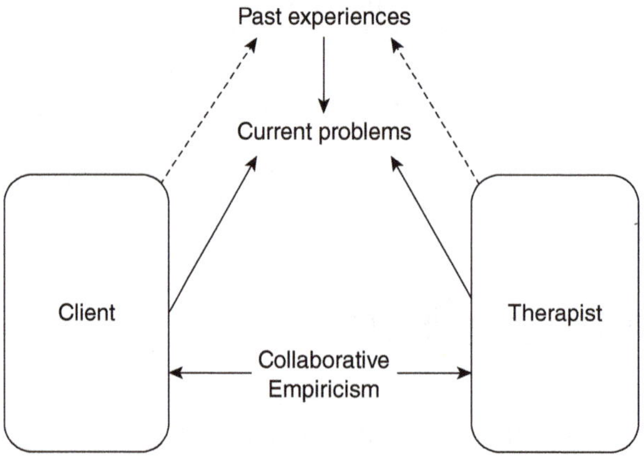

Figure 3.1 The therapeutic relationship in CBT for Axis I disorders

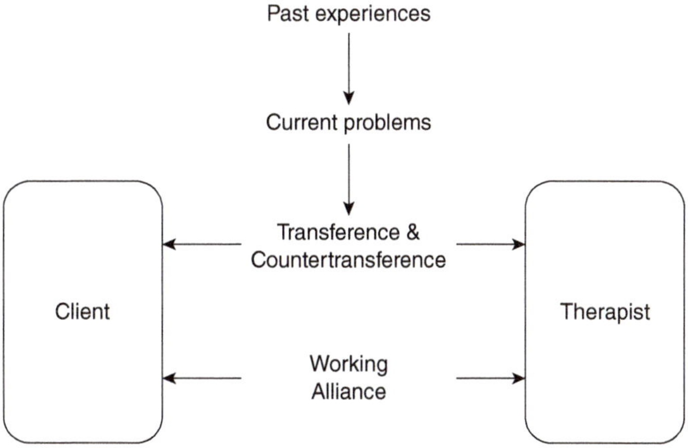

Figure 3.2 The therapeutic relationship in psychodynamic psychotherapy

(Moorey, 2014: 138–139). As a psychodynamic therapist has observed, psychoanalytic therapists allow the transference to grow 'and invite its expression' while CBT therapists try to reduce it through 'benign neglect or by challenging its interpersonal evidence' (Ivey, 2013: 234–235).

Despite features minimising transference, interpersonal problems still crop up in CBT and interfere with an external problem focus. A patient who believes they are incompetent and cannot function alone may have difficulty taking responsibility and becoming their own therapist, or a patient who wants to work on the extremely high standards they have for themselves and others may criticise the therapist for not being good enough. In these cases, it sometimes becomes necessary to address the therapeutic relationship directly. The more that patients express maladaptive personality traits, the more CBT may need to address these interpersonal beliefs and their impact on in-session behaviour.

The extent to which the patient's behaviour towards the therapist becomes a focus for change depends upon the disorder being treated and the goals of therapy. In general, Axis I disorders (DSM V) require a focus on an externalised problem (e.g. depression, health anxiety, panic, eating disorder), and the goals of therapy are to teach self-management skills to deal with the problem. Patients with Axis I disorders usually have had a time during which they have functioned reasonably well, so can draw on more positive memories. They also have a stable sense of self and can function in a more rational 'healthy adult' mode. Patients with Axis II disorders (e.g. dependent, avoidant or emotionally unstable personality disorder) may not have had a time when they functioned normally, so have little experience of effective problem solving to draw on. Their sense of self may be overly rigid or unstable, and their rational healthy adult is less well developed. Their problems are often in the interpersonal realm and so, in an Axis II disorder, the therapy relationship is a necessary component of treatment. Many patients fall between the straightforward Axis I

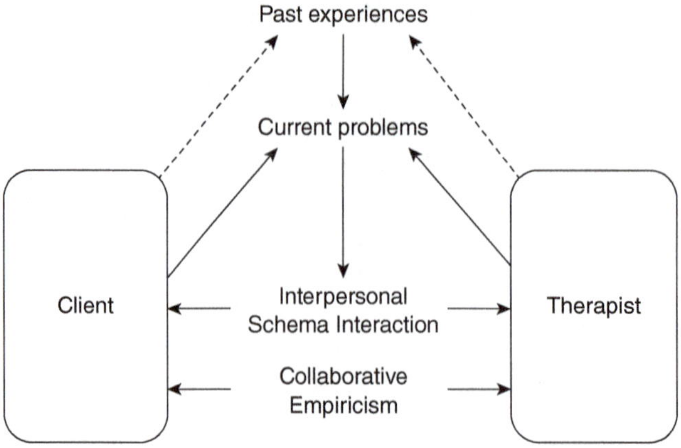

Figure 3.3 The therapeutic relationship in CBT patients with co-morbid Axis II traits

disorders and full blown Axis II personality disorders. Axis II traits will often interfere with the collaborative relationship. Attention to maladaptive patterns in the therapeutic relationship may then be essential in order to reduce therapy interfering behaviours and maximise collaboration. Figure 3.3 illustrates how the interaction between the interpersonal schemas of therapist and patient is an added factor in patients with co-morbid Axis II traits.

Reflective case example

Piers: predicting therapeutic challenges

We met Piers, a successful 30-year-old entrepreneur, in Chapter 1. He came to therapy because of lifelong feelings of dissatisfaction and self-hatred. He spent much of the therapy session either talking about the amount of money he was making, describing angry ruminations about the people who had put him down in his work and private life or subtly undermining the therapist's competence. Piers coped with his painful feelings through alcohol and cocaine use and compulsive use of prostitutes. Piers was an only child. His parents were cold and distant, gave him lots of material gifts but little love, and sent him to boarding school from an early age. His father was a high flyer in the City who expected him to succeed and so the only positive rewards he received were for success.

Imagine you are working with Piers. What might Piers' core beliefs about himself and others be? What interpersonal rules might he be living by? In what ways might Piers challenge the therapeutic alliance?

INTERPERSONAL SCHEMAS

Patients' therapy-interfering behaviours can be understood in terms of activation of interpersonal schemas (Safran and Segal, 1990; Scarvalone, 2005) and the therapeutic impasses that result as the interaction between the patient's and therapist's schemas (Leahy, 2003; Moorey, 2014). An *interpersonal schema* is a structure for interpreting and evaluating information about relationships. The schema integrates cognitive, affective, memory, behavioural and somatic elements of an interaction. Interpersonal schemas contain information about the self, the other and the relationship between them. This information is based on repeated experiences of interactions with other people encoded as declarative and procedural memories: implicit and explicit beliefs and rules about how relationships work. They are scripts for predicting the behaviour of other people and directing the individual's response, which function as 'if–then' rules (Baldwin, 1997):

> A woman might learn in her interactions with her husband that "If I get angry, then he will treat me with respect." A man might develop a relational schema for interactions with his boss, to the effect that "If I work late in the evening, then my boss will smile at me and call me a good worker." (Baldwin, 1997: 328)

The scripts may have a narrative quality as they describe an expected sequence of interactions. For instance, a patient with approval-seeking traits might demonstrate the following sequence: 'I believe I am unworthy, so I look for approval and try to please you, but you will act with disdain, and so prove my worthlessness.' As with any schema, these interpersonal schemas follow a confirmatory bias and so are self-fulfilling. Cognitive processes in operation in close relationships include *selective attention* to events confirming beliefs, *attributions* about the causes of events in the relationship, *expectancies* about the probability of events occurring, *assumptions* about how relationships work and *standards* for how relationships should be (Baucom and Epstein, 1990). The person who believes she is worthless, and that others will act with contempt, may misinterpret a friend glancing at her watch as a sign that she is not interested – 'I'm not worth bothering with.' Behavioural processes also contribute to schema-confirmation. The patient's obsequiousness may lead the other person to respect her less and so treat her with the disdain she expected. Through non-verbal and verbal behaviour, the other person is recruited into a role that confirms the individual's beliefs about the relationship. This can lead to a perpetuating vicious cycle or *cognitive-interpersonal cycle* (Safran, 1990). For instance, a depressed person may push others away (Kahn et al., 1985), confirming negative beliefs about his lack of worth, or elicit reassurance (Joiner and Metalsky, 1995), confirming his sense of helplessness.

Cognitive models of interpersonal relationships have actually been around for a long time. Freud believed that individuals had a relationship pattern, 'a stereotype plate (or several such), which is constantly repeated – constantly reprinted afresh – in the course of the person's life' (Freud, 1912: 99–100). Bowlby (1988) introduced the idea of 'internal working models' of the self, the world and the relationship between them, which are formed on the basis of perceptions and experiences with significant attachment figures. They comprise a model of the world – 'Who will care for me,

Box 3.1 Interpersonal schemas

- Structures for interpreting and evaluating information about relationships.
- Contain information about the self, the other and the relationship between them.

  I am incompetent and bad.
  Others are critical, rejecting and demanding.

- Integrate cognitive, affective, memory, behavioural and somatic elements of interaction.
- Can be seen as a 'programme for maintaining relatedness' but may have different aims – intimacy, power, attachment.
- Are scripts with a narrative quality, i.e. describe a sequence of interactions.
- Follow 'if–then' rules predicting the effect of your behaviour on others.

  If I show my real self, I will be rejected.

- Follow 'if–then' rules predicting others' behaviour and your expected response.

  People expect me to give them what they want. I must submit and please them.

- Are cognitively self-fulfilling – cognitive biases interpret relationships according to schema.

  My boss has asked me to see him. He's going to tell me my work isn't good enough.

- Are behaviourally self-fulfilling. Other person is recruited into a role that confirms the beliefs about relationships.

  Hide feelings, put on a front, give people what they want.

- May contain information about how to behave in both roles.

  Can sometimes be critical and rejecting of others.

where can I find them, and how will they treat me?' - and a model of the self - 'Am I acceptable to them?' Other psychodynamically oriented theorists have proposed cognitive models of relationships. Horowitz (1988, 1998) translated object relations into 'Role-Relationship Models.' Cognitive Analytic Therapy (CAT), influenced by Horowitz's writings, refers to these interpersonal processes as 'Reciprocal Role Procedures' (Ryle and Kerr, 2002). These theories all have a common theme: repeated experiences of a phenomenon leads to the creation of cognitive structures which guide future interactions. Box 3.1 summarises the features of interpersonal schemas. Where they differ from each other most significantly is in their conceptualisation of the motivational component of the schema. Some writers emphasise the importance of conscious life goals such as graduating or getting married (Cantor, 1990), others self-esteem (Greenberg et al., 1986) and others power (Jones and Pittman, 1982). Young's theory of Early Maladaptive Schemas (Young et al., 2003) explicitly defines schemas as arising from childhood needs that were not met. Safran and Segal (1990), drawing on Bowlby's attachment theory and Sullivan's interpersonal theory, define interpersonal schemas as 'programmes for maintaining relatedness'. Bowlby's model has been the most influential, and there is evidence for a connection between attachment style and relational schemas (Baldwin et al., 1993). Cognitive therapists have been less interested in the motivational aspects of relational models, but psychodynamic therapists see the wish (conscious or unconscious) behind an interactional pattern as central to the concept.

Therapist tip

When conceptualising a case:

- Core beliefs about the self and others will give indications of the self-other component of the patient's interpersonal schemas.
- Rules and assumptions will give an indication of beliefs about the relationship between self and other.
- Interpersonal strategies will follow from the 'if–then' rules and may either play out patterns confirming the beliefs, compensating for them or avoiding their activation.

TRANSFERENCE IN CBT

Within this more cognitive model of relationships, transference becomes less of a pathological phenomenon. It is merely a more emotionally charged version of what occurs in relationships all the time, i.e. we tend to react towards others on the basis of our expectations of how they will treat us. This will be based on past experience: the more the relationship is like key relationships from the past, the more we will react 'as if' they are the same. Transference reactions are 'habitual ways of thinking and acting that are recapitulated in the treatment setting' (Wright et al., 2017: 39). There is evidence from Susan Andersen's many years of social psychological research on this topic that everyday evaluations can be influenced by similarities of people we meet to important people from our past (Andersen and Cole, 1990; Andersen and Thorpe, 2009; Berk and Andersen, 2000). It is not surprising, then, that strong emotional reactions to the therapist can be evoked in the therapy setting, particularly if the therapy is set up in a way to promote these, as is the case with psychodynamic psychotherapy. Does transference occur in CBT? Gelso and Bhatia (2012) cite studies demonstrating the presence of transference in nonanalytic therapies. Connolly et al. (1996) used a method based on Luborsky's Core Relational Conflict Theme (CCRT: Luborsky and Crits-Cristoph, 1990) to look at transference in Cognitive Therapy (CT) and Supportive Expressive Therapy (SE) for opiate addiction. They identified narratives in the session about other people which followed the pattern of a wished outcome from the patient (e.g. to be asserting and separating), an expected response from the other person (e.g. watching and controlling) and then a response from the patient (e.g. asserting and separating). Similar narratives or interactions with the therapist were also extracted. Patients had between one and five distinct clusters of interpersonal patterns. For each patient, there was a main cluster with the greatest number of interpersonal narratives (the core maladaptive interpersonal theme). In both CT and SE, 60% of patients had an interpersonal theme that was also seen in their relationship with the therapist, i.e. a transference reaction. Bradley et al. (2005) found that ratings of transference by psychodynamic, eclectic and cognitive therapists treating patients with DSM IV personality disorders were basically similar and, on factor analysis, yielded five dimensions of patient affect and behaviour: angry/entitled, anxious/preoccupied, avoidant/counterdependent, sexualised and secure/engaged.

In schema terms, transference occurs when the patient–therapist relationship is being interpreted according to a pre-existing relational model. It becomes problematic when the patient's interpersonal schema is not updated to take account of the therapist's actual behaviour. As we have seen, by externalising the problem, encouraging joint work on problem-solving and being open and available, rather than distant and impassive, the CBT therapist increases the chances the patient will be able to relate to them on an adult–adult level. Misunderstandings of the therapist's motivations and intentions and thoughts about the patient are minimised. But transference can still arise when an interpersonal schema leads to a misinterpretation of the therapist's behaviour. This may be triggered by specific characteristics or behaviours of the therapist that activate implicit or explicit memories and beliefs about significant others in their past. The very activities that make the CBT relationship collaborative and problem-focused can be a source for a transference reaction: the structure of therapy can seem constricting and controlling to someone whose caregivers were overly strict, the expectations of self-help work may be extremely challenging for a dependent patient or the very thought of 'homework' might remind a patient of abusive school experiences.

Reflective case example

Piers: therapist emotional reactions

Piers finds it hard to keep focused during the session. He is easily distracted into complaining about his work situation, how he is not appreciated and is surrounded by incompetents. He tells you that setting an agenda cramps his style. He implies that CBT is too rational and objective and he has read about it and tried the techniques anyway. He is not very good at completing homework – too busy, had a heavy night! At other times, though, he can be very charming and amusing and gives you praise as a therapist – the other therapists he has met didn't know what they were doing. Less often, Piers becomes very dejected and seems like a helpless little boy. When he is like this, he reveals how empty his life feels.

What emotional reactions would you have if you were working with him?

Countertransference occurs when the therapist is no longer operating from a rational, healthy perspective but is either relating to the patient on the basis of their own maladaptive beliefs or is reacting to the patient's maladaptive interpersonal schemas. Although Haarhoff (2006: 127) defines countertransference from a CBT perspective as 'the therapist's cognitive, emotional, and behavioural reactions to the patient which are conscious and accessible to the therapist,' there is no reason to assume they are exclusively conscious. Implicit, procedural rules for behaving may still play a part. We may find we get angry with a patient who is not willing to take responsibility for themselves, but we do not necessarily link this to our personal rules that you should be self-reliant and not expect others to do your job for you.

Leahy has written in depth about transference and countertransference. In his book *Overcoming Resistance in Cognitive Therapy* he refers to transference as a form of 'schema resistance' (Leahy, 2003: 104–135) and outlines a number of strategies for working with the process. Prasko et al. (2010) reviewed the literature on transference and countertransference in CBT and made suggestions for how to manage various therapy interfering behaviours and how to respond to them. Prasko et al. advise the therapist to 'pay attention to any negative or positive reactions to him/her that arise' but not to 'deliberately provoke or ignore them.' They recommend vigilance for negative emotions, such as disappointment, anger and frustration, experienced by the patient in the therapeutic relationship but also for overly positive reactions such as idealisation, praise or attempts to divert the attention of therapy onto the therapist (Prasko et al., 2010: 190). Just as the therapist should look out for signs of hot cognitions in the session, he/she can look out for transference reactions:

> there may be a sudden change in the patient's nonverbal behavior: sudden change in expression, abruptly switching to a new topic, stammer, block, pauses in the middle of a train of statements, slumping posture, clenching fists, kicking, tapping foot and so on. One of the most revealing signs is a shift in the patient's gaze, especially if he/she has had a thought but prefers not to reveal it. When asked, the patient may say, 'It is not important.' The therapist should press the patient nonetheless, gently, as it might be important important. (Prasko et al., 2010: 190)

COUNTERTRANSFERENCE IN CBT

Countertransference arises when the therapist's cognitions about the patient are no longer based on rational, collaborative processing but have been hijacked either by the therapist's own personal agenda or by a reaction to the patient's schematic material. *Personal countertransference* can be understood to arise from the therapist's beliefs about therapy or about relationships in general. These are not mutually exclusive: therapist beliefs about the self and other people, e.g. 'If I upset someone it means I am a bad person' influence therapy specific beliefs, e.g. 'If I push the patient to do a challenging experiment they will be upset.' These beliefs can remain implicit and so create blind spots for the therapist. Therapist negative beliefs about exposure such as 'Compared to other psychotherapies, exposure therapy leads to higher dropout rates' and 'Conducting exposure therapy sessions outside the office increases the risk of an unethical dual relationship with the client' are associated with more cautious delivery of exposure therapy (Deacon et al., 2013; Farrell et al., 2013). McLean et al. (2003) have developed a Therapist Beliefs Scale which measures beliefs related to low tolerance of distress (I must not make mistakes in therapy, if I do then I've failed), rigid adherence to therapeutic model (If I deviate from the clinical model then I've failed), beliefs of responsibility (If my clients do not progress it is my responsibility) and need for control and understanding (I must fully understand my client or I won't feel effective). Therapist beliefs were associated with vicarious traumatisation and burnout. Another form of personal countertransference arises from therapist beliefs about particular groups of people. Because of her age and appearance, a patient may remind a therapist of their grandmother and so all the memories and associations, good or bad, may lead to erroneous assumptions about the patient. Strongly held beliefs about groups of people, such as the British National Party members or paedophiles, might generate strong emotions and assumptions that again may not necessarily be correct and can impede therapy.

A second type of countertransference arises from the interaction between the patient's and therapist's schemas. This can be termed *reciprocal countertransference* (Moorey, 2014). Similar schemas may be active in patient and therapist during a session (*schema congruence or schema fit*), which may be very adaptive if the schemas involve a shared view of the relationship as open, respectful and mutually helpful since this supports collaboration. But if, for instance, a depressed patient's hopelessness and helplessness becomes infectious, the therapist may buy in to the patient's belief system (Beck et al., 1979: 59) and become hopeless too (a form of empathic overidentification, as discussed in Chapter 1). Here, the therapist has attuned to the patient's internal world, 'from the inside,' and is experiencing some of the hopelessness with which the patient is struggling but has not been able to hold on to a separate awareness that these thoughts may not be facts. *Schema conflict*, in contrast, is a result of a mismatch between the patient's beliefs and the therapist's beliefs. Therapists may view depressed patients as 'wilfully passive, indecisive, and manipulative' (Beck et al., 1979: 58) and so fail to empathise; or a patient with a belief that 'I am special and the usual rules don't apply' may come up against a therapist with a strong belief that 'You should work hard and take responsibility for yourself.' Schemas may match or rub against each other, but they may also interact in a mutually confirming pattern. This *schema complementarity* is seen when the interpersonal beliefs and needs of patient and therapist create a self-perpetuating cycle: an example of Safran's cognitive-interpersonal cycle (Safran, 1990). For instance, when a patient with a dependency schema meets a therapist with an unrelenting standards schema, the therapist may work hard but end up looking after the patient. A narcissistic patient with entitlement beliefs may induce a therapist with a self-sacrifice or subjugation schema to treat them in a special way. Leahy (2003) describes 15 common therapist schemas, including demanding standards (I have to cure all my patients), being a special superior person (My patient should appreciate all that I do for them), excessive self-sacrifice (I should meet my patient's needs) and need for approval (I want to be liked by the patient) (Leahy, 2003: 256). Haarhoff (2006), using Leahy's Therapist Schema Questionnaire, found that the commonest schemas of CBT therapists were demanding standards, special superior person and excessive self-sacrifice.

Box 3.2 Leahy's Therapist Schemas (Leahy, 2003)

Special, superior person
Abandonment
Control
Need for approval
Witholding
Goal inhibition
Emotional inhibition
Judgmental
Rejection sensitive
Autonomy
Persecution
Need to like others
Helplessness
Excessive self-sacrifice
Demanding standards

Betan et al. (2005), in a study of North American psychiatrists and psychologists, identified eight countertransference themes: overwhelmed/disorganised, helpless/inadequate, positive, special/overinvolved, sexualised, disengaged, parental/protective and criticised/mistreated. When our own beliefs about relationships are activated, it can be difficult to disentangle what is me and what is the patient (Moorey, 2014). This underlines the importance of supervision and discussion with colleagues as a place where our feelings and automatic thoughts about our patients can be safely explored. Prasko et al. (2010) suggest some questions that therapists might ask themselves:

- What are my emotional reactions to this patient?
- Are they somewhat exaggerated?
- What is making me like or dislike this patient?
- What issues do I want or not want to discuss with this patient?
- What is making me feel uncomfortable?
- What were some signs of the patient's pathology that I had missed? What was it about me that made me miss them?

Good resources are now becoming available for therapists to reflect on their practice (e.g. Bennett-Levy et al., 2015). The rest of this chapter will introduce a method for mapping the therapy relationship that may be helpful in understanding and managing both transference and countertransference – *The Interpersonal Schema Worksheet.*

Box 3.3 Prasko's examples of countertransference (Prasko et al., 2010)

Moderate positive
Over-protective
Apprehensive
Distrustful
Competitive
Admiring
Erotic
Aggressive (invasive)
Derogatory

WORKING WITH INTERPERSONAL SCHEMAS

The Interpersonal Schema Worksheet (Moorey, 2013: Figure 3.4) offers a way to conceptualise the in-session thoughts, emotions and behaviours of patient and therapist and their respective rules for relating. The conceptualisation is best developed within supervision, where the therapist can explore his or her reactions with support from the supervisor who uses guided discovery to elucidate the interpersonal cycles being played out in the session. As we have seen, these reactions often occur because of our blind spots, and it is therefore helpful to have someone outside the therapy session to facilitate our understanding of them. It may be time-consuming to develop the whole worksheet in the supervision session, so the therapist is advised to complete as much as possible prior to supervision. As with much preparation for supervision, this may, in itself, answer the supervisee's question.

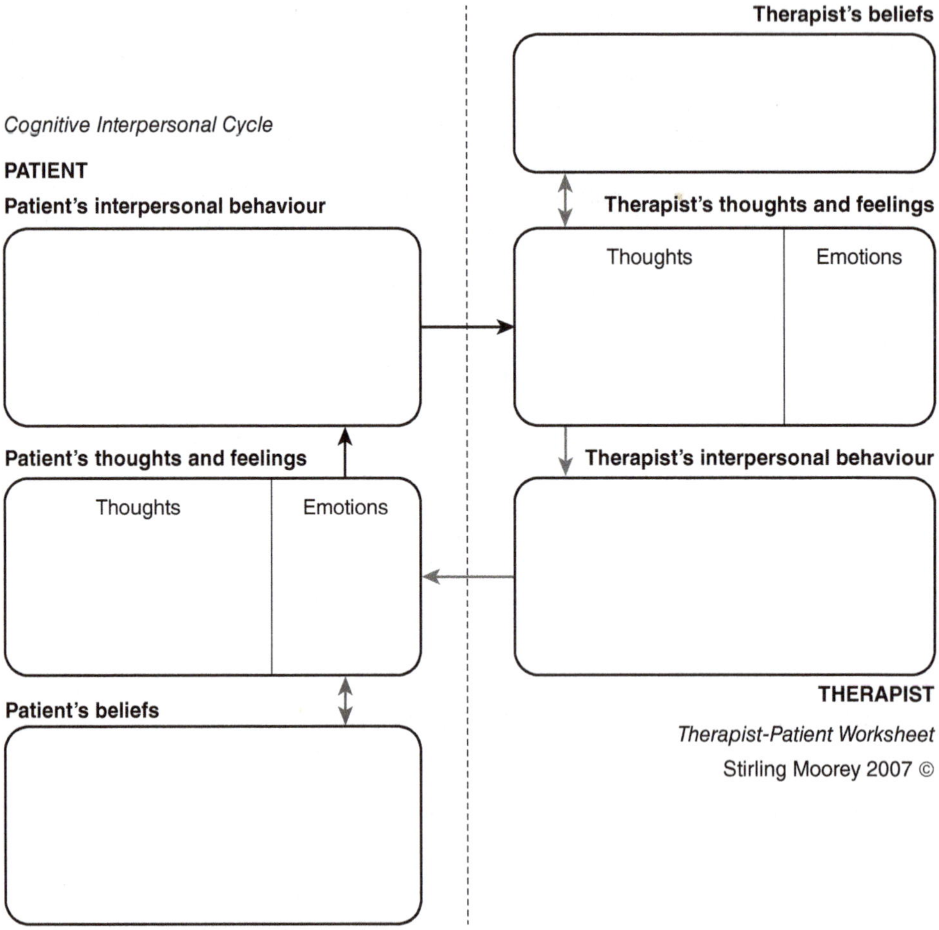

Figure 3.4 The Interpersonal Schema Worksheet

With the partially completed worksheet as a starting point, further exploration of what might be happening in the session can take place in supervision. The therapist can also use the worksheet as part of their own preparation for the therapy session. Let us use the worksheet to conceptualise a cycle that might play out between Piers and his therapist, Paul. It is possible to start at any point in the cycle, but the patient's behaviour and therapist's thoughts and feelings in response to this are usually where most evidence is available. Let us assume Paul is very aware of *most* of Piers' therapy interfering behaviour and identifies that he is:

- diverting the conversation, not following the agenda (avoidance)
- not completing homework assignments (avoidance)
- talking about all the money he is making (self-aggrandisement)
- complaining about work, blaming others for his problems (denigrating others)
- criticising CBT, and subtly demeaning the therapist (denigrating others)

Outside the session, Piers' use of cocaine and prostitutes is clearly an important avoidance/maladaptive self-soothing strategy; but it may also be interfering with his capacity to focus and preventing him from doing homework. In reaction to all this, the therapist feels angry, defensive and repulsed by Piers' narcissistic lifestyle. His automatic thoughts are:

- He's not doing any work. He's lazy and selfish → anger
- He's disgusting → anger and disgust
- He'll never improve → hopelessness
- I'm not good enough. He needs a more experienced therapist → dejection and helplessness

What is Paul doing in response to Piers' behaviour? Listening to a recording of a session reveals that Paul's voice barely conceals his irritation, and he falls back on reiterating the importance of doing homework and he tetchily reinforces the cognitive model. He sounds punitive and frustrated. But, at other times in the session, Piers appears more engaged and tells him what a good therapist he is. At this point, the therapist seems to be sitting back and enjoying the praise. As a result of supervision, Paul's behaviours are identified:

- rigidly reiterating the model and rationale
- becoming more didactic
- subtly criticising and silently disapproving
- accepting and colluding with praise

And another of Piers' strategies has become clear:

- flatter and praise (placation)

It may be difficult at this stage to be clear about what Piers is thinking in the session but we do know he has said various things, and behaved in ways, that allow us to hypothesise about some of his beliefs:

- If I succeed and do better than other people, I can feel OK about myself.
- If I tell people about my success they will admire me.
- People who fail are contemptible.
- I shouldn't have to do anything I don't want to do.
- I can't tolerate difficult feelings.

We can hypothesise that these beliefs and strategies are ways of compensating for the empty, despairing, self-critical state he occasionally displays in the session. In this state, he believes he is despicable and unlovable. The final component of the cycle is the therapist's beliefs. The therapist recognised a dichotomous belief: 'If a client isn't getting better either it's because I'm doing something wrong or the client isn't doing enough.' He was also rather surprised to discover that, despite thinking he was broad minded, there was something about Piers' libertarian lifestyle he found reprehensible. He strongly believed 'you must take responsibility for your actions' and he thought Piers was acting selfishly and irresponsibly. Box 3.4 summarises the steps in completing the worksheet.

Box 3.4 Guide for completing the Interpersonal Schema Worksheet

Step 1 – Choose a recurring difficulty you encounter in the therapeutic relationship.

Either (a) a recurring problem with a particular client **or** (b) recurring problems across a range of clients.

Step 2 – What is the salient feature of this problem?

Is it the client's behaviour (e.g. failing to complete homework), the thoughts and feelings evoked in you (e.g. irritability), the way you find yourself behaving (e.g. becoming controlling and demanding)?

Step 3 – Complete the interpersonal cycle, starting at the point identified in Step 2.

What is the client doing or saying, how does it make you think and feel, how do you react in the session, what effect does this have on the client's thoughts and feelings? It may be easier to recognise the client's behaviour and your emotions; your own thoughts and behavioural response may be less easy to recognise; and you may or may not have sufficient information to be sure of the client's thoughts and feelings – these may be speculative at this stage.

Step 4 – Fill in the boxes for client and therapist beliefs.

These may be specific beliefs about therapy or more general interpersonal beliefs. Do these fit with your conceptualisation of the patient or knowledge of yourself?

Step 5 – Examine the interpersonal cycle.

Is there an interaction going on that reinforces unhelpful behaviour from client and therapist?

Is there a conflict or collusion of therapist and client beliefs?

Step 6 – Develop a plan to break the cycle.

For example:

- Clarify the client's thoughts, feelings and beliefs about therapy if these are not clear.
- Draw out the maladaptive cycle in collaboration with the client and problem solve together.
- Reality test the client's thoughts and feelings about you or the therapy.
- Set up an experiment to test these or help the client experiment with alternative behaviour in the session.
- Place the beliefs and behaviour in the context of the overall conceptualisation.
- Examine and test your own thoughts.
- Experiment with an alternative attitude and behaviour towards the client that breaks the cycle.
- Develop and practice more adaptive therapeutic beliefs.

Figure 3.5 is a completed worksheet for the interaction between Piers and the therapist. By completing this, the therapist was able to see how Piers' automatic thoughts and behaviour were very much part of his set of defensive strategies to avoid some of his painful negative thoughts and feelings. Some of the methods described in Chapter 1, such as role play, exploring Piers' childhood experiences etc., can be used here to empathise with Piers' underlying feelings. The therapist could see how his countertransference reactions were leading him to focus too much on technique and become too directive and didactic in the session. His own morals and values were impinging on his ability to do therapy with the narcissistic patient. Recognising that most of this patient's behaviour could be understood as maladaptive attempts to manage a core pain from childhood, i.e. that he was unloved, that others were emotionally unavailable and that they were critical and demeaning, helped. So did the recognition of the function of this behaviour, whether it was avoidance, denigrating others and self-aggrandising to raise his self-esteem, trying desperately to soothe his pain or flattering to get acceptance. The therapist also saw that he and Piers were caught in a number of cognitive-interpersonal cycles in which one or the other would occupy a superior contemptuous position. Taking the stance that Piers' goals were legitimate (looking for happiness and building a sense of worth) but the strategies he was using were unhelpful allowed the therapist to explore the way in which these strategies played out in his life and also in the therapy session.

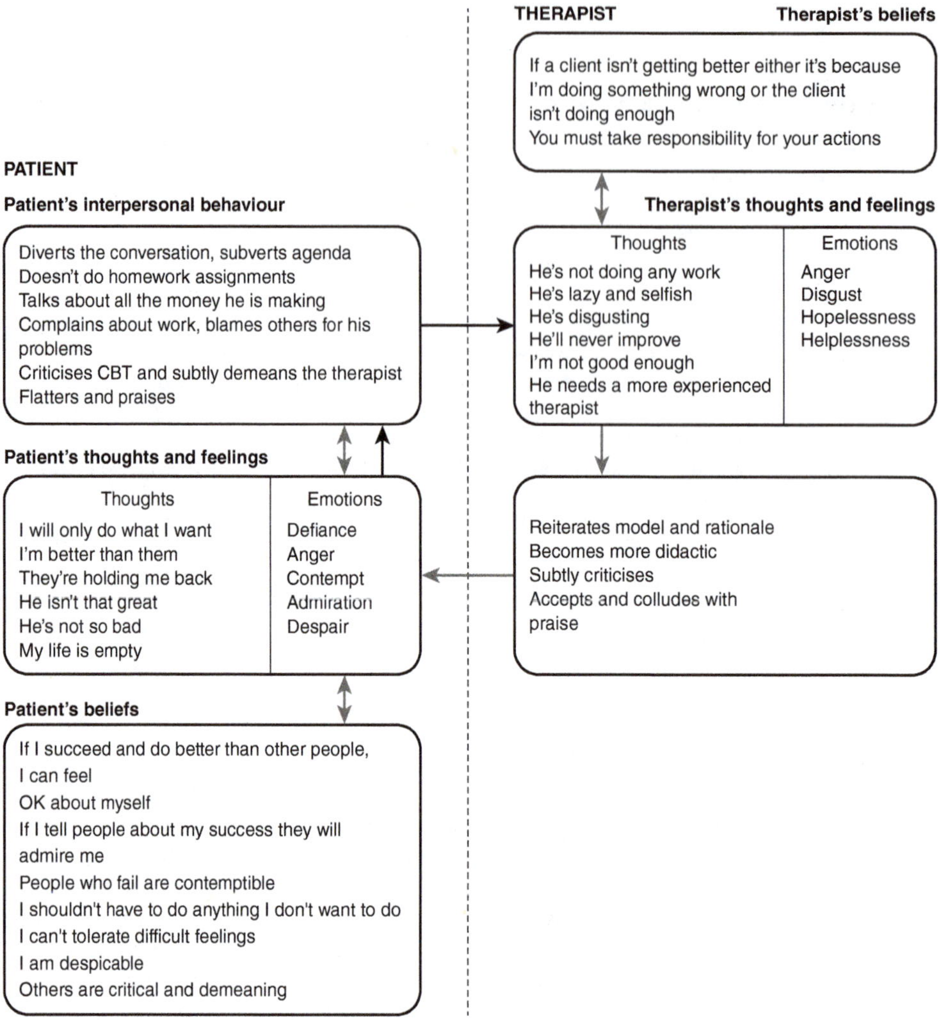

Figure 3.5 Piers' Interpersonal Schema Worksheet

CHAPTER SUMMARY

This chapter began by looking at the nature of the therapeutic relationship in CBT and suggested that the externalisation of the presenting problem, the structure of therapy and the collaborative approach all serve to reduce transference reactions. In more complex disorders, however, the patient's interpersonal difficulties may intrude on the therapy session. The interpersonal schema is used as a concept that can translate transference and countertransference into cognitive language. This also depathologises transference because it is conceptualised as simply a more emotionally charged version of what we do all the time, i.e. relate to other people on the basis of expectations based on past experiences with key figures. Through the chapter, we have used the example of a narcissistic patient to illustrate these ideas and a method for mapping the thoughts, feelings and behaviours of patient and therapist is described which may help clarify the unhelpful patterns we can sometimes fall into with challenging patients.

FURTHER READING

Leahy RL (2003) *Overcoming Resistance in Cognitive Therapy*. New York: Guilford Press.

Moorey S (2014) "Is it them or is it me?" Transference and countertransference in CBT In: Whittington A and Grey N (eds) *How to Become a More Effective CBT Therapist: Mastering Metacompetence in Clinical Practice*. Hoboken, NJ, USA: John Wiley and Sons.

Prasko J, Diveky T, Grambal A, Kamaradova D, Mozny P, Sigmundova Z and Vyskocilova J (2010) Transference and countertransference in cognitive behavioral therapy. *Biomedical Papers* 154(3): 189–197.

REFERENCES

Andersen SM and Cole SW (1990) "Do I know you?": The role of significant others in general social perception. *Journal of Personality and Social Psychology 59*: 383–399.

Andersen SM and Thorpe JS (2009) An IF-THEN theory of personality: significant others and the relational self. *Journal of Research in Personality 43*: 163–170.

Baldwin MW (1997) Relational schemas as a source of if–then self-inference procedures. *Review of General Psychology 1*(4): 326–335.

Baldwin MW, Fehr B, Keedian E, Seidel M and Thomson DW (1993) An exploration of the relational schemata underlying attachment styles: Self-report and lexical decision approaches. *Personality and Social Psychology Bulletin 19*(6): 746–754.

Baucom D and Epstein N (1990) *Cognitive Behavioral Marital Therapy*. New York: Bruner Mazel.

Beck AT, Rush AJ, Shaw BF and Emery G (1979) *Cognitive Therapy of Depression*. New York: Guilford Press.

Bennett-Levy J, Thwaites R, Haarhoff B and Perry H (2015) *Experiencing CBT from the Inside Out: A Self-Practice/Self-Reflection Workbook for Therapists*. New York: The Guilford Press.

Berk MS and Andersen SM (2000) The impact of past relationships on interpersonal behaviour: Behavioral confirmation of the social-cognitive process of transference. *Journal of Personality and Social Psychology 79*: 546–562.

Betan E, Heim AK, Zittel Conklin C and Westen D (2005) Counter transference phenomena and personality pathology in clinical practice: an empirical investigation. *American Journal of Psychiatry 162*(5): 890–898.

Bowlby J (1988) *A Secure Base*. London: Routledge.

Bradley R, Heim AK and Westen D (2005) Transference patterns in the psychotherapy of personality disorders: empirical investigation. *The British Journal of Psychiatry 186*(4): 342–349.

Cantor N (1990) From thought to behavior: "Having" and "doing" in the study of personality and cognition. *American Psychologist 45*(6): 735–750.

Connolly MB, Crits-Christoph P, Demorest A, Azarian K, Muenz L and Chittams J (1996) Varieties of transference patterns in psychotherapy. *Journal of Consulting and Clinical Psychology 64*: 1213–1221.

Deacon BJ, Farrell NR, Kemp JJ, Dixon LJ, Sy JT, Zhang AR and McGrath PB (2013) Assessing therapist reservations about exposure therapy for anxiety disorders: The Therapist Beliefs about Exposure Scale. *Journal of Anxiety Disorders 27*(8): 772–780.

Farrell NR, Deacon BJ, Kemp JJ, Dixon LJ and Sy JT (2013) Do negative beliefs about exposure therapy cause its suboptimal delivery? An experimental investigation. *Journal of Anxiety Disorders 27*(8): 763–771.

Freud S (1912) The dynamics of transference (J. Strachey, Trans.). In: Strachey J (ed) *The Standard Edition of the Complete Psychological Works of Sigmund Freud*. Vol. *12*. London: Hogarth Press, pp. 99–108.

Gelso CJ and Bhatia A (2012) Crossing theoretical lines: the role and effect of transference in nonanalytic psychotherapies. *Psychotherapy 49*: 384–390.

Greenberg J, Pyszczynski T and Solomon S (1986) The causes and consequences of a need for self-esteem: A terror management theory. In: *Public Self and Private Self*. New York: Springer, pp. 189-212.

Haarhoff BA (2006) The importance of identifying and understanding therapist schema in cognitive therapy training and supervision. *New Zealand Journal of Psychology 33*(3): 126–131.

Horowitz M (1988) *Introduction to Psychodynamics: A New Synthesis*. London: Routledge.

Horowitz M (1998) *Cognitive Psychodynamics: From Conflict to Character*. London: John Wiley & Sons.

Ivey G (2013) Cognitive Therapy's Assimilation of Countertransference: A Psychodynamic Perspective. *British Journal of Psychotherapy 29*(2): 230–244.

Joiner TE and Metalsky GI (1995) A prospective study of an integrative interpersonal theory of depression: A naturalistic study of college roommates. *Journal of Personality and Social Psychology 69*: 778–788.

Jones EE and Pittman TS (1982) Toward a general theory of strategic self-presentation. *Psychological Perspectives on the Self 1*: 231–262.

Kahn J, Coyne JC and Margolin G (1985) Depression and marital disagreement: The social construction of despair. *Journal of Social and Personal Relationships 2*: 447–461.

Leahy RL (2003) *Overcoming Resistance in Cognitive Therapy*. New York: Guilford Press.

Luborsky L and Crits-Christoph P (1990) *Understanding Transference: The Core Conflictual Relationship Theme Method*. New York: Basic Books.

McLean S, Wade T and Encel J (2003) The contribution of therapist beliefs to psychological distress in therapists: an investigation of vicarious traumatization, burnout and symptoms of avoidance and intrusion. *Behavioural and Cognitive Psychotherapy 31*(4): 417–428.

Moorey S (2013) The Interpersonal Cycle Worksheet. *Cognitive Connections*. Available at: http://www.cognitiveconnections.co.uk (accessed 22 May 2017).

Moorey S (2014) "Is it them or is it me?" Transference and countertransference in CBT: In: Whittington A and Grey N (eds) *How to Become a More Effective CBT Therapist: Mastering Metacompetence in Clinical Practice*. Hoboken, NJ, USA: John Wiley and Sons.

Prasko J, Diveky T, Grambal A, Kamaradova D, Mozny P, Sigmundova Z, ... and Vyskocilova J (2010) Transference and countertransference in cognitive behavioral therapy. *Biomedical Papers 154*(3): 189–197.

Ryle A and Kerr I (2002) *Introducing Cognitive Analytic Therapy: Principles and Practice*. Chichester: John Wiley.

Safran JD (1990) Towards a refinement of cognitive therapy in light of interpersonal theory: I. Theory. *Clinical Psychology Review 10*(1): 87–105.

Safran JD and Segal ZV (1990) *Interpersonal Process in Cognitive Therapy*. New York: Basic Books.

Scarvalone P, Fox M and Safran JD (2005) Interpersonal Schemas: Clinical Theory, Research, and Implications. In: Baldwin MW (ed) *Interpersonal cognition* (pp. 359–387). New York: Guilford Press.

Wright JH, Brown GK, Thase ME and Basco MR (2017) *Learning Cognitive-Behavior Therapy: An Illustrated Guide*. Arlington, VA, USA: American Psychiatric Pub. Inc.

Young JE, Klosko JS and Weishaar ME (2003) *Schema Therapy: A Practitioner's Guide*. New York: Guilford Press.

PART II

THE THERAPEUTIC RELATIONSHIP IN SPECIFIC DISORDERS

4

DEPRESSION

STIRLING MOOREY

CHAPTER OVERVIEW

Beck's cognitive therapy for depression (Beck et al., 1979) triggered the cognitive revolution in psychological treatment. It remains the basis on which modern CBT is founded. This chapter describes how the maintenance model (based on the triad of negative beliefs about the self, the world and the future) and the developmental model (particularly beliefs about relationships) can elucidate problems that arise in the therapeutic relationship. The chapter covers methods for engaging the depressed patient so that a collaborative partnership is built, using the formulation to predict, prevent and manage alliance ruptures.

THE COGNITIVE MODEL OF DEPRESSION AND THE THERAPEUTIC RELATIONSHIP

Wayne is a 40-year-old depressed, unemployed man. His mood is low, he gets little pleasure from anything and constantly feels tired and unmotivated. He wakes early in the morning, but his appetite is normal. Although he feels very hopeless, he does not feel suicidal. He has two children from a previous relationship whom he only sees occasionally. He has been with his current partner for two years, but she is getting frustrated with him because he no longer wants to socialise and seems to have given up on life. This depression has been getting worse over the last year since he was made redundant from his job as a porter in a local hospital. When he arrives for an assessment for cognitive therapy, he is unshaven and has clearly not been looking after himself well. He tells the therapist he desperately wants help but does not believe anything can be done. He says his chances of getting another job are close to zero and there seems to be no point in doing anything. He is 'just surviving' on benefits, not living. He is very angry at how life has let him down but also expresses thoughts that he is completely worthless.

Wayne's thoughts about himself, his world and the future illustrate Beck's depressive cognitive triad: the self is seen as worthless and/or helpless, the environment as unrewarding and the future as hopeless. Wayne's interpretation and evaluation of situations is skewed so that neutral or positive experiences are construed in a negatively biased fashion. Wayne sees himself as helpless and worthless in the face of a hostile world that no longer gives him the financial and occupational rewards he needs to make life worth living. Moreover, he sees little prospect of being able to change this in the future. CBT for depression aims to help Wayne recognise how his thoughts are skewed by his depressed state. His therapist will link Wayne's negative automatic thoughts to his behavioural avoidance and inactivity (social withdrawal and poor self-care) and work to break the cognitive-behavioural cycles maintaining his depression by testing his self-defeating beliefs, e.g. that he can get no pleasure from his current life and cannot achieve his goals for the future.

But, to start on this journey, Wayne needs to trust his therapist enough to take the risk of engaging in life again. The therapist needs to be able to understand and validate Wayne's negative experience, while also holding out hope that there might be other, more helpful, ways to think and act. This requires interpersonal skills that build the therapeutic alliance, as well as technical skills specific to the tasks and goals of CBT. Research has yet to clarify the relative contribution of these two skill sets (see Chapter 2 for a discussion of the research evidence regarding the therapy alliance in CBT for depression). Wayne and his therapist must reach a shared understanding of how homework assignments could be helpful. But Wayne's negative thoughts about himself may lead him to berate himself for not understanding or completing the homework assignments, while his hopelessness may lead him to believe he cannot benefit from therapy. The patient's pessimism can make it hard to establish a collaborative relationship, so fostering hope is one of the first goals of therapy. On the therapist's side, too much empathy for the depressed patient can create therapeutic hopelessness. Being with depressed people can be depressing: the therapist may not believe Wayne's negative automatic thoughts (NATs) but may still be dragged into despair ('I don't have the skills to get him better') – *overinvolved emotional empathy*. But the therapist may also start to believe Wayne's assertion that he will never get a job and is doomed to failure. As Beck observed: 'By stepping out of the role of scientific observer, the therapist may "buy into" the patient's distorted construction of reality' (Beck et al., 1979: 59) – *overinvolved cognitive empathy*.

Wayne's childhood was unhappy: his father was bullying, critical and sometimes physically abusive, and his mother could not stand up to him. He came from a deprived area in the North East where employment was low and was convinced from an early age that he would never make anything of himself. His older brother had worked in the steel industry but had been made redundant and now had significant alcohol problems.

Wayne believed he was a loser, that life was stacked against him and he would never get a break and so had always been somewhat truculent and dysthymic. The loss of his job confirmed these beliefs and set him off on a spiral of depressed mood, hopelessness and inactivity. The fact that he had thought this way for most of his life presented further challenges to the therapeutic relationship. Wayne was not convinced that a young, middle-class female therapist from London could understand where he was coming from, and he expected her to be judgemental and critical. His strong sense of having been deprived of the love, care and support he had needed also meant that he got stuck in angry ruminations about how the world was unjust: he could not, and should not have to, go through all this. Interpersonal beliefs can then interfere with the therapeutic bond through 'transference' (see Chapter 3). In this case, Wayne's beliefs contributed to him not feeling understood, feeling denigrated and also feeling resentful about having to go through the motions of therapy when it was the world that should change. These may cause alliance ruptures at any point in therapy.

Therapist tips

Remember that depression can challenge the therapeutic relationship in a number of ways:

1. The patient's negative thoughts about self, world and future can interfere with engagement in the tasks and goals of therapy – 'This won't work.'
2. The patient's negative thoughts about self and others can interfere with the therapeutic bond – 'The therapist thinks I'm rubbish.'
3. Overinvolved emotional and/or cognitive empathy with the patient can lead you to feel helpless and hopeless – 'The patient is right: CBT won't work for him.'
4. The patient's underlying assumptions about interpersonal relationships can challenge the therapeutic bond – 'If I get close to someone they will reject me.'

ENGAGING THE CLIENT

Depression will always pull the client into rumination and withdrawal, so the therapist needs to model optimism, curiosity and confidence. The best way to achieve this is through interventions that produce rapid symptom change, thus demonstrating that the therapist knows what she is doing and that the formulation makes sense. Fennell and Teasdale (1987) found that patients who had a positive response to the cognitive model followed by a successful first homework experience made more rapid recoveries, while Busch et al. (2006) found that improvement in mood after the first session and sudden gains in the first half of therapy predicted outcome. Small success experiences, e.g. scheduling three activities you used to enjoy but have been avoiding, demonstrate that change is possible. Sharing information about the nature of depression and the effectiveness of CBT can bring small rays of hope into the depressive's world – 'I don't know if this applies to you, but ...' The more the patient can see that they are not alone in their experience (checklists of depressive symptoms can be helpful here) and that others have benefited from therapy, the more likely they are to engage. This process requires the therapist to adopt an optimistic, warm and upbeat manner, while at the same time showing empathy with the patient's mood state. The therapist said to Wayne:

> I can see how life has been hard for you and things haven't gone the way you would have liked. You feel you haven't received the support or education that might have made life easier. I'm impressed with what you have been able to do despite this. How did you manage to make the move to London and find a job?

Identifying Wayne's strengths can help him recognise that he has overcome problems in the past. The therapist can then introduce the idea that it might be depression, rather than fate or inadequacy, that is holding him back:

> You put a lot of effort into finding work when you first came here, but right now it all seems too hard. We find this a lot in the depressed people we work with – depression robs us of energy, confidence and motivation. If we could help you feel less depressed perhaps you might be able to get back into the job market.

This is starting to generate an alternative explanation for Wayne's experience and hopefully makes him curious about how therapy can help. Beck emphasises the importance of this curiosity in hooking the depressed person so that they come back next week – curiosity about how their thoughts and actions might be making the depression worse, and curiosity about how they might change them. The early self-help assignments should be set up as success experiences to generate a sense of self-efficacy and build trust in the therapist and the therapy. They can be introduced as 'no-lose' tasks, where even if the outcome isn't what is expected, they will give information about the patient's negative thoughts. Finally, the general principles of setting homework apply in this setting. Homework tasks should be specific and meaningful to the patient, assigned collaboratively, agreed to be done at a specified time and obstacles predicted. Success at this stage will build trust in the tasks and goals of therapy and ultimately trust in the therapist. It is important to emphasise that disagreements over tasks probably arise more often from poor therapist technique than anything else. Assigning homework tasks that are too difficult for the patient's level of depression, not relevant to the patient's goals and not clearly and collaboratively derived can mean the tasks are not completed and the working alliance put at risk.

Therapist tips

When engaging the client:

1. Validate the client's experience of depression, but adopt a warm, hopeful attitude towards the possibility of change.
2. Find ways to encourage early gains – nothing succeeds like success.
3. Use psychoeducation to demonstrate that symptoms are a result of depression, not personal deficiency.
4. Troubleshoot obstacles to homework assignments.
5. Encourage curiosity about the way in which the client's thoughts and actions might be maintaining the depressed mood.
6. Ensure homework tasks are set collaboratively, relevant to the patient's goals and level of depression and derived from a shared formulation.

PREDICTING AND PREVENTING THREATS TO THE THERAPEUTIC ALLIANCE

As we have seen, the depressed person's negative mindset may present obstacles to engagement, but even if the therapeutic relationship gets off to a good start, setbacks can tip the patient back into a hopelessness. Warning that this might happen is an important part of socialisation to the cognitive model:

> Depression makes us think in a very negative way, and that can sometimes make us think negatively about therapy. We can think that we don't deserve help, that we're not able to do homework or that it will never work. It's very important that you tell me if these thoughts come up for you so that we can look at them together to see if they're realistic or if they're the depression talking.

Naming these possible roadblocks makes it easier to address them if they occur. In addition to factors arising from depressed mood and cognitions, the person's more general beliefs about relationships will also come into play. Beck's concepts of sociotropy (worth is determined by approval from others) and autonomy (worth is determined by internal standards) are useful in thinking about how these beliefs can impinge on the therapeutic relationship (Beck, 1983). Sociotropic individuals have beliefs such as, 'I can only be happy if I'm loved by someone' while autonomous people have beliefs such as 'I have to be successful to be worthwhile.' Autonomous patients may be more cautious and avoidant, and sociotropic patients more dependent and reassurance-seeking in the therapy. These interpersonal beliefs (Bieling and Alden, 2001) can lead depressed people to push others away (Kahn et al., 1985) or elicit reassurance (Joiner and Metalsky, 1995). Identifying autonomous beliefs about high standards, perfectionism or control and sociotropic beliefs about dependency, need for approval or fear of criticism allow the therapist to have a discussion about how these beliefs might interfere with the process of therapy.

For instance, with an autonomous patient the therapist might say:

> You've told me how important it is for you to be in control. You have been self-reliant all your life. I wonder if it may feel odd to share your feelings and in a way give up some of your independence in the therapy setting?

Or with a sociotropic patient:

> I understand how you've never felt able to stand on your own two feet and always relied on your husband. There may be times when you would like me to tell you what to do, but this therapy is very much about giving you tools you can use to cope by yourself.

The depressed patient's beliefs about relationships can potentially impinge upon therapy, so it is advisable to sketch out a working developmental conceptualisation early on. In Wayne's case, the therapist hypothesised that Wayne's childhood experiences had contributed to a belief that others could be bullying, critical and controlling (like his father) or weak and unable to help (like his mother). He had not overtly expressed these beliefs, so at this stage, they remained hypotheses. Wayne had, however, articulated a strong belief that he had been short-changed by life because of his upbringing, social status and lack of education.

Reflective question

Before reading further, consider how Wayne's experiences and beliefs might affect his relationship with the therapist, who was a 26-year-old, white, middle-class woman from the South of England.

What could the therapist do to prepare for potential problems?

PREDICTING PROBLEMS IN WORKING WITH WAYNE

Wayne's beliefs that he was helpless and hard done by in the face of a hostile and uncaring world could undermine the therapeutic alliance. His tendency to attribute blame externally could prevent him from taking an active role in the collaboration needed for effective therapy, thus exacerbating his helplessness and hopelessness. Moreover, the age, class and cultural differences between Wayne and his therapist could trigger angry, alienating thoughts ('She can't appreciate how difficult life has been for me') and angry, envious thoughts ('She's had an easy life!') (Figure 4.1).

The attitudes of Wayne's parents are likely to have shaped his views of others and, although it is speculation at this stage, the therapist can hypothesise a number of ways in which a 'negative transference' might play out. As an authority figure, the therapist could be seen as critical and punitive, like his father. If this were to occur, Wayne would feel more worthless and inadequate, and he might see the tasks and goals of CBT as controlling and unfairly demanding (Figure 4.2).

On the other hand, the therapist could be identified as being like Wayne's mother. In this case, he might emphasize how her youth, gender etc. mean that she could not possibly have the skills to help him i.e. she is weak and unavailable like his mother (Figure 4.3).

This formulation identifies some ways in which the working alliance could be affected:

1. The cultural gap between Wayne and his therapist makes it difficult for him to believe that she understands enough to help him (challenge to therapeutic bond).
2. Wayne perceives the therapist as superior, critical and demanding and so resists homework assignments (challenge to tasks, goals and bond).

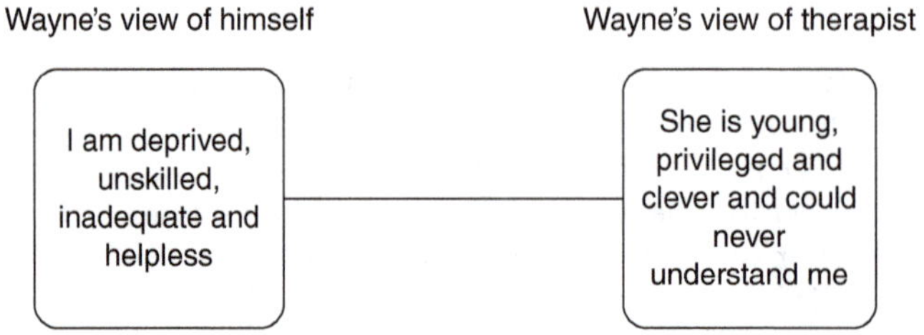
Wayne's view of himself
Wayne's view of therapist
I am deprived, unskilled, inadequate and helpless
She is young, privileged and clever and could never understand me

Figure 4.1 Wayne may feel the therapist cannot understand him

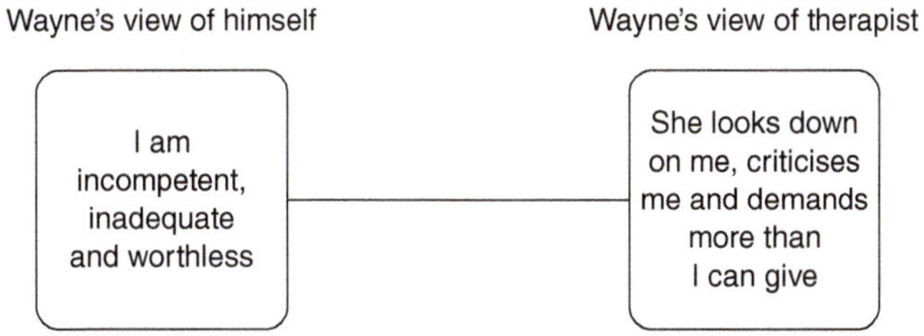

Figure 4.2 Wayne may see his therapist as contemptuous

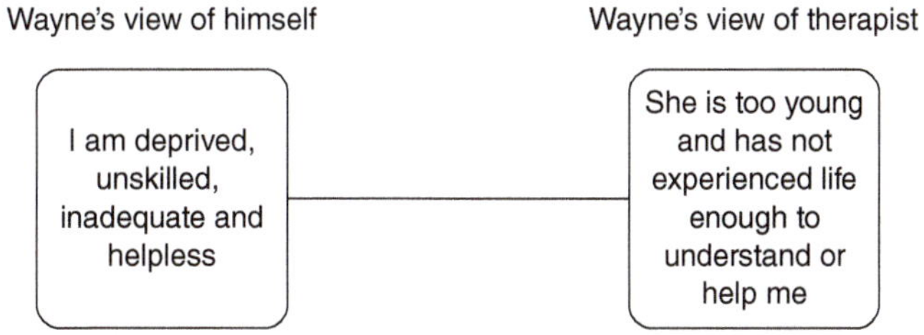

Figure 4.3 Wayne may believe the therapist is not able to help him

3. Wayne perceives the therapist as weak and inexperienced and so does not engage (challenge to tasks, goals and bond).

The standard features of good CBT minimise these threats, in contrast to more interpersonally based therapies that work directly with interpersonal conflict. CBT reduces transference by building a collaborative relationship, seeking feedback and constantly checking the patient's understanding and acceptance of the model. The therapist might ask Wayne if, given how strongly he feels about the way life has treated him, he might think she cannot understand his position. This could lead to an exploration and invitation for Wayne to really get across why he feels so helpless and angry, which the therapist can validate. The therapist can elicit any negative reactions to the structure and assignments involved in therapy, perhaps making reference to how Wayne has felt controlled and bullied in the past and assure him that the therapist wants to ensure he doesn't feel that way about therapy. And, finally, the therapist can ask Wayne how he feels about working with her and elicit any negative thoughts about her abilities and competence. Having elicited these doubts and hopefully dealt with them, it may be helpful to suggest to Wayne that there may be times during therapy when he doesn't feel understood, feels demeaned or fears his therapist can't help: when these occur they will need to work together in partnership to deal with them. This can all be brought together in a capsule summary:

> From what you have told me, life has not been easy for you. You feel you haven't received the sort of support and help you needed and you feel inadequate and unprepared for getting by in the world. This isn't surprising, since your father was very bullying and critical and your mother wasn't able to protect you from him. It's very

understandable that you feel helpless and lacking in confidence. I believe that critical voice of your father and your low mood may be undermining the abilities that you do have. I may be wrong, but would you be prepared to work with me to find out if you have more strengths than you think?

Reflective question

Consider a patient you are working with at the moment. What are his beliefs about himself, others and relationships? How might these appear and influence the patient's behaviour in therapy? Would they impact on the tasks and goals of CBT or on the therapy bond?

What could you do to prepare for potential problems?

WORKING WITH THREATS TO THE ALLIANCE

Naming potential threats can go a long way to preventing serious disruptions to the collaborative relationship. Having identified potential pitfalls at the beginning of therapy, it becomes easier to address them when they arise. But challenges to collaboration can arise nonetheless. The commonest cause is some external factor that triggers an exacerbation of the depression. As Beck observed: '... the patient may experience new disappointments or frustrations due to traumatic environmental events. If this should occur he may be flooded with a stream of negative cognitions which he automatically regards as valid without subjecting them to further consideration' (Beck et al., 1979: 59). This may lead him to conclude cognitive therapy is ineffective, that he is incurable or he may become disillusioned with the therapist. Predicting setbacks at the outset allows the therapist to remind the patient that these are not unusual in recovering from depression. The therapist models an unfazed, confident, warm manner and validates the patient's disappointment while labelling the setback as a lapse rather than a relapse.

Therapist:	When we spoke last week you were more hopeful about overcoming depression.
Patient:	I was just fooling myself. I'll never feel any better.
Therapist: (showing patient graph of scores)	It looks like the scores have been coming down over the last five sessions. Do we have an explanation for why they might be higher this week?
Patient:	As I said, the argument with my mother just knocked me back.
Therapist:	What was the effect of the argument on your thinking about yourself.
Patient:	I just thought how useless I am. I can't stand up to her and she's right when she says I'm a waste of space.

Therapist: So what she said confirmed your negative self-critical thinking about yourself. We have two possibilities here. One is that your mother is correct and this very punitive way of talking about yourself is valid. Another is that her continual criticism of you has created these beliefs that you're not good enough. Your default mode is harsh self-criticism.

Patient: I suppose so.

Therapist: How many years have you been working on that first assumption?

Patient: Too many.

Therapist: How long have you been exploring the second possibility, and what has been the effect?

Patient: I suppose I've only been working on this for a few weeks.

Therapist: Would you bc prepared to work on it a bit longer before concluding it's hopeless? Perhaps we could look more closely at what happened to see if your conclusions are justified and to see if there are ways you might handle her better in the future? These setbacks are very common in working with depression. You're not going to turn around these habits of thinking overnight.

Low mood is contagious and the therapist can become convinced the patient is right: they are not going to recover. The two keys to dealing with therapist hopelessness are returning to the cognitive model and bringing the feelings to supervision. CBT for depression is not about challenging all negative thoughts but about identifying which thoughts are realistic and which thoughts are distorted or unhelpful. For instance, realistic negative thoughts about your partner leaving you are addressed through acceptance and facilitation of emotional processing if the loss is recent and problem solving (taking steps to find a new partner) when appropriate. Distorted thoughts such as 'It's all my fault. I'm unlovable. I'll never find someone else at my age' can be examined and tested like any others. If the therapist steps back from the situation, she can often find distortions that go beyond the undeniably negative facts of a situation and expand the awfulness in terms of what it means about the person's worth and their ability to find happiness or achievement in the future. Supervision is invaluable in helping the therapist find a more objective vantage point. The Interpersonal Schema Worksheet (Figure 4.4) can be used to identify aspects of the patient's in-session behaviour that contribute to the therapist's feelings of despair and frustration, and therapist and supervisor can look for ways out of the unhelpful interpersonal cycles.

Wayne initially made some progress with activity scheduling and found himself a job as a volunteer, but he would often be late and sometimes miss a day altogether. He repeatedly told the therapist that she didn't realise how hard it was for him to motivate himself. Volunteering wasn't a real job. He believed it was too late for him to make anything of his life now so why bother. His therapist found herself becoming increasingly frustrated and veering between pushing him harder and just giving up. Her supervisor used the Interpersonal Schema Worksheet (Figure 4.4) to help her obtain perspective on the relationship. The supervisor first checked that Wayne understood the rationale and was not too depressed to carry out the homework assignments. Having clarified that Wayne understood the rationale and was able to do the tasks, therapist and supervisor listened to a recording of a recent session. The therapist was surprised to discover her voice sounded irritated and frustrated – she had felt that way but thought it didn't come across. She identified Wayne's behaviour, her own behaviour and her own thoughts but was less sure what Wayne was thinking. After listening to the session, recalling things Wayne had said and role-playing him in supervision, she was able to hypothesise about some of his beliefs and thoughts. She realised that Wayne's blaming the world was probably a strategy he had learned as an alternative to blaming himself and that, underneath his sullen facade, he was possibly more scared and self-hating than she realised. This helped her to have more empathy for her patient and to see that his aggression towards the world was a compensatory strategy that he used to avoid taking responsibility and

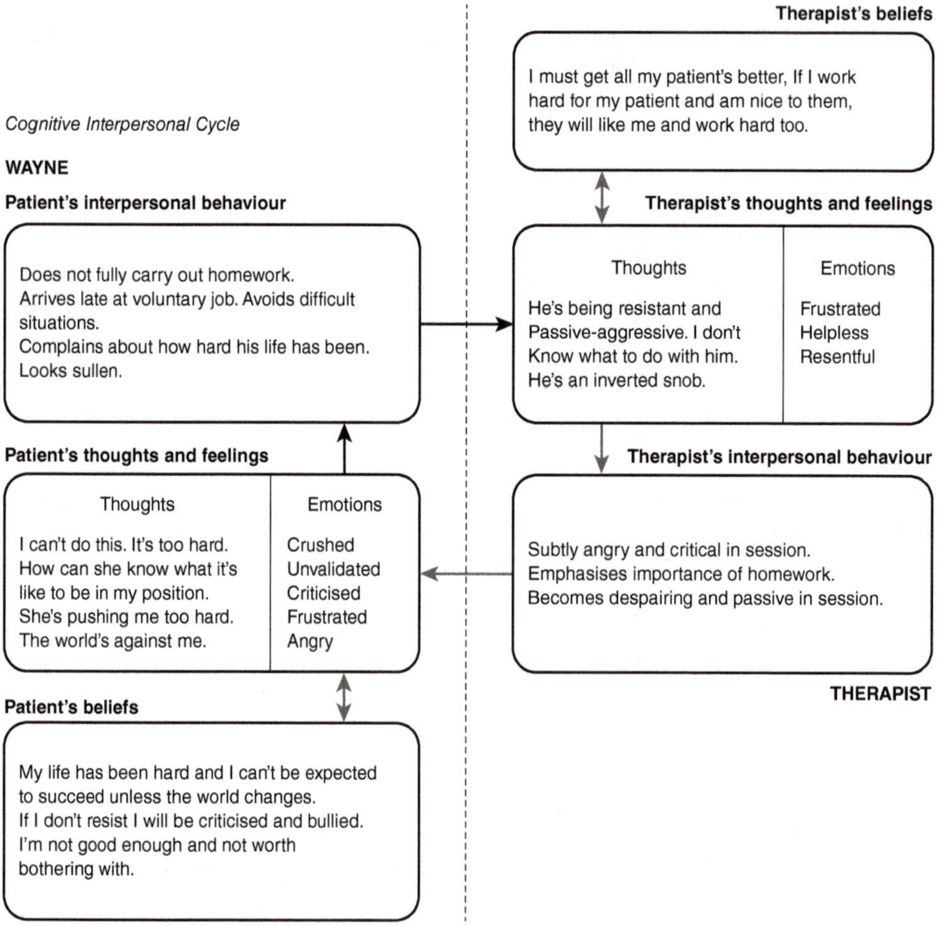

Figure 4.4 The cognitive interpersonal cycle of Wayne and his therapist

failing. She also recognised that she had been falling into the trap of acting just like Wayne's punitive, demanding father.

This allowed her to feel much less stuck and less annoyed with the ways in which he subtly put her down for not being working class. The dilemma remained that his coping mode was so well established he habitually made excuses and blamed others rather than himself. The therapist decided to share this dilemma:

Therapist: I've been thinking about your family and the tough time you had. It sounds like your father was always blaming you for things that went wrong.

Wayne: Yes, he always picked on me.

Therapist: Did he ever take responsibility when things went wrong.

Wayne: Never! It was always someone else's fault.

Therapist: So you grew up in a family where someone was always to blame if there was a problem. It's like it's either me or them. In my experience, it's seldom helpful to blame in this way.

Wayne: Why's that?

Therapist: If we blame ourselves, we can feel helpless and paralysed because we become very critical, but if we blame others, we're equally helpless because we can't force other people to be the way we want.

Wayne: I don't understand.

Therapist: How much of the time do you criticise yourself for not making more of your life?

Wayne: Quite a lot.

Therapist: How much of the time do you get angry with life for dealing you the wrong cards?

Wayne: Every day.

Therapist: Do those two ways of thinking help you?

Wayne: I suppose not.

Therapist: I find that when I ruminate like that I get quite tense and exhausted. You've mentioned a few times that I can't really understand how hard it's been for you.

Wayne: Yes.

Therapist: When you focus on that, how do you feel towards me?

Wayne: Quite angry I suppose.

Therapist: I think that has sometimes got in the way of us working well together. I can never fully understand what your life is like, but I hope I can understand enough to help you find ways out. Perhaps we can look at the effect of your blaming and getting angry with yourself and with the world. I think there might be another way of seeing things. You don't have to fall into your father's trap of always having someone to blame.

Wayne was intrigued. The therapist helped him to explore ways to understand and explain causality and responsibility that did not involve the all-or-nothing distortion of 'It's either my fault or theirs.' Finding more nuanced ways freed him from the straightjacket of blame and improved his collaboration in therapy.

ENDING THERAPY

Short-term interpersonally-focused psychotherapies pay a great deal of attention to termination. CBT places less emphasis on the ending of the relationship itself, but far more emphasis on the practical aspects of consolidating the lessons learned in therapy and preventing relapse. The brief, problem-focused nature of CBT minimises overt transference but focuses the patient's fears on whether or not they will be able to cope without therapy, rather than the loss of the therapist. As the patient comes to the end of a treatment they will usually have experienced an improvement in mood and have learned strategies for managing mood. The therapist will have been reminding the patient throughout that they are learning to become their own therapist. By presenting herself realistically, the therapist reduces 'positive transference,' demystifies therapy and reduces the patient's dependency (Beck et al., 1979: 317). Table 4.1 (see Beck et al., 1979: 318–322 for more on managing termination problems) outlines some of the challenges encountered at the end of therapy with suggestions for how to manage them.

Table 4.1 Managing endings

Problem with ending	Ways to manage
'I'm not completely cured.'	Help the patient understand that mood is on a continuum, not dichotomous. Therapy is 'work in progress:' skills learned will be built on when therapy ends. Each fluctuation in mood becomes an opportunity to practice these skills.
'I've not solved all my problems.'	CBT teaches you how to deal with problems and cannot necessarily resolve all your problems. Review problem-solving skills learned in therapy.
'I'm getting worse again.'	Reassure patient that this is common at the end of therapy. Identify possible misinterpretation of fluctuations in mood as sign of relapse. Review basic CBT skills for managing setbacks.
'I might relapse.'	Normalise fact that depression is a relapsing illness, but review evidence for CBT reducing relapse. Develop blueprint for relapse prevention.

If the patient brings up the loss of the personal relationship with the therapist, this can be acknowledged:

You have shared some very personal things with me over the last few weeks. I can see that opening up like that leaves one vulnerable and I'm honoured that you've trusted me enough to share that. I've enjoyed working with you and will miss the sessions too.

The therapist then moves back to emphasise the skills learned in therapy: it's not the personality of the therapist but the new ways of thinking and behaving that have got them out of the depression.

CHAPTER SUMMARY

This chapter has used the case example of Wayne, a depressed 40-year-old man, to illustrate challenges to the working alliance that can occur in CBT for depression. As well as methods for engaging and terminating therapy, attention is given to the way in which beliefs about interpersonal relationships can create roadblocks to progress. A method for mapping the therapeutic relationship (The Interpersonal Schema Worksheet) and ways to use this to predict and manage alliance ruptures are described.

FURTHER READING

Beck AT, Rush AJ, Shaw BF and Emery G (1979) *Cognitive Therapy of Depression.* New York: Guilford Press.

REFERENCES

Beck AT (1983) Cognitive therapy of depression: New perspectives. In: Clayton PJ and Barnett JE (eds) *Treatment of Depression: Old Controversies and New Approaches.* New York: Raven Press, pp. 265–290.

Beck AT, Rush AJ, Shaw BF and Emery G (1979) *Cognitive Therapy of Depression.* New York: Guilford Press.

Bieling PJ and Alden LE (2001) Sociotropy, autonomy, and the interpersonal model of depression: An integration. *Cognitive Therapy and Research 25*: 167–184.

Busch AM, Kanter JW, Landes SJ and Kohlenberg RJ (2006) Sudden gains and outcome: A broader temporal analysis of cognitive therapy for depression. *Behavior Therapy 37*(1): 61–68.

Fennell MJV and Teasdale JD (1987) Cognitive therapy for depression: Individual differences and the process of change. *Cognitive Therapy and Research 11*: 253–271.

Joiner TE and Metalsky GI (1995) A prospective study of an integrative interpersonal theory of depression: A naturalistic study of college roommates. *Journal of Personality and Social Psychology 69*: 778–788.

Kahn J, Coyne JC and Margolin G (1985) Depression and marital disagreement: The social construction of despair. *Journal of Social and Personal Relationships 2*: 447–461.

5

GENERALISED ANXIETY DISORDER

KEVIN MEARES, SUSAN HARRISON AND MARK FREESTON

CHAPTER OVERVIEW

In the treatment of most Axis I anxiety disorders, standard and skilful CBT generally takes care of the therapeutic relationship through the collaboration and structure that it provides. In the treatment of Generalised Anxiety Disorder (GAD), however, worry can hijack some aspects of therapy making it more difficult to establish and maintain a consistent working alliance. We will first reflect on the nature of worry and how it can affect the client's approach to therapy and then consider the various early-, mid- and late-therapy tasks. We will be considering typical challenges to the working alliance when worry gets in the way of the personal alliance or misaligned goals prevent effective task alliance. We will outline some typical patterns seen with this client group and offer tips about how to manage the interpersonal processes. We will also consider how therapist factors related to their own experience of worry can contribute to problems within the working alliance.

OVERVIEW OF THE MODEL OF GAD UNDERPINNING TREATMENT

There are several different contemporary approaches to worry that each have a different emphasis (see Behar et al., 2009 for an excellent review). These have been labelled the Avoidance Model of Worry and GAD (Borkovec et al., 2004; Newman et al., 2011), the Intolerance of Uncertainty Model (Dugas et al., 1998; Dugas and Robichaud, 2007; Wilkinson et al., 2011), the Metacognitive Model (Hjemdal et al., 2013; Wells, 1995), the Emotion Dysregulation Model (Fresco et al., 2013; Mennin et al., 2002) and the Acceptance-Based Model of Generalized Anxiety Disorder (Hayes-Skelton et al., 2013; Roemer and Orsillo, 2002, 2005). All of these treatment approaches have some empirical support, albeit to varying degrees (see Cuijpers et al., 2014).

All these treatments focus on the *processes* involved in worry rather than worry *content*. They all frame the central problem of GAD as worry rather than all the different things the person worries about. However, each approach proposes different ways of understanding and modifying the worry process. Whichever model the therapist is using, there will be common challenges as the worrier will approach therapy in much the same way. Regardless of the specific treatment model, we believe Intolerance of Uncertainty (IU) can inform an understanding of worry and is an important influence on the working alliance throughout the treatment of GAD.

INTOLERANCE OF UNCERTAINTY

IU has been variously defined (see Carleton, 2012 for a review) but, more recently, as 'an individual's dispositional incapacity to endure the aversive response triggered by the perceived absence of salient, key, or sufficient information, and sustained by the associated perception of uncertainty' (Carleton, 2016: 31). We would generally agree with this definition, or to express it in more straightforward terms, IU is a dispositional dislike of situations where the outcome is not yet known. This is expressed as a strong preference for knowing what will happen in the situation (and dislike of *not* knowing), a difficulty acting when the outcome is unknown and the emotional and body reactions to not knowing what will happen.

IU is increasingly believed to be transdiagnostic and observed across a range of problems, but we would argue that it finds its strongest expression in GAD. The IU model (Dugas et al., 1998) suggests that worry tends to happen in response to uncertain situations and that individuals who have problems tolerating the ordinary and universal uncertainty in everyday events experience excessive and, from the worrier's perspective, uncontrollable worry. This leads to powerful and unhelpful physiological, emotional, cognitive and behavioural responses. Individuals with GAD can be thought to have an 'allergy to uncertainty' (Dugas and Robichaud, 2007): when asked how they feel about uncertainty, worriers often reply saying they hate it and avoid it at all costs.

Consider an everyday situation such as a comment from one's manager about an upcoming deadline. For the worrier, this triggers a 'what if' type question ('just supposing...' 'imagine if...'). This leads onto further 'what if' questions and the stream of worry expands as the worrier attempts to identify all the things that could potentially go wrong, the possible solutions, the difficulties with these solutions and their possible failure, which in turn chains on to other worries. In this case, the deadline not being met leads to worries about losing one's job and this spirals into concerns about losing house, family, etc. The stream of worry can be experienced as overwhelming and leads to anxiety.

Anxiety is understood as the emotional states, physiological experiences and behavioural responses to worry. Worriers describe feelings such as anxiety, foreboding, edginess and dread. The anxiety is felt within the body as muscular tension, as gnawing sensations in the stomach or headaches. In this state of anxious apprehension, the worrier may be restless, have difficulty concentrating, may feel tired but have trouble sleeping and, unsurprisingly, may become irritable with people around them.

Worriers engage in a range of behaviours and cognitive strategies which are hypothesised to be attempts at managing uncertainty, dealing with unpleasant affect and even reducing worry. In general, however, the behaviours that worriers engage in, including worry itself, usually have significant personal and emotional costs and tend to exacerbate uncertainty and provoke more worry. For instance, if you worry that you have misunderstood something, you may repeatedly seek reassurance from a colleague and then feel stupid when you realise you had got it right anyway. The worrier may fear their colleague being short-tempered with them or judging them for continually seeking reassurance: this makes the work environment more subjectively uncertain and triggers more worry.

Scanning for problems, looking for answers, finding more problems and trying to control worry are energy demanding processes, and once the worry has passed, the worrier often experiences a sense of exhaustion. The worrier may also feel demoralised and 'beat themselves up' for having wasted another several hours worrying about things that never happened or chastise themselves for 'not coping.' Unsurprisingly, the comorbidity between GAD and depression is very high, and many clients arrive in therapy having been referred for depression (e.g. Kessler et al., 1996; Moffitt et al., 2007).

As with other disorders, the therapeutic relationship in GAD functions as both a container for working with the clients difficulties, distress and strengths, and a laboratory for therapy. It is highly likely that the worrier will worry during the session. This is helpful to the extent that we can observe and develop a formulation of the client's worry before helping them try different ways of responding. The roles therefore include containment, sitting back from worry, commenting on the processes, and then supporting experiments and changes in real life. However, the volume and detail of worry may overwhelm the therapist; while surface details of their worry are often accessible, the key central themes (usually about threats to things in their life that are most important to them) may be less accessible.

It is important for therapists to be aware that an apparently trivial day-to-day worry in the therapist's mind (e.g. being late for an appointment) is, in the worrier's mind, linked to a feared outcome that involves a threat to something that is central to their identity (see Provencher et al., 2000). So, while trying to avoid getting caught up in the detail of worry, it is important that the therapist recognises that, for the worrier, their worries reflect a perceived, if objectively unlikely, threat to what they value most; awfulness of threat always trumps likelihood. Further, the therapist may be able to be compassionate towards the experience of worry, rather than the specific details of the worry.

THE PARTICULAR CHALLENGES WHEN WORKING WITH GAD

The working alliance can be thought of as a fluid interpersonal framework within which the goals and tasks of therapy are enabled. In line with Bordin (1979) and Hougaard (1994), in this chapter, we make a distinction between the personal and task alliances (see Chapter 2). The personal alliance is about the emotional bond between the client and the therapist and includes qualities such as trust, confidence, containment and emotional attunement. The task alliance can be thought of as an agreement between the therapist and client about what needs to be achieved (goal) and how to go about it (task). In the treatment of GAD, the therapist and client might agree that, to help reduce worry (goal), it would make sense to find out about the client's worry by keeping a worry diary (task). In this conceptualisation, personal and task alliance are believed to feed off each other and lead to successful outcomes.

When working with GAD, some therapists report a good personal alliance but may struggle with establishing consistent task alliance when the volume and changing content of worry gets in the way. In other words, the therapist might get along with their client, and the client appreciates the containment and the opportunity to talk about their worries, but they mutually struggle to identify and engage in tasks. Other therapists may find that the continuous and ever-changing flow of worry content, and the sometimes apparently trivial content, limit their ability to maintain a compassionate, optimistic and effective personal alliance.

We will structure the rest of the chapter by considering the different stages of therapy, from before therapy through the early and middle stages to the final tasks.

BEFORE THERAPY

IU means that, for the client, 'therapy' starts well before the first assessment, as they have to recognise and accept that they have a problem and engage in finding help. People with GAD typically seek help after years of worry and distress. The client and the referrer may also wrongly believe that worry is an immutable part of their personality. Referrals may even be made at the point of exasperation. Alternatively, when a worrier presents at times of real crisis, the worry may be attributed to the situation: 'If I were in your shoes, I would worry about that as well.' Further, at times the crisis may have passed by the time they are eventually seen, and the longer standing pattern of worry may not be recognized by the person or the therapist. The referral may also be at the point where the worrier becomes depressed. Uncertainty about the nature of the problem or ambivalence about seeking help could mean that it often takes years for the person to find their way to therapy, further adding to unhelpful beliefs about their problem.

Once the referral is made, the effects of IU continue. The client who is uncertain about therapy might engage in help seeking and then disengage, or might repeatedly confirm and accept appointments, cancel at the last minute with an apology, then request another appointment. Or, motivated by wanting to reduce uncertainty, the client might seek detailed information about the service or the therapist. For nearly all clients, therapy is an unknown quantity: 'What will they ask, will they understand me, will I like them, what if they judge me? And what if I am late, what if they can't help, what if I can't do it, etc.' If uncertainty feels so unpleasant, the person may act impulsively and turn up unprepared, just wanting to do 'something' to reduce the uncertainty. The main goal at this stage is to help the client attend, help them engage in the process and importantly help them come back.

Therapist tip

Awareness of IU can help the therapist understand the sometimes contradictory behaviour or ambivalence that worriers may show even before therapy and help the therapist occupy a compassionate position and manage any irritation or frustration while also recognising the need to provide some relative certainty.

Therapist tip

Clear information and communication from the service will certainly help, but personal contact may be needed, either by the therapist or by administrative staff who have been suitably briefed.

EARLY STAGES OF THERAPY

The early stages of therapy are about building an effective personal alliance and working towards a shared understanding of the difficulties the worrier is experiencing.

RELATIVE STRUCTURE

In the initial stages, the therapist aims to provide reasonable certainty about how therapy will unfold while not painting themselves into a corner. The therapist needs to try to keep things 'tight–loose,' with enough structure to contain but enough room to move within. Therapist language is important to create and model relative certainty:

> Theorist: Generally speaking, the plan is that we will meet weekly (or otherwise) and for between (for example) 10–12 sessions. We'll make sure we keep track of what we have done, figure out together what we need to work on and then we will plan together the next step. We'll make sure each step is manageable.

The 'we' language is important here; it is the language of collaboration. And, if necessary: 'Although it *would* be nice to have a clear plan now until the end of therapy, unfortunately life doesn't work like that; but we will know on a week-to-week basis what we are doing.'

Therapist tip

Avoid guarantees, avoid too much detail. Questions do deserve a response if they seek new information that can realistically be provided. Repeated or increasingly detailed questions are likely to be driven by IU, the same reason why the person worries excessively.

With repeated questions, if they are a variant of the same question, or if the answer is currently unknowable, compassionate use of the 'broken record' technique can help establish the required relative certainty by repeating: 'Although it would be nice to have it all planned out in advance, experience shows that we can't; but we will make sure we both know what we are doing on a session-to-session basis.'

METAPHOR ABOUT RELATIVE CERTAINTY

> Tell me about going to the football.... (or going to the movies, going for a walk or even the supermarket for Saturday grocery shop, etc.). What time and day does it tend to happen? What time do you leave home? How do you get there? When you get into the ground, what's normally happening then? What's happening on the pitch? Then at 3 pm what happens? (i.e. the game starts, 45 minutes of football). Then what happens next? Will you know in advance what will happen? Until half time. What happens at half time? How long is half time usually? What do you usually do? Then there are another 45 minutes of football plus a variable amount of extra time. Then what happens? How do you go home? And so on.

In this metaphor, you can see relative structure and certainty about how the day unfolds, while part of it remains uncertain. The overall day is generally relatively structured and reasonably predictable, with some uncertainties about weather, traffic, exact timing etc. Then the football itself is quite uncertain; in fact, that is part of its attraction. So, in therapy, there are some things that we can be quite sure about (structure of sessions, time of sessions, where, how long, when to review, etc.) and there are more uncertain elements (the specific things we might work on together - that's the game of football).

INITIAL AGREEMENT ABOUT THE PROBLEM

Once the client has arrived for treatment, the early task for the therapist is to assess the client's problems, agree on an understanding and consider treatment choices. To offer treatment for GAD, the therapist needs to be sure that the client has GAD or excessive levels of worry, as misalignment at this fundamental level will threaten the alliance. Is the level of worry excessive? Or is the worry a normal, proportionate response to extraordinary circumstances (e.g. serious health problem, threat of redundancy, precarious living conditions, asylum seeker etc.)? Is the worry part of a long standing pattern or is it due to a current important stressor? Is GAD a reasonable hypothesis that accounts for their current difficulties as well as their history. Trying to treat GAD when it is not GAD (or not treating GAD when it really is) can strain the personal alliance, lead to task misalignment and jeopardise the client's willingness or ability to engage in therapy.

Therapist tip

Worry is a normal response to life stress and life events. GAD is about excessive worry. Use questionnaires (e.g. Penn State Worry Questionnaire) for general tendency to worry. Be curious about current life circumstances. Ask about their history of worry and the impact of worry.

Therapist tip

Ask them: 'Would you still worry/be a worrier if (the main problem(s) of the moment) suddenly went away?'

Finally, the therapist can check in with the client: does this understanding, based on the range and extent of their worries relative to their current circumstances, make sense?

Therapist: There seems to be a lot of things going on; you also seem to be worrying a lot about these things. The worrying seems to be having a big impact on you and how you feel and what you do. So, could we say that even though there are things going on in your life, worry about them is making it worse?

MANAGING THE FLOW

A challenge throughout is managing the flow of information. The therapist may report feeling overwhelmed or bogged down by the amount of information and worry recounted by the client. They might report struggling to find a consistent focus, as the content of the session can shift from moment to moment and week to week. Therapists may notice a range of negative emotions, such as feeling irritated

Therapist tip

Use frequent and accurate summaries, and be prepared to step in if needed.

Table 5.1 Questioning style in GAD

In typical CBT we might use the following sequence to navigate our way collaboratively through sessions:		**In CBT for GAD, because of the nature of worry we may need a slight modification so we can (collaboratively) stop worry hijacking the session:**	
Therapist:	(Socratic) question	*Therapist*:	(Socratic) question
Client:	Response	*Client*:	Flood of worry
Therapist:	(Socratic) question	*Therapist*:	Looks for an opening
Client:	Response	*Client*:	More worry
Therapist:	(Socratic) question	*Therapist*:	Is it OK if I just stop you there…?
		(perhaps several minutes later)	
Client:	Response	*Client*:	Stops, perhaps surprised
Therapist:	Summary, elicit feedback	*Therapist*:	Summary, elicit feedback on the *content* and the *conversation*

('Come on, we have talked about this'), exasperated ('Will he ever run out of things to worry about?'), disinterested ('I've heard it all ten times before') or powerless ('I can't help them with all this stuff'). Conversely, being overly empathic and connected with the client's worry ('This is terrible, how awful') can mean that the therapist is drawn into overidentifying with specific worries and thereby losing perspective on the central problem.

Stepping in may feel uncomfortable to do at first because of our normal expectations of turn-taking, but worry can pressure the client to keep providing more and more detail or chaining on to other worries. It may feel at first that the therapist is being directive rather than collaborative, but this is about creating some space, and importantly reflective space, to be able to work together (see Table 5.1). The first time the therapist does this, it's important to explain and check out the impact of the interruption:

Therapist: I'm aware that I've just interrupted you, but I wanted to make sure that I've properly understood what you have been telling me. I'd like to check out my understanding, is that OK?

The summary then starts by referring first to content, labelling the content accurately rather than entering into detail, so showing that therapist has been listening, empathising with the experience, then checking out understanding, and then the client's response.

Therapist: As I understand it, you are currently concerned about..., and about..., and about... That sounds very difficult and upsetting... Have I got that right?

Therapist tips

- The therapist's job is to collaborate with the patient, not the worry!
- If this happens again, the therapist can seek agreement about how to manage the flow when it becomes unhelpful.

Therapist: Once again it seems that we are talking about some really important (or upsetting or difficult) things here, but I just want to make sure that we're not getting caught up in it and missing the important parts... Is it OK if I stop you when I think this is happening? Then we can check out whether we are both understanding things the same way.

Once the therapist is able to manage the flow, they can use the reflective space created by the summaries to draw out patterns in the worry through the content-process shuffle.

THE CONTENT–PROCESS SHUFFLE

This is where the personal and task alliances come together. From the standpoint of the personal alliance, the worrier feels sufficiently understood, validated and contained and the therapist is empathic and attuned. Both are able to sit with the worries and uncertainty. From the standpoint of the task alliance, it is the ability to decentre, to notice being hooked into something, take a breath, and rather than being caught up in the process of worry, we can instead sit back and ask a question *about* the process and then make a choice about what to do next.

Without decentring or zooming out, it will be difficult for both client and therapist to understand the processes that according to each specific model maintain worry. Unless this is carefully managed, the client might feel that they have not been listened to, or their experiences dismissed, and so threaten the personal alliance. For the therapist, if they can't help the client move from worry content to worry process, therapy sessions can become frustrating and overwhelming; they risk experiencing the therapist's version of Groundhog Day, where each session seems a slight variation of the last.

Therapist: It sounds like you have had quite a week: your partner's new job and your *worries* about what this means for the school run, that you are *worried* you don't understand your 9-year-old's maths homework and that you have been dealing with some tough work issues that have led to some sleepless nights as you have been *worrying* about them... Lots going on, lots that you have been *worrying* about. Quite understandably, it seems like all the *worrying* seems to be getting you down.

Therapist tip

- Try to empathise with and emphasise the experience of worry, not the content of worry.
- Synthesising questions are part of the Socratic Method and aim to move clients into a reflective space. In the treatment of GAD, this equates to decentring and noticing, rather than just worrying out loud, starting to move from specific content to common process.

Therapist: We could unpack each of these..., or look at one in particular, but I am wondering if there is something in common between each of these?

Therapist: You have told me a lot today about your worries about your kids, I think we talked about this last session as well. Have you noticed that worries about your kids tends to lead onto worrying about your health? What does this tell us about what may be going on?

Therapist: If we rolled back a week, were you worried about the same sort of things? Or a month? If we rolled on a week, would it be the same? What might this tell us?

ESTABLISHING THEORY B

Like with other problems, this is often the turning point of therapy for GAD. It is possibly the essential task because moving further into therapy without a clear agreement about Theory B is usually unproductive (see Table 5.2). As far as is possible, guided discovery is probably best when trying to help the client understand Theory B. Importantly, the client does not need to believe Theory B at this point, but they do need to be curious about it and willing to work together to find out if this makes sense.

On the one hand, trying to get this alignment too soon, or by telling the client rather than guiding them towards it, risks the client believing that their therapist does not understand their difficulties. On the other hand, without agreement about the plausibility of Theory B, therapist and client are potentially trying to solve different problems. Both will have impact, whether direct or indirect, on the personal and task alliances.

MIDDLE STAGES OF THERAPY

While the early stages of therapy are characterised by establishing an effective personal alliance and shifting understanding to Theory B, the mid stages are about using the personal alliance to get on with the tasks of changing the behaviour that maintains worry. Depending on the model, this may be by reducing cognitive, behavioural or experiential avoidance, behavioural experiments to test beliefs about worry, addressing negative problem orientation, engaging in exposure to worry or dropping safety-seeking or uncertainty-reducing behaviours. These all involve the person stopping what they normally do (and probably have done for years) and/or doing something new. So whether IU is explicitly a focus of therapy or not, the worrier needs to move into what is, for them, uncharted territory.

Table 5.2 Reflecting on Theory A and Theory B

Theory name	Theory A	Theory B
Statement of theory	I have many things going on in my life that make me worry a lot	I worry a lot about the many things that are going on in my life
Impact	This is ruining my life (or making my life very difficult)	This is ruining my life (or making my life very difficult)
The problem is:	*All the things going on in my life*	*Worrying a lot*
Prediction	*If all these things stopped happening (or if me or someone could just fix them), I would worry less*	*If I could figure out how to worry less, I would be better able to deal with the things that are going on in my life*
Outcome	Life would be better	Life would be better

INTOLERANCE OF UNCERTAINTY AND CHANGE

Change strategies will lead to uncertainty, and the aversive feelings associated with IU can make the client feel uncontained and unsafe; the therapist's task is to help calibrate the dose of uncertainty in therapy. Not enough uncertainty means that there is insufficient challenge and no learning for the client. Too much may lead to preoccupation with details, 'new' worries or avoidance of therapeutic tasks. Both may become frustrated, which then threatens the personal alliance.

Within GAD, the IU has a particular way of playing out interpersonally. With GAD, the 'yes buts' have a distinctive feel. Rather than 'yes but,' the client might say 'yes, thank you ... but there is something else.' It is not a hostile 'yes but;' it may even be pleasant or grateful to start with. However, it may be experienced by the therapist as disempowering if interpreted as 'yes, thank you but.... you really don't understand me' or, more often, 'you do understand me, you are trying to be really helpful, but there is this other stuff that I need help with.'

Therapist tip

Whether or not the chosen treatment targets IU directly, it can be helpful to develop a shared understanding of how IU makes change feel difficult but that, by making changes, these feelings decrease or are easier to tolerate.

Therapist tip

Trust the process; the temptation when IU kicks in (for client and therapist) will be to change direction or try something else, normally returning to things that are familiar.

LATER STAGES OF THERAPY

Unlike people with panic disorder, who are often panic free at the end of treatment, people with GAD will still be worriers to a degree, just less so. The weeks and months following therapy will be uncertain, especially if therapy has gone well! People may be now exploring new possibilities after often years held back by worry.

CONSOLIDATION AND RELAPSE PREVENTION

Throughout therapy, especially at the start, the therapist has been providing structure and scaffolding the therapy process while providing relative certainty. Approaching relapse prevention as a process over several sessions, rather than as a focused session, will signal that the end is approaching. To help the client take ownership of their learning and its application in everyday living in a progressive way, it can be useful to develop the relapse prevention plan together from several sessions from the end.

The relapse prevention material, or 'emergency kit,' should focus on both general learning (e.g. my problem is worry) and specific skills that the client has developed (e.g. embracing uncertainty by... reduces worry). Key content includes predictions about the types of events or uncertainties that are likely to trigger worry, reasonable expectations that normal worry will fluctuate with events, the notion that worry should not become excessive or continue beyond the triggering event and clear identification of the strategies that have worked once and will work again. Completing the emergency kit together over the last few weeks and the client taking it away with them can be an important moment of handover.

SENDING PEOPLE OFF INTO AN UNCERTAIN FUTURE

A longstanding pattern of IU and worry about the future would predict that ending therapy may be difficult for the client, especially as the future with new possibilities may be objectively more uncertain. This may lead to a desire to have extra sessions or bring new opportunities as new problems. It is generally helpful to have a clear contract and agreement about how many more sessions are left and how they will be used throughout, but especially in the last third of therapy. The therapist may also need to consider whether their own IU or worry about the client and therapy (see below) may contribute to drawn out endings or extra sessions. It may be helpful to spread out the last few sessions to give greater opportunity for the client to generalise and consolidate. However, this needs to be a planned process with a clear plan and end date rather than fizzling out. Likewise, any follow-up plans should be clear, once again staying with the principle of relative certainty while the person gains confidence in their ability to manage alone the uncertainties of every-day life.

Therapist tip

Consider spacing out the last few sessions in a clearly agreed way.

Therapist tip

If your service allows, it might be better to say 'we will do a review in six months' rather than to say 'come back to therapy if you need to'.

THERAPIST FACTORS

THERAPISTS WHO WORRY

As members of the public, we would be happy for therapists to worry a bit. Not enough that it gets in the way of being an effective therapist, but enough to make sure they are concerned about doing a good job, thinking through the different options, trying to figure out the right thing to do (and thinking about what could go wrong) and showing genuine concern for us (or our family members). Therapists, in general, are likely to be close to the average, or even above average, as worriers as there is a fit between caring in mental health professions and some of the features of worry.

So, compared to some other mental health problems, there are probably many more therapists providing therapy for GAD who have first-hand experience of 'the problem.' On the up side is increased empathy; on the down side, worry may feel normal and so therapists may have difficulty seeing the processes as problematic compared with, for example, a panic attack. So, given that one of the roles of a therapist is to help clients decentre and see the processes as unhelpful, therapists who worry may implicitly or explicitly aim lower and try and help clients manage worry, tone it down a bit, or minimise its impact rather than help them fundamentally change their relationship to worry.

THERAPISTS IDENTIFYING WITH WORRY CONTENT

Almost everybody worries, and there is nothing especially distinctive about worry content in GAD. As therapists also have their own lives and care about their family, friends, their health and the health of those they care about, their job, the place they live, their community and broader society, the things that their clients worry about are also likely to resonate with them. On the plus side, this may help therapists empathise with their clients. On the down side, overly identifying with the content may disempower therapists and prevent them from decentring as they get hooked into the content and distracted from the process: 'That's terrible, I would worry about that too!'

THERAPIST'S BELIEFS ABOUT WORRY

Positive beliefs about worry are suggested by several models of worry; they include beliefs such as worry helps solve problems, motivates people or shows that one cares. The processes that maintain worry are also likely to be found among therapists and while, intellectually, one may 'know' that these beliefs contribute to worry, one may still 'feel' that worrying is the right thing to do.

THERAPIST INTOLERANCE OF UNCERTAINTY

IU keeps people sticking to the familiar, avoiding change and often making conservative, but less advantageous, decisions. Therapists who are high in IU may find it difficult to decide if and when to 'step in' to manage the flow, to know if the formulation is 'good enough,' whether to try new (and evidence-based strategies) from the different models or address difficult topics, or how and when to end therapy. The more common response to high IU is to delay, seek more information and think (or worry) a bit more, all of which will risk a slowed or stalled working alliance. However, when uncertainty becomes very aversive, we know that people make impulsive decisions to get rid of the unpleasant uncertainty feelings. The risk here is that an intervention is poorly timed, overplayed or not thought through, all of which may threaten the personal alliance directly through misunderstanding, or indirectly as the task alliance suffers.

IMPACT OF THERAPIST FACTORS ON THE WORKING ALLIANCE

Therapists' own experience of worry and IU may help them empathise, and indeed have some insight into the mind of the worrier, and so help the personal alliance. There may be a genuine connection around the experience of being a worrier and, indeed, around the content of worry or the dislike of uncertainty. However, these factors may prevent the therapist from helping the client decentre and be curious about worry and the different processes, and so reduce the ability to form an effective task alliance. Alternatively, if the therapist has a loved one or close friend who worries a great deal, the way the therapist deals with this person and their worries in their personal life may intrude into how they react to a person who worries in their professional life. If so, they could, for example, take an unhelpfully dismissive or directive stance that undermines the alliance. In CBT training, there is not a requirement for therapists to undergo therapy, but a compassionate and genuine response to any issues we bring is to practice what we preach on ourselves.

Therapist tip

Completing questionnaire measures developed for worry and GAD, such as the Penn State Worry Questionnaire (Meyer et al., 1990), the Intolerance of Uncertainty Scale (Buhr and Dugas, 2002) or the questionnaires used with the other approaches, may be helpful to start reflection about your own worry, IU, beliefs about worry, etc. If you find that you are scoring high on some questionnaires, you may wish to see if you can take yourself through a process of self-discovery or self-practice/self-reflection (see Haarhoff and Thwaites, 2015) or perhaps use a self-help book like *Overcoming Worry* (Meares and Freeston, 2015).

CHAPTER SUMMARY

We have seen how excessive worry and GAD may provide specific challenges to the working alliance, as worry itself and related processes may be present in session even at the end of therapy. We believe that understanding the phenomenology of worry and the role of IU are essential to the adjustments that may make the difference between successful and unsuccessful therapy, regardless of the specific treatment approach that is used. Interaction with therapist factors, notably their own worry and IU, should also be considered. When therapist and client can decentre from worry content and be curious about worry process, alternative responses to worry can be considered. Finally, it is important in the later stages of therapy to prepare the client for a future that may be objectively more uncertain.

FURTHER READING

Dugas MJ and Robichaud M (2007) *Cognitive-behavioral Treatment for Generalized Anxiety Disorder: From Science to Practice.* New York: Routledge.

Wilkinson A, Meares K and Freeston MH (2011) *CBT for Worry and Generalised Anxiety Disorder.* London: Sage.

REFERENCES

Behar E, DiMarco ID, Hekler EB, Mohlman J and Staples AM (2009) Current theoretical models of generalized anxiety disorder (GAD): Conceptual review and treatment implications. *Journal of Anxiety Disorders 23*(8): 1011–1023.

Bordin ES (1979) The generalizability of the psychoanalytic concept of the working alliance. *Psychotherapy 16*: 252–260.

Borkovec TD, Alcaine OM and Behar E (2004) Avoidance theory of worry and generalized anxiety disorder. In: Heimberg R, Turk C and Mennin D (eds) *Generalized Anxiety Disorder: Advances in Research and Practice*. New York: Guilford Press, pp. 77–108.

Buhr K and Dugas MJ. The intolerance of uncertainty scale: Psychometric properties of the English version. *Behaviour Research and Therapy 40*: 931–945.

Carleton RN (2012) The intolerance of uncertainty construct in the context of anxiety disorders: Theoretical and practical perspectives. *Expert Review of Neurotherapeutics 12*(8): 937–947.

Carleton RN (2016) Into the unknown: A review and synthesis of contemporary models involving uncertainty. *Journal of Anxiety Disorders 39*: 30–43.

Cuijpers P, Sijbrandij M, Koole S, Huibers M, Berking M and Andersson G (2014) Psychological treatment of generalized anxiety disorder: A meta-analysis. *Clinical Psychology Review 34*(2): 130–140.

Dugas MJ, Gagnon F, Ladouceur R and Freeston MH (1998) Generalized anxiety disorder: A preliminary test of a conceptual model. *Behaviour Research and Therapy 36*(2): 215–226.

Dugas MJ and Robichaud M (2007) *Cognitive-behavioral Treatment for Generalized Anxiety Disorder: From Science to Practice*. New York: Routledge.

Fresco DM, Mennin DS, Heimberg RG and Ritter M (2013) Emotion regulation therapy for generalized anxiety disorder. *Cognitive and Behavioral Practice 20*(3): 282–300.

Haarhoff B and Thwaites R (2015) *Reflection in CBT*. London: Sage.

Hayes-Skelton SA, Orsillo SM and Roemer L (2013) An acceptance-based behavioral therapy for individuals with generalized anxiety disorder. *Cognitive and Behavioral Practice 20*(3): 264–281.

Hjemdal O, Hagen R, Nordahl HM and Wells A (2013) Metacognitive therapy for generalized anxiety disorder: Nature, evidence and an individual case illustration. *Cognitive and Behavioral Practice 20*(3): 301–313.

Hougaard E (1994) The therapeutic alliance – A conceptual analysis. *Scandinavian Journal of Psychology 35*(1): 67–85.

Kessler RC, Nelson CB, McGonagle KA, Liu J, Swartz M and Blazer DG (1996) Comorbidity of *DSM-III-R* major depressive disorder in the general population: results from the US National Comorbidity Survey. *British Journal of Psychiatry Supplement 30*: 17–30.

Meares K and Freeston M (2015) *Overcoming Worry*. 2nd ed., revised. London: Robinson.

Mennin DS, Heimberg RG, Turk CL and Fresco DM (2002) Applying an emotion regulation framework to integrative approaches to generalized anxiety disorder. *Clinical Psychology: Science and Practice 9*: 85–90.

Meyer TJ, Miller ML, Metzger RL and Borkovec TD (1990) Development and validation of the Penn State Worry Questionnaire. *Behaviour Research & Therapy 28*: 487–495.

Moffitt TE, Harrington H, Caspi A, Kim-Cohen J, Goldberg D, Gregory AM and Poulton R (2007) Depression and generalized anxiety disorder: Cumulative and sequential comorbidity in a birth cohort followed prospectively to age 32 years. *Archives of General Psychiatry 64*(6): 651–660.

Newman MG, Castonguay LG, Borkovec TD, Fisher AJ, Boswell JF, Szkodny LE and Nordberg SS (2011) A randomized controlled trial of cognitive-behavioral therapy for generalized anxiety disorder with integrated techniques from emotion-focused and interpersonal therapies. *Journal of Consulting and Clinical Psychology 79*(2): 171–181.

Provencher MD, Freeston MH, Dugas MJ and Ladouceur R (2000) Catastrophizing assessment of worry and threat schemata among worriers. *Behavioural and Cognitive Psychotherapy 28*(3): 211–224.

Roemer L and Orsillo SM (2002) Expanding our conceptualization of and treatment for generalized anxiety disorder: integrating mindfulness/acceptance-based approaches with existing cognitive behavioral models. *Clinical Psychology: Science and Practice 9*: 54–68.

Roemer L and Orsillo SM (2005) An acceptance based behavior therapy for generalized anxiety disorder. In: Orsillo SM and Roemer L (eds) *Acceptance and Mindfulness-based Approaches to Anxiety: Conceptualization and Treatment*. New York: Springer, pp. 213–240.

Wells A (1995) Meta-cognition and worry: a cognitive model of generalized anxiety disorder. *Behavioural and Cognitive Psychotherapy 23*: 301–320.

Wilkinson A, Meares K and Freeston MH (2011) *CBT for Worry and Generalised Anxiety Disorder*. London: Sage.

6

PANIC, SPECIFIC PHOBIAS, AGORAPHOBIA AND SOCIAL ANXIETY DISORDER

RICHARD STOTT

CHAPTER OVERVIEW

Cognitive therapy has established itself as the first line treatment for anxiety disorders. The skilled therapist will not only be familiar with the specific theoretical models guiding their formulation and treatment approach but will learn how to apply *themselves* to the therapeutic process in a way that encourages rapport, motivates engagement and facilitates progress. Anxiety disorders present some particular challenges due to the powerful and pervasive nature of the human threat system and its consequences. The therapist often needs to work hard to develop and utilise the therapeutic relationship in order for the patient to have sufficient confidence to engage fully in the treatment. Ultimately, this will be a crucial determining factor in whether the promises of the theoretical models bear fruit.

ROLE OF THERAPEUTIC RELATIONSHIP AND PARTICULAR CHALLENGES

At a theoretical level, there is much in common between the various anxiety disorders, especially the presentations which are the subject of this chapter: panic disorder, specific phobias, agoraphobia and social phobia. Maintenance processes form the heart of the conceptualisation, with avoidance, safety-seeking behaviours, attentional biases, idiosyncratic appraisals and negative imagery typically playing a central role.

On paper, the models are relatively simple, coherent and easy to articulate. However, at a practical level, helping patients understand and then make changes to these maintenance processes can require significant interpersonal skill. A warm and friendly discussion about the patient's fears might be a necessary starting point but alone would not be sufficient to bring about the goals to which the patient aspires.

Sooner rather than later, the therapist is likely to need to suggest working with certain feared stimuli which have been loathed and avoided for years. Behavioural experiments will be designed which deliberately seek to activate the patient's anxiety system and challenge the patient's previous approach to interacting with the world around them. It is no simple task for the therapist to follow such strategies in a structured and timely manner, whilst maintaining the patient's engagement, trust and commitment.

ENGAGING THE CLIENT

READINESS TO CHANGE

Patients will start therapy with differing levels of commitment, understanding and clarity about what they would like to achieve. One patient has been recommended CBT by the doctor, and encouraged to attend by a loved one, but is sceptical about the value of talking therapies. He attends somewhat reluctantly, perhaps being open to a brief discussion of some 'top tips' on how to relax. Another patient has self-diagnosed with social anxiety disorder having struggled since childhood and, after losing an important relationship, has researched treatment extensively on the internet. She has made the choice to seek a specific course of treatment for this problem. Engagement of these patients requires different approaches.

Therapist: Can I ask you a little about your goals for therapy?

Patient: I don't know, to be honest - my partner suggested I come and see you. I don't know much about therapy.

Therapist: That's not a problem, we can definitely speak more about how therapy might work for you. First though, can I ask, what do you think was in your partner's mind?

Patient: Oh, she would tell you I'm really stressy, and I need to get it sorted - to be honest it's been causing quite a bit of friction.

Therapist: I'm sorry to hear that. But can I ask you what you think yourself - do you think you have problems with stress or anxiety at the moment?

Patient: I probably am a bit of a nightmare sometimes, yes okay I can freak out and lose the plot sometimes, yeah that's me, sure. But I've got to be honest, and not being funny, I'm sure you do some good work, but I can't see that talking about it is going to magically make it go away.

Even from this brief exchange, it is evident that the patient's readiness to change is in question. If the patient is not to drop out of therapy, the therapist must work efficiently in this first session to build trust and instil hope that the patient has indeed come to a place where their experiences can be understood, and where they can have confidence that their therapist can help them construct and work towards realistic goals in a non-judgemental manner. Therapeutic alliance is the major driving force here.

AVOIDANCE

Engagement should not be conceived as a one-time operation at the start of therapy, then taken for granted. Anxious patients frequently exhibit many manifestations of engagement difficulties, driven in particular by fear and avoidance processes. Examples of this might include late attendance, non-attendance or cancellation of sessions, non-compliance or procrastination with homework tasks and/or session content becoming dominated by tangential material in an attempt to avoid feared activities or discussion.

The therapist must address such issues, as failing to do so would be a collusion with the patient's avoidance system. However, it requires interpersonal sensitivity to achieve the right balance between firm guidance and not seeming critical or haranguing.

Therapist: So I'm interested to hear how you got on with the running experiments over the week?

Patient: Yeah, I've honestly been so busy this week, my wife's been working late so... but I did think about what you told me and I definitely will... I definitely am going to do it, I just need to get my head around all this a bit more.

Therapist: Okay, so it sounds like you've had your hands full this week - but you haven't done the experiment as we planned, is that right?

Patient: Not yet, no.

Therapist: I'm wondering whether, as well as being very busy this week, you think there was some avoidance going on perhaps?

Patient: Yes, there was probably an element... well, yes, I think so, yes.

Therapist: It's very good that you can identify that - and avoidance is extremely common, as we discussed last week - but what do you think are the advantages of engaging, even though it can feel scary?

Patient: You're right. Now I feel a bit stupid for not doing it, I guess I was scared.

Therapist: I don't think it is stupid at all. Like I said, avoidance is incredibly natural - it is one of the most frequent strategies people do when they are anxious, so you're not alone! But do you remember the problems with continuing to avoid?

Patient: It keeps the fear going in my head?

Therapist: Absolutely. And would you like us to work together to challenge and overcome that avoidance, a bit like you did so well in the session last week?

Patient: Well, yes, I guess that's what I'm here for.

Therapist: Great, so let's make a plan for what we're doing today, and then we'll make sure you've got a clear roadmap of what to do between now and next week's session – that way you can be confident you are working towards achieving your goals.

Patient: That sounds good.

By adopting a validating, normalising and non-judgemental stance, but also encouraging a structured and goal-driven approach, the therapist sets the tone early in the cognitive therapy process, and this can increase the bond between patient and therapist.

Reflective questions

- Consider a recent patient with an anxiety disorder.
- In what ways did avoidance manifest itself? Were any appointments missed or attended late, or homework not followed through?
- How did you handle this? When a similar situation next occurs, would you try to approach it any other ways?

MODELLING

Cognitive therapy for anxiety problems usually requires the therapist to become active in the session, often to model a particular exposure exercise or demonstrate an experiment. This can be helpful in several respects. Social learning theory has long been recognised as a key mechanism influencing the fear response, and seeing the therapist modelling engagement in a task without an undue fear response or adverse consequences can be helpful. Moreover, the patient has the opportunity to observe the detailed practicalities of engaging in the task, which will be more helpful than a purely verbal or textbook description. Also, the patient can be in the calmer, observer role which will free up more cognitive resource for them to shift perspective and attend to and process the realities of the benign or positive outcome.

Therapist: Okay, so in a minute, let's walk together down the high street where there will be plenty of passers-by. Can I first check, is there still plenty of water under my arms, and on my face?

Patient: Yes plenty.

Therapist: Okay, so let's walk [start moving]… and, as we go, I'd like you to be the observer – remind me of your prediction about looking sweaty around people?

Patient:	If you look sweaty, people will be disgusted and maybe laugh, definitely keep their distance.
Therapist:	Okay then, that's what you predicted isn't it, 75% I think - so, this group of people coming up.... please watch their behaviour and responses closely [passing on pavement very close to a group].
Patient:	...that's weird, they didn't register you - I think they were wrapped up in something, some conversation.
Therapist:	I suspect you're absolutely right. So did my incredibly sweaty arms and face draw their attention?
Patient:	No - and you went really close to them too, like they pretty much had to move so they didn't bump into you. But they didn't even look at you.

SUPPORT WITHOUT REASSURANCE

One of the therapist roles during engagement of the patient is to convey that therapy will be a supportive, non-judgemental space in which the patient can explore and overcome their fears. However, this should not be confused with providing constant reassurance to the patient that everything will be okay 100% of the time. Indeed, if the patient begins to rely upon the therapist for reassurance, this may become a safety behaviour which will inhibit, rather than aid, exploration and disconfirmation of fears.

Patient:	I can't believe I'm doing this - actually handling a real spider. Oh my God. Have you done this before with other patients?
Therapist: (showing calm)	Yes, absolutely. You're doing really well. Take your time. How anxious are you feeling right now?
Patient:	About 80. I'm thinking right now, what if it suddenly decides to jump out and crawl up my arm? Can you just tell me again, am I definitely going to be okay?
Therapist: (speaking calmly and slowly)	I'd just like you to take your time, focus here [pointing] on what's happening in reality in the box in front of you, and then follow my lead, putting your hand in just as I am.
Patient: (tentatively reaching forward)	I guess you seem calm and okay, so it can't be totally dangerous?
Therapist: (smiling calmly)	You're doing extremely well. Tell me what you see actually happening right now?

Patient: Well it's not jumping, actually it's kind of backing off or something.

Therapist: Yes, look at how it moves – I think maybe the spider is actually scared of us! How does that fit with your predictions?

In this extract, the therapist has not engaged directly with the patient's reassurance-seeking. However, a calm, encouraging tone and measured pace is adopted, and the patient's attention is directed to the evidence in front of them, following the experiment that was planned.

Therapist tips

1. Anxiety disorder patients will often benefit from seeing tasks modelled.
2. The observer role is helpful for the patient to begin with as it facilitates cognitive processing and a shift of perspective.
3. Seeing the therapist engage in a task with relative calm, and with no adverse effect, can be helpful and motivating.
4. Some experiments can be undertaken together, and/or the therapist can encourage the patient to follow through and try it out themselves.

PACING AND NON-VERBAL BEHAVIOUR

Whilst not specific to anxiety treatments, pacing and non-verbal behaviour are certainly important to consider in good therapeutic engagement. Some anxious patients will have pressured speech, and the therapist might wish, instead, to model a calmer, moderate pace to facilitate optimal cognitive processing and attention. Non-verbal behaviour is also important with anxious patients. A generally calm, curious and attentive stance is best. Many anxious patients will feel ashamed of expressing some of their fears, for example, considering a phobia to be childish or a panic problem to be a symptom of weakness. Nodding, smiling and compassionate body language may all be helpful in facilitating the engagement of the patient. Judicious use of humour and self-disclosure can also ensure the patient feels included and validated.

Good eye contact is typically a good feature of engaging non-verbal communication, although there are some specific exceptions. In particular, care should be taken with socially anxious patients in the early stages as excessive eye contact could be a trigger for the patient feeling scrutinised or judged. Indeed, socially anxious patients frequently overestimate the extent to which they are being stared at and may process direct eye contact in a threatening light. The therapist risks becoming an object of fear, rather than building the alliance required. Clinical experience has shown that patients engage better when making considerable use of a shared visual reference point, such as a piece of paper or drawing on a whiteboard, for example, in working through a recent example to help socialise to a cognitive model.

PREDICTING AND PREVENTING THREATS TO THERAPEUTIC ALLIANCE

Even when the anxious patient has been successfully engaged in the therapy, there are many potential pitfalls in the road ahead and threats to the therapeutic alliance.

THERAPIST ANXIETIES ABOUT STIMULI

The therapist might become aware early on that the focus of the patient's anxieties overlaps with their own fears. In specific height phobia work, for example, a therapist might be themselves uneasy with heights. Another therapist might be somewhat shy and feel unconfident in the knowledge that their socially anxious patient will need help speaking in front of groups.

Often, such an overlap of fears can be foreseen early on, at the referral or assessment stage. It is important for this to be considered, ideally in clinical supervision, so an appropriate decision can be made on how to proceed. If not addressed, there is a risk to the therapeutic alliance - sooner or later the patient will pick up on the therapist's unease and this could undermine their trust that the therapy is safe.

A therapist anticipating an extreme phobic response on their own part is probably best advised passing the case to a colleague. More common, perhaps, is the case where the therapist will have a mild level of anxiety response compared to that of the patient. In such cases, the therapist must be mindful not to collude with patient avoidance and to model engaging in experiments despite the fear.

THERAPIST CONCERNS ABOUT MAKING PATIENT DISTRESSED

Another common concern for therapists new to anxiety disorder treatments is of instigating components of therapy which might cause upset or distress. Warmth, genuineness and empathy, the bedrock of alliance, might come naturally to many therapists. However, when the therapist suggests to a socially anxious patient the idea of bringing a stranger into the room to chat with, a look of near terror crosses the patient's eyes. Proceeding will most likely be useful for the patient in their learning, but there is a significant chance the patient will be very uncomfortable and a possibility of getting tearful or even panicked. The therapist might question whether they are doing the right thing, given that their patient was quite calm a few minutes before. Handling this kind of moment therapeutically requires an established alliance and high levels of interpersonal skill.

Reflective questions

- Have you had any doubts when suggesting an exposure task or behavioural experiment for an anxious patient? Have you ever worried whether it is 'too much for them'?
- Do you think you have ever unwittingly 'colluded' with a patient's avoidance?

If so, you are not alone. Take a moment to consider your motivations, and think whether you would do anything differently given a similar presentation.

MINIMISATION AND LACK OF VALIDATION

Sometimes, even for therapists, it is easy to forget the world that an anxious patient inhabits. A severe spider phobic might enter a room treating every dark corner with an excessive focus of attention and suspicion. Their threat system might be triggered even by seemingly innocuous cues, such as a pencil sketch, a logo or a grotesque and caricatured plastic children's toy.

Even a well-meaning therapist might inadvertently slip into minimising language.

Therapist: Okay, so obviously we're going to work up to handling real spiders but today I've just brought in this little toy for you to look at, and all I want you to do is simply take a look and give me a rating from 0–10.

Patient: Um, actually... oh God, is that life size? I actually find that quite hard... I'm not sure I'm ready... okay I feel really stupid saying this, but that looks really big to me... and really real [shaking head]... I must sound like such an idiot.

The well-intentioned therapist was perhaps trying to reassure their patient, but in using the words 'just,' 'little' and 'simply,' the therapist has minimised the task demands and this risks the patient feeling misunderstood and possibly foolish. A skilled therapist can certainly rescue this situation before it develops into more of a rupture, but the lesson here is that validation of the emotional impact is highly important. For the therapist to encourage the patient beyond their 'comfort zone' is important, but only in a context in which the patient feels understood and supported.

A related pitfall comes when homework is not appropriately validated. In cognitive therapy, it is usual for homework tasks to be reviewed in the session. The therapist should be aware of the major emotional investment it can be for a patient to engage in a task which might seem trivial to others, including the therapist. Sometimes patients may themselves minimise their efforts, perhaps owing to shame about how trivial they might sound to others. The therapist should try to be aware of this, probing gently for details, praising the patient for their efforts and drawing out learning points or setting new goals as a result.

RATIONAL–EMOTIONAL DISSOCIATION

Very often with anxious patients there is a discrepancy between how fearful something feels and what they know about it rationally - a head–heart lag. This can easily lead to secondary appraisals, which may obstruct the therapeutic alliance, e.g. shame ('I feel so embarrassed telling you this') or craziness ('I think I'm losing my mind sometimes') or invalidity ('So many people have real problems, I feel bad for wasting your time').

Once again, the therapist needs to address such appraisals in order to keep the patient engaged and the alliance maintained.

Patient: The thing is, I really want to be able to be normal, go out, like other people, into normal places, like shopping centres. But I find this kind of blind panic comes on, it's so ridiculous, and every bone in my body is saying no, don't do it, don't risk it.

Therapist: And what is your worst fear if you were to go for a walk, right through the shopping centre this morning?

Patient: That's the thing, I know that nothing would happen, that's what's so stupid! My body starts shaking, I get absolutely terrified, but I'm so embarrassed even saying this because I know people are starving in the world and have real problems, and this is just... nothing, there's nothing bad. Little kids can go shopping, and I'm this jibbering adult - it's so embarrassing.

Therapist: It sounds like your rational voice says there's nothing wrong, but when you get into that situation, your emotional system is strongly active, have I got that right?

Patient: Yes completely.

Therapist: You put it really well - there's two different stories in your head, and actually, we're all built like that - with a rational part and an emotional part - and sometimes they seem to get rather disconnected.

Patient: That's exactly what's happening. But doesn't that make me crazy?

Therapist: Quite the opposite. The fact that you have a rational part and an emotional part shows me that your mind is built just fine! What we can help with in the therapy is to join the parts up a bit more - for example, so that when you enter the shopping centre and feel anxious, you become more connected with what that rational voice is saying - i.e. the evidence around you that you are safe in reality, and also that you could cope with the unexpected.

Patient: That would be good. Then I might feel a bit more normal again!

UNNECESSARILY STOKING WORRY

Some points of therapy might involve a more complex or demanding experiment or exposure exercise, and care needs to be taken not to overly stoke up worry in the patient with unnecessary build-up. For example, a therapist working with a panic patient might plan to introduce an experiment in which the patient pretends to collapse on the pavement, to test a theory about how others might respond. However, priming the patient in the previous session about this might be unwise. All this serves to do is to needlessly increase the levels of worry during the week and risk session cancellation or even drop-out.

New therapists will often fall into this trap, perhaps in part from their own anxiety about a particular experiment or technique, and perhaps because they are trying to 'soften the blow' by mentioning it in advance. However, unless genuine preparation is required or there is some other compelling rationale, it is best practice to introduce and execute tasks and experiments during the session, and not before.

Relatedly, even within the session, it is easy to overly build up experiments and drift into excessive discussion about the task, rather than actually getting on with doing it. Preparation for an experiment is important, certainly, including making and operationalising predictions and planning how the experiment should take place. But therapists need to be careful that this preparation is contained and does not dominate the session. The metaphorical image of the swan is useful for the therapist to keep in mind here - calm and serene on the surface, even if frantically busy beneath the surface. That is, the patient should experience the process of planning and executing the experiment as simply, straightforwardly and calmly as possible, even if, in reality, the therapist has done plenty of preparation and planning.

Therapist tips

1. Validate all efforts and homework tasks, however small, and try to avoid inadvertent use of minimising language.
2. The head–heart lag can be a source of confusion, or even shame, to some patients. Be prepared to address this directly.
3. Don't discuss upcoming tasks the week before (unless there is a good reason such as preparation or homework that is needed). To do so simply increases worry during the week for no benefit.

ENVY OR JEALOUSY

Social comparison is, to an extent, a feature of the human condition, and it is unsurprising that patients will, on occasion, contrast their own predicament with their perception of the therapist's life. For many, such thoughts will be fleeting and of little consequence. However, on occasion, a patient may be distressed by such ideas and even harbour feelings of envy or jealousy at what they see as the therapist's 'perfect life.' The patient might believe their life has been ruined by anxiety, or they might believe they have suffered, e.g. a lost relationship due to anxiety. The therapist needs to be attuned to the patient's appraisals in this regard.

Therapist: So you've observed me doing the 'collapsing on the pavement' experiment, and I'm wondering if you're ready to give that a try too?

Patient: Yeah, maybe... but I think it's different when it's me.

Therapist: Can you say a bit more about what you mean?

Patient: Thing is, it's easy for you, I mean you're a therapist, like, a professional, I mean, I watched you demonstrating it, okay, and I saw people came over to help, sure, but for me... no-one cares about an anxious wreck like me. I don't even imagine you ever get anxious do you anyway?

Therapist: Well, there's a couple of things there. In terms of anxiety, I certainly do get anxious sometimes. An anxiety system is something everyone is born with. In my experience, different things make different people anxious, and sometimes that anxiety can get too much, so that some help might be needed.

Patient: Okay, but I still think you are kind of, you know, an 'okay professional' if you know what I mean, so people will always help you, but I don't think they would for someone like me.

Therapist: I hear that is a strong belief in your head - but can we put it to the test? I'm wondering if we're more similar than that belief is telling you. After all, when someone's collapsed on the pavement, does a passer-by know who they are or whether they are a professional?

Patient: I guess not. But I find it so hard to think of myself as 'normal' like you. I guess I just assume that no-one would help, and that's what makes me so panicky.

Therapist: And what is the alternative perspective that we are going to test out?

Patient: That... people would try to help anyone in trouble, including me? It just seems so impossible!

Therapist: And that's why I'm really encouraging you to try the experiment - that way we can find out more about how the world really works - and not keep relying on that negative message which keeps going round in your head.

Patient: I get it. Yes, I'll give it a try I guess.

ENDING THERAPY

ROCKING THE BOAT

Often, anxious patients will make some good headway in therapy and reach a point where life is far more tolerable, whilst retaining significant residual symptoms and avoidance. The relief of this state can sometimes outweigh the perceived need to pursue the treatment goals further. Moreover, patients might fear pursuing more challenging tasks, lest there be a setback, and openly express that they do not wish to 'rock the boat.'

For the therapist, this presents a dilemma. There might be a strong temptation to go along with this view - to follow the path of least resistance. After all, there might not be many allotted sessions remaining, the patient seems happy with their progress and to suggest pursuing more experiments risks unnecessary distress or even a late-therapy rupture in the alliance.

However, the therapist is wise to consider the bigger picture here - what level of progress will provide the best life chances for the patient? What messages does the therapist wish the patient to leave with, concerning avoidance? Isn't 'rocking the boat' actually *exactly* what the patient needs, in order to discover their own resilience and to provide confidence that they can weather the uncertainties of life ahead?

TRANSITION TO INDEPENDENCE

When therapy ends, the patient will often benefit from continuing to set goals, pursue behavioural experiments or exercises and reviewing their progress on a regular basis. Essentially, they need the mindset and skills to be their own 'therapist' and become independent of the actual therapist. This needs careful thought on both a practical and emotional level.

On the practical side, the therapist needs not to micro-manage every aspect of the patient's therapy sessions right up to the final session; doing so will leave the patient ill-equipped to take on the work further. Instead, as the sessions progress, the collaborative relationship needs to gradually transfer the centre of gravity for planning the topics and tasks of therapy towards the patient's side.

On the emotional side, the therapist needs to be mindful of the feelings aroused by this gradual shift of responsibility within the therapeutic relationship, and the impending loss of the familiar therapy environment, as the sessions draw to a close. For many, there are positive feelings as the ending approaches; a sense of achievement, autonomy, liberation, optimism and pride at what they have achieved and the opportunities they see in the road ahead. For others, there may be trepidation or fear of having to 'go it alone,' or feelings of sadness and loss of the meaningful relationship they have formed with their therapist.

Reflective questions

Consider an anxiety patient you are working with at the moment.

- At this point, to what extent are they taking agency for their own progress, versus relying on you to guide them?
- Do you think it will be helpful to gradually shift the balance so that they take more ownership of their goals, progress and tasks? If so, when?
- What cognitions and emotions do you imagine they will experience when therapy draws to a close?

CHAPTER SUMMARY

This chapter has surveyed, with illustrative examples, a number of crucial areas for the therapist to consider when applying themselves to anxiety disorder work. Engagement processes were considered, including readiness to change, the role of avoidance, modelling, the importance of offering support without constant reassurance and non-verbal behaviour. A range of hazards were also outlined; areas where the therapeutic relationship could suffer if not handled well. Finally, the ending of therapy was considered, including the gradual transition to independence required to enable and empower the patient to continue the work beyond the timespan of the therapy sessions.

Anxiety disorder work can be exceptionally rewarding, perhaps especially when a therapeutic bond is formed which allows the patient sufficient confidence to explore their fears in new ways; feeling validated and not crazy, feeling supported but also challenged and feeling guided but also master of their own destiny.

FURTHER READING

Westbrook D, Kennerley H and Kirk J (2011). *An introduction to Cognitive Behaviour Therapy: Skills and Applications*. London: Sage

Clark DA and Beck AT (2011). *Cognitive Therapy of Anxiety Disorders: Science and Practice*. New York: Guilford Press.

7

OBSESSIVE–COMPULSIVE DISORDER (OCD) AND BODY DYSMORPHIC DISORDER (BDD)

LISA WILLIAMS AND DAVID VEALE

> To be honest I was petrified. I was deeply ashamed of my paedophilic thoughts and didn't know if I would be able to share them with a stranger. I needed help but every part of me was saying 'stay quiet.'
>
> I remember her smile. She sat with me and listened to my story. I wasn't rushed. It felt that she understood my pain and the effect it had had on my health, my relationships and living life. I felt safe. I started to open up and I knew that I wasn't alone on the journey.
>
> Anon (Resident from the Anxiety Disorder Residential Unit, Bethlem Hospital)

CHAPTER OVERVIEW

The origin of the word 'patient' is 'one who suffers.' It is worth remembering, therefore, that we are all 'patients.'

Even before the client enters the therapeutic space, he has perhaps built up in his mind an idea of you, his therapist, with whom he has been invited to share his inner world. Throughout life, the relationships we have with others, whether they be with family, friends, colleagues, mental health services or therapists, can either be experienced as safe, helpful and nurturing or, as so many clients describe to us, as sources of threat, mistrust, disappointment and fear.

The ways in which we relate to ourselves, others and the world are shaped by our life experiences. These often provide the internal and external maps which guide the thoughts, feelings and behaviours related to present experiences and, specifically, to the therapeutic journey the client is about to embark on with you, his therapist. If relationships and interactions with others have been experienced as externally threatening e.g. dismissive, sarcastic or judgemental, it is perhaps no surprise that the relationship we may have with ourselves is equally threatening and that feelings of shame, self-loathing, disgust and aloneness are commonplace (Gilbert, 2009). If we are able as therapists to engage with our clients compassionately, and to be aware of their and our own external and internal threat experiences, then we are perhaps optimally placed to understand how coping strategies to mitigate these threats have developed (Gilbert, 2009). We can then begin to walk alongside our clients, helping them to navigate the often challenging and painful paths of change.

In this chapter, we will be curious about how the therapeutic alliance can help clients suffering with Obsessive Compulsive Disorder (OCD) and Body Dysmorphic Disorder (BDD) to engage with cognitive behavioural interventions and succeed in meeting their goals for change.

INTRODUCING OUR TWO CLIENTS

LOUISE: BDD AND THE THERAPEUTIC RELATIONSHIP

Louise is a 28-year-old university student with BDD. She has isolated herself in her bedroom in her mother's home for two years and has withdrawn from all pleasurable activities. She has had to put university on hold. Although she feels hopeless, she does not feel suicidal. She is preoccupied with the symmetry between her eyes, which she believes are the windows to her soul. She believes that others will notice this and be able to recognise that she is a disgusting, worthless individual. She can no longer look at herself and has avoided all mirrors for two years. She avoids reflective surfaces, wears dark lensed glasses and has grown her hair long to cover her face. Louise has stopped contact with her friends and has withdrawn from all social media.

Louise has paid privately for scans to check the 'eye drop on her left side,' look for physical causes of her uneven eyes and is saving for cosmetic surgery.

When she arrives for an assessment for CBT, she tells the therapist that she desperately wants help but does not believe that she has a psychological problem. She is willing to delay cosmetic surgery until she has attended therapy but appears reluctant.

She witnessed her mother's death when she was nine years old and believes that she is a disgusting individual for not being able to save her. She was also bullied at school, which has impacted on her self-confidence. She berates herself daily with high levels of self-criticism.

Louise believes that her therapist will realise that she is a disgusting individual and will not want to support her. Louise is hypervigilant for how her therapist looks at her and what she says or doesn't say. Louise feels at first that she cannot trust her therapist and needs to protect herself from future hurt or pain. Louise is at first dismissive of a psychological basis to her problem and is reluctant to engage fully in therapeutic dialogue in session. The therapist reflects that she is 'peddling hard' in session to engage Louise and is aware that she often appears distracted and disinterested.

ROGER: OCD AND THE THERAPEUTIC RELATIONSHIP

Roger is a 29-year-old graduate with a longstanding history of paedophilic OCD. His mood is low. He lives on his own some distance from his family and friends and has isolated himself in his flat for the last nine months. Fearing that he may be a paedophile, he doesn't open his eyes in social situations and relies on others to be his guide. All photos, pictures, magazines, social media and TV are avoided, and he has stopped working. He has been with his girlfriend for two years but unable to travel on public transport or leave his flat. Their relationship has become very strained. He is suffering from depression, and although feels hopeless, is not suicidal. When he arrives for assessment, he is unshaven, has lost weight and clearly has not been caring for himself. He believes that he does not deserve care but should instead be punished for his thoughts.

Roger believes that the therapist will judge him negatively for his thoughts and once she is aware that they are paedophilic in nature will not want to work with him. He is highly ashamed and finds it really difficult to disclose his thoughts and feelings. Roger is concerned as to whether his therapist has her own children and does not wish to put them at risk. Understandably, he is highly anxious and seeks reassurance from the therapist about his risk to her and others.

The therapist is aware of Roger's distress and his need for reassurance. Initially, she notices that there is a subtle, yet significant, strain on the therapeutic relationship. She validates Roger's fears, and the function of reassurance and safety strategies he uses to cope, and meets his courage to engage in the therapeutic process with compassion. In this way, the therapist both supports and guides Roger into and through experiences that he finds distressing, without accommodating his OCD.

ROLE OF THE THERAPEUTIC RELATIONSHIP AND PARTICULAR CHALLENGES IN WORKING WITH CLIENTS WITH OCD AND BDD

In both BDD and OCD, it is the meanings underlying intrusive thoughts, the ensuing fears and the way they respond to the intrusions that drive and maintain clients' suffering (Veale and Willson, 2005). The client understandably engages in behaviours to ensure the feared consequence doesn't happen and to minimise their experience of anxiety. Typically, these maintenance processes include avoidance, negative appraisals, safety seeking behaviours, reassurance seeking and negative imagery. Although these behaviours are the client's best efforts to keep themselves safe, they maintain the disorder in the long term, severely impacting on functioning and on being able to live a meaningful life (Veale and Willson, 2005).

Whilst sharing and developing an idiosyncratic formulation of a client's difficulties is helpful to guide therapeutic understanding and direction of treatment, it is important to recognise that a conceptualisation is no more than a 'map' on its own. The skill is to engage the client and for them to trust in the journey ahead, to help motivate them to take unfamiliar or previously avoided paths, to be a guide helping them to navigate terrain that is uncomfortable, unfamiliar and often uncertain, and ultimately, to challenge the beliefs the client holds about themselves, others and the world around them (Gilbert, 2009).

THE THERAPIST'S AND CLIENT'S MINDS

If we were to take an overview of the therapy room, we would see two complex minds interacting. We are particularly interested in how a therapist's verbal and non-verbal communication can impact on the client and vice versa.

Aiming to be the best version of ourselves in the therapeutic relationship is often affected by the context in which we find ourselves as therapists. The self we take into the therapeutic space too often is one challenged by time, pressure to perform and lack of space to reflect. This raises the issue of how the body language and presence of the therapist may be interpreted by the client.

Reflective questions

Take a moment to reflect on your last therapeutic interaction.

- What was your body posture? Try to maintain relaxed shoulders and an open posture.
- Your breathing? Was it slow, deep and regular?
- Your facial expression? Warm smile on your face, relaxed eye gaze?
- Your thoughts? Critical? Or compassionate with a warm tone?
- How did you feel? Irritated? Bored? Engaged?

The version of ourselves that we take into the space we share with our clients may subtly, but significantly, affect the therapeutic alliance (Gilbert, 2005). The therapeutic environment may be interpreted as a safe space to 'share' and be vulnerable or, alternatively, as threatening, resulting in a desire to protect or defend oneself.

For example, Louise's behavioural experiment was to drop one of her safety behaviours, i.e. wearing glasses, which served as camouflage for her, and to be externally focused. She felt extremely distressed and thought her therapist would not want to treat her if she saw her eyes, as she believed her therapist would realise she was a disgusting human being. However, Louise discovered that she was not rejected upon taking off her glasses, and that her therapist instead offered compassionate understanding. Importantly, Louise also discovered that, although the therapeutic relationship was somewhat strained at the time of the exposure, her therapist stayed alongside her throughout, consistently offering support, curiosity and understanding, which served to strengthen her alternative beliefs and behaviours.

In our experience, because the building of rapport and trust can take time, if change strategies are introduced too soon, it may lead to a rupture in the therapeutic alliance and impede learning due to a highly activated stress response.

WHEN SHAME AND SELF-CRITICISM CAN BLOCK THE ABILITY TO MOVE TOWARDS THAT WHICH IS FEARED

For clients with OCD or BDD who may have high levels of shame and self-criticism, we have often found that the therapeutic relationship is a fundamental ingredient in helping them find inner strength and the courage to move towards that which is feared. It is perhaps particularly the early interactions with a therapist that form the basis of trust and safety in therapy and that may be the most enabling. The client and therapist work as a team, sharing responsibility for change, learning new skills and ways of being with self and others that can be transferred to situations and relationships outside of the therapy room.

The relationship the client has with themselves is also important. Being curious about how the client talks to themselves, especially prior to homework tasks, i.e. behavioural experiments, can enlighten both the client and therapist to the threat experienced prior to approaching that which is feared. For example, Roger, who has obsessional fears about being a paedophile, embarked on a behavioural experiment which involved walking past the school gates to look at school children without ritualising.

Therapist: I am interested to hear how you talk to yourself at those times prior or during a behavioural experiment.

Roger: Umm, let me think. Well, as I was approaching the school, I was saying 'Come on you idiot, dig deep you can do this. Come on where's your strength and courage. You're going to fail at this. You idiot.'

Therapist: I am wondering how you felt as you spoke to yourself in this harsh and critical way?

Roger: Well, thinking about it, it reminds me of how my father used to speak to me. It made me feel awful. Anxious. Afraid. I thought I was going to fail the task.

Therapist: I am wondering, if you were guiding me right now towards something I feared, how you would talk to me?

Roger: Well I wouldn't be negative that's for sure. I would say in a calm voice that you are doing well. That I know it is hard for you, but I am here with you. You are showing great courage. Keep going, you are doing great.

Therapist: Thank you. I would feel really supported by you and your kind understanding voice would be encouraging. I am wondering how the experience would be for you if you were able to adopt this approach for yourself rather than the harsh critical tones you have been listening to for so long?

Learning in this way to approach difficulties with a validating, kind empathic inner voice helps the client move towards that which is difficult rather than experiencing further threat from an internal hostile, critical voice.

WHEN SELF-CRITICISM AND SHAME ARE PRESENT IN THERAPY AND HOMEWORK TASKS

In CBT, it is usual for homework to be reviewed in session. For many, homework tasks are done alone in between sessions, and the client has to invest emotionally and summon great courage to engage with the task set. It is not uncommon for the client to minimise their successes or to hope that the session finishes without time to reflect on the task. It is important to be aware that shame and self-criticism may be blocking honest reflection e.g. 'I am so embarrassed that I cannot do the simple task of going into a public toilet. The therapist must think I am so stupid.'

It is important that the therapist makes time for a review of homework on the agenda, taking time to validate and to explore, praising the client for their efforts, being curious together about what has been learned and setting new, value-based goals and further tasks as a result.

Therapist tips

1. The client may have high levels of shame and self-criticism.
2. It is helpful to explore how the client speaks to themselves.
3. Shame may preclude the client from sharing homework tasks that he considers to be trivial.
4. Feeling safe and trusting the therapist allows the client to explore their inner world and approach that which has been avoided, i.e. internal or external threats.

WHEN KINDNESS FROM THE THERAPIST CAN BE AVERSIVE

The social safeness system may be activated when the client experiences being cared for by the therapist or when they perceive that the mind of the therapist is orientated towards them in a compassionate way. This can enable the client to feel safe enough to start to be curious about the world and start to explore it in a different way (Gilbert, 2005).

It is important, however, to keep in mind that this may be aversive for some clients, and that compassion may be, at first, very frightening (Lee, 2011). This was the experience reflected by Louise. When explored in therapy, it became clear that her early experience of school bullying had led to the formation of the belief that 'people are kind to you, but they can also exploit you.' This functioned as a filter through which she saw the world and acted as a block to her ability to receive compassion from others and offer herself compassion, generate alternatives to critical self-talk, receive positive feedback from her therapist and, importantly, feel safe enough in her relationships with others to trust and be vulnerable with her therapist.

Louise practiced using the positive relationship she had with her niece and role-played how she would talk to her if she was struggling or having difficulties. Louise reflected that she was able to offer her warmth and kindness, and that her intention was to help and support her through being reassuring, validating and helpful. She was able to reflect on how she showed her niece compassion through body posture, voice tone and facial expression. Role playing in this way enabled Louise to begin to recognise how she demonstrates compassion towards others. This enabled her to 'try on' and begin to embrace these qualities on herself and, importantly, recognise and begin to trust the caring intentions of her therapist to support her through her difficulties on the road to recovery.

GOAL SETTING AND MODELLING

Value-based goals are fundamental to overcoming OCD and BDD. The client must be aware of what they are aiming for and measure progress towards these on a regular basis. It is worth reminding the client that you will never ask them to do something that as a therapist you are not prepared to do yourself. Modeling the task first may help the client to approach that which is feared. For example, the therapist might model touching the toilet seat for five minutes and then not washing her hands afterwards.

It is important to choose targets that are challenging, but not too overwhelming, and that exposures are long enough, frequent enough and that safety behaviours are not present.

REASSURANCE

Clients suffering from OCD and BDD often experience discomfort and pain brought on by their intrusive thoughts, and they then do whatever they can to reduce the uncertainty. Clients then turn to compulsive strategies in an attempt to create an artificial sense of certainty (Veale and Willson, 2005).

It makes sense that if they are unable to make themselves feel sure internally about something, they will reach out for someone (either real or cyber) who is able to do this for them.

We know that the maintenance role of reassurance seeking means the solution soon becomes the problem and, although a temporary sense of assurance is provided, it is not long before the client needs more and more reassurance to 'feel assured' (Veale, Willson and Clarke, 2009).

This drive to achieve reassurance is strong in many of our clients and can be challenging for the therapeutic relationship to withstand. To see our clients suffering and in pain, and not to give them in that moment what they feel they need, can be seen as punishing by both client and therapist. It is important to consider the function of reassurance with the client and agree with them at the outset how you are going to respond or what may be most helpful in these moments. In this way, we are able, as therapists, to provide an alternative to reassurance by offering emotional support without the need to discuss the content of their worries.

Roger frequently asked for reassurance, and it would have appeared to be kinder to offer this to him in order to give immediate relief to his pain and suffering. However, the long-term effects of accommodating his OCD would have paradoxically meant that he would not have been able to discover and test the hypothesis that he didn't become a 'raging paedophile who would be locked up within hours' and build his self confidence and beliefs about coping with, and being around, children. Understanding the process of Exposure and Response Prevention (ERP) and the function of reassurance was important for Roger. Being able to feel warmth, non-judgement and support from the therapist helped him to drop safety behaviours and compulsions after exposure to children. Positive re-enforcement of his courage with compassion from his therapist also encouraged him to test out alternative beliefs to his fears.

Roger: Oh, my goodness, I am actually walking past the school gates. Are you sure this is safe for me to be here?

Therapist: (showing calm) Roger, as we discussed, let's keep walking past the school and look towards the children waiting for their bus. You are doing really well. Take your time.

Roger: (smiling calmly) I am doing it. My thoughts are screaming at me to run away, saying I am dangerous and need to be locked up. But we are here together, and you are not concerned. I can do this. Can't I? Do you think I am doing OK?

Therapist: Let's be curious about our thoughts and where our focus of attention is whilst we are at the school. You have been really courageous Roger.

In this extract, the therapist has not engaged in Roger's reassurance seeking directly. She has, in a warm encouraging tone, helped Roger to stay curious about the experiment that had been planned, directing his focus towards being near the school children without ritualising.

Reflective questions

- Have you ever offered reassurance when the client asked for it?
- Have you colluded with the client and pulled out of a behavioural experiment because the client was worried about it?

If so, it is not unusual. Reflect, and ask yourself the function of this behaviour or your motivations, and consider whether you could have done anything differently.

NOTICING SUBTLE CHANGES IN THE CLIENT AND OURSELVES

This requires micro skills and the engagement of the therapist with their own soothing system in order to notice nuances in clients' body language, changes in affect, e.g. a flush of cheek, change in focus or a skipping over of detail. A therapist who enters the therapeutic space feeling threatened themselves, rushed or stressed may not be in the most helpful mind set for optimal awareness of a client's subtle behaviours (Kolts, 2016).

Unresolved or feared issues in the therapist can also impact on sensitivity. A therapist who is uncomfortable talking about paedophilic thoughts, groinal sensations or disturbing images may guide a client away from their own distress and discomfort, rather than towards the client's pain.

High shame-prone clients like Louise and Roger may have become adept at hiding their shame, and therefore avoid disclosing important details of their inner worlds to the therapist for fear of judgement, ridicule or rejection. The client who is faced with a mechanical or technique driven therapist may find such important disclosure particularly difficult. It is therefore important for the therapist to sit with a client's distress and follow the emotion through Socratic dialogue, providing an environment of warmth, non-judgement and understanding in which key disclosures may take place in a shame-free manner (Gilbert, 2005).

EXPLORING SILENCE

With both Louise and Roger, the therapist explored the meaning of silence with them. Both clients were highly shame prone and often, when early shame memories were triggered, they would go into a 'shut down' freeze response and then enter a process of 'mindreading' with the therapist, trying to work out what they were thinking, in what ways they were being judged and what the therapist might be thinking of their 'frozen' state.

It was important for the client and therapist to discuss and be curious about these different states; for example, when silence is an opportunity to be with and explore feelings or when it means the client has switched to trying to mindread, is ruminating about what the therapist is thinking and feeling shame-based scrutiny.

With Roger, his thoughts were 'I think that you may be thinking that I am an abhorrent human being. I am thinking that you may be wanting to organise locking me up in a secure unit.'

Louise's thoughts were, 'you can see within me and recognise the traits that make me a disgusting individual. I cannot trust your words, and therefore will look for subtle changes in your body language that may confirm my belief.'

As therapists, we are listening and attending to what is said, as well as what is not.

VALUES

There are often two aspects of the suffering of clients. The first is the suffering from having to live with, and manage the symptoms of, their BDD or OCD. The second is the pain caused by the life not lived. Values are a way of being able to talk about the life a client wants to live, from a place of suffering (Harris, 2009).

This is true of the therapist also and the values that they may bring to the therapeutic relationship. Values are usually related to wanting to make a difference in someone's life, to alleviate suffering, to be genuine and to be able to support another to help them to get respite from their pain.

By declaring our values as therapists to our clients, e.g. 'I am committed to alleviating your suffering so that you can move towards a life that gives you purpose, fulfilment and meaning,' it can become a shared value, uniting both the therapist and client in a shared direction towards a life worth living.

OUR TRICKY BRAINS

A key message to someone with BDD or OCD is about the way that their brains have been shaped by the evolutionary problem of being human, combined with internal and external threats. In the case of BDD, symptoms are designed to keep them safe from social exclusion or rejection, and in the case of OCD, to keep either themselves or others safe from a perceived threat, e.g. contamination. This description of the evolutionary function of their symptoms gives the therapy a different stance and helps the client to recognise that much of what goes on in our minds is not our fault. In this way, we are able to sit alongside our client with the understanding that 'here we are together, with a tricky brain that we did not design.'

TRANSCRIPT: CURIOSITY

The below dialogue illustrates how we can be curious with our client and start to make links between a current sense of self and emotional memories of the past in a non-shaming, collaborative way.

Therapist: It is very understandable that, after experiencing being bullied and teased as a child, you began to feel different and separate from your peers. You told me that you felt alone, scared and rejected. It was then that you remember developing a negative felt sense of how you looked.

From this point, the therapist can engage in guided discovery.

Therapist: How might there be an emotional link between the image you have of your features and some of these difficult and painful memories?

Therapist: Is it possible that those fears of rejection, isolation and aloneness were drivers for your focus on appearance?

Therapist: I wonder what would happen if we could help you with the difficult memories that are still so painful for you and the shame that haunts you?

WORKING WITH THREATS TO THE ALLIANCE

At the start of therapy, it will be helpful for the client to be aware of the difficulties that may arise in therapy, especially with regards to behavioural experiments and exposure tasks.

It may be that the client has not first built up an internal feeling of safeness. If a client looks to the outside world to reduce threat but does not have an internal feeling of safeness, then he may experience head–heart lag, i.e. knowing cognitively that he can cope with an experience or situation but feeling unable to tolerate the distress.

If the therapist has not been explicit in exploring self-criticism, distress tolerance skills, matching or pacing exposure, and the 'temperature' is too hot, the client may not be able to complete the task and instead may be overwhelmed with self-criticism. This is likely to lead him to feel a failure, exacerbating his shame and concluding that therapy is ineffective or that he 'can never get better.' This sense of 'failing' and potential avoidance of further therapeutic interventions can impact on the therapeutic relationship, with both client and therapist feeling that they have reached an impasse.

TRANSCRIPT: UNINTENDED CONSEQUENCES

The following dialogue illustrates an understanding of our tricky brain and how it has functioned to keep Roger safe but has unintended consequences. The warmth and non-judgemental stance of the therapist allows a sense of collaboration and curiosity.

Therapist: So, Roger's threatened mind has been trying to keep you safe by being hypervigilant for danger, pointing out anything that could be related to children in your environment, such as images of children, children's toys or films that may have children featured. Your threat mind is doing what it has been designed to do, to ensure your safety and the safety of others. Is that right?

Roger: Yes, it's exhausting. From the time I first open my eyes until I turn the lights out at night, I am searching, making sure that there are no images of children nearby or listening to check there are no children playing in the street. Hypervigilance has become an obsession.

Therapist: It must be exhausting. I have observed you scanning the environment, becoming very distressed if you think an image of or a real child may be in your vicinity and asking others in the community for reassurance to confirm this.

Therapist: We have looked together at how your early experiences meant that you have never experienced a feeling of safeness, and that you were often alone and frightened as a child. You have worked so hard to keep yourself safe by checking. I am wondering, has this helped you achieve a feeling of safety?

Roger: No, my methods of trying to feel safe have made me more anxious. I just feel more scared.

Therapist: Ah, this is interesting. So, what you are saying is that your threatened mind is doing what it has been designed to do, but it has unintended consequences, i.e. you feel more anxious, you are exhausted, everything and everyone feels a threat, and you cannot engage in activities that give you a sense of meaning and richness. You are not able to grow the version of yourself that you would like to be.

RUPTURES IN THE THERAPEUTIC ALLIANCE

Ruptures in therapy are not uncommon. This is not surprising as the client may have been struggling for years with their difficulties and may believe that such entrenched patterns mean that change will be difficult, challenging and even threatening. As a result, the client may experience a range of emotions and behaviours in, and between, sessions that impact negatively on his progress, e.g. a fear of life without OCD/BDD.

SIGNS OF RUPTURE

These may be reflected in very subtle non-verbal cues related to emotional states, e.g. anger and distrust, or feelings expressed by you as a therapist, e.g. frustration or hopelessness. There may also be more overt signs, e.g. not doing homework or focusing on issues unrelated to the formulation as a function of avoidance.

It is important to name these impasses in therapy rather than hoping that they will change in time.

POSSIBLE CONSIDERATIONS IN THERAPEUTIC RUPTURE

WHAT FUNCTION DOES THE BEHAVIOUR HAVE?

For example, a BDD client may be hostile because he is protecting himself against rejection, or an OCD client may be reluctant to do exposure because of fears of being unable to cope with the distress afterwards.

WHAT FEARS MAY THE CLIENT HAVE ABOUT GETTING WELL?

An OCD client may be scared of the void left behind once there has be a reduction in OCD.

The skills to be reflective may be reduced due to feeling highly anxious, angry, ashamed etc ... and therefore less able either to reflect on emotion, or experience, or to engage in mentalisation processes.

WHAT ENVIRONMENTAL FACTORS MAY BE PLAYING A ROLE?

For example, an OCD client who returns to his home environment and is offered reassurance from his family or accommodations of his OCD.

HOW TO TACKLE THERAPEUTIC IMPASSES COULD INCLUDE:

- Revisiting the formulation and rationale for treatment.
- Asking the client to describe what they understand about the function and maintenance of their problem and the processes involved.
- Reviewing the pros and cons of change or no change.
- Reviewing values and goals.
- Validating the client's difficulties and finding ways to work together.
- Getting clients to talk to other sufferers about their struggles.
- Working on grounding techniques that can engage the soothing system, e.g. focus on body posture, facial expression, voice tone, soothing rhythm breathing (attention to breathing; slower, deeper and smoother than normal), mindfulness, external focus etc.
- Communicating using the client's language and using metaphors.

Therapist tips

- Be curious as to the function of silence.
- Consider your own values as well as your clients'.
- Be aware of blocks and ruptures to therapy in an open and curious way.

CHAPTER SUMMARY

It is often a very personal and intimate journey for the client to share their inner world with another. To turn towards our own suffering and to face feared situations takes courage and strength. We have explored how the relationship with our clients can create the conditions in which the patient can feel less threatened so that they can start to approach the thoughts and situations they fear.

CBT is committed to helping individuals overcome their difficulties by understanding the processes involved which have maintained behaviour and helping the client to adopt new ways of being with themselves, others and the world around them.

Working with clients who are suffering with OCD and BDD can be extremely rewarding. Often, clients have faced many years of isolation and disconnection from other people and the world around them, living in fear and exhaustion from behaviours intended to keep them safe.

This chapter has explored, with illustrative examples, a number of important areas for the therapist to consider, including how to mitigate ruptures and promote engagement in the therapeutic process.

To feel understood by a therapist can be an important vehicle for change for a client. Utilising CBT skills within a compassionate framework, we are perhaps enhancing the ability of clients to take the often difficult and courageous steps towards change, and helping them to move towards the version of themselves that they hope will flourish.

FURTHER READING

Gilbert P and Choden (2013) *Mindful Compassion. Using the Power of Mindfulness and Compassion to Transform our Lives*. London: Robinson.

Irons C and Beaumont E (2017) *The Compassionate Mind Workbook: A Step by Step Guide to Developing your Compassionate Self*. London: Robinson.

REFERENCES

Gilbert P (2005) *Compassion. Conceptualisations, Research and Use in Psychotherapy*. London: Routledge.

Gilbert P (2009) *The Compassionate Mind*. London: Constable & Robinson.

Harris R (2009) ACT Made Simple. An Easy-To-Read Primer on Acceptance and Commitment Therapy. Oakland, USA: New Harbinger.

Lee D (2011) *The Compassionate Mind Guide to Recovering from Trauma and PTSD Using Compassion Focused Therapy to Overcome Flashbacks, Shame, Guilt and Fear.* Oakland, CA: New Harbinger.

Kolts RL (2016) *CFT Made Simple: A Clinician's Guide to Practicing Compassion Focused Therapy.* Oakland, CA: New Harbinger.

Veale D and Willson R (2005) *Overcoming Obsessive Compulsive Disorder: A Self Help Guide Using Cognitive Behavioural Techniques.* London: Robinson.

Veale D, Willson R and Clarke A (2009) *Overcoming Body Image Problems including Body Dysmorphic Disorder: A Self Help Guide Using Cognitive Behavioural Techniques.* London: Robinson.

8

MEDICALLY UNEXPLAINED SYMPTOMS

DAVID MCCORMACK AND TRUDIE CHALDER

CHAPTER OVERVIEW

The therapeutic relationship is crucially important when working with people experiencing medically unexplained symptoms. Having a good therapeutic alliance and working in collaboration with the patient are not only important in the early stages of therapy, when the therapist is engaging and socialising the patient to the cognitive behavioural approach, but are necessary throughout therapy. This enables the patient to remain engaged and undertake the challenging cognitive and behavioural work which is essential for treatment to be effective. In this chapter, we aim to provide the reader with the key foundational ingredients to foster a good therapeutic relationship at each stage of therapy. We consider therapy to consist of three distinct stages: (1) engagement and assessment, (2) formulation and intervention, and (3) preparing for discharge. While these stages are distinct, there is invariably some interweaving; for example, one will often need to reassess when formulating, and one should be preparing the patient for the end of therapy and discussing relapse management right from the start of any clinical work. We will discuss how to maintain a working alliance at each stage of therapy and how to repair ruptures to the relationship should they occur.

MEDICALLY UNEXPLAINED SYMPTOMS/PERSISTENT PHYSICAL SYMPTOMS

Before we consider the therapeutic relationship when working with a person experiencing medically unexplained symptoms, it is important to clarify what is meant by this term. The first place to start is to recognise that 'medically unexplained symptoms' is not a discrete diagnosis. It is a broad umbrella term that is used to refer to a wide range of persistent symptoms and syndromes (e.g. non-cardiac chest pain, functional neurologic disorders, irritable bowel syndrome, fibromyalgia etc.). It is the opinion of the authors of this chapter that the term medically unexplained symptoms is inexact and can be unhelpful. While it is true that the persistent physical symptoms and syndromes mentioned here are not fully understood, particularly in terms of aetiology, it is not the case that they are always unexplained. Additionally, referring to a patient's symptoms as medically unexplained can connote or be interpreted by the patient as meaning that the symptoms are 'imagined' or 'all in the mind.' This is not the case. However, patients can have concerns in this regard (i.e. that their physical symptoms are seen as not being real or that they are being 'psychologised') and this can be a challenge when developing a therapeutic relationship (this will be discussed later in the chapter). Recent research has found that patients prefer the term persistent physical symptoms (Picariello et al., 2017). We believe that this is a more accurate term and, in our clinic, it seems to be acceptable to patients. However, the question remains regarding what has caused and is maintaining these symptoms and syndromes. Unfortunately, space does not permit a detailed discussion. In a nutshell, it appears that complex interacting physiological processes are involved, and associated cognitive and behavioural responses can exacerbate symptoms and associated disability (Henningsen and Creed, 2010; Chalder and Willis, 2017). Salkovskis et al. (2016) highlight how unhelpful thinking/negative appraisals and health anxiety, in particular, which can often co-occur with unexplained and persistent symptoms, may form part of the maintenance cycle for patients. It is important that any unhelpful cognitive and behavioural responses are addressed, as it should enable better management and amelioration of symptoms, lead to increased functioning and a better quality of life for patients.

In terms of models for persistent and unexplained symptoms, there are narrow models which focus on specific syndromes and broader/transdiagnostic approaches. There have been seemingly reasonable arguments made for developing models which focus on clustering a small number of symptoms into discrete syndromes and studying these in isolation with the notion that this may yield more fruitful findings than taking a broader perspective (Wessely and White, 2004). This 'splitting' approach may eventually lead to a better understanding of the aetiology and maintaining mechanisms of specific syndromes, and in time, it could be that the treatments developed using this narrower approach may prove to be more effective, and therefore this merits further investigation. Nonetheless, there are equally good reasons for pursuing a broader 'lumping' approach, the most important being that the specific syndrome approach has been unable to capture, or adequately account for, the clinical complexity of presentations seen in clinic. That is, the clinical reality is that persistent physical symptoms do not neatly cluster together into specific syndromes; symptoms overlap across the syndromes, comorbidity is common and similarities exist physiologically, cognitively and behaviourally (Deary et al., 2007; Kanaan et al., 2007). As a consequence, it has even been postulated that the many syndromes might actually be considered as one syndrome with various subtypes (Fink and Schroder, 2010; Wessely et al., 1999). However, while there are similarities, the evidence does not fully support classing the various syndromes as one disorder (Kanaan et al., 2007). There is, though, sufficient evidence to support taking a transdiagnostic approach to conceptualising persistent and unexplained symptoms and identifying the common processes that appear to be maintaining/exacerbating symptoms that the patient is experiencing (Chalder and Willis, 2017; Deary et al., 2007).

The Deary et al. (2007) model provides a hypothetical framework for understanding possible predisposing and precipitating factors as well as perpetuating factors (i.e. a theoretical autopoietic cycle of symptom maintenance is proposed). This model, as well as the Salkovskis et al. (2016) and Chalder and Willis (2017) models, can be adapted and tailored when working clinically with an individual patient. The therapist can adapt one of these models, or a hybrid of them, to collaboratively work with the patient and construct an idiosyncratic model and formulation (i.e. a shared understanding) which can guide interventions to overcome the symptoms experienced and associated functional impairment. These models lend themselves to a transdiagnostic approach. Throughout this chapter, the transdiagnostic approach is used when presenting cases.

ENGAGEMENT AND ASSESSMENT

Typically, a person who is experiencing medically unexplained symptoms will have seen a number of medical doctors prior to attending for CBT. This is a necessary part of the patient journey; their symptoms (e.g. fatigue, pain, limb weakness, gastrointestinal symptoms) need to be medically investigated and appropriately treated. If symptoms persist then the addition of CBT should be considered.

ENGAGEMENT

Given the very nature of the difficulties the patient is experiencing, namely, persistent physical symptoms, engagement in CBT can be tricky. Patients might be confused about why they are attending for a 'psychological therapy' when their problems are physical. This was best summed up by a patient attending our specialist clinic at the Maudsley Hospital in London, 'when you have a physical illness you should see a physician not a psychologist.' Given how CBT is strongly associated with the treatment of mental health problems, this is understandable but it is regrettable. It can make initially engaging in the approach a struggle for many patients. The biggest hurdle to overcome is the concern that their physical symptoms are going to be 'psychologised' – the fear that the medical professionals they have seen, and the CBT therapist in front of them, believe that their symptoms are not real, that they are imagined. Addressing this explicitly is of paramount importance, and it is vital to clearly state that you, as the therapist, believe that their physical symptoms are, of course, real, but it is because they are real physical symptoms that they are having a real negative impact on their life. Therapy is to try to help them to better manage symptoms, to overcome them if possible and improve functioning and their quality of life. Providing this message during the assessment, and throughout therapy, plays an important role in fostering engagement. An example of how a therapist might word this with a patient is presented below:

Therapist: I was wondering if you could tell me what brings you to see me today?

Patient: Well, I'm feeling really unwell... I'm in agony most days and it's hard to do anything.

Therapist: I am sorry to hear that. Can you tell me what the main symptoms are at the moment?

Patient: The main symptoms... where do I start?! The pain in my left arm is getting worse – it's been very sore over the past few days. Most of the time it feels weak but over the last few days it has been very painful. I also have this tight discomfort in my chest, just near my heart, which comes and goes. My GP and cardiologist say my heart is ok and they and the neurologist I saw can't really explain the pain. And the medication I've been given is not helping. And I have been so tired recently that I can't think straight during the day. It's hard to concentrate most of the time. I'm not sure what to do, I try sleeping whenever I can and I have tried taking ibuprofen and that co-codamol stuff but the pain just won't go and I feel so tired and unwell...

Therapist: I see, it sounds like you're suffering with quite a lot of pain and discomfort.

Patient: Yes, it's awful.

Therapist: Would it be ok if I summarise what you've told me just to make sure that I have understood what your main difficulties are?

Patient: Yes, of course.

Therapist: Ok – correct me now if I get anything wrong. From what you've told me, you have persistent left arm pain, which can be severely painful. In addition, you have frequent discomfort in your chest and you've been very tired and have had difficulties with concentrating. Are they the main symptoms?

Patient: Yeah, that's right.

Therapist: And you have been trying to manage these persistent physical symptoms by sleeping whenever you can and by taking pain relief medication, but these aren't really helping?

Patient: That's right. Sometimes the sleep helps with the tiredness but not the pain. The tablets aren't helping much at all anymore. Maybe they take the edge off the pain but that's about it.

Therapist: So, it sounds to me that you've been trying to cope and manage with these symptoms but so far what you have been doing doesn't seem to be helping that much.

Patient: Yep, that's about right. So, what should I do? How can a therapist like you help?

Therapist: I think a good place to start would be for us to spend a few minutes looking at your physical symptoms, how they are affecting your life and how you have been managing them in a little more detail. I find doing this often can help in working out ways to help better manage and cope with these types of physical symptoms. After all, you are experiencing very real symptoms and they are having a very real impact on your life. We need to take this seriously and find effective ways of managing them. Let's try and work together to firstly make sense of these symptoms, figure out what makes them worse and what helps, and once we've done that, we'll be in a better position to figure out how to manage these unpleasant symptoms and improve your quality of life. Does that sound ok?

ASSESSMENT

Carrying out a detailed and thorough assessment is essential. It is important to remember that the assessment will set the tone for any future sessions, and creating an atmosphere of collaboration is key (Carson et al., 2016). However, it is all too common, especially when one is under time pressures, to overly fixate on the goal of obtaining sufficient information (e.g. developmental history, symptom onset, what exacerbates symptoms etc.) and risk alienating the patient from collaborative engagement. That is, the patient may be engaged but only at the passive level; they may be answering the questions asked when a history is being taken but their level of engagement may be minimal and so an opportunity to socialise them to the therapeutic relationship can be missed. The traditional dynamic of physician and patient, which is the professional healthcare relationship patients are likely to be most familiar with, is often a passive one for the patient. The patient in such interactions provides answers to the questions asked and the doctor draws on their knowledge and experience and gives a diagnosis and prescribes a treatment. This doctor (expert) and patient dynamic is not the relationship that will lead to effective CBT. Instead, we want the patient to be actively engaged during the assessment phase and to collaboratively join the therapist in reviewing their history, to try to make sense of what is likely contributing to and/or exacerbating their symptoms, and what are the problems that the symptoms cause (i.e. what are the symptoms stopping the person doing). In so doing, by the end of the first assessment appointment this should have fostered the patient's curiosity regarding patterns and links between symptoms and their cognitive and behavioural responses to them. It should help to set up a collaborative atmosphere, to socialise the patient to the process of formulation and, in a very meaningful sense, the patient should have commenced at this early stage on the journey to become their own therapist, which is what therapy ultimately intends to achieve.

In our experience, the best way to structure the assessment is to start out by asking in detail about all of the physical symptoms the patient is experiencing and the negative impact they are having on functioning. We find that this invariably ensures patient engagement as it addresses the primary reason for their attendance and it offers opportunities to communicate that you as the therapist believe that the symptoms they are experiencing are, of course, real and, because they are real physical symptoms, they are having a negative impact on their functioning. This is important because, as mentioned earlier in the chapter, patients can be concerned that health professionals do not believe that their physical symptoms are real and are 'all in their mind.' This can be a potential barrier to engagement in CBT. Starting out by investigating the physical symptoms should help overcome this barrier. While doing so, it is crucial that one empathises with the patient, puts oneself in their shoes and tries to communicate this empathy in order for the patient to feel understood (see Chapter 1 of this book and Burns and Auerbach, 1996).

During the assessment phase, it is also important to assess motivation for therapy. Prochaska and DiClemente's (2005) stages of change model can be a useful framework to apply here to consider readiness to engage in therapy. For example, is the patient in the pre-complementation stage (not considering change), or the contemplation stage (considering change), or preparation stage (having tried experimenting with making change). If a patient appears to be in the pre-contemplation phase, it would be important to assess if they are able to consider making change (for example, it can be useful to ask how might they want their life to be different and what might they want to be doing differently). If the patient is able to identify that they would like to be able to do things they can't do now, better manage symptoms and/or have an improved quality of life, then you can use this to consider the benefits of making change with the patient and then develop general goals and, afterwards, specific therapy goals to be achieved.

However, if the patient is in the pre-contemplation phase (i.e. not considering change) then therapy is unlikely to progress until this is addressed. An example of this can be when a patient has been referred for CBT and, during the assessment appointment, it becomes clear that what they want is further medical investigations and pharmacological treatment. CBT may not be suitable for such a person at that point in time, and it might be better to review them at a later date to see if things have changed. Having said that, it is important not to give up too soon with such a patient. It might just be that they have never considered their symptoms as something that could be managed behaviourally, and that they could actually play an active role in doing this. Therefore, providing education and literature for them to read about how such an approach might be useful could enable them to be in the position to contemplate making change. It is often worth reviewing them again, even if only for a second assessment appointment, to discuss how the approach might be of benefit and to see if they are contemplating making change, or at least open to trying a cognitive behavioural approach.

Case example 8.1

John, aged 44, is referred for CBT. Since shortly after his fiancée ended their engagement two years ago, John has been experiencing non-cardiac chest pain, headaches, and pain and weakness in his left arm. He has been thoroughly investigated by a number of physicians. All tests and investigations have revealed nothing abnormal. There is no evidence of any disease. He frequently attends his GP and has attended the accident and emergency department six times in the past twelve months because of his symptoms. He states that he thinks that he is going to have a heart attack or a stroke. Most days, he stays at home and rests. He does not believe the doctors he has seen are taking him seriously, and he is not sure what CBT will involve.

Reflective questions

1. How might you go about introducing the CBT approach to John?
2. What questions might you ask John?
3. Can you foresee any challenges in establishing a therapeutic alliance with John? How might you manage this?

Simple Socratic questioning can be helpful to both assess readiness to change and also as a method to motivate the person to consider change. Motivational Interviewing can be useful here (e.g. see Miller and Rollnick, 1991), and the sample questions below draw on this approach:

1. What would be different if things were improved?
2. What would your life look like if the symptoms were better managed or less severe?
3. Can you think of any things that you are not doing that you would like to be doing?

One thing we have found helpful in creating a productive therapeutic relationship, and which can help motivate the patient to start considering change, is to set goals. Goal setting is, of course, a common feature of good CBT in general, and for patients with medically unexplained symptoms, it is essential. Initially, patients might have quite broad goals; for example, not to have persistent physical symptoms anymore, to not be depressed, have improved relationships and to be happy. We think these are fine goals to start out with, as who wouldn't want to be free from physical symptoms and enjoying life. However, in subsequent therapy sessions, these goals will need to be carefully operationalised (i.e. turned into a series of sub goals, which are specific, measurable, achievable and realistic). This process of goal setting, though, not only provides a direction for therapy and a way to measure if therapy is effective at achieving the patient's goals, but it also helps develop a collaborative relationship because it puts you alongside the patient as you are now both trying to figure out together how to achieve the goals for therapy.

Top tips for engagement and assessment

1. Remember to be collaborative. Encourage the patient to be actively engaged during the assessment phase.
2. Frame the assessment as a process where you are both working together (e.g. 'playing detectives') to look for what exacerbates and helps with the physical symptoms and for any patterns and links from the present and the past that might help you both understand the symptoms and the impact they are having on the patient's life.
3. Assess readiness to change, and set realistic goals for therapy, and promote the expectation that these goals can be achieved.

FORMULATION AND INTERVENTION

FORMULATION

The bridge between assessment and intervention is the formulation. It is the lynchpin that holds theory and practice together (Butler, 1998). Formulation is not merely a summary of the patient's problems, it is a hypothetical model which draws on clinical theory and research, developed by the therapist and patient, to help make sense of what may have contributed to the patient's persistent symptoms and what appears to be presently exacerbating and/or maintaining both the symptoms and associated difficulties (e.g. unhelpful thinking, distressing emotions and impaired functioning).

We find a simple formulation of maintaining cycles to be a helpful place to start (i.e. how the symptoms, thoughts and behaviours interact with one another). Patients typically seem to find this easy to engage with and, for some, it can be a revelatory experience as they may not have considered how their symptoms, thoughts and behaviour influence one another. It is important not to rush this and to ensure one is keeping pace with the patient. Asking open-ended questions can be helpful here in developing the formulation and checking on the patients understanding (e.g. What do you do when the symptoms are severe? What would you think then? What does this tell you?).

We recommend drawing out a diagrammatic formulation together with the patient and starting with a simple maintaining formulation. This fosters the collaborative relationship, ensures that the formulation is accurately capturing the patient's lived experience as they are constructing it with the therapist, and maintaining formulations are usually well understood by patients. In our experience, patients with persistent physical symptoms typically find it more acceptable if the maintenance model firmly places the symptoms at the centre (see Figure 8.1). We would recommend starting with the symptoms and the behavioural impact/ responses. Then enquire about any thoughts that they might notice and keep in mind that, for some patients with persistent and unexplained symptoms, associated thoughts and distressing emotions might not be as relevant as behavioural factors or it might take some behaviourally focused therapy for these to be observed by the patient (e.g. if behavioural activation is being tried you might ask the patient to keep a simple diary of thoughts and behaviours in response to situations/ symptoms).

As therapy progresses, the therapist and patient can develop a longitudinal formulation which encompasses pertinent aspects of the patient's history and possible predisposing and precipitating factors. When developing a formulation with people experiencing persistent physical symptoms, the therapist should draw on the cognitive behavioural models for persistent and unexplained symptoms and tailor these to the person and their presenting problems. Deary at al. (2007) and Chalder and Willis (2017) present hypothetical models which include predisposing, precipitating and perpetuating factors to consider. There is accumulating evidence to support these models. If health anxiety forms part of the presenting problem, the Salkovskis et al. (2016) model is also useful to consider. Based on these models, an idiosyncratic

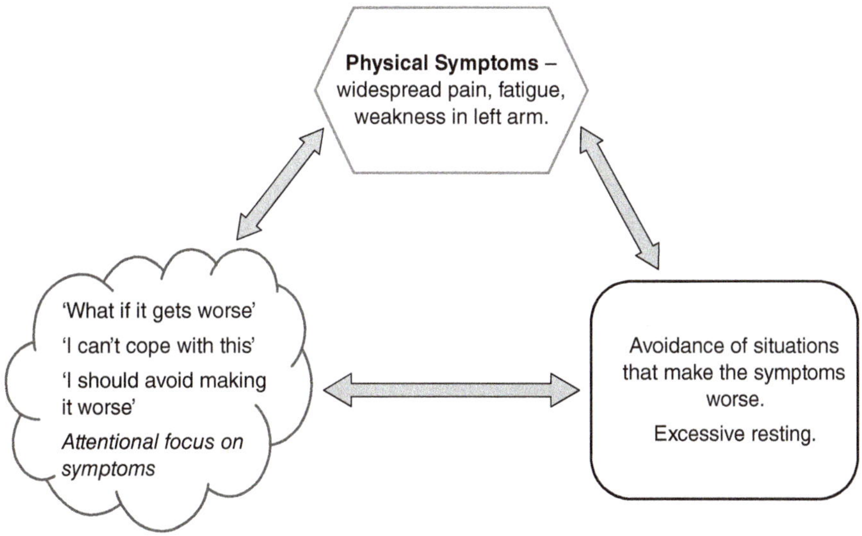

Figure 8.1 An example of a simple three systems diagrammatic formulation

model can be developed to make sense of the patient's symptoms and the associated difficulties. While we emphasised the importance of collaboration during assessment, when it comes to formulation, this is of paramount importance. It is crucial that the patient be actively involved at every stage of developing the formulation. It is something to be created together, rather than something to be presented to the patient.

The formulation should be returned to and further developed in sessions as more information comes to light (e.g. from discussions in session, information obtained from activity/daily diaries, behavioural experiments etc.). As formulation and intervention are only possible if collaboration is achieved, we find it helpful to communicate this explicitly to patients. That is, make explicit that you are wanting them to join you in the process of looking for patterns and links between their past experiences and their present circumstances/responses and symptoms. It can sometimes help to use a metaphor to help illustrate the process; for example, that you are two scientists or two detectives working together and coming up with theories/hunches of what might be contributing to the symptoms. We find that embarking on formulation in a collaborative manner provides an opportunity to further develop the therapeutic relationship. The therapist is able to communicate accurate empathy as both therapist and patient are working together to develop a model, which means that the therapist is continually checking that they understand the patient and the patient understands the model. This should help therapist and patient both reach a 'no-wonder' conclusion in terms of why the patient is responding in the way they do to their symptoms (see Case example 8.2).

Case example 8.2

Jane, aged 23, had leukaemia as a child and made a good recovery. At age 22, after an exceptionally distressing experience where she was misdiagnosed with cancer, she started experiencing heart palpitations, nausea and irritable bowel symptoms. When she first attended for therapy, after having first attended physicians who were unable to help, these symptoms were having a significantly negative impact on her functioning; for example, she avoided activities that were associated with symptoms worsening, which included work. She was excessively vigilant to physiological changes in her body and typically attributed any bodily sensations/symptoms as being either a sign of serious illness or directly caused by the situation or activity she had been engaging in. We developed the following formulation which draws on the Deary et al. (2007) model (see Figure 8.2).

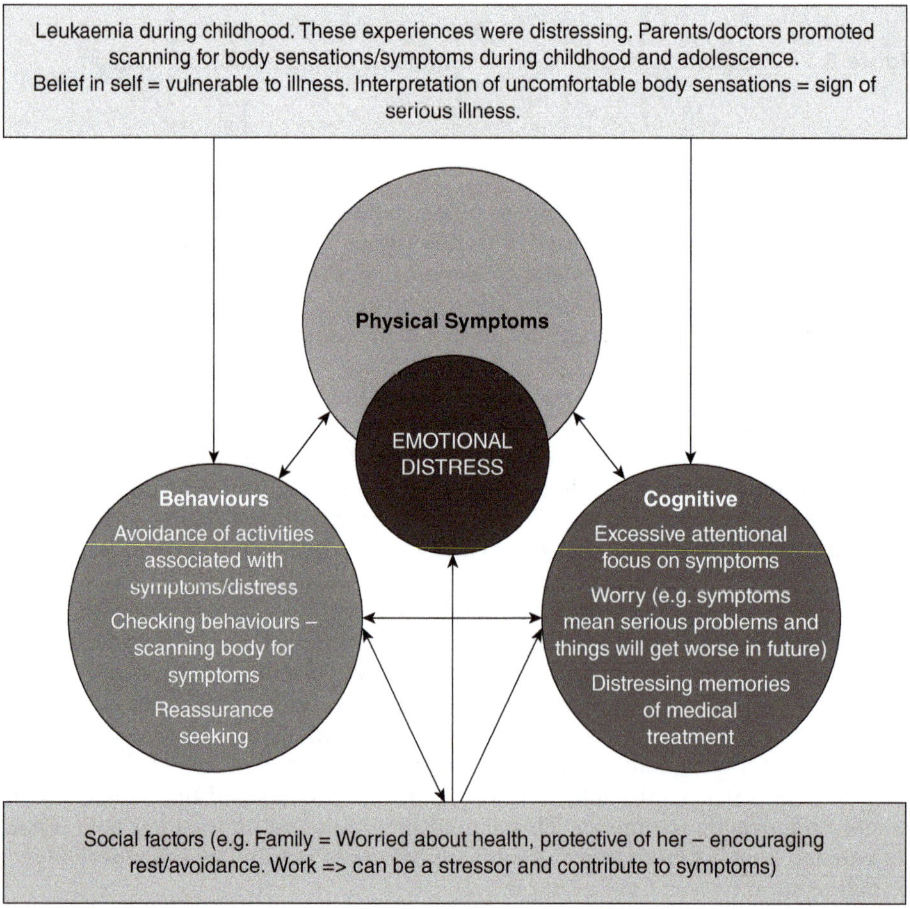

Figure 8.2 Diagrammatic formulation for Jane

INTERVENTION

Formulation should guide and inform intervention. For example, if it appears that excessively unhelpful thinking is exacerbating symptoms, or maintaining behaviours are stopping the person achieving their goals, then this should be apparent from the formulation and a clear rationale can be provided to the patient. This, in turn, should increase the patient's engagement in session and when carrying out any homework between sessions.

While early progress in therapy can strengthen the therapeutic alliance, it is important when carrying out any intervention to do so at a pace that the patient can tolerate and to consider possible unintended consequences of cognitive and behavioural change. When it comes to unintended consequences, this can vary from patient to patient. The consequences may be somewhat foreseeable (e.g. the symptoms the patient experiences may temporarily worsen when increasing a behaviour) or they can be less obvious (e.g. a patient who becomes more active and independent might have a partner who is not pleased about this change and their relationship may become strained as a result). It is important for the therapist to try and foresee potential unintended consequences and discuss with the patient the possibility that they may occur and how to manage the situation should this happen. For instance, explaining to the patient that increasing an avoided activity that they are worried about performing might likely temporarily cause anxiety, but that this should fade over time, ensures the patient is not surprised when anxiety occurs and it provides an opportunity to consider how the patient can best respond if this happens. When it comes to patients that experience fatigue and/or pain who want to increase physical activity, they should start with an achievable activity that will not be too exerting and they are quite confident that they can safely do (e.g. a five minute walk), and only once they have achieved this a number of times without problems should they experiment with very gradually increasing this, and they should monitor progress as they do so and adjust and modify activity in light of this.

Keep in mind that ambitious behavioural experiments that are too challenging for the patient to complete are likely to interfere with the therapeutic alliance (e.g. increasing activity while dropping safety behaviours as a first homework task). In such circumstances, it is all too easy for the therapist to be disappointed that the patient is not making sufficient progress and for the patient to become dispirited and feel like they have failed or that CBT is not effective for them or too difficult. This is particularly the case when the patient experiences a flare-up or a severe worsening of physical symptoms. An unhelpful dynamic can get set up in therapy as a result and a rupture in the relationship can occur. It is important to repair any ruptures as soon as one can. Acknowledging what has happened, discussing it in an honest and open manner, and then engaging in problem solving is often the path to repairing a rupture in therapy. Oftentimes, this can be helpful not just in therapy but it also models for the patient how to positively repair ruptures that might occur in their relationships with significant others. Having discussions and getting feedback from patients at the start and the end of sessions about how the therapy is progressing for them and how they are finding therapy provides a good opportunity for the therapeutic relationship to be discussed and for any problems to be addressed.

An example of what a rupture in the therapeutic relationship can look like in practice is provided below.

Elizabeth, aged 44, was a patient who felt that she was not making much progress in therapy and she became concerned that her therapist was negatively evaluating her for not making sufficient progress. The therapist had no such appraisal of the patient (in fact, he was himself engaging in self-criticism in regard to his skills as a therapist because the patient's condition was not improving). However, neither Elizabeth nor her therapist gave voice to their concerns. As therapy progressed, Elizabeth became convinced that her therapist was negatively evaluating her and started to miss appointments and turn up late. The therapist, not wanting to cause tension in the relationship, initially did not comment or address this directly. As time passed, the therapist became rather irritated that Elizabeth was not attending as planned. Elizabeth misinterpreted this irritation as evidence that the therapist was 'judging her for having failed at therapy.' The therapist, after talking the case through in supervision, decided to set aside time in subsequent sessions to discuss how they were both (patient and therapist) finding the process of therapy. This afforded Elizabeth the space to share her concerns and the therapist to clarify his perspective on how therapy was progressing. Speaking honestly and openly helped clarify misunderstandings and heal the rupture that had occurred. As a result, the therapeutic alliance was strengthened and therapy progressed effectively.

Top tips for formulation and intervention

1. Formulation is the lynchpin that holds theory and practice together.
2. Collaboration is key and simple diagrammatic formulations of maintaining cycles are the best place to start.
3. While early therapy gains are important, go at the patient's pace and repair any ruptures to the therapeutic relationship as soon as one can.

PREPARING FOR DISCHARGE

The ending of therapy should be carefully considered and well planned. A degree of dependence on the therapist can develop, particularly with those seen for long-term therapy and for those who have had a history of interpersonal problems. Preparing with the patient for therapy ending is important. Often, it helps to leave a longer interval between the last few therapy sessions to enable the patient to manage by themselves. This often provides a chance for the patient to better cope with setbacks and develop confidence in becoming their own therapist. Ideally, the therapist will have been promoting the idea of relapse management from early on in therapy and there may even have been some challenges and setbacks during therapy for the patient to practice how to manage these.

Developing a blueprint of therapy is important. That is, what has been learnt in therapy, how to maintain progress/make further improvement and how the patient can be their own therapist when they experience similar symptoms and associated problems in the future. Returning to the formulation can be helpful when having these discussions and thinking about how they can problem solve and get back on track to living their life to the full.

CHAPTER SUMMARY

Persistent and unexplained symptoms can have a negative impact on functioning and, without treatment, the prognosis may be poor. Initial engagement can be a challenge. As patients can be concerned that health professionals may not believe that their symptoms are real, it is important to stress that their physical symptoms are real. It is because the symptoms are all too real that they can have a negative impact on a person's functioning and quality of life. Collaboration is of crucial importance at every stage of therapy, including during assessment as this sets the tone for future therapy sessions. Formulation is the lynchpin that holds theory and practice together and simple diagrammatic formulations of maintaining cycles are often the best place to begin. It can help to start by looking at the negative impact that the symptoms are having on functioning and then explore what are the behavioural and cognitive responses to this. Throughout therapy, it is important to go at the patient's pace and to try to repair any ruptures to the therapeutic relationship in a timely manner. When it comes to preparing the patient for discharge, remember to develop a blueprint and plan with the patient for how they will manage flare-ups and setbacks.

FURTHER READING

Woolfolk RL and Allen L (2011) Somatoform and Physical Disorders. In Barlow DH (ed) *The Oxford Handbook of Clinical Psychology*. New York: Oxford University Press.

Kleinstauber M, Witthoft M and Hiller W (2011) Efficacy of short-term psychotherapy for multiple medically unexplained physical symptoms: a meta-analysis. *Clinical Psychology Review* 31(1): 146–160.

Lehn A, Gelauff J, Hoeritzauer I, Ludwig L, McWhirter L, Williams S, Gardiner P, Carson A and Stone J (2015). Functional neurological disorders: mechanisms and treatment. *Journal of Neurology* (263) 611–620.

Price JR (2006) Medically Unexplained Physical Symptoms. *Medicine* (40): 644–646.

Van Dessel N, Den Boeft M, van der Wouden JC, Kleinstäuber M, Leone SS, Terluin B, Numans ME, van der Horst HE and van Marwijk H (2014) Non-pharmacological interventions for somatoform disorders and medically unexplained physical symptoms (MUPS) in adults. *Cochrane Database of Systematic Reviews* [online]. Available at: 10.1002/14651858.CD011142.pub2/ (Accessed 12th May 2017).

REFERENCES

Burns DD and Auerbach A (1996) Therapeutic Empathy in Cognitive-Behavioural Therapy: Does it really make a difference? In: Salkovskis PM (ed) *Frontiers of Cognitive Therapy*. New York: Guilford Press.

Butler G (1998) Clinical Formulation. In: Bellack AS and Hersen M (eds) *Comprehensive Clinical Psychology*. Oxford: Pergamon.

Carson A, Hallet M and Stone J (2016) Assessment of patients with functional neurologic disorders. In: Hallet M, Stone J and Carson A (eds) *Handbook of Clinical Neurology*. Vol. *139*, Third Series. Amsterdam: Elsevier.

Chalder T and Willis C (2017) 'Lumping' and 'splitting' medically unexplained symptoms: Is there a role for a transdiagnostic approach? *Journal of Mental Health 26*(3): 187–191.

Deary V, Chalder T and Sharpe M (2007) The cognitive behavioural model of medically unexplained symptoms: a theoretical and empirical review. *Clinical Psychology Review 27*(7): 781–797.

Fink P and Schroder A (2010) One single diagnosis, bodily distress syndrome, succeeded to capture 10 diagnostic categories of functional somatic syndromes and somatoform disorders. *Journal of Psychosomatic Research 68*(5): 415–426.

Henningsen, P and Creed, F (2010) The genetic, physiological and psychological mechanisms underlying disabling medically unexplained symptoms and somatisation. *Journal of Psychosomatic Research, 68*(5): 395–397.

Kannan RA, Lepine JP and Wessely SC (2007) The association or otherwise of the functional somatic syndromes. *Psychosomatic Medicine 69*(9): 855–859.

Miller WR and Rollnick S (1991) *Motivational interviewing: Preparing people for change*. New York: Guilford Press.

Picariello F, Ali S, Foubister C and Chalder T (2017) 'It feels sometimes like my house has burnt down, but I can see the sky': a qualitative study exploring patients' views of CBT for chronic fatigue syndrome. *British Journal Health Psychology 22*(3): 383–413.

Prochaska JO and DiClemente CC (2005) The transtheoretical approach. In: Norcross JC and Goldfried MR (eds) *Handbook of Psychotherapy Integration*. 2nd ed. New York: Oxford University Press, pp. 147–171.

Salkovskis PM, Gregory JD, Sedgwick-Taylor A, White J, Opher S and Ólafsdóttir S (2016) Extending cognitive-behavioural theory and therapy to medically unexplained symptoms and long term conditions: a hybrid transdiagnostic/problem specific approach. *Behaviour Change 33*(4): 172–192.

Wessely S, Nimnuan C and Sharpe M (1999) Functional somatic syndromes: one or many? *Lancet 354*: 936–939.

Wessely S and White PD (2004) There is only one functional somatic syndrome. *British Journal of Psychiatry* (185): 95–96.

9

POSTTRAUMATIC STRESS DISORDER

NICK GREY, JENNIFER HOUSE AND KERRY YOUNG

CHAPTER OVERVIEW

This chapter considers the role of the therapeutic relationship in the treatment of Posttraumatic Stress Disorder (PTSD). While issues common to the therapeutic relationship in all psychological therapies apply to those with PTSD, there are aspects which are more specific to people with this presenting problem. The nature of evidence-based trauma-focused cognitive behavioural therapies (TF-CBT) presents challenges for both clients and therapists. TF-CBT requires the client not only to overcome avoidance to feared situations associated with the trauma but also to give up attempts to avoid internal reminders of the trauma, such as images, emotions and bodily feelings. For people who have experienced interpersonal trauma, such as physical or sexual assault in adulthood or childhood, trusting anyone can be difficult and will affect the therapeutic relationship. It will also be influenced by the experience of trauma-related shame. This chapter will focus on the skills needed to engage and maintain the alliance with traumatised clients.

TRAUMA-FOCUSED CBT FOR PTSD

PTSD is one of a number of disorders that can develop following exposure to traumatic events. PTSD is characterised by the presence of the following: (i) distressing intrusions, or re-experiencing symptoms, such as intrusive memories, dreams or flashbacks to the traumatic event; (ii) attempts to avoid thinking about or remembering the event, and attempts to avoid external reminders of it; (iii) negative shifts in cognition and mood; and (iv) persistent arousal, manifesting in symptoms such as hypervigilance (American Psychiatric Association, 2013; World Health Organisation (WHO), 1992). PTSD is associated with significant distress and/or functional impairment and comorbidity with other psychiatric disorders.

A classification of *Complex PTSD* (cPTSD) has been proposed for the 11th version of the International Classification of Diseases from WHO. People who meet proposed criteria for cPTSD are a subset of those who meet criteria for PTSD. cPTSD is associated with a history of multiple and/or sustained traumatic experiences, such as ongoing violence and abuse. Diagnostic criteria for cPTSD involve the core re-experiencing, avoidance and arousal symptoms of PTSD, along with problems with affect (emotion dysregulation), self-concept (negative beliefs about the self) and maintenance of interpersonal relationships. In contrast with the core symptoms of PTSD, these additional problems are not exclusively associated with trauma-related stimuli (Cloitre et al., 2013).

There are a number of evidence-based therapies based on cognitive behavioural models of PTSD. These include prolonged exposure therapy (Foa et al., 2007), cognitive processing therapy (Resick and Schnicke, 1992), narrative exposure therapy (Schauer et al., 2011), and cognitive therapy for PTSD (CT-PTSD; Ehlers and Clark, 2000). These treatments have differing emphases but many commonalities that are likely to influence the therapeutic alliance (Schnyder et al., 2015). These include the opportunity to provide people with a positive interpersonal experience characterised by empathy and a lack of negative judgement, the use of psychoeducation, exposure to trauma memories with appropriate emotional engagement and the use of cognitive therapy techniques to address the perceived meaning of traumatic events and their consequences (Schnyder et al., 2015).

Our experience in the UK National Health Service has been with CT-PTSD. Ehlers and Clark's (2000) model proposes that PTSD becomes persistent when traumatic information is processed in a way that leads to a sense of serious *current* threat. This can be a physical threat and/or a psychological threat to one's view of oneself. Due to high levels of arousal at the time of the trauma, the trauma memory is poorly elaborated, fragmented and poorly integrated with other autobiographical memories and can be unintentionally triggered by a wide range of low-level cues. In particular, there is no 'time-code' on the memory that tells the individual that the event occurred in the past. Thus, when the memory intrudes, it feels as if the event is actually happening again to some degree.

The persistence of the sense of current threat, and hence PTSD, arises from not only the nature of the trauma memory but also the negative interpretations of the symptoms experienced (e.g. 'I'm going mad'), the event itself (e.g. 'It's my fault') and sequelae (e.g. 'I should have got over it by now'; 'Others don't care about me'). Change in these appraisals and the nature of the trauma memory is prevented by a variety of cognitive and behavioural strategies, such as avoiding thoughts and feelings, places or other reminders of the event, suppression of intrusive memories, rumination about certain aspects of the event or sequelae and other avoidant/numbing strategies such as alcohol and drug use (see Figure 9.1).

The aims of CT-PTSD treatment are threefold:

1. To reduce re-experiencing by elaboration of the trauma memory and discrimination of triggers, and integration of the memory within existing autobiographical memory.
2. To address the negative appraisals of the event and its sequelae.
3. To change the avoidant/numbing strategies that prevent processing of the memory and reassessment of appraisals.

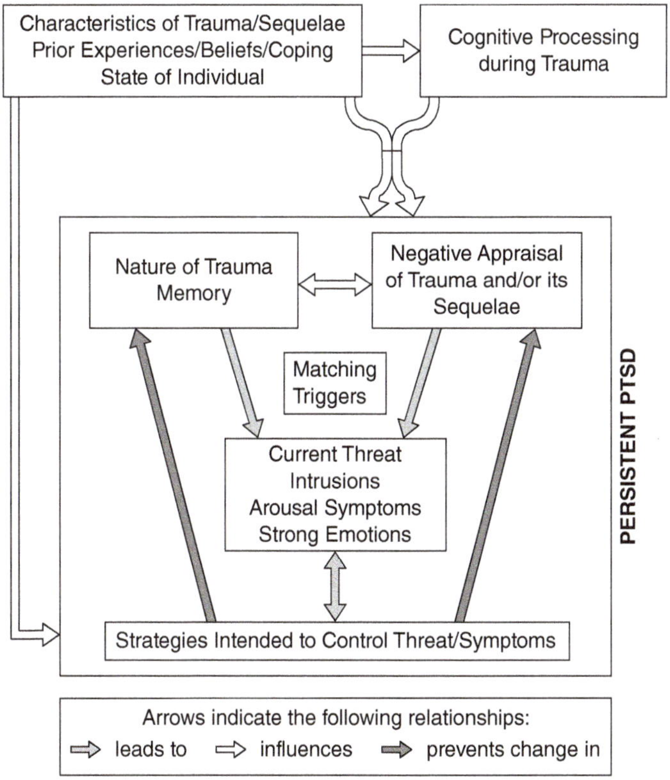

Figure 9.1 Cognitive Model of PTSD

Source: Reprinted from Ehlers and Clark (2000), with permission from Elsevier

A wide range of both general and PTSD-specific cognitive-behavioural interventions can be used to achieve such changes.

There are multiple strategies used to help address the nature of the trauma memory. The most commonly used is that of 'reliving' the event: imaging and describing the event in detail with eyes closed in the present tense. This is in order to identify the main cognitive themes activated during, and after, the event(s), rather than to promote habituation to fear. There follows an interweaving of reliving and cognitive restructuring. Ehlers and Clark's studies typically allow 12 sessions on a weekly basis. The total amount of reliving across all sessions is about 90 minutes. Compared to other published treatment trials, there are very low (< 5%) drop out rates in the treatment studies from Ehlers and Clark's group.

As with the PTSD treatments outlined above, psychological therapies for cPTSD involve processing of traumatic memories (UK Psychological Trauma Society, 2017). Memory processing in cPTSD usually forms the second phase of treatment, the first being a phase of stabilisation (focusing on risk management, management of symptoms and other stressors, and affect regulation). The third and final phase involves focusing on consolidation of treatment gains and social (re)integration (Herman,

1992). The relative timing of these three phases is flexible, and the focus of therapy can move between them as required. The need for a stabilisation phase in cPTSD treatment is still subject to empirical enquiry (De Jongh et al., 2016).

THE ROLE OF THE THERAPEUTIC RELATIONSHIP IN WORKING WITH PEOPLE WITH PTSD

The issues relating to the therapeutic alliance and *core* PTSD criteria also apply to the alliance in the treatment of cPTSD. Other sections of this book, such as the chapter on personality disorders (Chapter 13), may also be helpful when working with people with more complex presentations and difficulties with interpersonal relationships. Even those with severe PTSD symptoms can form strong therapeutic relationships (Callahan et al., 2003), and the presence of multiple traumatic experiences or comorbid disorders does not necessarily weaken the alliance (McLaughlin et al., 2014).

It has been suggested that the nature of TF-CBT could damage the alliance, as discussing the experiences and exposure tasks can be perceived as demanding and distressing for both the client and therapist. Perceived difficulties managing exposure can lead to reluctance to continue, which may compromise the effectiveness of therapy and the quality of the therapeutic alliance (McLaughlin et al., 2014; Ormhaug et al., 2015). However, research has found that the strength of the alliance in TF-CBT can be comparable to that in other, potentially more alliance-focused therapies (Capaldi et al., 2016; Gilboa-Schechtman et al., 2010; Ormhaug et al., 2014) and to that found during exposure work in non-PTSD samples (McLaughlin et al., 2014).

As PTSD is characterised by a sense of serious current threat, our key task as therapists is, therefore, to help the person to feel safe, both inter- and intra-personally. There are a number of ways this can be achieved, through both the 'physical' and the 'psychological' environment of the therapy. Physical factors will include: having longer sessions for reliving (up to 90 minutes, to ensure that the patient is able to return to a calmer state before leaving the therapy room); having a pleasant and open feel to the room (to emphasise to patients that they can leave if they want to); setting up the room to minimise the risk of dissociation; checking that the patient is happy with the gender of their therapist or interpreter (when present) and, if so, maintaining continuity by having the same interpreter in each session. More 'psychological' environmental factors might include: explaining to the patient about confidentiality; openly discussing trust issues; ensuring that the patient is able to make informed choices about the therapy and, finally, letting the client know that the therapist is comfortable with discussing the details of traumatic events. We will discuss some of these factors in more detail later.

ENGAGING THE CLIENT

There is evidence that working to achieve symptom reduction can result in a strong alliance and that a direct focus on the therapeutic relationship prior to this may not be necessary, or indeed as effective (Capaldi et al., 2016). A collaborative therapeutic relationship is important in CBT for any problem. In PTSD, the therapist must help the client to make an informed choice about whether they wish to engage in imaginal reliving of their traumatic experience. If the client feels coerced in any way, this will significantly damage the alliance. Equally, the therapist should not collude with unhelpful avoidance and should provide the client with a clear rationale for the therapeutic approach, information about what it will involve and evidence of its effectiveness. If available, sharing testimonials from previous clients is also helpful. This section outlines some common ways in which engagement is enhanced.

METAPHOR FOR RELIVING

The rationale for engaging in 'telling the story' is usually supported through the use of metaphors.

> Imagine that memory is a little bit like a cupboard. When you are involved in a trauma, it is as if someone runs at you with a huge, filthy duvet in their arms, screaming 'AAARGH... PUT THAT IN THE CUPBOARD RIGHT NOW!'
>
> You take the duvet reluctantly, you don't like touching it, and you stuff it in the cupboard, push the door shut and walk away, breathing a sigh of relief. As you do, the cupboard door opens and the duvet falls out onto the floor. The person screams again: 'PUT IT AWAY, PUT IT AWAY NOW!'
>
> You stuff it back into the cupboard but, every time you try to put it back in, it comes back out again. In the end, you find that you have to stand with your back against the cupboard door, keeping it closed – so you can't do anything else.
>
> This is what happens when you are involved in a traumatic event. The traumatic event is like the duvet, it is too big to fit into how you normally remember things (the cupboard). So, you might put it out of your mind because it is upsetting (stuff the duvet in). However, this does not work. The memory keeps coming back, in nightmares or during the day in the form of intrusive memories/flashbacks.
>
> What needs to happen for things to get better is for you to take out the duvet, smooth it down on the floor, fold it up properly, make space for it in the cupboard and then put it back in so that the door doesn't pop open.

The precise nature of the metaphor is not critical (others may describe objects falling off a conveyer belt or an over-stuffed filing cabinet), what matters is that the metaphor makes it easy for the client to see why it will be necessary to go through the details of the traumatic event.

PSYCHOEDUCATION

Providing clients with information about PTSD symptoms helps them to understand what they are experiencing and to consider alternative appraisals of the consequences of the trauma. Commonly, re-experiencing symptoms are interpreted by the client as signs that they are 'going mad,' or that they have been permanently damaged by their traumatic experience. Explaining early on that these are recognised, understandable and treatable symptoms can help reduce shame relating to the development of symptoms and address beliefs around the meaning of symptoms that might be contributing to the maintenance of PTSD. A written information sheet, detailing the common PTSD symptoms, how people may try to cope and the impact of this, is helpful and can be shared with others.

If dissociation is present and likely during TF-CBT, then it is important to discuss early on in the therapy process what dissociation is and how it can be managed. Giving the client such practical tools can also provide success, credibility and enhanced engagement (see Schauer and Elbert, 2010).

TRUST AND CONFIDENTIALITY

It is useful to discuss trust openly and to monitor it in the early stages of therapy - to make it easier for a client to admit that they don't trust their therapist.

> Many of the people that we see here find it difficult to trust us to begin with – it is unsurprising, given what has happened to them. So, we find that it helps to explain the rules about confidentiality and about what we do in this service.

> With your permission, I would also like to learn how to act in a way that makes it easier for you to trust me. I wondered if you would be willing to mark on this scale, here, how much you do/don't trust me at the beginning and then at end of each session.

Show the client a visual analogue scale with 'completely not trust' at one end and 'totally and completely trust' at the other.

> Each week, if my score has gone down by the end of the session, I will ask you about what I did to lower my score and then I will try not to do it again. Equally, if my score has gone up, I will ask why and try and do more of that behaviour!

WORKING WITH CPTSD

Fallot and Harris (2008) have proposed five areas to consider when working to establish a safe, collaborative and empowering therapeutic relationship with someone with cPTSD (UK Psychological Trauma Society, 2017). These are:

> the client's lack of trust following abuse or violence at the hands of authority figures or other adults; responding to hopelessness through establishing a basis for working together and instilling reasonable hope; developing safe and supportive boundaries; acknowledging and honouring loss, betrayal and injustice; [and] understanding and building on what matters to the individual and their sources of strength and resilience. (UK Psychological Trauma Society, 2017: 18–19)

Clear boundaries in the therapeutic relationship are particularly important for people with a history of abuse. When working with people with cPTSD, boundaries should be discussed and agreed collaboratively, formally contracted and consistently maintained to enable the client to understand what they can expect from the therapist and to help them to feel safe (UK Psychological Trauma Society, 2017).

Therapist tips

- Discussing the rationale for reliving with a client also acts as a useful reminder for you about why it is a useful and effective approach.
- Anticipating times when a client's resolve to continue with trauma-focused work may falter, ask them to write an encouraging note/draw an encouraging diagram for their future self. This will place them in control of encouraging themselves. The therapist can then bring out this document when needed. In our experience, putting it on colourful paper/card and/or laminating it can work well.
- Clarity and openness are important for PTSD work, particularly with cPTSD:
  - Openly address problems with trust, making it easy for a client to admit that they don't trust you – once you know that they don't trust you, then you two can start to work on it.
  - Openly address boundaries and why they are important.

PREDICTING, PREVENTING AND WORKING WITH THREATS TO THE THERAPEUTIC ALLIANCE

Potential threats to the alliance in TF-CBT can come from the nature of the trauma itself, the client, the therapist and/or the service in which treatment is taking place. Examples are outlined below, although in practice, they interact with each other.

THE NATURE OF THE TRAUMA

Common emotional reactions to traumatic experiences include shame and guilt. Shame is likely to result from sexual assault, torture and bodily reactions during traumatic events, such as loss of bladder control through fear or an unwanted sexual response during rape. Guilt is associated with the belief that one has behaved in an unacceptable way and/or caused harm to others. This may be experienced by people who acted instinctively to protect themselves rather than others in a life-threatening situation or may be linked to cases where people have intentionally or unintentionally caused harm to others, for example, during combat or in a road traffic accident.

Normalising clients' responses during traumatic events, and offering explanatory information about human physiology and behaviour at times of intense stress, can help people to understand why they may have reacted how they did, especially if this differed to how they believed they would react under such circumstances. This can then help with evaluating appraisals that may be associated with feelings of guilt or shame and may be maintaining PTSD. For example, normalising being paralysed with fear (due to dissociation) during rape, or explaining that torture can be designed to cause shame, can help to address clients' beliefs that they were to blame for what happened to them because they did not fight. Explaining relevant medical, legal or military procedures (which may require research) can also help the client to understand others' reactions during traumatic events. CBT techniques such as responsibility pie charts and correction of hindsight bias (Kubany and Manke, 1995) can be used to address excessive guilt, while if someone has caused actual harm, consideration of reparation may be appropriate.

CLIENT FACTORS

Clients' personal histories and trauma-related beliefs about other people can make placing trust in a therapist (or indeed anyone) challenging and make it difficult for clients to have faith in their therapists' ability to cope with the details of their traumatic experiences. Being open about difficulties with trust and about the rationale for trauma-focused therapy is essential. In our experience, some clients come from cultures where they expect their 'doctor' to tell them what to do and find the idea of collaborative working challenging. We suggest asking them to explain their model of how they expect a therapist to be and its origins. This can be compared with the therapist explanation of collaboration in a CBT model and its origins, with the aim to find a suitable compromise.

People who believe it would be dangerous to allow themselves to experience strong feelings (e.g. because they might 'go mad') may find the prospect of 'telling the story' frightening. It is important to acknowledge that some symptoms might temporarily increase and help them plan for how they will manage this. Clients may also have catastrophic mental images of themselves actually being overwhelmed by their symptoms. Once identified, the meaning inherent in these can be addressed.

Additional problems such as comorbid depression and substance misuse may also act as barriers to developing a strong therapeutic alliance, for example, due to impaired affect regulation and interpersonal functioning or because of anhedonia and low motivation (McLaughlin et al., 2014).

Therapists need to tell clients that they are comfortable with discussing details of traumatic events, and they can invite the client to use the therapeutic relationship as a crucible to test the client's concerns arising from shame or guilt.

Case examples 9.1

Jane had been sexually abused by numerous men who were meant to be caring for her during her childhood. She sought help after developing PTSD following an assault at work and felt let down by the way this had been handled. She described and demonstrated great difficulty trusting people – specifically, she felt vulnerable around men and was unsure whether any healthcare professional would care enough or understand her well enough to be able to help her. She found it difficult to trust her (female) therapist, which affected the extent to which she was able to engage in TF-CBT sessions. In one session, she experienced an episode of dissociation and felt faint and light-headed afterwards. She was distressed and described feeling weak and vulnerable. She did not feel well enough to take public transport home, and there was no trusted person available to collect her from the service. Her therapist arranged a taxi but was concerned about how she would feel if she was left to take a car journey alone with a male taxi driver while she felt compromised. The therapist therefore accompanied her on the journey. The following week, Jane returned to therapy and said that this had been a turning point for her in the therapeutic relationship, as she realised her therapist had listened to her fears and taken them seriously. She reported feeling safer and more able to engage in the sessions after this.

Brad was a retired fire fighter who attended an assessment at a specialist trauma service. The assessment was carried out by a young, female psychologist. During questions about the nature of his traumatic experiences, Brad became uncomfortable and was reluctant to disclose details. He said that the assessor looked like she was a similar age to his granddaughter and that he didn't want to make her cry by telling her about the terrible things he had seen. He explained that he had sought help 20 years previously and had seen a young, female counsellor at that time, who had become visibly upset when she heard about his experiences. This had made Brad feel so guilty that he avoided seeking help again for a long time. The therapist had to find a balance between explaining that he didn't need to protect her and that she had appropriate training, support and supervision to help her cope with her work, while still showing empathy and demonstrating, in a helpful way, that she wasn't totally unmoved by his traumatic experiences.

THERAPIST FACTORS

Therapists' beliefs about emotions and emotional avoidance will also be affected by their own personal histories. Exposure techniques are underutilised in the treatment of PTSD, despite their well-established efficacy (Van Minnen et al., 2010). This is generally due to therapists' concerns about client drop-out, or about revictimisation/exacerbation of symptoms or concerns that exposure might damage the therapeutic alliance (e.g. Cahill et al., 2006). Therapists may also doubt their own ability to cope with hearing the content of trauma narratives. These factors (among others) have the potential to influence therapists' level of adherence to the treatment model. Divergence from evidence-based trauma-focused treatments can have a negative impact on client outcomes *and* on the therapeutic alliance (van Minnen and Keijsers, 2000).

We should remind ourselves at all times that the trauma-focused approach is supported by evidence and that great treatment gains can be made. Indeed, we know that using evidence-based treatments for PTSD is associated with greater compassion and satisfaction and less burnout in therapists (Craig and Sprang, 2010). When working with people with PTSD, it is crucial that therapists use supervision to discuss their own emotional reactions to their clients' stories and any significant changes in their beliefs about the world as a consequence of the work. It is helpful for supervisors to ask about these directly, especially with inexperienced therapists who may fear being judged if they admit to finding the work emotionally difficult. Looking after yourself as a therapist may include knowing when to ask a colleague to work with a client if you are going to be very distressed by the detail (e.g. if you are pregnant and someone is referred due to traumatic childbirth).

Case example 9.2

Clara was a young woman who had experienced rape. When discussing 'reliving' in the first session with her therapist, she stated that she wouldn't be able to cope with this. She described images of having a complete mental breakdown or of dissociating permanently and never being able to re-engage with the present. In her images, both of these scenarios resulted in her being sectioned and spending the rest of her life locked in a psychiatric hospital. Her therapist noted that she had a history of dissociation, both during and after the rape, and that she had previously been admitted to hospital for psychiatric treatment. The therapist wondered if Clara might in fact be harmed by reliving and worried that she would be responsible if this did happen. She therefore agreed to spend a number of sessions working on other issues. Following supervision, the therapist's avoidance was highlighted, and she then returned to discuss this with Clara. They agreed that reliving was going to be important to move the therapy forward and developed a number of strategies to help Clara feel safe enough to attempt this. These included grounding strategies for coping with dissociation, agreement about what Clara would like the therapist to do and say if she became highly distressed, and an agreement that she would remain in control of the process and have the power to say stop if she didn't feel able to continue. In fact, Clara was then able to complete emotionally engaged reliving multiple times over a number of sessions, which led to a reduction in re-experiencing symptoms and helped identify key meanings that formed the focus of subsequent sessions.

SERVICE FACTORS

Some services have strict limits around the length and number of therapy sessions that can be offered or restrictions on treatment that is offered to people with uncertain immigration status. This may mean insufficient time is available to complete TF-CBT in a way that allows clients to feel safe. Alternatively, therapists fearing that they will run out of time to complete memory-focused work will avoid starting it. Therapists need to be clear with themselves and with the clients about service roles and limits; this might include what can realistically be achieved in the available time (part of informed decision-making). However, tight session limits may be a reason to more quickly engage with memory-focused work, rather than 'using up' sessions on other potentially less effective interventions.

The client's perception of healthcare services is also important; for example, refugees and asylum-seekers may find it difficult to trust NHS clinicians or services if they believe therapy notes might be passed to immigration services.

Case example 9.3

Yadumani was an asylum-seeker from Sri Lanka, who arrived in the UK hoping to find compassion, safety and support to rebuild his life after witnessing the murder of family members and experiencing torture back at home. His experience on arrival was far from what he expected, and for over a year, he had been trying to negotiate the system to obtain Leave to Remain. During an extended assessment at a specialist trauma service, he reported that his experiences since arriving in the UK had left him believing that no one in the world cared about him, and he felt angry and suicidal. His therapist thought that it was potentially going to be challenging to establish a helpful relationship under these circumstances, as she knew that the service where he was completing his assessment had a long waiting list for therapy, and the offer of treatment might be affected by the status of his ongoing asylum claim. After being upfront about the limits of what the service could provide, the therapist was able to give Yadumani the space to describe his traumatic experiences and hopes for the future, to express empathy and concern for his well-being, to ensure he was linked in with the appropriate services to help with his asylum claim, and to help him engage in activities that had the potential to reduce his sense of isolation and improve his mood. He was very emotional at the end of the assessment and said that it had been particularly upsetting to him previously that no one had listened to his story or shown him compassion when he arrived in the UK, and it was meaningful that his therapist had been able to do that for him. This highlights that a good relationship can be therapeutic, even when it is limited to the assessment stage.

Therapist tips

- Remember that threats to the alliance come from both the therapist and client.
- Ensure you get supervision from supervisors who are themselves trained in, and use, TF-CBT.
- Find ways to look after yourself, for your own well-being and the benefit of the therapeutic relationship.

Reflective questions

- Consider your own emotional responses to the stories you have heard. What has this 'pulled' you to do?
- Are you avoiding talking about the memory through your own anxiety?
- How might the therapeutic relationship be used actively to enhance the treatment of your client's PTSD?

ENDING THERAPY

As described elsewhere in this book, attention to the ending of therapy should be paid from the very beginning. No matter the degree of progress, it is routine to work with clients on a summary of their learning from treatment, a 'blueprint.' Such blueprints for people who have received treatment for PTSD will be similar in nature as for other presenting problems. This will cover key learning, what they have achieved and how, and how to make further concrete progress towards goals. This will include learning and reflection on the therapeutic relationship itself and the role of trust. A key addition is to ensure that there is some discussion of how the person would try to deal with any future traumatic experiences, what they may do the same as before and importantly what they would do differently.

We are all too aware that progress for many people we see is limited. A blueprint and summary of learning is still important. A more detailed discussion of how to manage such endings in CBT is provided by Worrell (2014).

Ending therapy is also an opportunity for the therapist to reflect, ideally with their supervisor, on their learning. This can include the impact of therapist reactions and the role of the therapeutic relationship, as well as application of specific techniques. Our experience and learning suggests that hearing the detail of traumatic experiences and reactions to them unlock key meanings and opportunities for progress. We have usually regretted delaying becoming memory-focused, rather than regretting doing this too soon.

CHAPTER SUMMARY

People who meet criteria for PTSD or cPTSD experience a sense of serious current threat, which may be both physical (the world is dangerous and I am at risk) and psychological (I'm weak and all alone). The key task for the therapist in TF-CBT is to help the person feel safe. Hence, the therapeutic alliance is crucial. The safety of the therapeutic relationship allows informed choices about engaging in memory-focused work, 'telling their story,' a crucial ingredient of the evidence-based TF-CBTs. The therapeutic relationship can be used to enhance treatment by using it to directly address features of PTSD, such as reduced trust in others and the experience of shame. Threats to the alliance can come from both therapist and client beliefs (usually fears) about memory-focused work and about one another (e.g. overprotection), and also from aspects of service organisation. Attention to these beliefs and factors allows important obstacles to the best outcomes to be addressed. This is aided by ensuring supervision routinely covers the therapist's reactions: emotional, cognitive and behavioural.

FURTHER READING

Ehlers A and Clark DM (2000) A cognitive model of posttraumatic stress disorder. *Behaviour Research and Therapy* 38(4): 319–345.

Grey N (ed) (2009) *A Casebook of Cognitive Therapy for Traumatic Stress Reactions*. East Sussex, UK: Routledge.

UK Psychological Trauma Society (2017) *Guideline for the treatment and planning of services for complex post-traumatic stress disorder in adults*. DO - 10.13140/RG.2.2.14906.39

REFERENCES

American Psychiatric Association (2013) *Diagnostic and Statistical Manual of Mental Disorders*. 5th ed. Arlington, VA: American Psychiatric Publishing.

Cahill SP, Foa EB, Hembree EA, Marshall RD and Nacash N (2006) Dissemination of exposure therapy in the treatment of posttraumatic stress disorder. *Journal of Traumatic Stress 19*: 597–610.

Callahan KL, Price JL and Hilsenroth MJ (2003) Psychological assessment of adult survivors of childhood sexual abuse within a naturalistic clinical sample. *Journal of Personality Assessment 80*: 173–184.

Capaldi S, Asnaani A, Zandberg LJ, Carpenter JK and Foa EB (2016) Therapeutic alliance during prolonged exposure versus client-centred therapy for adolescent posttraumatic stress disorder. *Journal of Clinical Psychology 72*(10): 1026–1036.

Cloitre M, Garvert DW, Brewin CR, Bryant RA and Maercker A (2013) Evidence for proposed ICD-11 PTSD and complex PTSD: a latent profile analysis. *European Journal of Psychotraumatology 4*: 10.3402/ejpt.v4i0.20706

Craig CD and Sprang G (2010) Compassion satisfaction, compassion fatigue, and burnout in a national sample of trauma treatment therapists. *Anxiety, Stress & Coping 23*(3): 319–339.

De Jongh AD, Resick PA, Zoellner LA, van Minnen A, Lee CW, Monson CM, Foa EB, Wheeler K, ten Broeke E, Feeny N, Rauch SAM, Chard KM, Mueser KT, Sloan DM, van der Gaag M, Rothbaum BO, Neuner F, de Roos C, Hehenkamp LMJ, Rosner R and Bicanic, I.V.A (2016) Critical analysis of the current treatment guidelines for Complex PTSD in adults. *Depression and Anxiety 33*: 359–369.

Ehlers A and Clark DM (2000) A cognitive model of posttraumatic stress disorder. *Behaviour Research and Therapy 38*(4): 319–345.

Fallot RD and Harris M (2008) Trauma-informed services. In: Reyes G, Elhai JD and Ford JD (eds) *The Encyclopedia of Psychological Trauma*, pp. 660–662. Hoboken, NJ: John Wiley.

Foa EB, Hembree EA and Rothbaum BO (2007) Prolonged exposure therapy for PTSD: emotional processing of traumatic experiences: therapist guide. New York: Oxford University Press.

Gilboa-Schechtman E, Foa EB, Shafran N, Aderka IM, Powers MB, Rachamim L, Rosenbach L, Yadin E and Apter A (2010) Prolonged exposure versus dynamic therapy for adolescent PTSD: a pilot randomized controlled trial. *Journal of the American Academy of Child & Adolescent Psychiatry 49*(10): 1034–1042.

Herman J (1992) *Trauma and Recovery: The Aftermath of Violence – From Domestic Abuse to Political Terror*. New York, USA: Basic Books.

Kubany ES and Manke FP (1995) Cognitive therapy for trauma-related guilt: Conceptual bases and treatment outlines. *Cognitive and Behavioural Practice 2*(1): 27–61.

McLaughlin AMA, Keller SM, Feeny NC, Youngstrom EA and Zoellner LA (2014) Patterns of therapeutic alliance: rupture-repair episodes in prolonged exposure for PTSD. *Journal of Consulting and Clinical Psychology 82*(1): 112–121.

Ormhaug SM, Jensen TK, Wentzel-Larsen T and Shirk SR (2014) The therapeutic alliance in treatment of traumatized youths; relation to outcome in a randomized clinical trial. *Journal of Consulting and Clinical Psychology 82*(1): 52.

Resick PA and Schnicke MK (1992) Cognitive processing therapy for sexual assault victims. *Journal of Consulting and Clinical Psychology 60*(5): 748–756.

Schauer M and Elbert T (2010) Dissociation following traumatic stress: Etiology and treatment. *Journal of Psychology 218*: 109–127.

Schauer M, Neuner F and Elbert T (2011) *Narrative Exposure Therapy. A Short-term Treatment for Traumatic Stress Disorders*. 2nd ed., revised and expanded ed. Göttingen: Hogrefe.

Schnyder U, Ehlers A, Elbert T, Foa EB, Gersons BPR, Resick PA, Shapiro F and Cloitre M (2015) Psychotherapies for PTSD: what do they have in common? *European Journal of Psychotraumatology 6*(1): 28186.

UK Psychological Trauma Society (2017) *Guideline for the treatment and planning of services for complex post-traumatic stress disorder in adults*. DOI: 10.13140/RG.2.2.14906.39

van Minnen A, Hendriks L and Olff M (2010) When do trauma experts choose trauma therapy for PTSD patients? A controlled study of therapist and patient factors. *Behaviour Research and Therapy 48*: 312–320.

van Minnen A and Keijsers GPJ (2000) A controlled study into the (cognitive) effects of exposure treatment on trauma therapists. *Journal of Behaviour Therapy and Experimental Psychiatry 31*: 189–200.

World Health Organisation (1992) *International Statistical Classification of Diseases and Related Health Problems 10*th *revision*. Herndon, VA, USA: Stylus Publishing, LLC.

Worrell M (2014) What to do when CBT isn't working. In: Whittington A and Grey N (eds) *How to Become a More Effective CBT Therapist*. West Sussex, UK: Wiley.

10

PSYCHOSIS

REBECCA KELLY, ANNIS COHEN AND EMMANUELLE PETERS

CHAPTER OVERVIEW

This chapter will describe the critical role of the therapeutic relationship in CBT for psychosis (CBTp). As described in previous chapters, the therapeutic relationship involves both a strong bond between the therapist and client and agreement on the specific goals and tasks for therapy. In CBTp specifically, it has been emphasised that a trusting relationship is a crucial foundation (Brabban et al., 2017), particularly for the challenging work involved when addressing psychotic symptoms and experiences such as delusional beliefs or voices (e.g. Wright et al., 2014).

CBTp requires a very explicit focus on engagement. Engagement is a broad concept, encompassing the development of the therapist–client bond, specific therapeutic procedures and activities that the therapist utilises, as well as the extent to which the client actively participates in the therapy process. This chapter will consider some of the unique challenges to engagement that arise when working with individuals with psychosis and how therapists can manage these challenges, illustrated by case studies. We will then describe why the therapeutic relationship is so critical in CBTp and how paying specific attention to the first two aspects of engagement, in particular (the therapist–client bond and therapeutic procedures that facilitate engagement), can facilitate the development of a positive and effective therapy relationship.

CBTP MODEL

CBTp is not based on a single psychological model and includes a combination of elements and therapeutic activities (Morrison and Barratt, 2010). The specific model used depends on what the primary difficulties are (e.g. delusions, voices, emotional difficulties). Nevertheless, each model emphasises the important role of appraisals of, and responses to, particular experiences, as well as a person's previous experiences and their beliefs about themselves, the world and others (Garety and Hardy, 2017).

Successful implementation of CBTp involves both skilful application of therapy techniques and adherence to the underlying values and principles of offering hope, and a recovery-oriented perspective; listening to and collaborating with the service user; and validating and supporting the 'making sense' process of the service user's experiences (Brabban et al., 2017).

COMMON CHALLENGES IN CBTP AND THEIR IMPACT ON THE THERAPY RELATIONSHIP

There are a number of common challenges that can represent potential obstacles to developing a therapeutic relationship in CBTp. Individuals with psychosis often experience considerable anxiety, often due to past experiences of trauma and victimisation. They might feel anxious about meeting the therapist, particularly if they hold distressing beliefs, for example about being watched or influenced in some way. Understandably, they might fear the therapist could be (or could become) involved with things that they believe are happening. Individuals who hear voices might struggle to talk about these experiences or the content of the voices might prevent them from doing so. They might also anticipate that the therapist will see them as mad or foolish, or not believe what they say. They might fear being admitted to hospital if they speak honestly. Or, clients might adopt a 'sealing over' recovery style in order to regulate distress and avoid overwhelming affect (Gumley and Schwannauer, 2006), fearing things will 'unravel' if they begin to speak about their difficulties.

A particular challenge is the so-called 'lack of clinical insight' i.e. when clients believe their main concerns are entirely external and therefore not amenable to therapy (e.g. harassment by neighbours cannot be fixed by CBT) or when their goals do not match the therapist's goals (e.g. a client who wants the therapist to provide evidence in their case against perceived persecutors). CBTp is somewhat unique in that many clients do not see their difficulties as being mental-health related; in this sense, CBTp is closer to psychological therapies for physical health-related problems, such as chronic fatigue, than for emotional problems. A key challenge for the therapist and an early task of therapy is to try to relocate the problem from 'A' (the experiences) to 'B' (the appraisal) and, importantly, to do so without invalidating the client and their experiences.

A further challenge is the extreme nature of the appraisals and resulting fear held by some clients, which can make devising and conducting experiments difficult. For example, experimenting with responding assertively to commanding voices, or even just going outside, can feel like taking a huge risk if the person fears for their or their loved ones' safety from the voices and/or persecutors. Clients must have complete trust in their therapist, who therefore needs to attend closely to engagement when undertaking challenging work such as exposure or behavioural experimentation.

Reflective question

Think of a client you're currently working with whose paranoid beliefs make them highly anxious and fearful. What do they think would happen if they stopped avoiding the source of their fear? How strongly do they believe this?

Now, think of the experiments you would like them to do to test this fear. If you held this belief with as much conviction as they do, would you be willing to try this experiment? What would your therapist need to do or say for you to trust them enough to give it a go?

Different models of explanation can also present unique challenges. For those clients who adopt a 'medical model' of their difficulties, they might not see how a talking therapy could improve a biological illness. For others, psychological therapy could be seen as part of a psychiatric system they see as irrelevant or unhelpful (e.g. Messari and Hallam, 2003).

Lastly, individuals with psychosis often have a significant trauma history (Varese et al., 2012). In addition, experiences of psychosis and their sequelae, such as terrifying visions or involuntary hospital admissions, may also have been traumatising (Rodrigues and Anderson, 2017). Individuals with psychosis often feel socially victimised (e.g. Selten and Cantor-Graae, 2005) and experience further disempowerment and stigmatisation following diagnosis (González-Torres et al., 2007). These difficulties can also affect the therapeutic relationship through a lack of trust and attachment difficulties (Berry et al., 2007; Gumley et al., 2014).

Despite the range of potential difficulties, there is no evidence that clients with psychosis cannot form therapeutic relationships: good levels of therapeutic alliance, comparable to non-psychotic populations, have been found (Evans-Jones et al., 2009; Svensson and Hansson, 1999). Interestingly, no association has been found between client ratings of the therapy alliance and measures of severity of psychotic symptoms and clinical insight (Couture et al., 2006; Evans-Jones et al., 2009).[1]

THE CASE OF 'MARY'

Mary is a 30-year-old woman with a diagnosis of paranoid schizophrenia who experiences distressing voices and beliefs that she is being followed by a past abuser. She believes she has mental health difficulties and finds her antipsychotic medication helpful in reducing her arousal and distress. However, she does not believe that her voices are caused by her mental health problems. She lives alone, but with family nearby. She manages a few simple daily tasks, but very few meaningful activities, and is unable to work.

Mary was sexually abused by a neighbour during her teens. In her early 20s, she began hearing a threatening derogatory voice, which she believed was that of her abuser.

Mary now hears a number of additional male and female voices. She is unsure of their identity but believes they may be friends of the abuser. Most of the voices threaten to 'get' her, attack and kill her. They call her derogatory names, such as 'slut,' and comment negatively on her day-to-day activities. They tell her that people hate her, disbelieve her and blame her for the abuse. Mary also hears voices that

[1]There is often disparity between client and therapist ratings of the therapeutic alliance in CBTp, with clients generally rating the alliance more positively than the therapists. Therapist ratings have been found in some studies to correlate with measures of insight, symptom severity and indices of suitability for therapy (e.g. Couture et al., 2006). However, client ratings of alliance tend not to correlate with these variables.

> give her seemingly friendly warnings such as 'don't trust her' and 'don't go out.' At times, however, she wonders whether these voices are just trying to isolate her.
>
> Mary knows that the abuser is in prison but believes he is conspiring to track her down and kill her. She thinks he may be kept informed of her whereabouts via her neighbours, who may be using cameras or bugs to watch her.

In an attempt to reassure or alleviate distress, health professionals or family members may explain voices or other distressing experiences as simply symptoms of schizophrenia that are not real and therefore need not be feared. However, because these experiences *feel* incredibly real and frightening, this message can be experienced as an invalidation of their reality. In contrast, CBTp seeks to develop a shared understanding of their experiences, rather than impose a particular explanation. This is a critical first step in establishing a therapeutic relationship where individuals feel safe to talk and do not feel invalidated or disbelieved.

CBTP CONCEPTUALISATION

Below in Figure 10.1 is an example of a simple conceptualisation that the therapist might draw out with Mary, highlighting the role of appraisals and responses to experiences in maintaining distress. Useful shared formulations should draw on the key CBTp models (Garety et al., 2001; Morrison, 2001) and the most important maintenance processes, but will often take the form of simple 'hot-cross bun' or ABC formulations, at least at the outset.

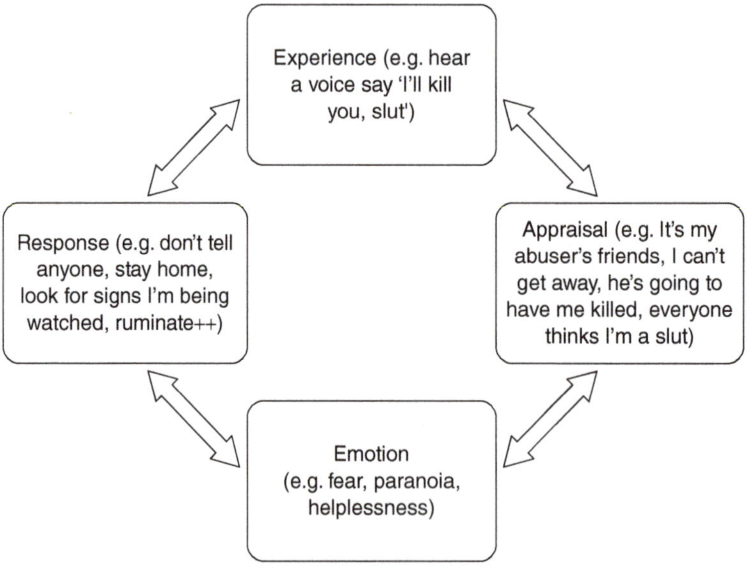

Figure 10.1 Simple Maintenance Formulation

The process of formulating these difficulties with Mary highlights several important ways that the therapist can develop the therapeutic relationship. Conceptualising Mary's difficulties in this way allows her therapist to use the CBT model to both validate and normalise her difficulties, e.g. no wonder she feels distressed if this is what she is experiencing, that it must be terrifying and that it is understandable that she feels frightened of others. The therapist can also share information with Mary on how common the experience of voice-hearing is, especially following trauma. The therapist aims to get across the idea that Mary is a reasonable person trying to make sense of her experiences and deal with them as best she can, rather than dismissing them as a symptom of a mental illness. Highlighting the impact of factors such as rumination and avoidance can help Mary to consider that, even if it is not possible to get rid of the voices, it might still be possible to reduce the distress and fear she experiences so that she can start to achieve her valued goals.

Therapist tip

Initially, the CBT conceptualisation should be used to normalise and validate, and create a shared understanding with the individual. Using the conceptualisation to immediately start challenging thoughts can be invalidating and damaging to the therapy alliance.

First-person accounts have emphasised the importance of this formulating and 'sense making' process for both the relationship with the therapist and for good outcome in therapy; 'therapy helped me see that psychosis is quite a logical process and that I had a definite road to psychotic crisis... [The therapist] talked about lessening distress and never talked about fixing a disorder or dealing with maladaptive coping strategies' (Sen, 2017).

Qualitative research has highlighted other factors that clients perceive to be important in enabling them to engage with therapy and develop a relationship with their therapist, including trusting the therapist (Coursey et al., 1995; Kilbride et al., 2013), feeling liked and respected (Coursey et al., 1995), having a sense of control over the process (Kilbride et al., 2013), having difficult experiences listened to and taken seriously (McGowan et al., 2005), therapists being genuine and non-judgemental and able to tolerate their distress (Wood et al., 2015).

ENGAGING THE CLIENT IN CBTP: PREDICTING AND PREVENTING PROBLEMS

THERAPY STYLE AND ADAPTATIONS

Given the challenges outlined above, CBTp therapists often need to do more than simply rely on their interpersonal skills to develop a rapport with their client. Competent therapists (e.g. R-CTPAS; Startup et al., 2007) must pay particular attention to issues that facilitate engagement and increase the client's ability to work collaboratively within the session. Difficulties can often be prevented if the therapist strives to maintain the client's sense of control over the process of therapy as far as possible. Therapists often need to be flexible with timing, pace or location of sessions and discussing explicitly the rationale of therapy. Therapists should be prepared to take more responsibility for the session and to apologise and give reassurance if things are misinterpreted (Johns et al., 2014). Individuals with psychosis can sometimes misinterpret social situations and may have experienced many social setbacks, and so the therapist needs to ensure that sessions are as positive and even pleasant as possible (Hoaas et al., 2011).

> At the outset of therapy, Mary's therapist negotiated some ways of making Mary feel safe. They agreed that they could arrange the therapy room with their chairs spaced apart, and with Mary sitting close to the door. Through asking about Mary's concerns and the particular behaviours that might make her feel anxious, the therapist realised she needed to be particularly cautious not to make any sudden movements, and to give Mary some warning when she moved to get something out of her bag Mary's therapist ensured she adopted an open, interested and respectful stance, and spent time at the start of therapy empathising and validating Mary's distress. When Mary asked her therapist if she thought she was crazy, she did not dodge the question or treat it as unhelpful 'reassurance-seeking,' but answered 'No, not at all.' The therapist took time to describe openly her role, and that of her team, and the aims of CBTp. She was clear that she could not promise that CBTp would get rid of Mary's voices but hoped that she could reduce Mary's distress and help her achieve her goals. The therapist also told Mary that she knew that, sometimes, voices might say things to clients about the therapy or therapist. She encouraged Mary to let her know if this happened, so that she could reassure her or pass a message on to the voices if needed.

PREDICTING AND PREVENTING PROBLEMS IN ACTIVE THERAPY

Typically there is a 'change of gears' after the early engagement and assessment sessions, where therapy enters a more 'active' phase of trying to implement change. In order to keep the client engaged, it is critical that a shared goal has been agreed and to ensure that therapy is collaborative and problem-oriented (Morrison, 2017). Goals should be measurable and achievable, and focused on alleviating distress and improving functioning.

Therapists can prevent problems by thinking carefully about the sequencing of interventions, for example starting with normalisation and coping strategy enhancement. Normalisation can be a helpful early strategy to alleviate distress. For example, Hoaas et al. (2011) suggest therapists emphasise how stress can contribute to the development or worsening of psychotic symptoms; or provide information about how psychotic symptoms often emerge during certain conditions e.g. sleep deprivation, extreme isolation, such as being a hostage or solo-sailing around the world, or substance use; or demonstrate that experiences such as voice hearing are common in the general population and are not necessarily always associated with distress or dysfunction (Baumeister et al., 2017; Woods, 2015).

Therapist tip

Research suggests some clients can find case formulation a negative experience (Chadwick et al., 2003). In psychosis, particularly, formulations need to be clearly linked to the client's current problems as they experience them. Formulation at a level helpful to the therapist, but not the client, can be damaging to the relationship (Gumley and Schwannauer, 2006). For example, linking past experiences to the formation of distressing beliefs might be unhelpful when a client's conviction in a belief is very high and the client therefore sees it as their reality and not as a belief. In this case, a more helpful formulation might be to have the persecution as the 'event' (A) and the appraisal (B) as 'I must fight them/clear my name/keep safe,' leading to confrontations/isolation (behavioural C) and anger/distress (emotional C). This type of 'vicious cycle' formulation can then lead to considering alternative appraisals (e.g. 'the best way to deal with bullies is ignore them and get on with my life') that may help the client achieve their valued goals and reduce distress, without invalidating their reality.

Try to ensure that formulations:

- include only aspects that are likely to be helpful and accessible to the client
- are collaboratively drawn out rather than simply presented
- clearly highlight potential strategies to escape vicious cycles, so as to offer hope

Ensure you also consider the potential emotional impact, for example of referring to and linking in past trauma.

When working on appraisals and beliefs in CBTp, therapists need to be mindful to question gently, using the client's own words, and avoid trying to persuade the client of an alternative view. For example, therapists might use the Theory A/Theory B strategy to present the cognitive model as an alternative rather than the absolute truth. Therapists might need to float suggestions and alternatives, but also need to be prepared to back off. Challenging beliefs is likely to create 'psychological reactance' i.e. increase conviction and intensity of beliefs in the long term. Using the client's own language, and referring to what the client 'experienced' or 'knew' rather than what they 'thought' or 'felt' was happening, at least at the start, can support this non-confrontative style (see Johns et al., 2014 for further suggestions). Whilst clients might initially express curiosity about the therapist's view of what could be going on, try to avoid getting 'caught' in long discussions or debates that can easily become ruminative and impact unhelpfully on the relationship.

In terms of behavioural work, it is best to introduce low risk, win-win experiments at the start and move on to more challenging experiments, such as dropping safety-seeking behaviours, later (Morrison, 2017), when the client feels more confident and there is a strong foundation of trust.

MANAGING DIFFICULTIES IN THE THERAPY RELATIONSHIP

THE CASE OF 'PETER'

Peter is a 45-year-old white British male, who lives alone and was formerly employed as a teacher. He has a diagnosis of delusional disorder and is not willing to take antipsychotic medication. He is heterosexual but believes that people are spreading rumours that he is gay and pays men for sex. Peter believes they were started by ex-colleagues but that now almost everyone he comes into contact with (e.g. neighbours, shopkeepers, bus drivers) is either actively involved in spreading the rumours or has heard about them.

Peter reports that this began five years ago when he was the subject of a disciplinary procedure after being accused of sexual harassment. He was eventually cleared but found the process so stressful that he resigned. He believes that his colleagues started the rumours out of revenge and that they were also jealous of his intellect, education and attractiveness to women. Most of the persecutors do not really believe he is gay but are simply using the conspiracy as an effective way of slandering him, preventing him from getting a job or a girlfriend and isolating him from friends. He also thinks the persecutors may be aiming to get him injured in a homophobic attack, and consequently Peter is very anxious in the street.

Peter cites a range of behaviours as evidence of people's involvement in the persecution, including hostile or disgusted looks, avoiding him or, conversely, smiling or overt friendliness, especially from men. However, Peter's main evidence is that he just 'knows:' there is a particular atmosphere present when someone is involved, which he is able to detect as he is highly intelligent and a good reader of people.

Peter avoids going out socially as places such as bars or restaurants would be particularly easy for the persecutors to 'frame' him. He also avoids what he feels to be stereotypically 'gay' areas of London or areas where he thinks there will be a lot of men, such as gyms. He avoids sticking to a set routine: for example, he will frequent far-away shops, so that he cannot be watched and it cannot be predicted when he will arrive home.

Peter spends almost all of his time thinking about the persecution, either planning his day-to-day activities around avoiding giving the persecutors a chance to frame him or in trying to work out how he can defeat them. Peter spends much time writing to authorities (e.g. MP, police, housing officers) about the persecution, which he describes as time-consuming and exhausting. His main aim is to convince mental health professionals that he is not delusional, so that they will advocate on his behalf with police and housing officials. He wants the therapist to help with this.

Peter's case illustrates some potential obstacles to the development of a therapeutic relationship. Clients with such a presentation might present initially as frustrated and hostile towards mental health services in general or the therapist themselves. They might make explicit demands that the therapist feels unable to fulfil. The therapist might feel overwhelmed by the all-encompassing nature of the delusion or might think that therapy seems unlikely and that they won't be able to help.

Therapists might also worry about how to avoid colluding with the client's beliefs on the one hand, whilst also avoiding misleading the client or 'stringing them along' on the other.

The therapist can try to overcome these challenges by validating the distress and adopting an open-minded position when asked directly if they believe the client (e.g. 'I'm not sure if this is going on, as I haven't seen it myself, but I certainly believe that you are noticing these things and finding them distressing'). Even if, initially, the client's goals do not seem to match with a CBT approach, therapists can try to support clients to identify positive goals that focus on increasing their sense of control, understanding or ability to cope. It is important to persevere and be patient. The pace is often slower than CBT for anxiety and depression, and the therapist will often need to provide support to enable clients to identify shared, achievable goals and maintain motivation to work on these goals. Critically, the therapist needs to be transparent about what they can and cannot do for the client.

After some discussion, Peter and his therapist agreed the following general goals for therapy.

- To go through Peter's story in detail and think about his evidence and what might have caused the difficulties in convincing other people.
- To help Peter cope with the distress caused by the current situation, particularly in how it is affecting his sleep and ability to relax.
- To start to think about Peter's broader goals in life, which are to get back into teaching and to have a relationship.

The therapist started with coping strategy work with Peter, using CBT approaches for sleep difficulties and anxiety management. Peter found this helpful, especially to manage his preoccupation with the persecution during a stressful period.

Therapist tip

Coping strategy work often aids engagement early on but can later be used to reframe key appraisals (e.g. relating to power or control over distressing experiences). For example, with voice hearers, if reading aloud reduces the intensity of voices, ask the client what this means for their belief that they have no control over the voices. Or, for Peter, if he is able to use strategies that successfully reduce his anxiety and improve his sleep, does this suggest it might be possible for him to improve his quality of life, even if the persecution hasn't stopped?

The therapist then began to work with Peter on pursuing his value-directed goals, despite the persecution. For example, Peter identified a local walking group where he thought he might be able to make female friends and was able to attend this on a few occasions. Whilst he did not feel able to 'risk' going to new places where there might be lots of men, this group was predominantly female and so he felt quite safe. Peter and the therapist agreed that he would experiment with not looking out for signs that people know the rumours, and looking out for neutral and friendly gestures and facial expressions instead. Peter reported finding this helpful and encouraging.

Therapist tip

Delusions can often be highly resistant to change. However, some behaviour change might be possible even if the belief does not change.

Try to find out what might be possible 'in spite of' what the client believes is going on – starting with small steps and building up to bigger experiments if the client is willing.

Remember, the goal is not necessarily to reduce the client's conviction in their belief but their levels of preoccupation and distress, and impact on functioning i.e. 'working within the delusion.' Trying to reduce the client's conviction in their belief might actually lead to more distress if they cannot identify any plausible alternative explanations.

Based on a shared formulation, Peter's therapist then attempted some strategies to effect cognitive change. Peter's therapist tentatively used a 'better safe than sorry' model to introduce the idea that his previous difficulties might make him particularly vigilant and that, in his day-to-day encounters with strangers, he might be sometimes assuming that people are involved when they are not. Peter accepted that recent difficult experiences might mean he is more likely to look out for signs of people being involved but was certain that, because of his skill at reading atmospheres, there was still no possibility that he was ever mistaken. Peter seemed irritated by this discussion, so the therapist, mindful of the need to protect the therapy relationship, apologised and changed tack. The therapist suggested that they return to the initial goals and decide together what they could work on next, and asked Peter for some feedback on the therapy so far.

Peter said that he felt satisfied with his goal to retell his story; he fed back that he appreciated being listened to. However, he no longer wanted to work on the goals of coping with distress and focusing on his broader life aims; he decided that attempting to 'live well despite the persecution' would constitute giving up and accepting an injustice.

When the therapist asked if there was anything Peter had found unhelpful, Peter asked the therapist again whether she would be willing to speak to the police. The therapist explained that she was unable to help him with his goal of persuading the authorities to act to stop the persecution. She expressed that she understood how distressed he felt but could only pass on the information that he had given her, and therefore could not provide any further proof that the harassment was going on. She was also honest that she was not sure it would be helpful for her to do so and reminded Peter of the nature and limits of her role as his clinical psychologist. The therapist offered some suggestions of things she could try to help with, but Peter declined, so they mutually decided to end therapy at this point.

This case illustrates an important issue: CBTp requires the therapist and client to identify a collaborative goal. Good outcome is contingent on clients moving past the assessment and engagement phases and engaging with 'change strategies' (Dunn et al., 2012). Inability or unwillingness on the client's part to engage in active attempts to make progress towards a collaborative goal, such that sessions do not progress beyond just talking about difficulties, can potentially make things worse. Long discussions can become ruminative, and clients can become more preoccupied with their beliefs. For these reasons, if it is not possible to establish a collaborative goal, or if a client decides they no longer wish to work on previously agreed goals, sometimes it might be better, and more empowering for the client, to agree to end therapy. This ending can be managed in a way that protects the relationship as far as possible and leaves open the possibility for the client to change their mind and pursue CBT again in future.

In their final session, and in an ending letter to Peter, his therapist focused explicitly on his strengths and positive qualities, praising him for trying out new coping strategies and successfully improving his anxiety and sleep. She acknowledged the risk he took in trying out the walking group and reflected this might suggest that, even with the persecution going on, he was able to do some things that he enjoys and finds valuable. She thanked him for being honest about wanting to end therapy and encouraged him to try to access therapy again in future if he wishes.

Reflective questions

Consider a client you are working with who has a distressing belief.

What might be the meaning of this belief for the client? Do you have any hypotheses the client might not be able to access or disclose (e.g. sexuality, self-esteem or trauma)? What personal difficulties, failures or losses might the belief be providing an explanation for, or what might the client lose if they were to give up this belief?

Is there a way to communicate these hypotheses to the client sensitively or address them indirectly (e.g. adopting a gay affirmative stance (e.g. Davies, 1996))? If not, can you work on putting things in place that might replace those losses or mitigate against difficulties, before/rather than addressing the belief directly?

ENDING THERAPY

As with CBT for other difficulties, it is important to prepare clients for therapy ending from the start, when the therapist needs to be clear that CBTp is a time-limited intervention. The main focus for ending CBTp is on consolidating new learning and planning how to manage setbacks in future. Often this involves relapse prevention and sharing those plans with key people in the client's support network. The end of therapy represents an important opportunity to counter experiences of disempowerment and invalidation by highlighting the client's strengths and resilience, and offering recognition and praise for their hard work in therapy.

Clients might feel understandably anxious about coping without the therapist once therapy ends. The therapy relationship might have been one of very few positive experiences of relating to others, and being listened to and believed. The therapist can help the client prepare practically for how they will continue to use helpful strategies and work towards goals that they have been making progress with; for example, using a blueprint and developing a pack of resources that they can refer to in future. Clients with psychosis often have memory and cognitive difficulties, and attention may need to be paid to what support or resources the client might need to rise to the challenge of being their own therapist. For example, audio recordings or a CD summarising the key messages of therapy; coping cards; brief and clear blueprints and relapse prevention plans can all be useful.

The therapist might also, if appropriate, support the client to reflect on their experience of the relationship with the therapist and whether this experience has provided any new learning or evidence to counter previous beliefs and appraisals. For example, the therapist could help the client draw out key messages such as: 'I've learned I'm not crazy,' 'I've learned I can relate to others despite my difficulties,' 'I might assume others won't believe or understand me, but I might be wrong,' 'I know now that not everyone intends me harm.' This use of the therapy relationship as a place to test interpersonal beliefs may be especially useful for clients experiencing paranoia. The therapist might be able to help the client reflect on changes in the relationship with the therapist over time (e.g. 'were you able to trust me more than you had anticipated?' or 'did I respond differently to things you shared than you had expected?'). For more on interpersonal beliefs and schemas, please refer to Chapter 3 in this text.

CHAPTER SUMMARY

Many people with psychosis experience stigma and can be overwhelmed and frightened by their experiences. Paying close attention to the therapeutic relationship is essential if the therapist is to create an atmosphere of trust, empathy and validation. However, in CBTp, the therapeutic relationship cannot merely be achieved in the engagement phase and then taken for granted. The therapist must continue to be mindful of challenges to the relationship, which may occur due to fluctuations in symptoms or past difficulties with relationships. In particular, the therapeutic relationship is vital when working with the client to create a helpful psychological model of their difficulties without invalidating their own deeply held understanding. It is also vital in moving to an intervention stage, where the therapist is asking the client to take significant risks in the face of frightening and overwhelming experiences. Despite the challenges, evidence and clinical practice show that excellent therapeutic relationships can be formed in CBTp and are the basis of successful therapy.

FURTHER READING

Brabban A, Byrne R, Longden E and Morrison AP (2017) The importance of human relationships, ethics and recovery-orientated values in the delivery of CBT for people with psychosis. *Psychosis* 9: 157–166.

Describes the central values underpinning CBTp.

Chadwick P (2006) Relationship building, therapist assumptions and radical collaboration. In: Chadwick P (ed) *Person-Based Cognitive Therapy for Distressing Psychosis.* Wiley: London, UK.

Guidance on building open and collaborative relationships in CBTp.

Johns L, Jolley S, Keen N and Peters E (2013) CBT with People with Psychosis. In: Whittington A and Grey N (eds) *How to Become a More Effective CBT Therapist: Mastering Metacompetence in Clinical Practice.* Wiley: London, UK.

Provides a detailed description of CBT for psychosis.

REFERENCES

Baumeister D, Sedgwick O, Howes O and Peters E (2017) Auditory verbal hallucinations and continuum models of psychosis: A systematic review of the healthy voice-hearer literature. *Clinical Psychology Review 51*: 125–141.

Berry K, Barrowclough C and Wearden A (2007) A review of the role of adult attachment style in psychosis: unexplored issues and questions for further research. *Clinical Psychology Review 27*(4): 458–475.

Brabban A, Byrne R, Longden E and Morrison AP (2017) The importance of human relationships, ethics and recovery-orientated values in the delivery of CBT for people with psychosis. *Psychosis 9*(2): 157–166.

Chadwick P, Williams C and Mackenzie J (2003) Impact of case formulation in cognitive behaviour therapy for psychosis. *Behaviour Research and Therapy 41*(6): 671–680.

Coursey RD, Keller AB and Farrell EW (1995) Individual psychotherapy and persons with serious mental illness: The clients' perspective. *Schizophrenia Bulletin 21*: 283–301.

Couture SM, Roberts DL, Penn DL, Cather C, Otto MW and Goff D (2006) Do baseline client characteristics predict the therapeutic alliance in the treatment of schizophrenia? *The Journal of Nervous and Mental Disease 194*(1): 10–14.

Davies D (1996) Towards a model of gay affirmative therapy. In: Davies D and Neal C (eds) *Pink Therapy: A Guide for Counselors and Therapists Working With Lesbian, Gay, and Bisexual clients.* Buckingham, England: Open University Press, pp. 24–40.

Dunn G, Fowler D, Rollinson R, Freeman D, Kuipers E, Smith B ... and Bebbington P (2012) Effective elements of cognitive behaviour therapy for psychosis: results of a novel type of subgroup analysis based on principal stratification. *Psychological Medicine 42*(5): 1057–1068.

Evans-Jones C, Peters E and Barker C (2009) The therapeutic relationship in CBT for psychosis: client, therapist and therapy factors. *Behavioural and Cognitive Psychotherapy 37*(5): 527–540.

Garety PA and Hardy A (2017) The clinical relevance of appraisals of psychotic experiences. *World Psychiatry 16*(2): 140–141.

Garety PA, Kuipers E, Fowler D, Freeman D and Bebbington PE (2001) A cognitive model of the positive symptoms of psychosis. *Psychological Medicine 31*(2): 189–195.

González-Torres MA, Oraa R, Arístegui M, Fernández-Rivas A and Guimon J (2007) Stigma and discrimination towards people with schizophrenia and their family members. *Social Psychiatry and Psychiatric Epidemiology 42*(1): 14–23.

Gumley A and Schwannauer M (2006) *Staying Well After Psychosis: A Cognitive Interpersonal Approach to Recovery and Relapse Prevention.* Chichester, UK: John Wiley & Sons.

Gumley AI, Taylor HEF, Schwannauer M and MacBeth A (2014) A systematic review of attachment and psychosis: measurement, construct validity and outcomes. *Acta Psychiatrica Scandinavica 129*(4): 257–274.

Hoaas LEC, Lindholm SE, Berge T and Hagen R (2011) The therapeutic alliance in cognitive behavioural therapy for psychosis. In: Hagen R, Turkington D, Berge T and Grawe R (eds) *CBT for Psychosis: A Symptom-based Approach.* London, UK: Routledge.

Johns L, Jolley S, Keen N and Peters E (2014) CBT with People with Psychosis. In: Whittington A and Grey N (eds) *How to Become a More Effective CBT Therapist: Mastering Metacompetence in Clinical Practice*. Chichester, UK: John Wiley & Sons.

Kilbride M, Byrne R, Price J, Wood L, Barratt S, Welford M and Morrison AP (2013) Exploring service users' perceptions of cognitive behavioural therapy for psychosis: A user led study. *Behavioural and Cognitive Psychotherapy 41*(1): 89–102.

McGowan JF, Lavender T and Garety PA (2005) Factors in outcome of cognitive behavioural therapy for psychosis: Users' and clinicians' views. *Psychology and Psychotherapy: Theory, Research and Practice 78*(4): 513–529.

Messari S and Hallam R (2003) CBT for psychosis: A qualitative analysis of clients' experiences. *British Journal of Clinical Psychology 42*(2): 171–188.

Morrison AP (2001) The interpretation of intrusions in psychosis: an integrative cognitive approach to hallucinations and delusions. *Behavioural and Cognitive Psychotherapy 29*(3): 257–276.

Morrison AP (2017) A manualised treatment protocol to guide delivery of evidence-based cognitive therapy for people with distressing psychosis: learning from clinical trials. *Psychosis 9*: 1–11.

Morrison AP and Barratt S (2010) What are the components of CBT for Psychosis? A Delphi study. *Schizophrenia Bulletin 36*: 136–142.

Rodrigues R and Anderson KK (2017) The traumatic experience of first-episode psychosis: A systematic review and meta-analysis. *Schizophrenia Research 189*: 27–36.

Selten JP and Cantor-Graae E (2005) Social defeat: risk factor for schizophrenia? *The British Journal of Psychiatry 187*(2): 101–102.

Sen D (2017) What stays unsaid in therapeutic relationships. *Psychosis 9*(1): 90–94.

Startup M, Jackson M, Rollinson R, Smith B, Jolley S, Steel C, Onwumere J and Fowler D (2007) *Revised Cognitive Therapy For Psychosis Adherence Scale Manual.* Unpublished material.

Svensson B and Hansson L (1999) Therapeutic alliance in cognitive therapy for schizophrenic and other long-term mentally ill patients: development and relationship to outcome in an in-patient treatment programme. *Acta Psychiatrica Scandinavica 99*: 281–287.

Varese F, Smeets F, Drukker M, Lieverse R, Lataster T, Viechtbauer W, ... and Bentall RP (2012) Childhood adversities increase the risk of psychosis: a meta-analysis of patient-control, prospective-and cross-sectional cohort studies. *Schizophrenia Bulletin 38*(4): 661–671.

Wood L, Burke E and Morrison A (2015) Individual cognitive behavioural therapy for psychosis (CBTp): a systematic review of qualitative literature. *Behavioural and Cognitive Psychotherapy 43*(3): 285–297.

Woods A (2015) Voices, identity, and meaning-making. *The Lancet 386*(10011): 2386–2387.

Wright NP, Turkington D, Kelly OP, Davies D, Jacobs AM and Hopton J (2014) *Treating Psychosis: A Clinician's Guide to Integrating Acceptance and Commitment Therapy, Compassion-Focused Therapy, and Mindfulness Approaches Within the Cognitive Behavioral Therapy Tradition.* Oakland, California: New Harbinger Publications.

11

EATING DISORDERS

ULRIKE SCHMIDT

CHAPTER OVERVIEW

This chapter starts with an introduction to eating disorders (EDs) and their treatment. It then reviews illness-specific features that influence the therapeutic relationship and also therapist factors. This is followed by an overview of process and process-outcome studies assessing the impact of the therapeutic relationship in different EDs, across different types of therapies, but with emphasis on CBT. The chapter finishes with a review of factors that help build and maintain the therapeutic relationship in EDs and recommendations for therapists.

EATING DISORDERS AND THEIR TREATMENT

The EDs, anorexia nervosa (AN), bulimia nervosa (BN) and binge eating disorder (BED), are common mental disorders affecting mainly young women in their teens and twenties. EDs can be conceptualised as being on a spectrum of over- and under-eating. This is associated with changes in weight and in how salient/rewarding food is to the person. The latter manifests in a number of ways, for example, as a dread of food or a phobic avoidance of eating or of fullness or fatness. Alternatively, there may be an excessive desire to eat, eating large quantities of highly palatable foods with a sense of loss of control, or a mixture of both dread and desire and over- and under-consumption. In addition, an overvaluation of body weight, shape and appearance is usually present. In a proportion of patients, there are other symptoms designed to counteract the effects of eating, such as self-induced vomiting, over-exercise or purging. Effective treatments are available for some of the EDs. A specific ED-focused form of CBT (enhanced CBT or CBT-E; Fairburn, 2008), delivered face-to-face or via various self-care formats, is the treatment of choice for adolescents and adults with BN and BED, with good acceptability and efficacy (National Institute for Health and Care Excellence, 2017).

While family-based interventions are generally recommended in the treatment of adolescents with AN (Treasure et al., 2015; Zipfel et al., 2015), for adults with AN there is a range of individual psychological therapies with comparable efficacy but putative different mechanisms of action. These prominently include CBT-E, the Maudsley Model of Anorexia Treatment for Adults (MANTRA; Schmidt et al., 2014, 2015, 2016), Specialist Supportive Clinical Management (SSCM; Byrne et al., 2017; McIntosh et al., 2006), and focal psychodynamic psychotherapy (Zipfel et al., 2014) (for review see Brockmeyer et al., 2017).

What follows will mainly focus on AN, which is arguably most challenging to therapists. However, where available, evidence related to BN and BED will also be presented.

FEATURES OF EDS THAT INFLUENCE THE THERAPEUTIC RELATIONSHIP

ILLNESS AND PATIENT FEATURES

Anorexia nervosa is a highly visible illness, which elicits strong emotional responses from others ranging from admiration, concern and compassion to shock, horror and disgust.

Aspects of the disorder often become highly valued by the person, including issues of control, safety, predictability, conveying the visible message that all is not well and the numbing of emotions. These valued features may lead to the formation of meta-beliefs about the utility of the illness to the person (e.g. 'anorexia keeps me safe and tells others that I am not well,' 'without anorexia I'd be lost;' Schmidt and Treasure 2006; Schmidt et al., 2014). It follows that people with AN are reluctant to change, and it is often close others who are concerned and urge the person into accepting treatment.

People with AN have broad impairments in recognising, allowing, managing and expressing emotions, and this profoundly affects their relationships (Davies et al., 2016; Oldershaw et al., 2011; 2015; Treasure and Schmidt, 2013). This may make it difficult for them to read and process others' expressions of emotions (including their therapist's) but also makes it difficult for the therapist to assess the emotions of the person sitting in front of them. Patients with AN may wrongly be seen as 'ice queens,' as on the surface they may display little or no emotions whereas underneath they have very strong and intense emotions. They often hold beliefs suggesting it is not safe to express their emotions (Oldershaw et al., 2015). Examination of the core schemata prevalent in AN include defectiveness, subjugation and social isolation as the ones most commonly endorsed (Oldershaw et al., 2015). Thus, in terms of their interpersonal behaviour, people with AN often try to please and placate others, whilst privately 'seething.'

In addition, certain cognitive features are common, most prominently cognitive rigidity and an exaggerated focus on detail at the expense of the bigger picture (Treasure and Schmidt, 2013; Wu et al., 2014). These are often underpinned by highly perfectionist traits with extreme and unrealistic personal standards and a fear of making mistakes (Lloyd et al., 2014). Extreme criticism of self and (often somewhat hidden) also of others may make the therapist feel under scrutiny.

Together, these factors present the therapist with a formidable challenge in building a relationship, with significant potential for misunderstandings and subsequent ruptures in the therapeutic relationship. Ruptures may take time to heal, as patients may feel very hurt, distrustful and bear grudges. As EDs affect mainly adolescents and emerging adults, therapists are often seen as powerful authority figures. This view may be further enhanced by desperate family members who threaten the person with AN that if they continue to lose weight they will be 'locked up' in hospital and 'made to eat.'

THERAPIST FACTORS

STIGMATISATION

All EDs are highly stigmatised, with males displaying more stigmatising attitudes than females (e.g. Griffiths et al., 2014). Thus, therapists may also hold stigmatising views. Compared to people with major depression or schizophrenia, ED sufferers are viewed as being to blame for their condition, as attention-seeking and as less impaired (e.g. Ebneter and Latner, 2013). Those with AN are seen as vain and irritating but also as admirable, with aspects that are worth emulating. In contrast, those who are overweight or obese are seen as lacking self-discipline (Ebneter and Latner, 2013). Thus therapists, especially those who are struggling with their own weight or have never been concerned about their weight and eating, will need to be aware of any stigmatising attitudes they may hold.

CLINICIAN BELIEFS, ATTITUDES AND EMOTIONS ABOUT EDS AND THEIR TREATMENT

Key features of CBT for EDs include regular collaborative weighing at the beginning of each session (e.g. to disconfirm unhelpful beliefs about small changes in food intake leading to massive weight gain) and the introduction of regular meals to help normalise weight and reduce the likelihood of binges. For some patients, these aspects of treatment are difficult and anxiety provoking. This may, in turn, contribute to therapists' preference for other elements of therapy (e.g. understanding the patient's background, focusing on motivation) and avoiding therapy elements focusing on behaviour change, and labelling them as potentially alienating, distressing or threatening the therapeutic relationship (Waller, 2016).

WHAT DO WE KNOW ABOUT THE THERAPEUTIC RELATIONSHIP IN EDS?

PROCESS AND PROCESS-OUTCOME STUDIES

Across different studies assessing therapy process in different psychotherapies, there is consensus about the importance of the therapeutic relationship as central to a successful treatment of AN (e.g. Oyer et al., 2016; Sibeoni et al., 2017; Zainal et al., 2016).

Likewise, a small qualitative study of bulimia patients treated with CBT-E suggested that a good therapeutic relationship is a key feature, highlighting both expertise and empathy as contributing to this (Onslow et al., 2016).

Early studies on the associations between the therapeutic relationship/alliance and outcome in EDs have had contradictory findings (Brauhardt et al., 2014; Zaitsoff et al., 2015). Some authors found that the alliance is not, or is negatively, associated with outcome (Brown et al., 2013a,b) whereas others found the opposite (Mander et al., 2017; Tasca and Lampard, 2012). These discrepant results may be due to methodological differences such as patient demographic and illness characteristics, treatment type and setting, drop-out rates and rater perspective.

A recent meta-analysis of ED studies examined the relationship between symptom change and alliance over time (Graves et al., 2017). The study found a bi-directional relationship between symptoms and alliance. Irrespective of ED diagnosis and treatment type, overall symptom change and, in addition, specifically early symptom change were associated with subsequent alliance ratings. Conversely, early alliance changes also predicted later symptom changes. Early alliance showed weaker associations with symptom change in more behaviourally oriented therapies. Early alliance was particularly strongly related to symptom change in younger patients and in those with AN (Graves et al., 2017).

Three further studies addressed links between alliance and symptom change in different ED populations and found either an impact of the alliance on outcome (Accurso et al., 2015; likewise, Tasca et al., 2016) or a reciprocal relationship between alliance and symptoms (Vrabel et al., 2015).

A large transdiagnostic study of patients with EDs, depression or somatoform disorders found that patients in all three groups experienced similarly positive alliances and showed similar alliance outcome associations (Mander et al., 2017). This study also examined correspondence between patients' and therapists' alliance ratings and found some disorder-specific differences. The authors conclude that feedback about any such (in)congruence might be helpful for therapists, as previous meta-analyses of studies of alliance trajectories and their correspondence found that the stronger the correspondence, the better the outcome (Mander et al., 2017).

WHAT CAN BE DONE TO BUILD THE THERAPEUTIC RELATIONSHIP IN EDS?

THERAPIST AWARENESS OF THEIR OWN ATTITUDES TO EDS AND THEIR TREATMENT

A key issue for therapists working with EDs is to reflect on their own attitudes to underweight and overweight/obese patients and their own eating behaviours. Like many people in modern society, psychotherapists also often struggle with their weight and eating and may have unresolved 'hang-ups' about these.

Answer the questions in the text box below to assess whether you hold unhelpful beliefs that may interfere with the treatment of a particular patient. If so, consider discussing this in supervision.

Reflective questions

- Do I secretly admire my patient's underweight figure?
- Am I critical, or even contemptuous, of my obese patient because of their weight and eating?

- If you draw a blank with these overt questions, try the following: What adjectives would I use to describe my patient's appearance to myself? Do these provide pointers towards attitudes I hold, e.g. overprotective, admiring, critical, shocked, horrified or disgusted? How do these attitudes affect my behaviour towards this patient?
- What are my views about my own weight, shape and behaviour? Do I have issues around my own appearance that I find hard to deal with? Do I ever eat chaotically, unhealthily, too much or too little? Do I drink too much? What are my views on physical activity and exercise? Do I have a healthy lifestyle? How does that affect the way I talk with my patients and the advice I give them?
- Am I frightened of offering and being firm around potentially helpful interventions (i.e. focusing on behavioural change) because I fear the patient will 'run a mile.' What does that say about me and my attitudes to them? Who am I protecting here?
- Am I mirroring my patient's perfectionist attitudes and therefore delaying introducing certain therapeutic procedures (e.g. working on the case formulation) because I feel I do not know enough about the patient yet and need to strive harder to provide them with the perfect formulation?

BUILDING A SHARED UNDERSTANDING OF RECOVERY AND CARE AT THE BEGINNING OF TREATMENT

A recent study of patients who resisted engagement in therapy suggests that a shared understanding between patients and health professionals about the function of the ED may avoid conflict and provide a pathway to treatment and to building the therapeutic relationship (Musolino et al., 2016), a view that is echoed by others (Sibeoni et al., 2017). The distinctive therapeutic style and well-defined clinical procedures of motivational interviewing (MI; Miller and Rollnick, 2012) may be helpful in facilitating a shared understanding of recovery and care. MI encompasses a collaborative conversation style for strengthening a person's motivation and commitment to change. It combines relational (empathy, respect for patient autonomy) and technical elements (open questions, affirmation, simple and complex reflections, summarising) to create a safe atmosphere for patients to verbalise personal values, capacities and reasons regarding behaviour change. The key mechanism is thought to be increasing 'change talk' and reducing 'sustain talk.' Whilst a collaborative and empathic style is also part of CBT, the distinctive therapeutic style and well-defined clinical procedures of MI are not necessarily inherent in the routine practice of CBT (Wilson and Schlam, 2004). The therapeutic scenario below illustrates how MI can help the therapist make their opening moves during the initial assessment with a reluctant patient. Commentary on what the therapist is trying to achieve is inserted after each segment. However, a full explanation of a MI style and technique is beyond the scope of this chapter. The interested reader is referred to the classic text by Miller and Rollnick (2012).

Case study

Building a shared understanding of recovery and care at the beginning of treatment

Chloe is an 18-year-old first year economics student who has been referred by her GP to the ED team. Shortly after she started her course and moved away from home eight months ago, her father had a heart attack and nearly died. Since then, Chloe has become obsessed with living healthily and has increasingly restricted her food intake and walks and cycles three hours a day. She has steadily lost weight and her current BMI is 16 kg/m^2. Prior to starting university, her weight was normal. Her GP has diagnosed anorexia nervosa. She is now attending an outpatient assessment with a view to starting outpatient psychological therapy.

Therapist: Thank you for coming to the appointment with me today. I wonder whether you could tell me how you came to be here?

Chloe: I very nearly didn't come. I didn't want to come.

The therapist starts with an open question.

Therapist: I appreciate you being so honest with me and letting me know that you really, really don't want to be here.

The therapist reflects on the patient's emotion and they also exaggerate Chloe's reluctance (in the hope that this will allow her to reduce this or expand on it).

Chloe: I am really just here because of my mum – she made me come because she was worried. She had been on at me for quite a while, saying that I am not eating properly and that I am too thin. In the end I couldn't take her nagging any more and I went to see our GP with her and he wrote the referral to you. I know I have lost some weight, but I don't really think there is anything wrong with that. I am perfectly fine. I think I am wasting your time.

Therapist: So what you are saying is that you just played along with the referral to keep your mum and your GP happy and that you don't have a clue what all the fuss is about.

The patient minimises any concerns. The therapist again reflects on the patient's emotion and minimises more (again in the hope that this will allow her to expand and express some concerns). Note, the therapist does not go down the route of exploring the mother's or the GP's concerns which, from the patient's perspective, might easily be perceived as everyone 'ganging up against her.'

Chloe: That's right.

Therapist: That must be confusing, other people around you are concerned and you don't have any concerns whatsoever.

The therapist again reflects on the patient's emotion and minimises more. With very ambivalent patients, there is often this delicate dance at the beginning of the meeting.

Chloe: Well, sometimes I am a bit worried because since I started losing the weight I get tired quite easily now.

Therapist: Can you tell me a bit more about that?

Now, for the first time, Chloe expresses a concern, i.e. her tiredness. The therapist uses the opportunity to get her to expand.

Chloe: Well, I am supposed to study for my first year exams at Uni, but I can't really concentrate on my studies at all. I sit down for 15 to 20 minutes at a time and that's it. My brain just goes fuzzy.

Therapist: That sounds really tough, with you trying so hard to study and not managing to. Are there other changes that you have noticed since your weight has gone down?

The therapist empathises with Chloe's concern, and then broadens the conversation to elicit other concerns. This avoids a premature focus on just one concern. Note also the therapist's use of language here, which is neutral, i.e. 'change' rather than 'concern.'

Chloe: Well, I do feel really cold all the time; at home it is alright, I can put the heater on full blast, but in my student lodgings at Uni, I am never warm enough.

Therapist: That sounds rather miserable to feel so cold all the time.

Chloe: Yes!

Therapist: Do you mind me asking about a couple of other things that people often say they notice when they have lost some weight?

The therapist then systematically asks about a whole range of life domains that may be affected by AN, including physical and psychological health, family, social and romantic relationships, work and study and other aspects of life. By now, Chloe is more willing to be open about how her AN is affecting her. The therapist also asks whether there are any positive aspects of AN. This whole sequence may take 10 to 15 minutes to complete, and at the end, the therapist summarises their understanding, maintaining a respectful, tentative stance.

Therapist: If I have understood you right, your dad's heart attack has really made you rethink your own lifestyle and has made you determined to live what you have called 'super-healthily' and you have cut out increasingly more things from your diet and got into a very strict daily exercise routine. From what you were telling me, part of you feels proud and pleased about this, and you have felt very safe with your new found routines. At the same time, you have found yourself getting tired and cold a lot, you have noticed that your hair is falling out, that your nails are brittle, you no longer sleep so well and your periods have stopped. There have been arguments at home about you losing weight, and you have been concerned about how this is affecting your dad in particular. You no longer enjoy seeing your friends and find it a struggle to keep up with university assignments. You have also noticed that you are constantly thinking about food, what to eat, what not to eat, are constantly checking calories and your weight, and this is wearing you down and making you confused and exhausted. Have I got this right? Is this a fair summary of our discussion?

Chloe: Yes, it is. Whoa, when you say it like this, I can see how much all of this has been affecting me. What can be done about it?

Therapist: Well, in the first instance it would be really important for us to talk more about how things got to this point, and also for me to get a colleague to check your physical health, so that we then can make a good plan together where to go from here? How does that sound? Are you ok with that?

The therapist provides the beginnings of a shared understanding of what is the problem and sets the tone for all further interactions between Chloe and her therapist. Critically, this emphasises the therapist's willingness to respect the patient's autonomy, checking in with them, giving them options and providing advice after obtaining the patient's permission to do so. In what follows, the therapist can then probe a lot more into how AN has helped or hindered the patient in their life, what mattered to the person before the onset of their illness and what are their hopes and aspirations for the future.

STRENGTHENING THE RELATIONSHIP DURING THERAPY

As treatment continues, a collaboratively constructed case formulation, from which the focus, goals and tasks for the treatment emerge, will be developed. Very often what emerges from this is that AN seemingly provides a solution to some of life's problems, whilst also getting in the way of the person's aspirations and the kind of person they want to be. Once this has been laid out, questions can be asked on how the patient might be able to get what AN provides them (e.g. to feel safe, to feel noticed or special, to get others to see their distress) in different ways and how they can start mapping out a path towards fulfilling their aspirations (i.e. getting a bigger life). This then paves the way for getting to an agreement on the need to include gradual behavioural change, i.e. working on regaining a healthy or healthier weight and eating, with specific goals and tasks relating to this as an important part of the focus of the work. However, it is the jointly agreed overall direction of travel (i.e. determined by the patient's aspirations for their life) together with a consistent motivational stance of the therapist that underpin all the smaller process goals and shore up the therapeutic relationship when the going gets tough and the patient gets more anxious about change. In this context, Dr Lucy Serpell (personal communication), an ED researcher who has done a lot of work understanding how patients perceive the pros and cons of AN and associated decision making (Serpell et al., 2003, 2004), typically asks her patients whether today/this week is a day/week for pushing forward or for going more slowly. Whilst, in working towards behavioural change, consistency is important, this question puts the patient in the driving seat and gets them to reaffirm their commitment to change.

THERAPIST WRITINGS

Therapist letters to the patient, to summarise the case formulation and again to say goodbye at the end of treatment, are part of cognitive analytical therapy and the Maudsley Model of Anorexia Treatment (Schmidt et al., 2015, 2016). Qualitative studies of patients receiving MANTRA suggest that they highly value receiving formulation and end of treatment letters. Two studies (Allen et al., 2016; Simmonds et al., in preparation) have examined the quality of these letters using a specifically designed rating scheme that assessed model adherence, content and therapist stance. Formulation letters that paid attention to the patient's story and development of their ED were associated with greater treatment adherence, and those that had a more reflective or respectful tone were associated with better ED outcomes (Allen et al., 2016). End-of-treatment letters that were more affirmative were associated with better outcomes at one-year follow-up and similar trends at two years (Simmonds et al., in preparation). Taken together, these findings provide preliminary evidence to suggest that therapist writing is valued by patients, that the style of writing matters and that writing is helpful in building a stronger alliance and improving outcome. The text box below illustrates elements of the quality assessment of therapeutic letters and what constituted high quality in relation to writing about the patient's story, a reflective and respectful or affirming style.

Examples of more or less helpful style in therapist writing (from Allen et al., 2016)

Developmental aspect: The letter mentions 'what the patient brings to the illness' i.e. traits, key challenges in their life, strengths and supports. Where this is done well, this will go beyond description of the patient as anxious or perfectionist but will give some illustration of the extent of this and where this has mattered in their life.

- 0 = no mention of this
- 1 = description or list without illustration or without mentioning the impact on the patient's life
- 2 = illustration of the extent OR impact on life
- 3 = fully including illustration of BOTH the extent and how this has impacted e.g. 'even as a child you always were anxious about pleasing people, which included eating healthily in order to please your parents. Over your lifetime, this characteristic has often caused you to be upset about having possibly offended or hurt someone, and currently, this opens the door to binges when you are upset about this.'

Reflective, respectful of patient's views, and/or adopting one-down position (e.g. 'this is my attempt to understand you ... I may not have got it all right ...' Includes using tentative language, putting forward hypotheses, e.g. 'I wonder ...', 'I sense ...'... 'Perhaps' .....).

- 0 = language placing the therapist as the expert
- 1 = no use of one-down position or tentative language
- 2 = some use of one-down position or tentative language but somewhat formulaic
- 3 = reflective, respectful, one-down position permeates the letter, e.g. 'I look forward to our future sessions where we will work towards your goals and aspirations, should you feel that you are now ready to allow anorexia to loosen its grip.'

Affirming stance: Use of affirmation, i.e. positively and warmly connoting the patient's efforts (e.g. 'I have been very impressed by ...')

- 0 = presence of any negative statements/connotations
- 1 = no affirmative statements
- 2 = some use of affirmative statements but somewhat formulaic
- 3 = affirmation permeates letter, e.g. 'I have been very impressed with how, despite your difficulty with opening up to others and accepting help, you have made use of your best friend for support. Moreover, despite your misgivings of letting your mum into things, you have gone to stay with your parents twice over the summer and this has gone much better than you thought. You allowed yourself to be guided by your mum with regard to your eating and felt physically much better as a result.'

THERAPIST SELF-DISCLOSURE

Therapist self-disclosure is a controversial topic in psychotherapy. Two studies have suggested that therapist self-disclosure may be helpful in building a positive alliance in EDs (Oyer et al., 2016; Simonds and Spokes, 2017), in particular therapists' expressing positive feelings towards the participant, talking about their therapeutic orientation/training, their life experiences, personal background and mistakes they had made. The latter, in particular, is of interest in the context of modeling 'being good enough' to what are often highly perfectionist patients.

CHAPTER SUMMARY

Whilst there is a bi-directional relationship between the therapeutic alliance and treatment outcome in EDs, the strength of the alliance early on in treatment seems to matter particularly in AN and in younger patients. This is unsurprising, as symptoms in AN are often valued and patients often feel pushed by others into accepting treatment, and unless this is addressed early on, it will get in the way of treatment. It is therefore vital to spend time building a joint understanding of recovery and the model of care. Therapists can use the techniques and stance of MI as a complement to CBT to start building a shared conceptualisation of what the problem is and how it might be tackled. Additional techniques, such as therapeutic letter writing, may also be helpful in building and maintaining a helpful alliance that allows patients to make necessary changes.

FURTHER READING

Allen KL, O'Hara CB, Bartholdy S, Renwick B, Keyes A, Lose A, Kenyon M, DeJong H, Broadbent H, Loomes R, McClelland J, Serpell L, Richards L, Johnson-Sabine E, Boughton N, Whitehead L, Treasure J, Wade T and Schmidt U (2016) Written case formulations in the treatment of anorexia nervosa: Evidence for therapeutic benefits. *International Journal of Eating Disorders* 49(9): 874–882.

Graves TA, Tabri N, Thompson-Brenner H, Franko DL, Eddy KT, Bourion-Bedes S, Brown A, Constantino MJ, Flückiger C, Forsberg S, Isserlin L, Couturier J, Paulson Karlsson G, Mander J, Teufel M, Mitchell JE, Crosby RD, Prestano C, Satir DA, Simpson S, Sly R, Lacey JH, Stiles-Shields C, Tasca GA, Waller G, Zaitsoff SL, Rienecke R, Le Grange D and Thomas JJ (2017) A meta-analysis of the relation between therapeutic alliance and treatment outcome in eating disorders. *International Journal of Eating Disorders* 50(4): 323–340.

Waller G (2016) Treatment Protocols for Eating Disorders: Clinicians' Attitudes, Concerns, Adherence and Difficulties Delivering Evidence-Based Psychological Interventions. *Current Psychiatry Reports* 18(4): 36.

REFERENCES

Accurso EC, Fitzsimmons-Craft EE, Ciao A, Cao L, Crosby RD, Smith TL, Klein MH, Mitchell JE, Crow SJ, Wonderlich SA and Peterson CB (2015) Therapeutic alliance in a randomized clinical trial for bulimia nervosa. *Journal of Consulting and Clinical Psychology 83*(3): 637–642.

Allen KL, O'Hara CB, Bartholdy S, Renwick B, Keyes A, Lose A, Kenyon M, DeJong H, Broadbent H, Loomes R, McClelland J, Serpell L, Richards L, Johnson-Sabine E, Boughton N,

Whitehead L, Treasure J, Wade T and Schmidt U (2016) Written case formulations in the treatment of anorexia nervosa: Evidence for therapeutic benefits. *International Journal of Eating Disorders 49*(9): 874–882.

Brauhardt A, de Zwaan M and Hilbert A (2014) The therapeutic process in psychological treatments for eating disorders: a systematic review. *International Journal of Eating Disorders 47*(6): 565–584.

Brockmeyer T, Friederich HC and Schmidt U (2017) Advances in the treatment of anorexia nervosa: a review of established and emerging interventions. *Psychological Medicine 11*: 1–37.

Brown A, Mountford V and Waller G (2013a) Therapeutic alliance and weight gain during cognitive behavioural therapy for anorexia nervosa. *Behavioural Research Therapy* 51(4–5): 216–220.

Brown A, Mountford VA and Waller G (2013b) Is the therapeutic alliance overvalued in the treatment of eating disorders? *International Journal of Eating Disorders 46*(8): 779–782.

Byrne S, Wade T, Hay P, Touyz S, Fairburn CG, Treasure J, Schmidt U, McIntosh V, Allen K, Fursland A and Crosby RD (2017) A randomised controlled trial of three psychological treatments for anorexia nervosa. *Psychological Medicine 29*: 1–11.

Davies H, Wolz I, Leppanen J, Fernandez-Aranda F, Schmidt U and Tchanturia K (2016) Facial expression to emotional stimuli in non-psychotic disorders: A systematic review and meta-analysis. *Neuroscience & Biobehavioural Reviews 64*: 252–271.

Ebneter DS and Latner JD (2013) Stigmatizing attitudes differ across mental health disorders: a comparison of stigma across eating disorders, obesity, and major depressive disorder. *The Journal of Nervous and Mental Disease 201*(4): 281–285.

Fairburn CG (2008) *Cognitive Behaviour Therapy and Eating Disorders*. New York: Guilford Press.

Graves TA, Tabri N, Thompson-Brenner H, Franko DL, Eddy KT, Bourion-Bedes S, Brown A, Constantino MJ, Flückiger C, Forsberg S, Isserlin L, Couturier J, Paulson Karlsson G, Mander J, Teufel M, Mitchell JE, Crosby RD, Prestano C, Satir DA, Simpson S, Sly R, Lacey JH, Stiles-Shields C, Tasca GA, Waller G, Zaitsoff SL, Rienecke R, Le Grange D and Thomas JJ (2017) A meta-analysis of the relation between therapeutic alliance and treatment outcome in eating disorders. *International Journal of Eating Disorders 50*(4): 323–340.

Griffiths S, Mond JM, Murray SB and Touyz S (2014) Young peoples' stigmatizing attitudes and beliefs about anorexia nervosa and muscle dysmorphia. *International Journal of Eating Disorders 47*(2): 189–195.

Lloyd S, Yiend J, Schmidt U and Tchanturia K (2014) Perfectionism in anorexia nervosa: novel performance based evidence. *PLoS One 9*(10): e111697.

Mander J, Neubauer AB, Schlarb A, Teufel M, Bents H, Hautzinger M, Zipfel S, Wittorf A and Sammet I (2017) The therapeutic alliance in different mental disorders: A comparison of patients with depression, somatoform, and eating disorders. *Psychology and Psychotherapy 90*(4): 649–667.

McIntosh VV, Jordan J, Luty SE, Carter FA, McKenzie JM, Bulik CM and Joyce PR (2006) Specialist supportive clinical management for anorexia nervosa. *International Journal of Eating Disorders 39*(8): 625–632.

Miller WR and Rollnick S (2012) *Motivational Interviewing: Helping People Change*. 3rd Edition. Guilford Press, New York.

Musolino C, Warin M, Wade T and Gilchrist P (2016) Developing shared understandings of recovery and care: a qualitative study of women with eating disorders who resist therapeutic care. *Journal of Eating Disorders 16*(4): 36.

National Institute for Health and Care Excellence (2017) Eating Disorders: Recognition and Treatment. *NICE guideline (NG69, May 2017)*.

Oldershaw A, Hambrook D, Stahl D, Tchanturia K, Treasure J and Schmidt U (2011) The socio-emotional processing stream in anorexia nervosa. *Neuroscience & Biobehavioural Reviews 35*(3): 970–988.

Oldershaw A, Lavender T, Sallis H, Stahl D and Schmidt U (2015) Emotion generation and regulation in anorexia nervosa: A systematic review and meta-analysis of self-report data. *Clinical Psychology Review 39*: 83–95.

Onslow L, Woodward D, Hoefkens T and Waddington L (2016) Experiences of enhanced cognitive behaviour therapy for bulimia nervosa. *Behavioural and Cognitive Psychotherapy 44*(2): 168–178.

Oyer L, O'Halloran MS and Christoe-Frazier L (2016) Understanding the working alliance with clients diagnosed with anorexia nervosa. *Eating Disorders 24*(2): 121–137.

Schmidt U and Treasure J (2006) Anorexia nervosa: valued and visible. A cognitive-interpersonal maintenance model and its implications for research and practice. *British Journal of Clinical Psychology 45*: 343–366.

Schmidt U, Magill N, Renwick B, Keyes A, Kenyon M, Dejong H, Lose A, Broadbent H, Loomes R, Yasin H, Watson C, Ghelani S, Bonin EM, Serpell L, Richards L, Johnson-Sabine E, Boughton N, Whitehead L, Beecham J, Treasure J and Landau S (2015) The Maudsley Outpatient Study of Treatments for Anorexia Nervosa and Related Conditions (MOSAIC): Comparison of the Maudsley Model of Anorexia Nervosa Treatment for Adults (MANTRA) with specialist supportive clinical management (SSCM) in outpatients with broadly defined anorexia nervosa: A randomized controlled trial. *Journal of Consulting and Clinical Psychology 83*(4): 796–807.

Schmidt U, Ryan EG, Bartholdy S, Renwick B, Keyes A, O'Hara C, McClelland J, Lose A, Kenyon M, Dejong H, Broadbent H, Loomes R, Serpell L, Richards L, Johnson-Sabine E, Boughton N, Whitehead L, Bonin E, Beecham J, Landau S and Treasure J (2016) Two-year follow-up of the MOSAIC trial: A multicenter randomized controlled trial comparing two psychological treatments in adult outpatients with broadly defined anorexia nervosa. *International Journal of Eating Disorders 49*(8): 793–800.

Schmidt U, Wade TD and Treasure J (2014) The Maudsley Model of Anorexia Nervosa Treatment for Adults (MANTRA): Development, Key Features and Preliminary Evidence. *Journal of Cognitive Psychotherapy 28*: 48–71.

Serpell L, Neiderman M, Haworth E, Emmanueli F and Lask B (2003) The use of the Pros and Cons of Anorexia Nervosa (P-CAN) Scale with children and adolescents. *Journal of Psychosomatic Research 54*(6): 567–571.

Serpell L, Teasdale JD, Troop NA and Treasure J (2004) The development of the P-CAN, a measure to operationalize the pros and cons of anorexia nervosa. *International Journal of Eating Disorders 36*(4): 416–433.

Sibeoni J, Orri M, Valentin M, Podlipski MA, Colin S, Pradere J and Revah-Levy A (2017) Metasynthesis of the Views about Treatment of Anorexia Nervosa in Adolescents: Perspectives of Adolescents, Parents, and Professionals. *PLoS One 12*(1): e0169493.

Simmonds J, Allen, K, O'Hara CB, Bartholdy S, Renwick B, Keyes A, Lose A, Kenyon M, DeJong H, Broadbent H, Loomes R, McClelland J, Serpell L, Richards L, Johnson-Sabine E, Boughton N, Whitehead L, Treasure J, Wade T and Schmidt U (2018) Therapist Written Goodbye Letters: Evidence for Therapeutic Benefits in the Treatment of Anorexia Nervosa. (In preparation)

Simonds LM and Spokes N (2017) Therapist self-disclosure and the therapeutic alliance in the treatment of eating problems. *Eating Disorders 25*(2): 151–164.

Tasca GA and Lampard AM (2012) Reciprocal influence of alliance to the group and outcome in day treatment for eating disorders. *Journal of Counseling Psychology 59*(4): 507–517.

Tasca GA, Compare A, Zarbo C and Brugnera A (2016) Therapeutic alliance and binge-eating outcomes in a group therapy context. *Journal of Counseling Psychology 63*(4): 443–451.

Treasure J and Schmidt U (2013) The cognitive-interpersonal maintenance model of anorexia nervosa revisited: a summary of the evidence for cognitive, socio-emotional and interpersonal predisposing and perpetuating factors. *Journal of Eating Disorders 1*: 13.

Treasure J, Zipfel S, Micali N, Wade T, Stice E, Claudino A, Schmidt U, Frank GK, Bulik CM and Wentz E (2015) Anorexia nervosa. *Nature Reviews Disease Primers 1*: 15074.

Vrabel KR, Ulvenes PG and Wampold B (2015) Alliance and symptom improvement in inpatient treatment for eating disorder patients: A study of within-patient processes. *International Journal of Eating Disorders 48*(8): 1113–1121.

Waller G (2016) Treatment Protocols for Eating Disorders: Clinicians' Attitudes, Concerns, Adherence and Difficulties Delivering Evidence-Based Psychological Interventions. *Current Psychiatry Reports 18*(4): 36.

Wilson GT and Schlam TR (2004) The transtheoretical model and motivational interviewing in the treatment of eating and weight disorders. *Clinical Psychology Review 24*(3): 361–378.

Wu M, Brockmeyer T, Hartmann M, Skunde M, Herzog W and Friederich HC (2014) Set-shifting ability across the spectrum of eating disorders and in overweight and obesity: a systematic review and meta-analysis. *Psychological Medicine 44*(16): 3365–3385.

Zainal KA, Renwick B, Keyes A, Lose A, Kenyon M, DeJong H, Broadbent H, Serpell L, Richards L, Johnson-Sabine E, Boughton N, Whitehead L, Treasure J, Schmidt U; MOSAIC trial group (2016) Process evaluation of the MOSAIC trial: treatment experience of two psychological therapies for out-patient treatment of Anorexia Nervosa. *Journal of Eating Disorders 4*: 2.

Zaitsoff S, Pullmer R, Cyr M and Aime H (2015) The role of the therapeutic alliance in eating disorder treatment outcomes: a systematic review. *Eating Disorders 23*(2): 99–114.

Zipfel S, Giel KE, Bulik CM, Hay P and Schmidt U (2015) Anorexia nervosa: aetiology, assessment, and treatment. *Lancet Psychiatry 2*(12): 1099–1111.

Zipfel S, Wild B, Groß G, Friederich HC, Teufel M, Schellberg D, Giel KE, de Zwaan M, Dinkel A, Herpertz S, Burgmer M, Löwe B, Tagay S, von Wietersheim J, Zeeck A, Schade-Brittinger C, Schauenburg H, Herzog W; ANTOP study group (2014) Focal psychodynamic therapy, cognitive behaviour therapy, and optimised treatment as usual in outpatients with anorexia nervosa (ANTOP study): randomised controlled trial. *Lancet 383*(9912): 127–137.

12

PHYSICAL ILLNESS AND PALLIATIVE CARE

STIRLING MOOREY AND KATHY BURN

CHAPTER OVERVIEW

This chapter will describe how the therapeutic relationship can be established, focusing on the important balance between empathy and validation on one hand, and effective problem-solving on the other. The value of including physical symptoms in the formulation from the outset is emphasised. CBT in physical illness requires the establishment of an empathic relationship in which the client feels understood but is also able to explore how their thoughts about their illness and their ways of coping may be contributing to their distress. Methods for preventing and managing alliance ruptures are discussed.

WORKING WITH PEOPLE WITH PHYSICAL ILLNESS

Most of us have had experience of illness ourselves or through an acquaintance, friend or family member. All of us will face our own death one day and lose those important to us. Working with people with life-altering or life-ending conditions evokes memories, fears and fantasies that can have a profound effect on how we relate to our patients. In Chapter 1, we explored some of the ways in which empathy can become problematic, such as when we over-empathise or empathise inaccurately. Empathy can be both a strength and a vulnerability when we work with physically unwell people. *Emotional empathy* - our innate capacity to resonate with another person's feelings - is vital to establish rapport. But, when a person is dying or their life situation is challenged, we may empathise and identify too closely with their sadness and become overwhelmed. We work in this field as we are empathic practitioners and much of what we see, or are alongside, is distressing. As our mood mirrors our patient's, we can lose our therapeutic optimism and be flooded with negative thoughts about the patient's condition, the relevance of therapy and our competence as a therapist. In the face of another's painful thoughts and feelings, we may react in one of two ways. We may either feel hopeless and distressed ourselves, or distance ourselves and cut off from the patient. We become less available as therapists, either because we feel low or overwhelmed and so cannot distance ourselves enough to think clearly, or because we have distanced ourselves too much as it is painful, so that we cannot be with the patient and show them that we are in tune with their distress. Another complication is that (because our feelings may be mirroring the patient's) we may assume that we know what they are thinking but, in fact, we are *mind reading* on the basis of our personal beliefs and fears. The 'closer to home' or more 'usual' the situation, the easier it is to slip into this trap. This is perhaps seen most starkly in the way we face the existential threat of death when working with dying patients. For instance, if we are working with a patient with cancer in palliative care, we may assume that, because we fear a particular aspect of death, this is what is driving the patient's fear. In fact, the concerns of people with advanced cancer are very varied (De Faye et al., 2006): 48% are worried they will be a burden to others, 42% are concerned about weakness and 17% are concerned for the future well-being of family members. Concerns about one's own death and dying are found in 40% of people; these include not being ready to dic, uncertainty about time/manner of death, being alone, concerns about an afterlife and concerns about not actually being dead. Each situation and each person's concerns are unique. It is therefore essential to allow space for the patient to express their feelings, and for them to explain the cognitive as well as the emotional content of their fears. The question can be phrased:

> 'Many of us have fears about dying, but for each of us they may be different. What is it about dying that is most frightening for you?'

Jenny had small cell lung cancer with brain metastases and was very breathless and unwell. She had finished chemotherapy and had a prognosis of a few weeks.

Many breathless people fear dying at the height of a breathless episode, breathing so fast their 'breathing switches off,' or their heart beats so fast 'it can't go on and so stops.' After careful listening, empathy and validation of her feelings, the therapist gently explored her worst fear. At the height of the breathless attack, her actual fear was that she would not get enough oxygen in her lungs and that this would cause long-term brain damage. Her worst fear was not of dying but of living in a vegetative state for years, unable to communicate her wishes: this was, in fact, what had happened to one of her family members.

Therapist tip

You can never assume or guess what someone's most distressing 'hot' thought or fear is! Always listen actively and thoroughly, with the aim of understanding truly. Empathise and validate well and continue gently to 'unpeel the onion.'

Ben feared that, when he was very breathless and his heart was beating fast, he could 'die of fright.' Ray's panic, in contrast, was when his breathing was *gentle, calm and relaxed*. Ray had heart failure and feared that when his breath slowed it too would 'fail and switch off' – he was terrified he would literally forget to breathe.

Believing we understand the thoughts behind the patient's distress is an example of how we may accurately empathise emotionally but fail to empathise cognitively (see Chapter 1).

Cognitive empathy refers to our capacity to understand the patient's inner world. However, even if we do truly understand the situation from the patient's perspective, we can run into therapist traps. As well as buying into their emotions, we can also buy into, and believe, their thoughts and thus their sense of hopelessness. Our past experience and personal beliefs about illness and suffering may get in the way of both accurate empathy and therapeutic hopefulness. Box 12.1 lists some therapist beliefs that may interfere with effective therapy.

Box 12.1 Therapy interfering beliefs

- If someone is physically fatigued or disabled, there's no point in using behavioural activation.
- Anxiety and depression in physical illness are different.
- If someone is going to die, then of course they will be depressed.
- It's cruel to challenge negative thoughts in someone who is very ill.
- Dying patients need TLC not CBT.
- Asking lots of questions and using assessment tools is intrusive and unkind.
- Reality is bad, thoughts are true, and there is no place for CBT.
- If I enquire about their fear of death, it will make them worse.

Jason had been the victim of a car accident aged 48 and was left quadriplegic. He lived in a nursing home with few people under 65, was ventilated with a tracheostomy and received one-to-one 24 hour care. He could not sleep at night and only ever left the nursing home to attend medical appointments. He was described as disruptive, aggressive, angry and unreasonable. It would have been very easy for the therapist to fall into the trap of thinking that this was in fact a hopeless situation and he could never feel any better than this. He could communicate one letter at a time, using his eyes. He slowly spelled out how hopeless, sleep deprived and depressed he felt. Despite his disability, he was able to complete a HADS (Hospital Anxiety and Depression Scale; Zigmond and Snaith, 1983) and also an activity record and to rate his mood. He filled it in electronically and in a detailed way, saying 'Why not? I have nothing else to do!' He recorded a pleasure rating of 6/10 for a trip out in the fresh air for a smoke with a friend who visited.

This was the starting point for his therapist to help Jason become a detective, to discover any other small things that lifted his mood. His diary gave both him and the therapist hope that his mood could shift in the same way as someone in less extreme circumstances. This led to a change from lying in bed all morning, declining to wash, to a day of planned activity: a trip to the pub with a carer and a friend was organised, and a taste of a burger (with all the awareness of the risks of aspiration attached) generated a pleasure rating of 8/10! He managed to engineer things so he missed the bus back and got to stay out for longer. He scored this very highly on achievement!

He then helped construct a letter to his GP and the nursing home, explaining the medical need for therapeutic trips to places other than hospital consultations. This was not straightforward, but with carers and friends, and night sedation (allowing him to wake earlier and have a longer day), he discovered some hope for a new and very different life, one with some reward, pleasure and achievement. He now lives in his own flat, with two carers he employs, and goes out daily. He applied for and got a job as an inspector of nursing homes and hopes to visit prisons to lecture on hopelessness and not giving up!

ENGAGING THE PATIENT

Ruth was certain her pain was entirely physical. Dan was convinced his bowel was narrowing, gradually blocking so that his intestines would become completely obstructed. Jan had a lump in her throat, was certain her cancer had spread and that she would gradually become unable to swallow at all and would die struggling for breath. Distress in people with medical conditions often arises from very real physical symptoms and a simple ABC model (Situation - Thoughts - Emotion) does not do justice to the centrality of pain, discomfort, nausea etc. in their suffering. The five areas model, which gives equal weight to physical, cognitive, emotional and behavioural factors, is therefore especially helpful in medical settings. The acknowledgement of the importance and influence of physical symptoms allows the therapist to start working from where the patient perceives their problem to be, i.e. their illness. After active listening and allowing the patient to relate their experience, it is a natural and unthreatening progression to ask about the emotions, behaviours and thoughts associated with the pain, the bowel problems or the lump in their throat. This prevents the sort of impasse that can occur if the patient gets the idea the therapist thinks their problem is 'all in the mind.' Forming an alliance through gentle exploration allowed Ruth to express her fear that she believed the pain meant the cancer was 'on the move.' In order to monitor her condition and to reassure herself that she was OK, she avoided taking her painkillers if at all possible. To guard against the pain, she moved less and had become almost immobile. This meant she had little to do, lots of time on her hands and so she focused on the pain even more. Figure 12.1 illustrates the interaction between Ruth's pain and her thoughts, emotions and coping behaviours.

The therapist asked our second patient, Dan, to share his thoughts and images of his blocked bowel. He had a picture of his bowel becoming bloated and bursting. He was understandably frightened to eat much and kept his bowel empty; each day he was terrified until he had had his bowels open, and most days he would check his rectum internally to reassure himself. Figure 12.2 illustrates how Dan's behaviour reinforced his fears.

The therapist's sensitive listening allowed Jan to be open about her fears about her throat: something she had been unable to do with her family or medical staff. She spoke of her huge anxiety (despite negative scans) that the cancer had spread to her throat. Her belief the cancer had spread was causing her to monitor how her throat felt and to frequently check by feeling her throat, swallowing, drinking and clearing her throat. She told the therapist how the lump came and went and how this was her 'barometer' of how anxious she felt (see Figure 12.3).

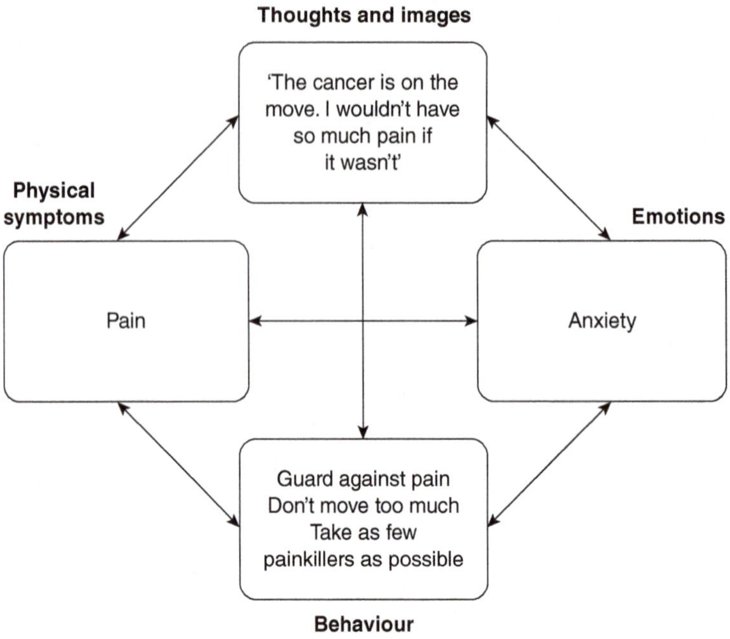

Figure 12.1 Ruth's pain

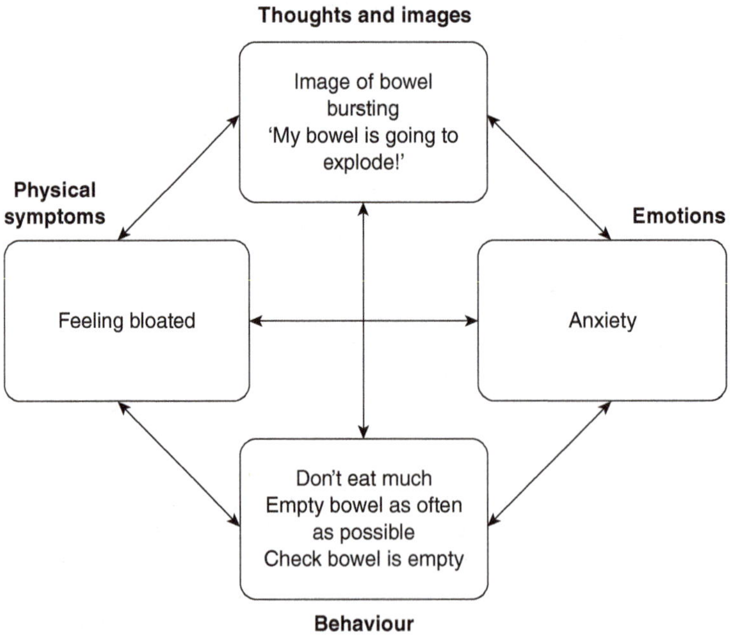

Figure 12.2 Dan's bowel symptoms

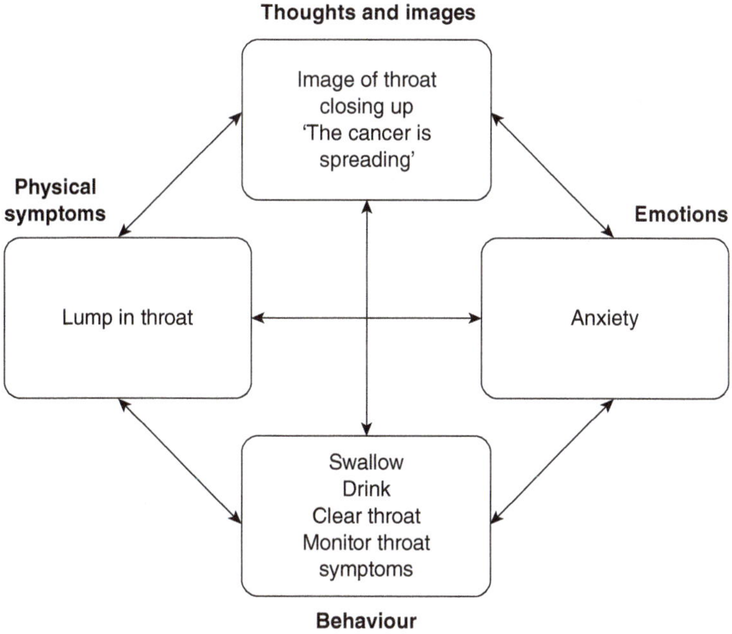

Figure 12.3 Jan's lump in her throat

Drawing out the links between physical symptoms and thoughts, emotions and coping behaviour is a simple, descriptive, non-judgemental way of exploring how thoughts can lead to unhelpful emotional and behavioural reactions. When this is mapped on paper, the confusing, overwhelming feelings can be seen in perspective, and many patients are able to see how their legitimate attempts at coping may be less helpful than they initially appear.

> **Therapist tip**
>
> Allowing the person time and space to fully tell their story, and non-judgemental open, active listening, will allow the person to move from the physical to its impact on thoughts, feelings and emotions, while validating their concerns.

PREDICTING PROBLEMS IN THE THERAPEUTIC RELATIONSHIP (TABLE 12.1)

Paul had been locked in a coal shed as punishment when he was a child. He had undiagnosed dyslexia and, as a result, was bullied and called 'thick and stupid' at school. He presented as always angry, expecting to be let down, treated as insignificant, expecting the worst, for example, his medical notes to be lost or his appointment to be delayed. He expressed his anger at the world everywhere he went. Very few people were in his inner 'circle of trust,' and now he was becoming weaker and less well. The medical staff found Paul very difficult to manage. His hostility to them meant that they avoided interaction with him, and the hostility of some of the staff to him was palpable. The therapist recognised that his issues with trust could become a problem in any attempts to help him. The more ill he became, the more he would have to depend on others, and the more distrustful and resentful he might get. The therapist decided to address this potential problem compassionately from the outset:

Therapist: You've had a tough start in life, haven't you? From what you've told me about it, you've been let down by lots of people over the years.

Paul: Everyone lets you down in the end.

Therapist: It must be very hard to trust anyone.

Paul: Yes it is. You see, even here you can't expect people to do their job properly. They cancelled my appointment last week and I had to call to find out what was going on. They take me for a fool!

Therapist: That must be very frustrating. When you're ill, you need to rely on people and it's hard if you can't trust them. If we're going to work together to help you feel less stressed, I guess you might have to gradually trust me. Do you think this might be a problem?

Paul: Yes, I think it could.

Therapist: Trust comes over time. I'll do my best, but are there any things that might help you to trust me?

Paul: You need to do what you say you'll do and not mess me about.

Therapist: I'll do my best to always be honest with you. And I hope you feel I treat you with respect. If you feel I'm letting you down in some way or not treating you respectfully, will you tell me?

The therapist talked with Paul about how his past experiences had contributed to beliefs that no one could be trusted, people let him down and to expect people to treat him with contempt. She suggested that his 'radar' might be very good at spotting people who said one thing and did another. Paul agreed to tell the therapist if he found staff treating him this way, including her. Naming the trust issue from the beginning of therapy allowed them to identify early, and deal with, hiccoughs in the therapy relationship and, more significantly, in the relationship with medical staff, as they arose. It also allowed Paul to begin to learn that it may be possible to enter into a relationship where he was treated openly with respect and where his opinion was listened to and valued. He was able to see that he perhaps found fault rapidly and responded explosively to minor let downs, and begin to recalibrate his radar a little.

Trust can be a significant problem for people with serious physical illness because they are inevitably more vulnerable and can often be dependent on others. If it is suspected that a patient has issues with trusting others, this can be addressed directly, as with Paul, and also worked with through being as open as possible, being as collaborative as possible, seeking regular feedback and emphasising you are not expecting them to take anything on trust, as they need to test this for themselves. In CBT, the 'proof of the pudding is in the eating.' People who cannot trust others often cope through excessive self-reliance. A need for control and self-reliance may be a problem in itself. Many people have lived their lives through taking responsibility for themselves and keeping everything in order for themselves. The uncertainty and vulnerability inherent in having a physical illness robs them of this sense of control.

Mary was a successful CEO who had prided herself on how she was a self-made woman. She had believed almost magically that she was strong, could handle anything and that her life was charmed. She was a super problem-solver. When she developed cancer, although she was given a good prognosis, she collapsed into depression. She was convinced that she would be dead within the year. She had a helpless/hopeless adjustment to her cancer (Moorey and Greer, 2012), and she told the therapist she felt completely adrift because this was something she couldn't control. Her usual strategies were of no benefit in this situation. She was 'at the mercy of the cancer which could return and she couldn't stop it.' The therapist recognised there might be a dilemma for Mary: on the one hand, she felt helpless, yet she was also so self-reliant that she might resist if the therapist was too directive, as she needed to feel in control. She therefore empathised and emphasised from the outset how Mary had not lost her problem-solving ability, and helped Mary to focus on her inner resources and strengths that she had used in many previous situations. Asking for feedback in session, and allowing Mary to set the agenda and lead, prevented a potential alliance rupture that might have occurred if Mary had felt too controlled.

Patients who have been used to being in control of their lives can feel helpless and 'completely lost at sea' when they become ill and must depend on others. Their usual coping strategy of independently doing it all themselves no longer works. People with dependent traits may also feel out of control, but they look to others for the solution to their problems. They apply their coping strategies (seeking reassurance and looking for support) even more strongly. This can create problems in a short-term therapy such as CBT where we are asking patients to become their own therapists. Val had stayed with an unsupportive husband and had cooked and cleaned for him throughout her chemotherapy. She felt unable to see how she could get through the illness alone. From the beginning, the therapist considered how to use the therapy tools to foster independence and nurture confidence. Together, they decided to keep a notebook of what Val was learning and her progress. This included her writing short bullet-point summaries of what had been worked on in each session. Val and her therapist agreed clear, manageable goals and measured and reviewed progress. This helped her grow in confidence, and she used the notebook to build up a therapy blueprint for how she could continue to cope when therapy ended.

Val: I can't manage to keep this up without seeing you.

Therapist: It seems you feel you can only do this with my support?

Val: I've made all this progress because you understand me and can support me.

Therapist: So it sounds like the tasks and activities we've done, you've only been able to do because we set them up together?

Val: Absolutely!.............

Therapist: I wonder how much you believe that thought?

Val: Well certainly 80%

Therapist: And I wonder how we could find out whether it's true?

By easing Val towards setting goals and experiments for herself, regular review of progress and her having a written record of what she had achieved, independence was fostered. Val and her therapist decided together to spread out the last two appointments and the end-of-therapy review so that, like a learner driver, she was moved from 'L Plates' to newly qualified 'P Plates' so she could learn to work alone for a few weeks before discharge.

MANAGING ALLIANCE RUPTURES

Alliance ruptures can occur through disagreements about the goals and tasks of therapy or the relationship itself (see Chapter 2). One area in which there may be a mismatch is between the type of therapy a therapist is keen to deliver (e.g. a problem- or goal-focused approach) and a patient who is expecting a more person-centred, less goal orientated, supportive model of therapy. The latter is often encouraged by the way in which referrals are made from medical and surgical departments to psychological therapy departments. Patients are often told they are being referred for 'support' or they may have previous experience of counselling of a non-directive nature. This can usually be clarified in the engagement phase of therapy, but for some patients, it may be a persistent problem leading to continued difficulties with the alliance, the structure and the aim of therapy. Beliefs about being 'unable to cope on my own' may underlie this (see above discussion of dependency). Another underlying cause may be resentment of *having* to cope. This can be seen in patients with entitlement beliefs but more commonly is seen in people who have been trying hard and are just exhausted by the hard work of being ill and want a safe space to 'fall apart.' For instance, part way through CBT, a patient may have a relapse of their multiple sclerosis or rheumatoid arthritis, a hospital admission or a recurrence of cancer. Thoughts like 'I can't do this anymore', 'I'm too tired' or 'I shouldn't have to keep fighting like this' may bring resistance and reluctance to engage in homework tasks. In this case, it is vital to acknowledge and validate these feelings of anger and wishes to be left alone. It may even be appropriate sometimes to allow the person to 'take time out from the struggle' (Ruth Williams, personal communication). When they have expressed their feelings, it may then be possible to gently explore the pros and cons of the therapist simply listening versus the patient building on their coping skills. Usually, patients will admit that what they have been doing has been helpful so far and that they will get further if, following a little respite, the therapy returns to a problem-focused mode. Sometimes, they may feel differently and an experiment may be needed to discover the way forward or even take a break from therapy before continuing. The best way forward can be worked out together using the CBT formulation and goals. Similar difficulties can arise when the patient does not feel understood and interprets the structure and goal/intervention focus of therapy as a sign the therapist is cold or uncaring. This is usually found when we slip into a way of relating that is too business-like, trying too hard to get the patient to manage negative thoughts or develop new coping behaviours. This illustrates the importance of being sensitive to the balance between warmth, empathy and validation on one hand and approaches which focus on formulation, goals and problem-solving on the other (see Moorey, in press, for a discussion of some of these issues in patients facing adversity). Actively seeking both positive and negative feedback each session will pick this up and allow it to be discussed. Giving people time to talk is vital, so that they can verbalise thoughts, doubts about therapy and fears that have been on their minds. The concern that the therapy will 'make them feel worse' or 'open Pandora's Box' is rarely borne out but is best shared then formulated together, as it is likely to have a huge impact on engagement. Very occasionally, however, patients can be overwhelmed as they explore their thoughts and fears about the future. For instance, when a woman talked about her worst fears, it emerged that she had witnessed a lot of death and was distressed by real images she had seen laying out 'boney bodies and a fungating tumour;' she felt this was too difficult a subject and that the trauma of having shared her memories and fears was too great. She did not want to become that distressed again and avoided returning to this, yet it was terrifying for her. It required discussion to reassure her that she was in charge of the pace, topic and goals of therapy, and that she was not going to be forced to discuss these difficult areas unless she wanted to. She was given clear permission to return if she wished, and therapy then redirected towards her goals. After a few sessions, she came back to the frightening thoughts and images in her own time. The therapist was then able to help her decatastrophise them and also to assist with practical advance care planning for her future. She was then able to put these fears and images to rest.

John was a 75-year-old man with advanced lung cancer. He was depressed and had given up on the life that was left to him. Despite his family pushing him to look after himself, he could not manage to get up, shave or wash. They were angry and frustrated that he had given up and was unable to help himself and that he did not want to see his grandchildren. After one session of CBT, he was able to see, via a simple maintenance formulation, how his negative thoughts and mood were reinforced by his behavioural withdrawal. He began to try to be more active and agreed to wash, shave and even consider coming to the hospice gym. His family felt useless and bitter: 'why hadn't he been able to do this when they told/asked/begged him to?' Their resentment sabotaged further input until the therapist, with his permission, shared the CBT model with them and explained the vicious cycle that had been keeping him stuck. They were then able to understand why his engagement with life had altered so much. Because, fortunately, most of us do not have to cope with physical illness alone, the involvement of family/friends can be both a tremendous help and a potential hindrance to the therapeutic collaboration. Bringing family members or a friend into the session as co-therapists or supporters, with the patient's consent, can provide information to help the formulation, give them an understanding of what their loved one is going through and ideas about how best to help and support them. They can be engaged as co-therapists on many levels, to assist with activity diaries, to support activity planning or to help with behavioural experiments (Moorey and Greer, 2012).

ENDING THERAPY

Ending therapy in people who are physically ill requires the same sensitivity as with any patient group. In some way it may be easier, since many of the patients we work with have previously been good at coping and managing their lives but have decompensated because of their illness. A brief intervention can help them recover their equilibrium and return to their previous level of functioning surprisingly quickly. In this case, the end of therapy is not a hugely significant issue since they feel able to cope without the therapist. However, in some cases, as with Val, the patient may feel that their progress has been achieved by the therapist, not themselves, or they may fear that if their disease worsens they do not have the skills to weather the storm. It is important to recognise that, in a vulnerable state, many people really value the personal relationship with the therapist, and this must be acknowledged while at the same time emphasising the nature of CBT as a brief therapy that aims to make the patient their own therapist. A feature of CBT in physical illness that is different from CBT in other conditions is the fact that therapy may need to end, to be interrupted because the patient is too unwell to continue, or each session to be shorter due to fatigue or other physical symptoms. Therapeutically, we would seek to treat every therapy session (even the assessment) with someone who is seriously ill as if it was their final session, i.e. maximising the gains in the session, summarising learning, planning an initial step forward and emphasising how these can be continued over the next week or longer. If a patient does not return for the rest of therapy, then a brief intervention of value will have been delivered and can be added to, if possible, in the future. An ending may sometimes be a phone call, an email or a letter as a way to manage a goodbye when therapy is incomplete.

CHAPTER SUMMARY

Working with people with life-threatening and life-limiting illness can be extremely rewarding as well as challenging. Our own beliefs about illness, death and dying can interfere with our ability to accurately empathise with patients, while our natural compassion may sometimes lead us to accept the patient's hopelessness as a realistic view of their situation. Paying attention to our 'countertransference' can keep us from falling into these traps. Engaging patients in therapy requires sensitive, empathic listening to their stories about their illness, followed by an exploration of how the cognitive model may help them to understand and find a way forward out of their distress. Using the five areas model and starting with physical symptoms such as pain or fatigue is a good way to engage patients so they do not feel we are telling them it is 'all in the mind.' Challenges to the therapeutic alliance can come from several areas. Patients with physical illness are in a highly vulnerable position where their coping strategies may no longer be working for them. Issues of trust, control, loss of self-reliance and dependency may interfere with collaboration but can usually be managed if the therapist uses a compassionate conceptualisation as a guide.

Table 12.1 Common therapy interfering beliefs and behaviours

Theme	Beliefs	Behaviour	Tips for therapist response
Trust	If I trust someone, I will be hurt or let down	Reluctance to talk about thoughts and feelings about the illness; acting in a guarded way; expressing doubts about therapy or therapist	Empathise with vulnerable feelings behind the mistrust; emphasise collaborative nature of therapy; set up tasks as experiments
Excessive self-reliance and/or need for control	If I don't look after myself, no one will do it for me If I'm not in control, something bad will happen	Reluctance to engage in tasks of therapy; reluctance to reveal vulnerability in session; trying to direct and control the session	Conceptualise origins and benefits of self-reliance and need for control; introduce possibility of balance between dependence and self-reliance; set up experiments to test giving up control
Dependency	If I try to cope on my own, I will fail	Over-reliance on therapist; failure to complete homework assignments; expressing fear of therapy ending	Name dependency; emphasise therapy as a process of learning skills; graded approach to independence (L-plates)

FURTHER READING

Moorey S (in press) Socratic Methods in Adversity. In: Padesky and Kennerley H (eds) *The Socratic Method in CBT*.

Moorey S and Greer S (2012) *The Oxford Guide to Cognitive Behaviour Therapy for People with Cancer*. Oxford: Oxford University Press.

REFERENCES

DeFaye BJ, Wilson KG, Chater S, Viola RA and Hall P (2006) Stress and coping with advanced cancer. *Palliative & Supportive Care 4*(3): 239–249.

Moorey S (in press) Socratic Methods in Adversity. In: Padesky and Kennerley H (eds) *The Socratic Method in CBT.* Oxford: Oxford University Press.

Moorey S and Greer S (2012) *The Oxford Guide to Cognitive Behaviour Therapy for People with Cancer*. Oxford: Oxford University Press.

Zigmond AS and Snaith RP (1983) The hospital anxiety and depression scale. *Acta Psychiatrica Scandinavica 67*(6): 361–370.

13

PERSONALITY DISORDERS

ANNA LAVENDER AND HELEN STARTUP

CHAPTER SUMMARY

Individuals with personality disorders present frequently to psychological services, often undiagnosed and requesting help for Axis I disorders such as depression and anxiety. This being the case, as clinicians working in almost any context, we can expect to encounter patients with personality disorders through our years of practice. Indeed, within the UK's Increasing Access to Psychological Therapies (IAPT) services, designed primarily to treat anxiety and depression, around two thirds of patients will have at least some features of personality disorder (Hepgul at al., 2016), the presence of which will be associated with poorer treatment outcomes (Goddard et al., 2015).

CBT was not originally conceived to treat individuals with personality disorders. Its time-limited nature and focus in its classical form on overt symptoms, and the necessary establishment of early treatment goals, mean that individuals with personality disorders often fail to engage. Or, where these early hurdles of engagement are well negotiated, later on in treatment, the requirements of relatively accessible cognitions, quite rapid behavioural change and reliance on the capacity of a patient to engage fairly quickly with, and then maintain, a good working relationship with her therapist will often mean that the individual with a personality disorder and her therapist struggle to make headway (Goddard et al., 2015).

However, since the early 1990s, there has been much work to expand the strengths of CBT to working with individuals with personality disorders, with the above factors in mind. There has been a particular emphasis on conceptual and strategic approaches, not only in developing and maintaining the therapeutic relationship but using it as a vehicle for change in therapy. One of the key models in this movement is Young's schema therapy (Young, 1990; Young et al., 2003), in which the nature and role of the therapeutic relationship are core, both conceptually and clinically.

This chapter is aimed at the cognitive therapist who is not a specialist in personality disorders but who recognises that, when individuals with these difficulties are encountered in clinical practice, consideration of the therapeutic relationship will be helpful to enable therapy to progress towards successful outcomes. We will consider the importance of, and issues that arise within, the therapeutic relationship with individuals with personality disorders, and how these can be conceptualised and worked with using concepts from schema therapy to augment short- to medium-term CBT.

WHY IS THE THERAPEUTIC RELATIONSHIP SO IMPORTANT WHEN WORKING WITH PEOPLE WITH PERSONALITY DISORDERS?

It will first be useful to establish what we mean by personality disorders, and how these individuals present in therapy. It is not usually our role as therapists to diagnose personality disorders and is often of limited utility clinically to think in terms of diagnostic categories. However, it will be helpful to consider what the range of patients we meet may present with in structured terms, in order to guide our thinking about how this is likely to impact on the therapeutic relationship and what patients' needs within therapy and the therapeutic relationship are likely to be. It is also worth noting that many individuals present with traits, but not full criteria, for a personality disorder, and we include this group implicitly in our thinking within the chapter.

DSM V clusters personality disorders into three groups. The first of these is Cluster A (odd or eccentric disorders), which include paranoid, schizoid and schizotypal personality disorders. Individuals with these disorders often present as particularly suspicious and mistrustful, disinterested in social relationships or experiencing extreme discomfort socially, with distorted interpretations of social interactions. Cluster B (dramatic, emotional or erratic disorders) includes antisocial, borderline, histrionic and narcissistic personality disorders. These patients have intense difficulties interpersonally, often displaying emotional and behavioural patterns that make it difficult to maintain relationships at any level and lead to actual or perceived rejection by others. Cluster C (anxious or fearful disorders) includes avoidant, dependent and obsessive-compulsive personality disorders. For this group, relationships with others are governed by fear of negative evaluation or rejection or of involving an unacceptable lack of control. These patients can be overly compliant, submissive or rigid in their interactions with others.

In summary, disturbances in interpersonal relationships are a hallmark of individuals with personality disorders; relationships are indeed what this group usually find most difficult and distressing. Given that a strong working relationship with a therapist is a requisite of successful therapy (Martin et al., 2000), it becomes clear why it is so important to consider how we can best engage our personality disordered patients, develop and maintain these relationships and then use them to enhance clinical outcomes.

In working with individuals with personality disorders, then, it is important to find a way to formulate relationship difficulties and to develop a shared language to talk about these in therapy. This is necessary more generally within a formulation that captures as fully as possible the scope of the patient's difficulties, but it is also vital within the context of the therapeutic relationship to allow a dialogue about processes that arise within it.

Within the formulation of interpersonal difficulties, given the lifelong nature of personality disorders, it is also helpful to include a greater emphasis on the developmental origins of these, relating to attachment patterns, unmet need and early childhood experiences more generally. This can help in understanding a patient's relationship problems generally, but also provides a framework to explore how these patterns manifest within the therapeutic relationship.

Personality disordered patients are often a challenge for us as therapists on a personal level. Individuals with disturbed relational patterns bring these to therapy, and the processes that ensue within the therapeutic relationship can trigger strong emotional responses in us, including difficulties with empathy, feelings of incompetence, frustration, general 'heartsink' and many others. Having a way to understand the developmental origins and functions of an individual's relationship difficulties offers a framework for how these difficulties are activated within the therapeutic relationship. Paired with a conscious awareness of our own trigger points, this can assist immeasurably in working through our own responses in a way that remains therapeutic for the patient and emotionally sustainable for us as therapists.

HOW CONCEPTS FROM SCHEMA THERAPY CAN HELP

SCHEMAS LINKING TO UNMET NEED

Schema theory suggests that all children have a set of core emotional needs. These include the needs for security, safety, acceptance, nurturance and the development of autonomy, competence and identity. When these needs are not met, children and adolescents may form early maladaptive schemas. Schemas are defined as broad, pervasive themes, comprised of memories, emotions, cognitions and physical sensations, related to the self and one's relationships with others, developed in childhood and elaborated throughout one's lifetime, and which are significantly dysfunctional (Young et al., 2003).

Schemas affect adult relationships in that they are the 'lenses' through which an individual makes sense of the motivations and intentions of others, which then organise their behaviour accordingly. If one has endured significant childhood unmet need in the domains of safety and security, for example, then the schemas that develop - initially to help the young child make sense of, and cope with, their difficult experiences - go on to form the bedrock of the adult's relational expectations. A 'mistrust/abuse' schema will render it almost impossible for the individual to form basic trust. In their earlier life, it might have been adaptive to follow any number of 'relational scripts' in order to survive, such as when individuals avoid relationships altogether or enter familiar, yet abusive, relationships or even, in some cases, start acting out their abusive experiences on others.

Describing an individual's core schemas also offers a window into the terrain of someone's early life. Schema theory encourages a compassionate and empathic stance between patient and therapist by conceptualising these in regard to chronic unmet need. Schemas fight to keep that person safe as though their historical terrain is still active, meaning that, for individuals who experienced limited, conflictual or harmful early life experiences, schemas struggle to update despite new and more hopeful landscapes. Thus, whilst it can feel initially baffling to be faced with someone who, for example, avoids closeness altogether, pausing and viewing their relational expectations through their 'lenses,' formulated as a response to chronic unmet need, enables both empathy and sense of genuine connectedness to form.

COPING STYLES

Unhelpful schemas are largely maintained because the individual has had limited exposure to experiences that could correct them. The patient had to adapt to whatever early life experiences were endured in order to survive. At that time, the behaviours, interpersonal and otherwise, that this involved may have been the most adaptive way to deal with whatever kinds of situations and relationships they were exposed to.

Once formed, the schemas and an individual's ways of coping with them are carried forward, into adulthood. However, in their current life, where there are new possibilities, these behaviours may be far from ideal and only serve to maintain the patient's schemas and suffering. Essentially, there are three ways in which one copes with schemas: surrender, overcompensation and avoidance. In the short term, these ways of coping offer some relief, but over time, they keep the patient stuck and bewildered because these schema activations and ways of coping are usually not under conscious control.

Thus, a first step is to make these schemas and coping responses explicit to the patient, and schema monitoring can enhance this. When a patient surrenders to a schema, they act in accordance with that schema and adapt their feelings and responses to be in line with the schema. In a patient with an abandonment schema and a tendency to cope by surrendering to this, they may enter relationships that are inconsistent in some way, thereby eliciting this familiar pattern. They would then feel the emotional impact of abandonment over and over again.

When a patient engages in avoidance in relation to an abandonment schema, they do whatever is necessary to avoid its activation. So, they may avoid intimacy to minimise the risk of their core pain being activated, or they may choose a partner who is kept at emotional distance, such as by residing in another country, and then struggle with a sense of emptiness and desolation.

Where a patient is seen to overcompensate, they do the opposite to their schema, again in order to cope with, or avoid, its activation. This often leads to some type of 'over the top' response, such as in the case of an abandonment schema, seeking excessive reassurance of love and loyalty and expecting 'perfect care.'

Coping styles are relational, in that one is always coping in relation to someone else or between parts of the self. Thus, identifying dominant coping styles begins to make conscious the very processes that maintain difficult relational styles and the sense of stuckness.

SCHEMA MODES AND SCHEMA MODE FORMULATION

Where individuals present with high levels of complexity, therapists often report that their patients have an abundance of 'core beliefs' and, in schema theory terms, score highly across all maladaptive schemas. This can lead to the patient (and therapist) feeling overwhelmed and bewildered as to what to focus on in therapy.

Schema therapy adapts to this complexity via the concept of schema modes. Whereas schemas are the stable and enduring 'traits' that govern behaviour and feeling states, modes can be conceptualised as 'states', which encompass an individual's active schemas, along with their coping responses and feelings, at any particular moment. These can usefully be considered and spoken about in therapy as parts of the self, which the individual can move between.

Schema theory suggests a vulnerable child mode which 'houses' the individual's core pain, dysfunctional parent modes (the punitive and demanding parents) which attack the vulnerable child, an angry child mode which responds with anger to core unmet needs, maladaptive coping modes in which the individual behaves in ways to avoid (the detached protector), overcompensate (the overcompensator) or surrender (the compliant surrenderer) to the schemas activated within the vulnerable child. In addition, there are the healthy adult mode, the part of the individual which is functional and adaptive, and the contented child mode, in which the individual's core needs feel met and she feels at peace.

Individuals on the higher functioning end of the spectrum tend to have well integrated schema modes that communicate well with each other. Indeed, with brief consideration of ourselves, we are likely to recognise a number of these modes, as it is normal to move between different states of being during the course of our daily lives.

However, for individuals with a more complex profile, we tend to see rapid shifting between states with minimal helpful correspondence between each mode (i.e. partially dissociated states). Thus, for example, when one is overwhelmed with feelings of rejection and abandonment, this is all-consuming and there is little soothing from a more 'adult' mode, hence the depths of despair that can be experienced.

Where a patient is seen to shift rapidly between partially dissociated states, classic CBT strategies for formulating and working may be disrupted because how the individual experiences the self, the world and others is variable, depending on the 'mode' that is most present. With this type of profile, it isn't uncommon for a patient to suddenly experience the therapist or others in their life as hostile or persecutory in some way, if for example, an 'abused child' mode is activated. Formulating according to modes enables a patient to start to track their state shifts, which promotes integration and also enables the therapist to identify, name and intervene with any modes and their associated behaviours that impede the therapeutic relationship.

This also opens a window for working directly with relational styles that are ignited in the therapeutic relationship that cause difficulties in broader life, as well as in the therapeutic relationship. It offers the opportunity for the therapeutic relationship to become a live 'workshop' for the activation, recognition, naming and discussion of, and working with, the modes in a way that, because of the direct repeated linking with the unmet needs of the child, remains empathic and de-shaming.

In order to understand and contain these modes, a shared formulation is required. The schema mode formulation is not disorder specific (i.e. describing the processes maintaining a single presenting problem) as in classic CBT formulations, but rather can accommodate and describe adequately a breadth of symptoms, coping styles and relational patterns. This is not to say that it is incompatible with disorder-specific cognitive models; because schema therapy is a development of CBT, a modal model incorporating broad relational patterns is not inconsistent with the concepts of CBT, and the two can sit alongside each other in therapy.

For example, Jenny, a severely depressed patient with personality disorder traits experienced intense and prolonged activation of her vulnerable child mode. She tried to cope with this through smoking cannabis (avoidant coping in the detached protector mode) and submissiveness in her relationships in an attempt not to be abandoned (compliant surrenderer mode). She experienced harsh internal criticism from her punitive parent mode and bouts of rage when she felt how unfair it all was and moved into her angry child mode. In treatment, Jenny worked well with all the evidence-based strategies that we would normally employ for treating depression (e.g. thought records to monitor her critical voice/negative automatic thoughts and restructuring of these, teaching assertiveness within her relationships, working towards reducing cannabis use), with the modal formulation providing an overarching conceptualisation for understanding the rapid shifts between states and extreme nature of her symptoms.

Reflective questions

- What are my patient's key maladaptive relationship patterns, and how do these manifest within the therapeutic relationship?
- When might it be useful to use a schema mode formulation with my patient, in addition to a disorder-specific formulation?

IDENTIFICATION OF SCHEMAS AND MODES

There are a range of formal measurement tools to assess an individual's repertoire of schemas (such as the Young Schema Questionnaire, Young, 2005) and modes (such as the Schema Mode Inventory, Young et al., 2007). There are various useful published summaries of what is available and their psychometric properties (i.e. Sheffield and Waller, 2012).

However, in clinical practice, our experience is that relevant schemas will emerge naturally as therapy evolves, and where schema modes are relevant, they have the tendency to 'pop out' as the therapeutic relationship becomes more trusting and the patient allows different sides of the self to be seen. A combined approach of allowing schemas to emerge organically from exploration of an individual's earlier life and associated areas of unmet need, and modes to be shaped and named collaboratively as therapy becomes more 'active' and dynamic, in addition to use of the formal measurement tools, is likely to be a useful strategy to bring these concepts into therapy and use them successfully.

LIMITED REPARENTING

The concept of 'limited reparenting' has sometimes been viewed as controversial amongst those needing to work within tight time limits and with concrete goals in mind. Therapists have expressed concerns about promoting dependence in patients, fearing connotations of regression or, because of the use of 'parenting' in this context, being viewed as infantilising. However, limited reparenting within schema theory and therapy is quite simply the involvement of the therapeutic relationship as an active vehicle for change by going some way (hence the 'limited') to meeting the unmet needs of the patient in the present moment.

So, Sam, a patient who was invalidated and punished as a five-year-old when he expressed fear or sadness, is responded to by his therapist when in his vulnerable child mode (evidenced by tearfulness, a curled body posture, palpably intense sadness) with a level of attunement, empathy and warmth in keeping with the needs of his younger self. Thus, the tone of voice used and body language Sam's therapist uses are consistent with how one might literally respond to a frightened five-year-old.

Using one's imagination to act 'as if' one is responding to a young child further promotes this reparenting stance. It is important to note that the therapist does not interact with Sam in this way all the time, but *only when he is in his vulnerable child mode*. This is a point that has been misunderstood by some therapists in the past and has led to the concern about limited reparenting being infantalising or patronising.

Below is an example of Sam's therapist employing a limited reparenting stance with him.

Sam	(curled forward in his chair, crying, not speaking)
Therapist: (posture learning forward, tone compassionate and comforting)	Sam, I can see you feel so sad and scared right now. My heart goes out to you, because I can see you're in such pain. This feels to me like it links right back to those times when you were a child when you felt pain like this and there was nowhere to go with it, no comfort.
Sam:	It's just that I'm so alone, so scared, no one will ever love me, how could they?
Therapist:	Sam, you are so worthy of love. I can see such good things in you, but you were made to feel so bad about yourself as a child, this badness feels true. But Sam, you didn't deserve that treatment. You're a warm, kind, lovely man. I can see and feel that in our sessions together, and my hope is that, over time, you'll begin to see and feel that too.

The therapist uses the accessibility of Sam's vulnerability to draw on other means to support and heal this part of him. For example, Sam's therapist might offer between session contact (via phone, text or email) or a transitional object (such as a special therapy pen, a found object like a stone or shell). Instead of written flashcards, it can also resonate more at an emotional level to have an audio flashcard recorded to the patient's phone that follows the format of a typical flashcard but using the soothing and compassionate tones of her therapist. Asking the patient to bring in a photo of himself to therapy, so that the therapist and he can both focus compassionately on the younger self, can also be useful.

'Limited reparenting' can involve the therapist offering greater self-disclosure than might be typical in standard CBT, when this feels relevant to the patient's unmet needs. For example, where a patient experienced a parent as closed and 'unreachable,' the therapist might offer a (carefully considered) anecdote from their day to bring connectedness and playfulness into the room. In addition, of course, the therapist is continuously paying very close attention at all times not to repeat any of the harmful ways of responding the patient experienced as a child.

Where there has been chronic unmet need and life-long relational struggles, the ending of therapy (if, indeed, the patient has engaged with therapy at an emotional level) will be painful. We believe that keeping in mind the early attachment unmet needs of our patients, naming these collaboratively and offering a compassionate and reparenting stance in relation to these fears around the ending of the therapeutic relationship are critical to validating the core pain of some of our patients.

Stephanie had been in and out of foster homes throughout her younger life. Over time, she gradually developed trust in her therapist, with whom she shared an abundance of painful memories and became very attached to him. As ending approached, strong memories of being 'dropped' by her parents just when she most needed them surfaced and a surge of abandonment feelings became overwhelming.

Her therapist responded with compassion and close attunement, validating the strength of feeling by making links to her unmet need. Together, they came up with a range of methods for helping Stephanie to 'keep in mind' her therapist as the ending approached. These included an audio recording in the style of a flashcard for triggers of abandonment, a 'loveability box,' which Stephanie decorated and to which she added reminders of how loveable she can feel (postcards from friends, a lovely note left by a colleague, a photo of a happy day out) to help her keep in touch with other sides of herself when abandonment engulfed her. With Stephanie's needs in mind, a further offer of ten sessions was made and the final five sessions were spaced out. Sometimes, the reality for our patients is that the therapeutic relationship is the first, or only, relationship in which they have dared to attach. We need to be mindful about abrupt and inflexible endings, where service constraints allow this, and not get caught up in our own fears about promoting 'dependency.'

Therefore, as a therapist, if you are organised by the unmet needs of your patient and your own compassionate humanity, and you remain boundaried (i.e. you realise this is not actual parenting) and realistic (by only offering something that fits with what is feasible for you, both in terms of your therapy timescale and personal resources), it is hard to go far wrong. In our experience, using a limited reparenting approach with individuals with personality disorders or traits with longstanding relationship difficulties allows us to relate to our patients in qualitatively more enriched ways that enhance the therapeutic relationship, clinical practice and outcomes.

Reflective questions

- What are my patient's core unmet childhood needs?
- How can I use a limited reparenting stance, keeping in mind the timescale of therapy I am working with, to meet these and provide a reparative experience in therapy?
- How can I use my knowledge of my patient's attachment history and unmet needs to compassionately talk about and manage the ending?

EMPATHIC CONFRONTATION

Empathic confrontation refers to the schema therapy strategy of confronting the patient with her unhelpful behaviour patterns, whilst remaining compassionate, and linking current behaviour with past unmet need. This can be focused on behaviours occurring external to therapy, such as with family members or at work, and also within the therapeutic relationship.

Within therapy, empathic confrontation can be one of the most powerful tools with which to use the therapeutic relationship as a vehicle for positive change; in our experience, it can lead to sudden and lasting shifts in patients' understanding of how their behavioural patterns impact on others and provide a strong motivation for working towards changing these.

For example, James was referred to CBT for his depression. One of the maintenance factors he and his therapist had identified was his sense of isolation and loneliness that resulted from his difficulties with making and maintaining relationships with friends or partners as, once he got close to people, he felt things tended to 'blow up' and they left him.

James had experienced severe emotional deprivation and abandonment as a child. His father had been an alcoholic, swinging between violent physical and emotional abuse to James and buying him expensive presents occasionally to make up for it. His mother had been emotionally absent and self-absorbed. One of his key memories was of his pain and shame in her never attending his primary school plays, meetings with teachers and other events, and his sense of sadness and longing when observing other children's attentive and loving interactions with their parents.

James' therapist had to cancel a session at late notice for personal reasons but rearranged to see him the following day. James attended but was, from the start, critical and attacking towards his therapist. Faced with this barrage of anger and hostility, the therapist responded to James saying:

> James, I can see you feel really angry and let down by me. I can understand this, because it links in so closely and painfully to your experiences of being let down and not cared for properly by your parents. When I cancelled the session, I wonder if it brought all this up for you. But James, when you shout at me and criticise me, I feel attacked, and my emotional response to that is to start feeling angry and anxious, so that a part of me wants to run from you right now. But, there's a larger part that really cares about you, and I want to stay with that and try to help you. This is so hard for you because it brings back all the pain from your past. I wonder if we can use this to try to understand better what happens with other people when you feel abandoned or let down by them? Does our experience here feel like it fits the pattern you've told me about with others?

In interactions such as this, tone is all-important. It is easy for a patient to feel patronised and invalidated, particularly if their mistrust schema has been activated, as is likely in the example above. It is vital to remain compassionate, but firm, and whilst not allowing your response to be governed by your own emotions in terms of acting these out, to share your emotional response in a way that is clear to your patient. It is important to make a direct link with the individual's childhood experiences to show that their behaviour is understandable, but remains unhelpful in the present day. This is vital in order to de-shame the interaction for the patient.

Some helpful phrases that can be useful in situations such as these are:

> When you speak to me like that I feel pushed away by you and unable to access the enormous warmth I can so often feel towards you, and which I know you long for

> I'm finding it hard to keep empathising with you in the way you deserve when you're saying that to me ...

> hiding away behind intellectualised tones leaves me out in the cold and distanced from you, when I know only so well how the more vulnerable sides of you long for closeness and warmth....

> I need you to know that I am here for you and that I understand the pain you are in right now, but that this behaviour (hitting the table and banging his head against the wall) is not acceptable to me......

CHAIR WORK

Within schema therapy, chair work is one of the major strategies for therapeutic change, and there are many variants on how it may be incorporated into therapy and its potential targets for clinical change. It is a technique that lends itself well to shorter term work and can usefully be embedded within shorter term CBT. For a full account of this, and also for detail regarding the clinical technique, we refer you to Kellogg (2004).

For the purposes of working directly to enhance the therapeutic relationship, one of the most valuable applications of chair work is to enhance patients' 'meta-awareness' in relation to their mode flipping (i.e. rapid shifting between parts of the self). For example, where a patient has a tendency to shift from feeling desolate and vulnerable one moment to self-attacking and self-loathing the next in an abrupt fashion, it can be useful to introduce one chair that represents each of these two parts of the self. These parts of the self should be named as part of a wider formulation or, at a minimum, a discussion beforehand. There is no need to label them as 'modes' if you have not used this concept in therapy; calling them 'parts' or 'sides' of the self is fine.

For example, for an adult patient, Jackie, her vulnerable mode could be 'Little Jackie' on one chair, and on another, her critical mode, 'The Bully.' Essentially, the patient is then guided to move between the chairs as the state shifts occur. The rule is for the patient to sit in the chair of the mode they are currently in.

The role of the therapist is to be curious with your patient about triggers for the mode shift (such as finding vulnerability too exposing or shaming) and to discuss relevant origins (such as having been bullied at school) which can help them begin to develop compassion for themselves, greater tolerance to 'stay with' vulnerability and to feel more contained within the therapeutic relationships because the state shifting becomes less bewildering and more a shared process to be understood and contained.

Many of our patients with complex needs can fail to fully engage with a therapist because they are flooded with self-loathing, sometimes to the degree they can barely engage with much else. For these patients, it can be enormously valuable to 'place' their critical mode in an empty chair and then for the therapist to speak directly to the chair, to challenge the harshness of the tone and the unfairness of the demands, and also to talk directly to the originator of that voice (a bully, parent, abusive partner) to stick up for the patient.

This exercise is more than thought challenging and more than role play. It has the potential to be a moving first experience for some of our patients to have someone actually be on their side. Over time, having experienced the therapist take their side, protect them and value them, many patients can begin to take over and respond themselves to their critical mode in an assertive, compassionate or forgiving manner (whichever feels it addresses the unmet need most closely). The rule here is not to talk in assertive tones to the chair in which the patient is sitting, as this could be experienced as a direct attack. The therapist always speaks assertively to the empty chair.

For example, Jackie and her therapist had established that her critical mode, 'The Bully,' was an amalgamation of messages from her abusive father and bullies at school. Whilst 'Little Jackie' sat in one chair, her therapist spoke to `The Bully':

> *The Bully* (Jackie in the Bully chair): Jackie you're just bloody hopeless. You're fat and ugly, and you'll never get anywhere in life. No one will ever want to be with you because you're such a complete loser. What a waste of space.

At this point, the therapist asks Jackie to move chairs and sit in the Little Jacky chair. The therapist then addresses the empty chair Jackie has just left.

Therapist: (to empty Bully chair) I'm here to tell you that you need to back off and stop attacking Jackie. She doesn't deserve what you do to her, and the things that you say to her are lies, and hurting her terribly. We know where you come from: you're the messages Jackie got from her dad when she was little. But Jackie's dad was wrong: he was a bad parent who didn't look after, or care about, Jackie in the way he should have done. Jackie was so little and vulnerable that she took all this in and believed it, but it's not true. I'm not going to allow you to hurt Jackie any more. So just go away and leave her alone!

The therapist then turns to Jackie in the Little Jackie chair.

Therapist: (to Little Jackie) Little Jackie, what was it like to hear that. How did it feel?

Jackie: (in the Little Jackie chair) It was weird. It felt odd, but good. No one ever spoke to my dad like that. I was a bit scared he'd be angry with you, but also I felt good that you were standing up for me, telling him I'm not bad. I feel a bit lighter, a bit stronger just now.

It is important to use the patient's own vocabulary within this kind of interaction and to put significant emotion into it; this is an emotion-focused technique in which the therapist is using the therapeutic relationship very directly to restructure the patient's internal framework, and the patient needs to experience the therapist as being sufficiently emotionally involved in the process in order for this to happen effectively.

IMAGERY

Imagery work is another core strategy within schema therapy that the therapeutic relationship may be used to enhance. Imagery is used widely and increasingly within CBT, with a range of different presentations and in numerous ways, for example, with imagery rescripting techniques in posttraumatic stress disorder. Imagery within schema therapy is used to achieve goals broader than, and different to, those focused on within classic trauma work.

In schema therapy, imagery rescripting is used often to provide alternative emotional 'memories' that a patient can access, to counter existing damaging and painful memories of childhood experiences. The main aim is to change the emotional tone of a painful memory in a way that promotes the meeting of the patient's needs. Within the context of an established and trusting therapeutic relationship, the therapist can 'enter' a rescripting of an early memory and alter events in order to meet the needs of the child within it. This differs from more conventional CBT rescripting in that the therapist may have a key role in the reparative function of the rescripted memory. It is also not important whether the worked-on image is an actual memory or a troublesome recurrent image. The issue is whether it is associated with painful emotions associated with unmet need. The therapist entering a memory rescript can nurture, comfort and care for a child, directly confront an abuser, protect him from harm and remove him to safety.

For example, Alfred and his therapist had identified a particularly painful early memory of him being five years old, at home in bed waiting for the sound of the front door to click, knowing this would signify the return home of his drunk father and turbulent, violent rows between his father and Alfred's mother. He had a vivid memory of listening to the abuse of his mother knowing that, once this changed into the sound of heavy boots on the stairs, he would be next for abusive treatment. Alfred and his therapist had identified his unmet needs for safety, protection, nurturance. Most pronounced in their work had been Alfred's core pain that his suffering had gone unnoticed. One piece of powerful imagery work he and his therapist engaged in was for Alfred to recount (with his eyes closed and as though it was happening right now) the painful image/memory and then, with his permission, to allow his therapist to 'enter' the image and to speak directly to the abusive father in a firm and confrontational manner in order to prevent the violence and then to 'remove' Alfred from the terrifying situation (meeting his need for protection). Alfred requested that he be taken to his aunt's house, which for him, was the only place he ever felt safe.

The aim of this type of work is to identify the unmet need of 'little Alfred' (to be protected and out of harm and to feel safe and cared for) and to change the script of the memory in order to make this happen (whilst being guided in how best to achieve this by your patient). For example, although Alfred could identify his aunt as a person of safety, some patients have no one. For these patients, it is fine to use whatever your imaginations can come up with to guide the image to a place of safety.

Leanne, another patient with similar childhood parenting experiences but with no protective others in her life, wanted to be taken to a house in the woods where she could be protected by the animals (because, for her, only animals were truly to be trusted not to hurt you). The rule is that if the patient's need is met by the re-script (and this will be clear because you will notice an often quite stark affect shift), the imagery work is done from a genuine place of emotional connectedness (rather than the patient merely recounting a series of events in a detached mode) and the image ends at a point of safety for the patient, then it is likely to be effective. This can be an extremely useful tool for altering the emotional tone of painful childhood memories via 'reparenting' in imagery and going some way to meet the unmet needs of the patient.

Another application for imagery work can be to bypass an avoidant mode that can sometimes be responsible for a 'stuckness' in therapy. Alan tended to be guarded and intellectualised in sessions with his therapist. This had been conceptualised as a 'detached protector' part of him that functioned to keep others at 'arms-length' for fear of being shamed (as his mother had always made him feel). Alan had carried out all his CBT homework perfectly (an overcompensatory mode) and, despite focused CBT treatment for his anxiety and depression, he remained symptomatically unchanged.

To begin to get to know his 'detached protector' a little better, his therapist asked Alan to gather an image of this side of him, which he described as a fortress with a moat around it. He described how lonely and desolate he felt all by himself in the fortress but terrified to let others in for fear of being attacked and ridiculed. This enabled the therapist (who had previously felt herself quite cut off during sessions with Alan) to feel an increase in connectedness and compassion for Alan, and for the first time, Alan got in touch with some of the emotional pain of his experiences. By exploring this image, she also learned that Alan first retreated to his fortress when he was just two years old, which enabled Alan to challenge his view that it was his fault his life was 'in this mess.' Over time, this work spring-boarded a shift in Alan, first to recognise when he was in his 'fortress' mode (as it came to be named) and then, slowly, to dare to let other parts of himself to have a 'voice' in therapy (such as 'Little Alan'), which led to a closer therapeutic alliance, greater emotional connectivity in his CBT work and opportunities for some powerful reparenting.

Reflective questions

- How might I use chair work and imagery with my patient to help foster change at an emotional, in addition to a rational, level?
- Which of my patient's 'parts' – schemas, modes or deeply held beliefs – might be most useful to restructure using chair work or imagery?
- How does this fit with my formulation? What aspects of maintenance am I addressing with these?

CHAPTER SUMMARY

In this chapter, we have sought to identify and elucidate some of the ways in which the therapeutic relationship can be affected by the relational patterns our personality disordered patients bring to therapy, and how the therapeutic relationship may be used positively to help meet their needs using concepts and strategies from schema therapy. We hope that we have successfully communicated our overarching message: that with compassion, an attunement to historical unmet need and bringing the concepts and strategies we have discussed to our work with personality disordered patients, we can help them to thrive in therapy and move towards the growth and healing they need.

Therapist tips

- When it becomes difficult to empathise, imagine the patient as the child they were, whose core emotional needs were not met. Most challenging behaviours and interactions developed as strategies for a young child to cope with this, and to keep themselves safe from further pain.
- When difficulties in the therapeutic relationship arise, try to identify whether these are part of wider relational patterns. Name them and develop a language to talk about them as soon as possible so they can be worked with. Trying to 'plough on' and ignore it risks significant rupture and disengagement, as well as missed opportunities for valuable work.
- Where the patient presents with rapidly shifting self states and an Axis I formulation just doesn't 'cut it,' consider a schema mode formulation to contain and talk about the complexity.
- If your patient appears to be 'going through the motions' of therapy but making little symptomatic change, consider whether they are operating from a detached part of the self. Try naming this and working with this side directly using imagery or chair work.
- Keep closely in mind the relational unmet needs of your patient that are relevant to the ending of therapy; consider a reparenting and compassionate stance.

FURTHER READING

Rafaeli E, Bernstein DP and Young JE (2011) *Schema Therapy: Distinctive Features*. London and New York: Routledge.

Young JE, Klosko JS and Weishaar ME (2003) *Schema Therapy: A Practitioners's Guide*. New York: Guilford Press.

REFERENCES

Goddard E, Wingrove J and Moran P (2015) The impact of comorbid personality difficulties on response to IAPT treatment for depression and anxiety. *Behaviour Research and Therapy 73*: 1–7.

Hepgul N, King S, Amarasinghe M, Breen G, Grant N, Grey N, ... and Wingrove J (2016) Clinical characteristics of patients assessed within an Improving Access to Psychological Therapies (IAPT) service: results from a naturalistic cohort study (Predicting Outcome Following Psychological Therapy; PROMPT). *BMC Psychiatry 16*(1): 52.

Kellogg S (2004) Dialogical encounters: Contemporary perspectives on 'chairwork' in psychotherapy. *Psychotherapy: Theory, Research, Practice, Training 41*: 310–320.

Martin DJ, Garske JP and Davis MK (2000) Relation of the therapeutic alliance with outcome and other variables: a meta-analytic review. *Journal of Consulting and Clinical Psychology 68*(3): 438–450.

Sheffield A and Waller G (2012) Clinical use of schema inventories. In: van Vreeswijk M, Broersen J and Nadort M. *The Wiley-Blackwell Handbook of Schema Therapy: Theory, Research, and Practice*. pp. 111–124.

Young JE (1990) *Cognitive therapy for personality disorders: A schema-focused approach*. Sarasota, FL: Professional Resource Exchange, Inc.

Young JE (2005) *The Young Schema Questionnaire*. New York: Schema Therapy Institute.

Young JE, Arntz A, Atkinson T, Lobbestael J, Weishaar ME, Van Vreeswijk MF and Klokman J (2007) *The Schema Mode Inventory*. New York: Schema Therapy Institute.

Young JE, Klosko JS and Weishaar ME (2003) *Schema Therapy: A Practitioner's Guide*. New York: Guilford Press.

PART III

THE THERAPEUTIC RELATIONSHIP IN DIFFERENT CLIENT GROUPS

14

CBT WITH YOUNG PEOPLE

LORNA TAYLOR AND TROY TRANAH

CHAPTER OVERVIEW

The past decade has seen the publication of numerous randomised control trials evaluating the effectiveness of CBT with young people with a range of disorders. Typically, models and techniques developed for work with adults have been modified and applied to children. However, cognitive therapy with young people differs from that with adults, and the need to adapt intervention to the cognitive, developmental and verbal needs of the young person has been recognised (Ronen, 1998). Within this consideration, there is vast clinical variation and the individual presentation of each young person must be considered to determine the relative focus on cognitive and behavioural aspects of CBT to be offered and thus enable effective engagement. This chapter discusses the importance of the therapeutic relationship with young people undertaking CBT and considers the challenges and barriers before outlining therapeutic skills that may support the development and maintenance of an effective and positive therapeutic relationship.

OVERVIEW OF THE MODEL

There is no specific model for working with adolescents within a CBT framework and models used with adults are often, flexibly applied. The key tenets of CBT for adults remain, with an increased focus on the environmental contingencies and impact of the wider system with the family, educational and social contexts.

In contrast to adults, very few young people attend therapy on their own volition, and frequently they are referred to therapy because their psychological difficulties create a problem for the system around them (e.g. school, home). They may not recognise their difficulties and, even if they do, they may not want to engage in an often stigmatised process of seeking help from a professional. A small, but growing, number of studies highlight that therapeutic relationship variables, including alliance, are important in establishing engagement in therapy and are associated with better outcomes in children and adolescents (Shirk and Karver, 2003; Shirk et al., 2011). A positive alliance promotes participation in therapy sessions and therapy completion (Kendall, 2006), and alliance has been demonstrated as a factor directly related to CBT treatment outcome (Kazdin et al., 2005). The engagement with a young person in CBT is therefore understood to be challenging and a key determinant of the success of therapy.

Young people do not exist in isolation, and their engagement is frequently determined by the engagement and participation of the adults around the young person; from practically attending sessions and this being prioritised, to others feeling that therapy is useful and effective. It is important that the clinician is aware of the family structure, the systematic implications of any interventions and psychosocial factors that may impact on therapy with children and adolescents (Stallard, 2006).

ENGAGING THE CLIENT

> Sophie is a 14-year-old female with depression and self-harm behaviours. She has started to disengage from education and has little motivation to engage in any activities, preferring to be alone at home. Sophie's parents believe that she is not going to school because of difficulties getting along with the teachers. She has received detentions since Year 7 and teachers have expressed concern about her behaviour, stating that she appears unmotivated and can become oppositional. Sophie feels that she hasn't been able to settle into the new school and has found it difficult. She finds it hard to concentrate in class and has been repeatedly told off for distracting others and not completing work. Sophie has found it difficult to make new friends at the school and has been bullied. She sought help from her school counsellor in Year 7 but felt that they did nothing to help her. She was teased by peers following them being aware of her speaking to the counsellor at school and she only attended on one occasion. She wants to do well in her exams next year but doesn't feel able to manage. She tells teachers she doesn't care. Her non-attendance is a source of anxiety and she feels like a failure and is increasingly hopeless. She feels that she has let her parents down and finds it hard to tell them that she has been having difficulties. Her mother has had depression since the birth of her sister five years ago. Her parents are aware that she has started self-harming. Whilst her parents want her to stop, Sophie doesn't want to, as she feels it is the only thing that helps her feel better when she is upset. She doesn't think that they understand and that they see her as being a 'difficult teenager.'

A strong therapeutic alliance is essential for adolescents, who often present with high levels of hopelessness and isolation like Sophie (Brent et al., 1998). A genuine, caring and empathic therapist will enable Sophie to attend therapy and be exposed to, and actively engage with, the CBT intervention. Problems with the therapeutic alliance and relationship, more than other factors, are associated with early termination of therapy, and thus the therapeutic relationship is critical to the success of therapy (Garcia and Weisz, 2002). Older children are less likely to report close relationships with their therapist compared to younger children (DeVet, 2003), and engaging adolescents in therapy poses unique difficulties related to the development of the therapeutic relationship. The role of communication, exploring motivation, adapting session delivery and involving others will be outlined.

COMMUNICATION

Whilst adolescence is a time when young people are separating from parents, adults and figures of authority, they want someone to understand, listen and attend to what they have to say (Rice and Dolgin, 2008), and the utilisation of a Motivational Interviewing (MI) approach has been shown to be effective with adolescents who demonstrate reluctance to engage (Naar-King and Suarez, 2011). Taking an open-minded, non-judgemental stance and listening reflectively can avoid the push towards change that a young person may expect in therapy and may frequently 'push back' against, leading to disengagement. The approach involves attempting to understand the young person's perspectives and helping them feel understood, so that they can identify personally meaningful goals and help them to evaluate their current difficulties.

The use of reflective statements alongside open-ended questions is a way of providing balance. Certain open-ended questions can be particularly helpful for eliciting information and such questions can take the focus away from the young person and enquire about other people in the person's life. The use of well-timed affirmations can highlight a young person's strength and increase positivity in the engagement process. The use of stems ('what you're saying is ...', 'it sounds like ...') is common when reflecting but can often take away from the content of the message or provide unnecessary words in an interaction and often portray a sense of formality. This can be annoying for a young person, and therapists are encouraged to drop the stems, or avoid overuse, in interactions with young people.

Therapist: Hi Sophie, thanks for coming to see me today.

Sophie: I didn't want to and I won't be coming back. I don't want to talk.

Therapist: Ok. Lots of people that come to see me say that. It's not an easy thing to do. Do you know why it is you don't want to talk to me?

Sophie: What's the point? I am only here because Mum said I have to.

Therapist: Ah ok, so you didn't really want to come today. Thanks for telling me that. It's great that you did. Is there something that Mum is concerned about for her to want you to come here?

Sophie: She's not worried about me.

Therapist: So you don't feel she's worried about you. Has something happened recently for Mum to think coming to see me would be a good idea?

Sophie: She's getting on my case because I haven't been going to school.

MOTIVATION TO ENGAGE IN THERAPY

Risk behaviours are frequently prioritised as a goal for therapy by therapists and the wider system around a young person given their impact on a young person's safety. However, young people may not always view such behaviours as a treatment target.

Sophie is reluctant to address her self-harm behaviour as she perceives it as helpful in managing her emotions. MI skills could be utilised by her therapist to allow consideration of her reduced ability to generate goals due to her belief that things cannot change and allow for an open exploration of thinking about how things could be different, encouraging the expression of her view and perceptions of events, while her therapist listens for, and reinforces, signs of motivation. The approach can address the challenges faced by Sophie regarding her belief that others don't understand her emotional difficulties, and that they are primarily concerned about her behaviours due to their impact on educational engagement.

Young people may often present as reluctant to engage as they have little confidence that they can make meaningful changes to address their patterns of anxiety, depression or distress. For Sophie, it would be important to explore whether she genuinely doesn't want to give up her self-harm or, more likely, whether she feels that she can't cope without it and doesn't know how she would manage her emotional difficulties without self-harm.

There are times when, due to a lack of motivation or ability to generate a response or communicate this effectively, a young person may find it difficult to answer open-ended questions, and more resistant adolescents may not want to answer these types of questions. Multiple choice questions can provide a helpful, structured alternative. Providing a structure for the conversation and exploring motivation whilst offering choice can be helpful.

Sophie: I don't know why cutting myself is a problem. It helps me chill out and I've never had to go to A&E.

Therapist: You've never really had any problems because of your self-harm?

Sophie: It isn't a problem. I don't do it a lot, it helps me feel better. Loads of people do it worse than I do.

Therapist: Of course. It really is your choice about whether or not you are going to stop self-harming. Whilst people can try to stop you, it has to be your decision.

Sophie: Yes.

Therapist: Can you tell me why self-harm is helpful for you?

Sophie: I don't know.

Therapist: Some people say that it can help them feel better when they feel rubbish, or that it can be a way of showing other people when they are stressed out. Do either of those seem right for you?

Sophie: I don't show other people!

Therapist: No, you don't do you. Is self-harm a way of feeling better when you're stressed and low?

Sophie: Yes.

Therapist: That makes sense when you've told me how hard it feels when you are feeling that way.

Therapist tip

During points of frustration or resistance from a young person, take time to step back and assess what is going on for them in that moment. Consider potential difficulties prior to session and plan ahead to enable you to be most effective in the moment and not pulled in to a battle!

It is essential to outline a framework for the therapeutic relationship that allows the adolescent to make autonomous decisions but also establishes clear boundaries and expectations. The tasks of establishing rapport, setting clear boundaries and expectations, whilst also allowing for autonomy can present challenges. The use of transparency and honesty in anticipating therapy interfering factors and negotiating ways to manage these in advance can be beneficial. Naar-King and Suarez (2011) provide helpful practical guidance regarding the application of MI with young people to facilitate engagement. Table 14.1 provides some ideas to facilitate motivation and collaboration.

Table 14.1 Promoting motivation through collaboration

What to do	What not to do
Support autonomy	Take responsibility or control
Guide	Prescribe
Evoke intrinsic motivation and confidence	Tell the young person why and how to change
Create an atmosphere of warmth and acceptance	Focus on behaviour change or problem solving at the expense of expressing empathy
Elicit discrepancy between the young person's behaviour and their goals	Emphasise external demands in your reasons to change
Actively listen	Convince or interpret
Promote behaviour specific optimism and hope	Focus on global factors or undermine self-efficacy and ability to change with unrealistic goals
Collaborate with the young person regarding the goals and tasks of treatment in the initial encounter	Assume to know what the 'real' problem is or assume to have the 'best ideas' on how to fix the problem

NON-VERBAL SKILLS AND ADAPTATIONS

Concrete techniques with clear and simple instructions are beneficial when working with young people. The challenge for working with this client group can often be how to translate abstract concepts into simple and understandable examples. Therapy materials and concepts should be presented at an appropriate level for the young person's ability (Young and Brown, 1996). There can be a need to develop suitable therapeutic materials, and imaginative and creative approaches can often increase motivation and engagement. Thought bubbles, cartoons, imagery and metaphors based upon the child's everyday life are helpful. Alternative methods of conveying the concepts of CBT through, for example, play and puppetry, could be explored for use with younger children. The use of movies, social media and music may also facilitate engagement and interaction.

Language can be a barrier to engagement, so adapting tasks to match language abilities is essential. The pacing and structure of sessions should always be matched to the young person's abilities and needs to support their engagement. Of caution, young people may be more likely to present as tangential and wanting to use the therapist for wider social support that may not always be therapeutically relevant. It is important that the therapist carefully navigates the need to express interest and care with adherence to a therapeutic agenda and structured focus on goals. An awareness of this issue, appropriate boundaries and transparency around the relationship between client and therapist can also be beneficial in preventing issues that may arise at the end of therapy, for example, young people viewing a therapist as a friend and wanting to maintain contact.

ENGAGING THE SYSTEM

In contrast to adults, young people are likely to be more immersed in wider systems such as families, peer networks and schools. The focus of CBT lies with providing intervention for young people within these environments (Ronen, 1998), and it is imperative that therapists appreciate the complex systemic issues that surround a young person and design interventions accordingly. The systems in which the young person functions can reinforce or extinguish adaptive coping and functioning developed within therapy. Family and school involvement and consultation, alongside consideration of peer influences, can be critical for the successful generalisation of progress in therapy.

PARENT/CARER ENGAGEMENT AND ALLIANCE

Parental involvement in the young person's therapy is related to therapeutic outcomes and increases the likelihood that the young person attends therapy consistently, completes homework tasks and generalises skills learnt in therapy to the home environment (Diamond et al., 2000). In addition, there is recognition that there is a relationship between parent–therapist alliance and early termination of therapy with young people (Garcia and Weisz, 2002). Whilst there is indication that the importance of parental involvement is greater with younger children, this is not always the case and several factors determine the extent to which a therapist may involve parents in the therapy (e.g. developmental profile, parental mental health and resource, relationship dynamics with parents). In engaging parents and carers, it is important to consider the relationship dynamics and beliefs of parents regarding the young person's difficulties. Parents may present as feeling responsible for the difficulties, they may feel judged by professionals or may minimise the difficulties faced by the child. All of these require careful formulation and consideration to enable engagement and co-working.

PARENTAL ROLE IN SUPPORTING ENGAGEMENT

The actual role and extent of parental involvement varies considerably. Stallard (2006) highlights numerous potential roles, including facilitator, co-therapist or client in their own right. The focus and emphasis can vary depending upon the chronological age of the young person, their developmental and social abilities, their willingness to involve parents in their therapy and the willingness and resource of parents to play an active role.

The most explicit role of parents relates to the role of reinforcement and contingencies based on behavioural principles. Therapists can support the appropriate use of rewards to communicate expectations and increase motivation. The ability of a system to reward may facilitate engagement and utilisation of therapy skills outside of sessions. For Sophie, the therapist may encourage her parents to spend time with her following sessions or schedule a positive activity together to demonstrate their encouragement of her attendance. They may also be encouraged to take an active role in checking in with a positive activity schedule or homework tasks and praising or paying attention to their completion.

PARENTS AS FACILITATOR AND CO-THERAPISTS

Parents commonly assume a role of facilitating treatment and the engagement of a young person with their therapy within and beyond the therapy room, and there is emerging evidence that this is beneficial (Reynolds et al., 2013).

Parents can have a role as a co-therapist within sessions, providing prompting and supporting a young person's engagement more directly. This may involve the therapist directly involving parents in discussion of the young person's perspective, asking parents to support reflection and generation of information that the young person may find difficult. Commonly, parents are educated into the treatment rationale and the transfer of skills from clinical to real-life situations can be encouraged. Parental involvement is highlighted as facilitating continuation of improvement after the intervention has ended (Spence et al., 2000; Stallard, 2005).

The importance of parental psychopathology, parenting approach and management has been emphasised, particularly within anxiety disorders and the role of parents in maintenance of difficulties (Barrett et al., 1996). Spence et al. (2000) states that interventions that do not attempt to address parental behaviour and approach are likely to be ineffective. High levels of parental psychopathology and stressful life events are likely to impair the quality of the therapeutic relationship by reducing available emotional and social resources and attention to devote to therapy for the young person. Sophie's mother is experiencing depression and the family have a younger child to care for; both factors may limit the time and resource that parents have to support Sophie to attend session, consider any difficulties in therapy and to generalise skills outside of session. Where parental resources are limited, the therapist may seek to identify alternative adults or systems that can provide support.

It is important to be transparent with the young person about the role of parent working and agree their parents' involvement, particularly with adolescents. The therapist will need to carefully consider how to work with Sophie to enable her mother's engagement. It is often helpful to explore with the young person what they think their parents' view of their difficulties is and to suggest that they agree to the therapist working with parents to increase each other's understanding of the difficulty from each perspective. It is not uncommon for communication to break down between a young person and their parents, and the therapist can provide a useful means of addressing barriers within the parent–child relationship. In the example of Sophie, the therapist could state that they are interested to know why her mother is 'always on her case,' validating that this must feel difficult and intrusive for her and suggesting that the therapist could work with her mother to explore this.

PREDICTING AND PREVENTING THREATS TO THE THERAPEUTIC ALLIANCE

SOCIAL AND COGNITIVE SKILLS

Consideration of Sophie's cognitive and social abilities will be important in establishing a comprehensive understanding of her presentation and adapting therapy to enable her to engage with it meaningfully and effectively. Whilst her difficulties at school may be attributed to her depressive symptoms, they may precede the depression and be important factors in the onset and maintenance of her current presentation. Whilst consideration of chronological age is important, it is nonspecific, and it is important that her therapist pays adequate attention to developing an individual formulation and understanding of wider social, emotional and cognitive functioning within a longitudinal formulation. This will determine whether Sophie is able to engage in sophisticated techniques requiring monitoring, reflection, exploration and rational analysis or benefit more from simple cognitive strategies and behavioural intervention. Language ability, perspective taking, reasoning and verbal regulation are all highlighted as key factors when undertaking therapy with young people (Ronen, 1998). Consideration of such variables early in therapy will avoid potential resistance or avoidance that could occur should the therapy demand exceed the abilities of a young person and enhance engagement.

For young people with comprehension or concentration difficulties, the use of two-way feedback at regular intervals may be increasingly important for successful ongoing engagement, particularly when important, confusing or emotionally charged information is being addressed. Major summaries should also occur at the beginning and end of sessions as routine, led by clinician or adolescent, to help reinforce and consolidate material discussed.

VIEW OF THE DIFFICULTIES

In some cases, young people may not possess the level of insight required to understand a need for behavioural or emotional change, and consequently, they may be less willing to engage in therapy. Whilst those around them may be considering the long-term impact of their mental health difficulties and related reduction in engagement in education or social activities, young people are frequently unable to consider the impact beyond the immediate here-and-now. Therapy may be best based on an experiential here-and-now approach, and connecting coping skills to concrete actions is likely to help a young person attend to, recall and use coping skills developed in therapy.

The level of insight and reflection demonstrated by a young person may improve with age as they learn more sophisticated cognitive processes and engage in social comparisons (Lamb et al., 1999), and it has been predicted that engagement in therapy and the therapeutic bond may increase with age due to increased insight into their difficulties and resultant increased motivation to change (Shirk and Saiz, 1992). As outlined in Chapter 2, tasks, goals and the direct bond between therapist and client are important factors in the alliance. Whilst we may expect a young person's ability to understand therapy tasks and goals to improve with age, the relationship between bond with a therapist and age may be more complex.

AUTONOMY

During adolescence, emerging issues of autonomy and independence may make a young person unwilling to participate in therapy that other adults, including parents, may have suggested. Relationships with peers are a crucial part of development, and an understanding of peer relationships is required for meaningful assessment and intervention. The positioning of the therapist as someone who promotes collaboration, listens to and incorporates information brought by the young person whilst also teaching without a didactic approach is likely to support a young person to maintain their independence but access information and support.

Reflective question

What is your stance as a therapist? Do you adopt different roles with different young people? If so, do you have any thoughts on why this may be?

PAST EXPERIENCES

For both children and adolescents, the ability to enter into a relationship with a therapist is influenced by the young person's relationships and experiences of adults to date, including parents. Stable and positive relationships with parents, teachers and other adults in early life play an important role in the development of a therapeutic relationship (Rubin and Niemeier, 1992). Sophie has positive relationships with her parents and teachers despite more recent difficulties. Sophie's therapist needs to explore any previous help-seeking behaviour and any cognitions or beliefs, positive or negative, that may impact on her willingness to engage. Whilst the exploration of relevant beliefs and perceptions of help-seeking may be relevant to any adult receiving CBT, the on-going development and formation of such beliefs with young people presents a different challenge.

WORKING WITH THREATS TO THE THERAPEUTIC ALLIANCE

Progress in therapy is often disrupted by obstacles and barriers to engagement. Some key barriers and suggested solutions are presented in Table 14.2. The individual formulation is important in predicting obstacles, to enable the therapist to shape the intervention plan to prepare for and negotiate any therapeutic impasses.

Sophie has difficulties with concentration that have led to behavioural difficulties in school. Anticipating difficulties in engaging in long sessions, checking in on the need for breaks and frequently checking understanding will be important in engaging Sophie during the intervention. The therapist should consider the language used in therapy, simplifying language and ensuring it is accessible to Sophie's level of development. The amount of material covered in sessions and expectation on Sophie will be important during agenda setting, and sufficient time should be allocated to checking in on each therapeutic task. This will be important in avoiding challenging behaviour or a breakdown of engagement in sessions.

Helping Sophie to explore the impact of her difficulties without exacerbating her anxiety will be difficult. She is likely to be avoidant of discussing her self-harm behaviour and her difficulties with managing her low mood and anxiety. It will be important to anticipate this and normalise the difficulties in a confident and containing manner during the beginning of work together, whilst also holding and validating the difficulties that she is experiencing. Sophie may have a sense that 'no one can help' or want to help her, given her past experiences with teachers and school staff. The belief that change is possible is an important motivator for successful change. It is important to help adolescents to be hopeful and confident about their ability to impact their own future in a positive way.

Parental work may also present challenges. Sophie's parents' understanding of her behaviour and its relationship to her emotional functioning will require exploration and careful formulation. Consideration of her mother's depression may be important and parents' support of her attendance at school may be problematic. Sophie's mother may find it difficult to support the therapy and increase her use of positive activities. A separate session with Sophie's parents may be helpful as the formulation is likely to indicate that her parents' expectations and management of her difficulties may be acting to reinforce her beliefs about the possibility of change and benefits of therapy.

Sophie is motivated to engage in education. However, she doesn't believe that she can manage, and her confidence to re-engage is going to be important. Additionally, she fears negative evaluation from peers and teachers. Establishing a relationship with her teachers may be useful. We would likely discuss the mental health needs with those working with Sophie to develop their understanding of her behaviour and support them to effectively manage her in the classroom. Increasing her teacher's awareness of her anxieties related to her performance would be beneficial.

Table 14.2 Threats to the alliance with potential solutions

Problems	Ways to manage
Why should I see you if Mum isn't seeing anyone? It's not just me.	Focus on what is within the young person's control with recognition of the wider system.
I have school work to do.	Consider the impact of difficulties on education.
	Discuss the importance of emotional well-being in the future with consideration of beyond the here-and-now.

Problems	Ways to manage
Not wanting to come because parents want them to.	Explore motivation. Highlight autonomy and decision making. Resist pushing back.
Therapy doesn't help. My friends have had CBT and it was rubbish/didn't help.	Validate and explore concerns. Discuss the collaborative role of therapy and that it requires active engagement.
I always feel worse after sessions. It's too hard.	Practical management strategies for distress following sessions. Explore difficulties within a CBT formulation.

Reflective question

Consider a client you are working with at the moment. What are their beliefs about their difficulties? How might these appear and influence their behaviour in therapy? Would they impact on the tasks and goals of CBT or on the therapy relationship? What could you do to prepare for potential problems?

ENDING THERAPY

The ending of therapy is a time for reflection on progress made and the planning for sustaining any positive changes achieved in therapy. The role and perception of the therapist may be important for young people as they move towards managing without formal therapeutic support. The positioning of the therapist throughout the work together will impact on the young person's confidence that they are able to sustain progress without therapy. It is important that the therapist supports the young person to become their own therapist, both throughout therapy and, more explicitly, during the development of relapse prevention plans at the end of therapy. By positioning oneself as a coach and support, and encouraging a young person to be active in therapy, the therapist will be in a good position to encourage the idea that the next task is to manage difficulties as they arise, utilising skills and techniques learnt together in therapy and seeking support where needed from those around them. Being transparent about the goal of managing without therapy from the outset of therapy can be particularly helpful for young people. Some young people may wish to maintain contact with a therapist following the end of therapy and conversations regarding this can be challenging as the therapist balances a need to communicate genuine care versus a need for a clear and well managed ending.

CHAPTER SUMMARY

This chapter has discussed the challenges and tasks associated with engaging young people, using Sophie as an example of the complexity of adolescence and the importance of developmental and systemic considerations. In addition to considering the variety of challenges to engaging young people and those around them, the specific skills in interacting with young people and engaging them in intervention are outlined with examples. The importance of being transparent, reflective of therapeutic positioning and open to true collaboration in agreeing goals and monitoring progress is outlined, alongside consideration of the role of parents/carers.

FURTHER READING

Kendall P (2006) Guiding theory for therapy with children and adolescents. In: Kendall P (ed), Child and Adolescent Therapy: Cognitive-Behavioral Procedures. 3rd ed. New York: Guilford Press, pp. 3-30.

Naar-King S and Suarez M (eds) (2011) *Motivational Interviewing With Adolescents and Young Adults*. New York: Guilford Press.

Stallard P (2005) A Clinician's guide to think good-feel good: Using CBT with children and young people. Chichester, UK: John Wiley & Sons.

Stallard P (2009) Cognitive behaviour therapy with children and young people. In: Beinart H and Kennedy D (eds) *Clinical Psychology in Practice.* BPS Blackwell, pp. 117-126.

REFERENCES

Barrett P, Dadds M and Rapee R (1996) Family treatment of childhood anxiety: a controlled trial. *Journal of Consulting and Clinical Psychology 64*: 333–342.

Brent D, Kolko D, Birmaher B, Baugher M, Bridge J and Roth C (1998) Predictors of treatment efficacy in a clinical trial of three psychosocial treatments for adolescent depression. *Journal of the American Academy of Child & Adolescent Psychiatry 37*: 906–914.

DeVet K, Kim Y, Charlot-Swilley D, Ireys H (2003) The therapeutic relationship in child therapy: perspectives of children and mothers. *Journal of Clinical Child & Adolescent Psychology 32*: 277–283.

Diamond G, Diamond G and Liddle H (2000) The therapist–parent alliance in family-based therapy for adolescents. *Journal of Clinical Psychology 56*: 1037–1050.

Garcia J and Weisz J (2002) When youth mental health care stops: Therapeutic relationship problems and other reasons for ending youth outpatient treatment. *Journal of Consulting and Clinical Psychology 70*: 439–443.

Kazdin A, Marciano P and Whitley M (2005) The therapeutic alliance in cognitive-behavioral treatment of children referred for oppositional, aggressive, and antisocial behavior. *Journal of Consulting and Clinical Psychology 73*: 726–730.

Kendall P (2006) Guiding theory for therapy with children and adolescents. In: Kendall P (ed), *Child and Adolescent Therapy: Cognitive-Behavioral Procedures*. 3rd ed. New York: Guilford Press, pp. 3-30.

Lamb J, Puskar K, Sereika S and Corcoran M (1998) School- Based intervention to promote coping in rural teens. *The American Journal of Maternal/ Child Nursing 23*: 187–194.

Naar-King S and Suarez M (eds) (2011) *Motivational Interviewing With Adolescents and Young Adults*. New York: Guilford Press.

Reynolds S, Clark S, Smith H, Langdon P, Payne R, Bowers G, Norton E and Mclwham H (2013) Randomized controlled trial of parent-enhanced CBT compared with individual CBT for obsessive-compulsive disorder in young people. *Journal of Consulting and Clinical Psychology 81*: 1021–1026.

Rice F and Dolgin K (2008) *The Adolescent: Development, Relationships, and Culture*. 12th ed. Boston: Allyn and Bacon.

Ronen T (1998) Linking developmental and emotional elements into child and family cognitive-behavioural therapy. In: Graham P (ed) *Cognitive Behaviour Therapy for Children and Families*. Cambridge, UK: Cambridge University Press, pp. 1–15.

Rubin S and Niemeier D (1992) Non-verbal affective communication as a factor in psychotherapy. *Psychotherapy: Theory, Research, Practice, Training 29*: 596–602.

Shirk S and Karver M (2003) Prediction of treatment outcome from relationship variables in child and adolescent therapy: a meta-analytic review. *Journal of Consulting and Clinical Psychology 71*: 452–464.

Shirk S and Saiz C (1992) Clinical, empirical, and developmental perspectives on the therapeutic relationship in child psychotherapy. *Development and Psychopathology 4*: 713–728.

Shirk S, Karver M and Brown R (2011) The alliance in child and adolescent psychotherapy. *Psychotherapy 48*: 17–24.

Spence S, Donovan C and Brechman-Toussaint M (2000) The treatment of childhood social phobia: The effectiveness of a social skills training-based, cognitive-behavioral intervention, with and without parental involvement. *Journal of Child Psychology and Psychiatry, 41*: 713–726.

Stallard P (2005) *A Clinician's Guide to Think Good–Feel Good: Using CBT with Children and Young People*. Chichester, UK: John Wiley & Sons.

Stallard P (2006) The involvement of parents in child-focused cognitive behaviour therapy. *Hellenic Journal of Psychology 3*: 23–38.

Young J and Brown PF (1996) Cognitive behaviour therapy for anxiety: practical tips for using it with children. *Clinical Psychology Forum 91*: 19–21.

15

OLDER ADULTS

DEBORAH WALKER AND CHARLOTTE GARDNER

CHAPTER OVERVIEW

This chapter will focus on the specific factors that may arise when working with an older adult population and how this can impact on the development and maintenance of a therapeutic alliance during CBT. It will not address disorder-specific factors, as these will be covered elsewhere, but these should be considered in conjunction with this chapter.

Our current older adult population represents those born in the 1920s to 1950s. However, with every passing year, it shifts to encompass a gradually shifting group of people. Some of the challenges faced in older age may persist across these generational changes, but others are a facet of the time span into which people are born and raised. This chapter focuses on those older adults that have lived through, or been influenced by, the wars, political, social and technological changes that have occurred in the past 100 years.

MODEL UNDERPINNING TREATMENT

A CBT MODEL FOR OLDER ADULTS AND THE THERAPEUTIC RELATIONSHIP

Robert is a 72-year-old retired gentleman. He is highly anxious, low in mood and has stopped doing his regular activities. He is preoccupied with anxiety symptoms and fears he may not return to the life he had before. His anxiety started following an episode of physical ill health and being in hospital for three months. He has recovered physically but fears this will be the onset of further illness. This feels unbearable for him, as he's always seen himself as strong and dependable, which he equates with being well. He associates being ill with being a weak person who can't look after himself. Robert retired aged sixty-five and now has a part time job, which he has not felt able to return to since being physically unwell. His only previous experience of mental ill health was overhearing neighbours talking about a neighbour's wife taken to an asylum in the 1950s, after which she was never seen again.

Robert lives with his wife and has four adult children that he sees regularly. His children want to help but think he should slow down and not devote so much time to his part time job and other pursuits. He has always been the breadwinner in the house and views himself as the provider and protector of the household. Robert says that now he's become 'just another grumpy old man,' something he has fought against, having observed his own father become a 'grumpy old man.' He wonders if his family would be better off without him but doesn't have any plan to harm himself.

Robert represents an older adult client who has been referred for a course of CBT for depression. In considering how best to conceptualise Robert's difficulties and the likely impact on therapeutic alliance, the cognitive behavioural model of Laidlaw et al. (2003) can help to consider both disorder-specific and age-specific factors and how they may impact on the willingness of clients from this cohort to engage in therapy.

At the heart of this model is Beck's traditional framework (Beck, 1979): our early life experiences help us to form our core beliefs; these may not present in a problematic way until a specific event/series of events acts to trigger them, with the resulting negative automatic thinking and emotional reaction. Laidlaw has developed a broader framework around this, taking an older adult focus, which also considers cohort beliefs, role investments, health status, intergenerational linkages and the sociocultural context (Laidlaw et al., 2003). When working with Robert, the factors shown in Table 15.1 may impact on his engagement and adherence to a course of CBT.

Table 15.1 Engagement factors

Factors that may impact on Robert engaging with CBT
• Beliefs about mental health = madness = taken to an asylum
• View of himself as breadwinner, provider and protector for the family
• His children's view that he should slow down and fully retire
• Belief that unhappiness is a normal part of ageing
• Experience of physical illness requiring a three month hospital admission

Reflective question

Consider your own cohort beliefs about mental health difficulties and think about how these may affect your views on the effectiveness of therapy with an older adult client.

ENGAGING THE CLIENT

The assessment, engagement and socialisation of older adult clients to a course of CBT may benefit from taking place over a greater number of therapy sessions than with a younger person. They may be less familiar with mental health care pathways and the content of psychological therapies, which may give rise to a number of problematic myths about these services.

Robert's beliefs about mental health may be influenced by his limited awareness of people with mental health problems and his one notable experience being of someone being sent away to an asylum and not returning. When clients hold these types of beliefs and fears then it can impact on their willingness to be open in sessions. Successful engagement depends on gently exploring them at the start of therapy and allaying those fears as much as possible, without misleading.

Therapist: I wonder if talking about these feelings is difficult for you?

Robert: I've always been a strong person.

Therapist: What does being a strong person mean to you?

Robert: Being capable, independent. Not having to rely on others.

Therapist: So coming here and meeting with me, how does that feel?

Robert: That I've failed; I'm weak now and not able to look after myself.

Therapist: That must be frightening for you. I wonder if it's also frightening to talk about these fears?

Robert: I'm worried you'll think I'm mad. If I'm not able to look after myself, will you get me sent to the psychiatric hospital?

Therapist: Many patients I see have that fear, but stays in inpatient wards are always the last thing that are considered, when everything else has been tried. Currently, we believe people recover better from anxiety and depression when they stay at home and are seen in an outpatient clinic.

Giving a more realistic view of the workings of mental health services can work towards dispelling clients' concerns and a greater feeling of control over their treatment. Myths about what therapy can achieve can also impact on engagement. Establishing realistic goals for therapy should take the normal form of SMART (Specific, Measurable, Achievable, Realistic, Time-limited) goal development but also take into account any restrictions that physical health may impose and challenge any myths about what is, and isn't, attributable to age. In Robert's case, he is invested in his role as breadwinner and being a strong person without 'weaknesses.' This may lead him to believe that the only satisfactory outcome is to be entirely rid of any illness, physical or psychological. But he may also be wedded to ideas about whether change is actually possible if he overidentifies his difficulties as being due to old age. The belief that being old means change is impossible is a common myth, more likely to be found in an older adult population than a younger one. Spending time in the engagement sessions looking at the pros and cons of changing and exploring motivation and willingness to try behavioural changes are essential in order to foster engagement in therapy and work towards the client's goals.

Therapist: What would you like to gain from these sessions?

Robert: Not to be feeling miserable any more, get my health back. But I suspect this is all part of getting old, so I'll just have to get used to it.

Therapist: A common myth is that unhappiness is a normal part of getting old. If you weren't depressed, what would you be doing differently?

Robert: I'd be back doing my part time job, feeling like my old self.

Therapist: What one small change would you like to make as a result of therapy that would mean to you that you are moving towards 'being your old self'?

Robert: If I could get back to playing golf. I used to really enjoy meeting friends for a round, but I can't go back while I'm feeling like this.

Therapist: That sounds like a great goal; let's think together about what you could work on in therapy to help you reach that goal.

Whilst, in general, it is important not to rush the socialisation stage, particular care may need to be taken when the psychological component may not be so obvious, e.g. when it accompanies a physical health difficulty. CBT approaches for physical health conditions are commonplace in current NHS practice, but this has only emerged in recent decades. The average older adult has known a health service for a far greater period of time when the only treatment approach for physical health conditions was a medical one. Some older adults may have the experience of being a passive receiver of treatment, with the 'expert' (doctors) directing their treatment. CBT, in contrast, intrinsically entails a greater degree of collaboration, which may be a new concept for many older adults. From the very start, the therapist should seek to highlight the collaborative nature of therapy and dispel myths about the therapist holding all the expertise. This could entail taking the position of non-expert and asking a client to explain their medical condition, emphasising that they have a greater knowledge in this area. The therapist can introduce collaborative working by describing the specific CBT knowledge they have and how it may sit alongside their explanation.

Alan is 68 years old, married to Betty. He had to retire early from his job as a scaffolder due to his physical health. A year prior to retiring, he was diagnosed with chronic obstructive pulmonary disease (COPD). He coped well initially, keeping busy with his garden and picking up and looking after their two grandsons after school. He and Betty also enjoyed taking trips to the coast, Alan driving them by car.

However, his daughter and wife noticed he started to make excuses as to why they couldn't take their trips out, he became reluctant to go out in the car and was starting to neglect his garden, something he was previously extremely proud of. There was a marked decline in his physical health; despite recovering well from a chest infection, he was becoming much more breathless, wanting to stay at home more and becoming generally less active. A review in the chest clinic noted his COPD remained unchanged, but they noted his mood was low and he was getting panic attacks. The chest clinic decided to make a referral for CBT, but Alan is unclear why he is being seen by a therapist as he thinks it's understandable to be feeling low in mood as he's physically unwell and life doesn't hold much for someone of his age.

Socialising Alan to a CBT approach would benefit from starting from a point of purely being curious about the impact of COPD on Alan's life and when he has struggled more, or less, with this condition. Rushing straight to psychological symptoms can risk alienating older adult clients with clear physical health difficulties. So, a more gradual process of looking for consistencies and inconsistencies in their response to their physical health difficulties may be more useful.

Therapist: Alan, can I check your understanding of why you have been referred to a therapist?

Alan: I'm not sure to be honest. I have a chest complaint, I'm not mad.

Therapist: I know you have a very real medical problem that makes you breathless, and sometimes, when people have breathing difficulties, it causes a lot of worry. Can you tell me what aspects of your illness cause you worry?

Alan: I get very breathless when I have to do things. When it occurs, I stop what I'm doing and take a rest, as I worry I may not be able to catch my breath if I carry on.

Therapist: I see, and I understand you were particularly unwell recently?

Alan: Yes, I had a chest infection and couldn't do anything at all.

Therapist: And now that the infection has cleared, have you started doing more?

Alan: Not really.

Therapist: Why is that?

Alan: I'm worried that, if I do too much, I might not be able to catch my breath, so I prefer to play it safe.

It has been well documented that, when socialising older adults to a CBT model of their difficulties, it is beneficial to share ideas with the client as soon as possible, but perhaps initially through using simple conceptualisations (Figure 15.1) involving a few components of the model (Charlesworth and Reichelt, 2004).

Alan's simple conceptualisation: *Activity = Panic = Avoidance activity*

Figure 15.1 Simple CBT conceptualisation

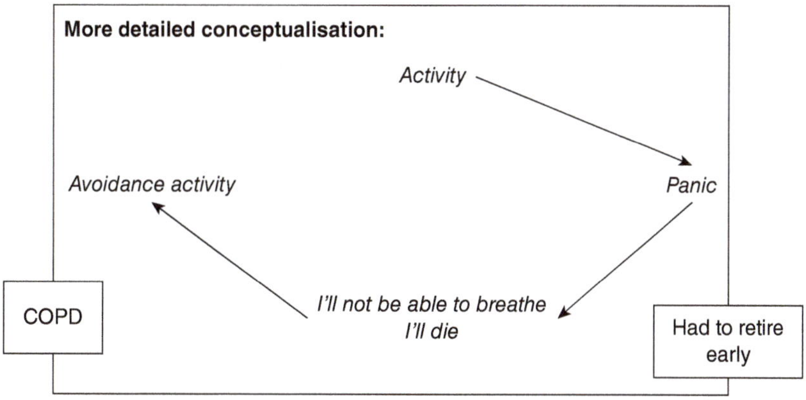

Figure 15.2 Expanded CBT conceptualisation

Then, therapy can proceed by presenting this to the client and using it to pose further questions, in order to build a fuller understanding of their difficulties (Figure 15.2).

This type of simple conceptualisation helps older adult clients to begin to show some curiosity towards a psychological understanding of their difficulties and is more effective than introducing a comprehensive formulation. It is helpful to notice the client's own language to describe their emotional states and initially use these in conceptualisations. Many older adults describe their anxiety or depression using somatic terms, for example, 'pain in my stomach.' The therapist needs to be aware of this and to ensure their own language is matched to this, with the avoidance of 'psychobabble' jargon. The word 'homework,' as used in CBT, meaning between-session work to test out new coping strategies, may mean something completely different to an older person who may have had a difficult schooling experience (e.g. interrupted by World War II) where 'homework' became synonymous with failure and criticism.

Therapist tips

When engaging older adult clients:

1. Don't rush socialising to CBT model, emphasise collaboration and use adapted formulations.
2. Explore myths and negative beliefs about ageing and change and the ability to engage in therapy.
3. Be sensitive to labels used to describe homework tasks and language of distress.

PREDICTING AND PREVENTING THREATS TO THE THERAPEUTIC ALLIANCE

The potential for threats to the therapeutic alliance bear many similarities to working with younger adult populations. However, some factors are more likely to occur with an older adult population. Some may be unavoidable and leave a permanent fracture in the alliance, e.g. a prolonged hospital stay or decline of their physical health to the extent engagement in therapy is impossible. For many clients, ensuring you have understood their individual needs before commencing therapy can help to predict possible threats that may arise and minimise their impact on the therapeutic alliance.

In our assessment of Robert, we took care to identify how his beliefs could impact on his ability to engage in therapy, but it may also have been helpful to consider how the beliefs of his family could impact on the success of any therapeutic goals. Robert's children wanted to help but also thought he should slow down and not devote as much time to his job and other pursuits. This could create a conflict if CBT goals were directed towards him increasing his activity levels or re-engaging with his part-time job. It would be important to explore this possible conflict between Robert's wishes and those of his children's in order to ascertain whether goals needed to be changed or if Robert needed support in asserting his plan to his children.

We have also considered how Alan and Robert's beliefs about psychological models being helpful and the possibility of change in older adults can impact on engagement. However, the therapist also needs to be aware of and, if necessary, question their own beliefs and prejudices about ageing and potential for change. For example, a therapist may think 'I'm not surprised Alan is panicking and depressed, I would be too if I was in that situation.' These types of beliefs are likely to hinder a therapist's ability to maintain a working therapeutic alliance with an older adult client. Whilst they may generally be more common with therapists new to working with older adults, it is important that any therapist regularly checks their own age-related biases.

More generally, older adult therapy assessments should include enquiries about sensory and cognitive impairments, as well as physical health difficulties. Sessions can be adapted to ensure hearing impairments are accommodated for through the use of therapy spaces that have minimal auditory distractions, that hearing aids are worn if needed and that rooms with hearing loops are used if they add benefit. If the client has visual impairments, ensure the room has sufficient light. If they need spectacles, they should bring and wear them, and diagrams or charts should be enlarged if necessary. By regularly checking in with clients, by clarifying their understanding of what has been discussed in therapy, and through asking clients to verbally report their understanding of information discussed, we can reduce the risk of misunderstandings.

If there is uncertainty about cognitive impairment, therapists could consider referring clients for a comprehensive assessment of cognitive abilities or, if this has already been completed, ensure that the extent of difficulties is clarified with previous records and with the client. A client with even mild cognitive impairment may have difficulty remembering the content of sessions from week to week or within session. Although memory impairment should not rule out therapy, the therapist needs to work with the client to establish the best memory tools to use. This could include taping sessions or writing summaries during the session and ensuring that diaries are used to record future appointments or to aid recall of between-session tasks. In agreement with the client, it may also be helpful to include available family members as co-therapists to assist with prompting the client to attempt between-session tasks or to use thought-challenging tools.

In later life, the likelihood of a client having a co-morbid physical health difficulty is high, partly due to increasing frailty and partly because the impact of declining physical health on mental health may be the precise reason that they have been referred for psychological therapy. In terms of frailty, the location of therapy may need to be adapted, e.g. providing home visits, ensuring clinics are on the ground floor, facilities have wheelchair access etc. The sessions may need to be scheduled for particular times of day or length of appointment to maximise clients being sufficiently alert to engage in therapy. It is important to ensure that the impact of physical health on mood is included in formulations and that the relative impact of physical health in relation to more long-standing patterns of dysfunction is understood.

When presented with a client with multiple physical health difficulties, or deterioration in their physical health, a therapist may conclude that this will automatically lead to deterioration in mental health. However, the impact of physical health on mental health is variable and dependent on protective factors. These include the client's perception of control over their condition, the chronicity of the condition, pain associated with the condition and impact on functional abilities, also the amount of support that they have in managing the condition, either from health professionals, family or friends.

Therapist tip

When predicting therapeutic alliance risks:

1. Assess for sensory impairments.
2. Assess for cognitive impairments.
3. Clarify physical health difficulties and their specific impact on the client and their ability to engage in talking therapy.

WORKING WITH THREATS TO THE ALLIANCE

Fatemeh is an 82-year-old widowed lady who up until three years ago was leading a very active life with involvement in local politics, fundraising and church activities. However, she now spends the majority of her time at her home, either in bed or watching TV. She has difficulties mobilising due to arthritis, and this led to a fall, which left her with a broken hip. Up until that point, she had been coping well with the arthritis symptoms and was able to continue with her activities, but since the fall, she has gradually lost confidence in going out and no longer sees the point in engaging in the activities she had previously enjoyed. This has left her low in mood and isolated from the friends that she used to see regularly, as she doesn't like them to see her at her home in her current condition and doesn't feel motivated to go out to meet with them. Therapy sessions occur at Fatemeh's home in her lounge, which serves as her bedroom, and every time you arrive, she offers you a drink which you decline. She says that she would like to engage in therapy but you notice that, as sessions progress, it is increasingly difficult to maintain a CBT focus to your sessions as she appears more comfortable talking to you about the politics of the week rather than staying on track with the CBT session.

Maintaining a therapeutic focus to CBT sessions can be particularly difficult when working in a client's home, and although this is not exclusive to working with older adults, it is more common. Add to that the possibility of you being the only social contact, or one of a limited pool of contacts, and there is a risk that therapy sessions may become an opportunity for a social chat. Socialising a client to the format of CBT at the beginning may go some way to pre-empting this difficulty, but if it continues to reoccur, then it should be brought up as a discussion point to enlist the client's help in staying on track.

> *Therapist*: Fatemeh, I've noticed that although we start out talking about how low mood has impacted on you this week, we often get diverted to talking about what's been happening in the local news. That may be because you tell me watching the news makes you feel low, but it may also be because politics has been of such interest to you in the past? I find myself very interested in what we're talking about but I wonder if it's getting in the way of us working on your goals for therapy? I wonder if we could think together of a way that we could both stay on track with the goals that you had for therapy?'

Sharing the responsibility for going off track minimises the client feeling that they have got something wrong and reinforces the collaborative nature of CBT. Sometimes, the process of noticing and naming the 'going off track' can be helpful, as can being more specific at the agenda setting point. Setting time limits for general updates can also ensure that therapy remains focused on what is most helpful to the client. In some circumstances, it may be necessary to weigh up with the client whether it is truly therapy the client wants or, more specifically, social contact. From a therapist's point of view, CBT may seem like a good choice of treatment for the low mood symptoms that Fatemeh is experiencing. Seeing her friends again could either be a method for resolving low mood or a successful outcome of therapy. However, if Fatemeh is not on board with this method of overcoming her difficulties, then the weekly CBT contact may begin to serve as more of a social outlet. In this case, redirecting the client to other services, such as befriending, may meet a client's goals more effectively.

When working with older adults with chronic physical health difficulties, there is always the possibility for the therapeutic alliance to be ruptured by further declines in physical health. It is helpful to retain a flexible stance to the progress of therapy. It may be helpful to consider putting therapy on pause for a brief period and providing the client with written material which they can access until their physical health improves. Alternatively, goals may need to be revised if the physical health decline makes initial goals no longer achievable.

ENDING THERAPY

Good CBT practice suggests that the end of therapy should be discussed from the start, that clients should be aware of how many sessions they will attend, that follow-up sessions are used and a collaboratively produced relapse plan developed.

Therapy with older adults requires this approach, but particular care should be taken to reinforce clients becoming their 'own therapist.' Older adults can be more likely to take a view of medical professionals as holding all the expertise, so this approach reduces the likelihood of the therapist being seen as the expert with the answers. Clients invested in their therapist as an expert may find the discharge process more challenging. Typically, the end of CBT would include follow-up appointments (often one or three months) after discharge. However, for some clients, the discharge may need to take place over a longer period, with the appointments spaced further apart to allow the client to disengage from the therapeutic relationship more gradually. Gallagher and Thompson (1998) found that more gradual terminations were easier for clients to adjust to and were associated with more long-term gains.

Rosemary had made significant gains in her therapy coping with worry; however, as discussions of therapy ending were broached, it was noted she became more worried again. The therapist explored with Rosemary what the next six months would be like after sessions ended and discovered that it was not the worry that was the issue, but the thought of worry. The usual three month follow-up appointment was booked, but instead, the therapist also offered the option for Rosemary to call should she need a telephone session before this appointment. At the follow-up session, it was noted that Rosemary had not needed to call her therapist, proof that she was able to cope without the session. This information made ending therapy easier for Rosemary.

Due to the nature of ageing, and possibly declining physical health over the course of therapy, older adult clients may report feeling worse at the end of therapy. This can be difficult for both the novice therapist and the client, as expectations are generally that people feel better by the end of a course of CBT. This can be ameliorated by reviewing skills learned over the course of therapy and applying these to ever changing situations. If therapy sessions were interrupted by setbacks in their health, it may be helpful to use these occasions to learn how to manage these problems, so that they can still function to their optimal level, rather than curing them of these problems.

Occasionally, the ending of therapy when working with older adults can be as a result of the death of the client - this may be expected or unexpected. Nevertheless, it is something that needs to be considered when working with ageing clients. Having good, regular supervision and an opportunity to reflect on this and its impact on the therapist is an important consideration when working therapeutically with older adults.

CHAPTER SUMMARY

This chapter has looked at four cases presenting issues specific to working with older adults that may impact on establishing and maintaining a therapeutic relationship. The importance of taking time to engage this client group is discussed, as well as ending therapy, which may require a slightly adapted approach to working with younger adults. The significant impact of physical health, and the myths and beliefs which both clients and therapists may hold, which are potentially threatening the therapeutic alliance, are explored. A specific CBT model that was developed by Laidlaw et al. (2003) to work with older adults is described.

FURTHER READING

Knight BG (2004) *Psychotherapy with Older Adults*. California: Sage.

REFERENCES

Beck AT, Rush AJ, Shaw BF and Emery G (1979) *Cognitive Therapy of Depression*. New York: The Guilford Press.

Charlesworth G and Reichelt F (2004) Keeping conceptualizations simple: Examples with family carers of people with dementia. *Behavioural and Cognitive Psychotherapy 32*(4): 401–409.

Gallagher D and Thompson LW (1998) *Depression in the Elderly: A Behavioural Treatment Manual*. Los Angeles: University of Southern California Press.

Laidlaw K, Thompson LW, Dick-Siskin L and Gallagher-Thompson D (2003) *Cognitive Behaviour Therapy with Older People*. Chichester: Wiley.

16

TRANSCULTURAL ISSUES IN THE THERAPEUTIC RELATIONSHIP

PATRICIA D'ARDENNE

CHAPTER OVERVIEW

This chapter continues with the necessary and sufficient conditions of the therapeutic relationship (Moorey and Lavender, Chapters 1 and 2) and threats to the alliance but, in addition, focuses on the CBT relationship with clients where therapists are working with one cultural model with someone from another. Such an alliance requires further transition and translation. There is a growing evidence base of successful adaptations of CBT in other cultural or ethnic settings (d'Ardenne et al., 2007; Graham et al., 2013; Hays and Iwamasa, 2006; Janelle et al., 2014; Robjant and Fazel, 2010). CBT has universal applicability as long as the values, history and beliefs of all parties are acknowledged and used within the therapeutic relationship. There may be a need for literal interpretation (spoken) or translation (written), requiring the therapist to invest in training in the use of interpreters and translators, and to incorporate them ethically and effectively into the therapeutic process without intruding on the therapeutic relationship (d'Ardenne and Farmer, 2009; Mailloux, 2004). Readers will be given guidelines on how to use interpreters better for CBT. Then, there are black and minority ethnic clients, who have many experiences of racism, as well as those people who live with prejudice and social exclusion, whether on the basis of sexual orientation, disability, economic or educational privation – all of whom may perceive professionals and their organisations as 'establishment.' This chapter describes racism in mental health practice, as well as the origins and development of anti-discriminatory relationships in CBT. This chapter will propose CBT relationships can be better developed for all these client groups to promote engagement and trust and prevent alliance rupture. Examples will be given of how service users from other cultures, if given the opportunity, have helped clinicians find more appropriate metaphors and approaches in CBT. Finally, readers will have a chance to consider the supervision, training and personal development requirements likely to improve their relationships working outside their own culture.

INTRODUCING TRANSCULTURAL PSYCHOTHERAPY

CBT developed in the twentieth century within an individualistic, Western culture in which concepts like introspection, autonomy, self-determination and personal growth were assumed to be shared goals by therapists and their client populations. Dudgeon and Kelly (2014) called CBT 'culturally unaware' and 'not culturally responsive.' The needs of other cultures may not have been a priority in developing evidence-based practices. Indeed, Truax and Carkhuff (1967) made no reference to 'race' or 'culture' in their seminal *Towards Effective Counselling and Psychotherapy*.

But the Civil Rights movement in the United States led to anti-racist practice in psychiatry and psychotherapy, seeking to depathologise what was alien and to challenge the institutional and personal prejudices of those in power who had failed (increasingly) large numbers of the community in providing psychotherapy. In short, white folk got talking therapy; black folk were more likely to be diagnosed with psychosis and offered medication in hospital or prison. And the numbers, both in the United States and in Europe, proved it (Bhui and Bhugra, 2007; Fernando, 2010).

Alongside this, since the 1980s, the *User Movement* has spread from the United States and Europe to a global culture of involvement of the patient (Walcraft and Bryant, 2003) for support, information and empowerment of patient experts. The movement had criticised psychiatric services for not addressing inequality of access to services, misdiagnosis due to cultural or racial bias or patients being marginalised in our culture through the psychiatric referral and treatment process. User involvement is closely linked with Human Rights. Through information sharing, social networking, the expansion of research on patients as experts, good psychological and psychiatric care is deemed *a basic human right* (Patel et al., 2001; Silove, 2011). Therapists cannot proffer their own ignorance or refer to 'language barriers' as a reason to refuse care.

The challenges of developing a therapeutic relationship outside your own culture in CBT are always relative. Lago (2011) refers to seven dimensions of identity - gender; race; class; sexual orientation; disability; religion; and age - all the objects of anti-discriminatory practice. Our clients may define themselves culturally by many more - birth order; economic status; education; social networks; political beliefs; moral code; or football team!

CBT is a successful therapy precisely because it embodies a number of universally applicable psychological strategies, such as problem solving, identifying negative thoughts and images, linking thoughts with emotions and testing out thoughts in everyday life to see if they hold true (behavioural experiments). CBT encompasses key interpersonal therapeutic elements of empathy, goal setting, collaborative relationships, positive regard, genuineness and getting client feedback, as well as being empirically supported by studies with Ugandan, Australian Aboriginal, Inuit, Middle Eastern, Indian, Nigerian and Bangladeshi communities - to name but a few (Hays and

Iwamasa, 2006). The tide is changing. In Chapters 1 and 2 (Moorey and Lavender), we have already seen how CBT requires the clinician's *curiosity* to understand the client's emotions without judgement, in order to make sense of how clients are caught up in their problems. Does the transcultural therapeutic relationship mean that judgement is suspended until the therapist has grasped the full personal meaning of a problem? Is it robust enough to enable therapists to imagine situations beyond their direct experience, e.g. the horrors of war or the humiliations of racism?

Cross cultural models begin with therapists recognising, accepting and working from their own cultural framework, rather than assuming that CBT is culturally independent or neutral. Psychological theories may have universal application, but their practice is mediated by our own language, history, values and beliefs. Cross cultural relationships require the practitioner not just to meet clients with a shared language but to demonstrate enough respect, curiosity and trust to commence an effective therapeutic partnership. Although this model applies to all therapeutic relationships, this chapter will primarily concern itself with differences in transcultural settings (D'Ardenne and Mahtani, 1999).

ENGAGING THE CLIENT

Case example

You are assessing a black South African client who survived the Apartheid years and now suffers depression. On his ethnic monitoring form he indicates simply that he is a Communist; you ask him about this and he replies that it is his political identity, not his colour, that has shaped his struggle against the white supremacist regime.

Therapist tips

- Research the history of the South African Communist Party – from the client and elsewhere.
- Find out if other black clients prefer not to record their colour on your forms, and why not?
- Review ethnic monitoring in the light of this information.

The terms 'culture,' 'ethnic group,' and 'race' have created much heated discussion, not least because they have been used to subjugate, discriminate and exaggerate difference (Fernando, 2010). One definition of 'culture' could be limited to *the shared history, practices, beliefs, and values of a racial, regional or religious group of people* (D'Ardennne and Mahtani, 1999). In this model, all therapy is cross cultural, since our clients differ from us all the time - in cultural degree, rather than in absolutes. There are organisational and institutional barriers to the cross cultural client that can be addressed, in part, by the practitioner and which transcend local Equal Opportunities Policies and ethnic monitoring.

Therapist tips

- Are you happy with the cultural ethos of your organisation?
- Do its communications, policies, staff profile, referral criteria and policies tackle barriers to inclusion and engagement? Do you?
- Research your catchment area, its cultures, history and the existing community resources.
- The individual practitioner can act on these from the start of her employment and the cultural priorities she brings to her work, and in her supervision and training.

The practitioner is well placed also to identify who are the non-attenders/non-responders, and are they over represented among certain cultural groups? Therapists from BME backgrounds (Mahtani, 2003) are more likely to have experienced racism and unequal access to services; therapists from the dominant culture can learn from them. They can also draw on their own cross cultural resources (d'Ardenne et al., 2007). Examples of these include learning a second language, travel, religious or spiritual experiences in another culture, healthcare, sport, the arts and entertainment and local connections to community groups, as well as tackling personal prejudice and racism within supervision.

Tips and reflective questions for engagement

- Audit all your clients by ethnic and/or language origin, which will allow you to see which clients are more at risk of non-engagement.
- Evaluate how your client from another culture is made to feel welcome at the service. Good examples include images, photographs and welcome signs that extend beyond a white, English-speaking world.
- Is your booking system sensitive to holy days and festivals?
- Do you have end of morning or evening sessions for those who find strict timekeeping more of a challenge?
- Could there be provision for children to play? For nursing mothers? Increased access for disabled?
- Is there any space in the waiting room for relatives, advocates and interpreters?
- Is information about your service provided in community languages?

We know that cross cultural adaptation to the needs of minority clients improves engagement (Tribe and Morrissey, 2004), and this may link to entirely practical matters. If the service offers flexible appointments for those who cannot keep to strict time, attendance will be better. If the service proactively translates its policies into the main community languages and displays them prominently in clinic and on its website, the client will feel less alienated. These service requirements predicate how well you will be able to engage your clients in a relationship within transcultural CBT.

Case example

After audit, you notice that referrals for CBT from the Bangladeshi community significantly defaulted more than others on first appointments. Letters had been sent in English and Bengali. You contact these people directly, who explain that first appointment letters were thrown away because they were seen as 'too official or too complex.' Letters were identified with trouble. But, when pressed, defaulters said they would have attended if sent texts, emails or telephone calls. You try this for a year, auditing any changes, and establish significantly improved attendance and engagement for CBT.

INTERPRETING – THE RIGHT TO BE UNDERSTOOD

Case example

A young French-speaking client from Rwanda is referred to you for panic attacks. The referrer indicates that she speaks enough English to work with you and she arrives for her first appointment, accompanied by her husband, a charming, chatty man who holds his wife's hand and insists on attending with her. You look at her and she nods furiously, indicating that she will only go in if accompanied, and you take them into your consulting room where they sit side by side. She begins speaking French and he immediately takes over as her interpreter. He smiles, makes eye contact with you. She does not and appears to be more anxious than ever, as he speaks for much longer periods than she does, adding his own observations about his wife's difficulties.

Reflective questions

- How has this situation arisen?
- What are the risks to the therapeutic relationship?
- How can this situation be renegotiated?
- Why has the client reverted to French? Is she ashamed of her imperfect English or afraid of her husband?

Therapist tip

Relatives make inappropriate, untested and partial interpreters or translators and should not be used. They may also be part of the problem, and in the above case, it would be appropriate to negotiate even the last part of the initial session with the client alone and to establish her interpreting needs for the next appointment.

Local policies ensure that referrers have evaluated this need beforehand, to accelerate engagement between the client and eventual therapist. Professional interpreting services with a good knowledge of the local community, and preferably with mental health training and support, work best (Tribe and Morrissey, 2004). Therapists themselves may be a barrier to engagement in the therapeutic relationship if they do not know how to use interpreters or advocates, but they can learn how to use interpreters and advocates (D'Ardenne and Farmer, 2009) and schedule time with them before the client enters the room.

Interpreters are not centre stage, but like good waiters, they are constantly available but not part of the therapeutic alliance. Interpreters can sit in a triangle between therapist and client, accountable for providing face-to-face verbal communication, non-verbal communication and additional cultural information for the therapist. A diplomatic model (D'Ardenne and Mahtani, 1999) for interpreted therapy places the interpreter just behind the client or clients – speaking into the ear of the client but able to face the therapist and allows the therapist and client to maintain eye contact and speak to each other, face to face. The diplomatic model permits this kind of contact once clients have become accustomed to having a voice behind them doing the interpreting. Sequential interpreting is always used in one-to-one therapy as it allows each party to speak in chunks, pause and speak in turn. It is slower than simultaneous interpreting, which is better for groups or conferences. Interpreters can also translate documents when homework sessions are completed or forms filled in. Back translation entails re-translating back to the original language to ensure that the original meaning has been maintained. It is ideally done by a second translator and is useful for standardised assessment forms or psychometric tools, where systematic errors can develop.

Interpreters/translators themselves do not always have support or supervision for dealing with serious mental health issues. They may, indeed, have experienced similar hardships, exile, war or trauma as the people they are trying to assist. Some services that use many interpreters have developed their own protocols and provision of support and supervision in-house. (D'Ardenne and Farmer, 2009), but the clinician also has some responsibility for the processes in therapy and their impact on all those in the room. It is at least recommended that the clinician ascertains that the interpreter/advocate has not had experiences that are likely to be painful during therapy, e.g. the reliving of loss or trauma with the client that resonates past history and which would affect impartiality.

Case example

You are assessing a Syrian woman, Ayla, who was gang raped during the civil conflict there and who is now too anxious to leave her home and receive the healthcare she needs. After several attempts to engage her, she arrives and accepts (at the last minute) a much older, female, Arabic-speaking interpreter. You have had no opportunity to brief or screen her. The client begins to provide you with a history of her assault. As you listen, you are able to see each of their faces and notice immediately that the interpreter has started to shake her head. She is distressed, although able to continue interpreting, and fails to make eye contact with you for the rest of the session. As your client leaves, she begins to speak directly to your client in Arabic, putting her arms around her and trying to comfort her, making no eye contact with you.

Therapist tip

Stand up immediately and invite your client to return to the waiting room, and sit down with the interpreter for a debrief.

Therapist: I'm sorry I did not have the chance to prepare you before this afternoon's client. How do you think it went today?
Interpreter: Oh, very well. I really felt I understood that poor woman.
Therapist: Great! But I lost the last few minutes and wondered if you could tell me in direct speech exactly what the client said?
Interpreter: I got carried away. But I understood Ayla's sense of shame and felt I had to speak directly to her.
Therapist: You felt her suffering and wanted to comfort her directly. I do understand that. But it seems that you stopped interpreting, and that is what I needed from you.
Interpreter: It's very hard ... I was raped myself and I felt her suffering.
Therapist: I am so sorry. We should have selected an easier case for you and made sure you get some support for yourself.
Interpreter: You are very kind. I want to see her again.
Therapist: But you must stay as my interpreter please?
Interpreter: Of course – thank you!

Tips for using interpreters

- Consider current affairs, e.g. a Turkish interpreter may be unacceptable to a Kurdish client.
- Keep interpreters, ideally, in separate waiting areas from clients.
- Allow at least 50% extra time for an interpreted session.
- Check on the day that the interpreter speaks the same language/dialect as the client and is fluent in English.
- Ascertain that the interpreter is impartial and accurate with CBT terms. If uncertain, rehearse!
- Be willing to send the interpreter away and reschedule another.
- Insist on direct speech, in the same tense as given – essential for reliving.
- Use simple language – short sentences with one main clause are best.
- Monitor the body language and eye contact of interpreter and client.
- At the end of the session, escort the client out of the room, checking client's comfort with the process, explaining that the interpreter will stay on.

PREDICTING AND PREVENTING THREATS TO THE ALLIANCE

In East London, we encourage practitioners to learn another language - and to value the insights this provides. An obvious one is that *linguistic equivalence* does not always apply across languages (D'Ardenne and Farmer, 2009). Then, there are variations in the wider English Language world and with non-standard forms of English. English is a language rich in the vocabulary of thought and mood but there are big differences in how psychological ideas are shared and understood. D'Ardenne et al. (2013) assessed the needs of CBT therapists in Uganda, attempting to achieve a culturally appropriate training in trauma-focused CBT. Emphasis was on finding local metaphors about traumatic memories that could be understood and accepted by Ugandan clients, a task judged by African clinicians as critical in establishing credibility and trust in the CBT relationship. Here are some examples of what they proposed:

> A memory is like a snake, that cannot be killed, and has got into your house. The temptation is to flee, but is better to return to the house, hunt it, put it into a cage, and keep it safe.
>
> An unprocessed memory is like an infected boil and hurts all the time. It must be examined and lanced, causing even more pain until healing and the development of a clean scar.
>
> Un-shed tears cause internal organs to 'rot'
>
> (i.e. unprocessed memories lead to the development of PTSD) (d'Ardenne, 2013).

Threats to the alliance in cross cultural settings are best prevented at referral stage but may only emerge at assessment or during treatment. Clients arrive with many expectations about CBT, and the relationship can be used to establish early on what these might be. One misconception is that the therapist has superhuman powers; so, if she fails, she is useless, with no other explanation. Careful preparation is also needed on issues of privacy and confidentiality - difficult for any client. But these become magnified by minority ethnic clients who are more often marginalised, excluded, criminalised or have refugee status and fear the State and the organs of the State, including the NHS.

All CBT clients need to have the boundaries of therapy properly explained, including the difference between secrecy and confidentiality. Such nuances - especially sharing information only with those who have a right to know - place a responsibility on the practitioner and her organisation to check that clients understand this before disclosures are made. Extra effort will be required for anyone outside mainstream communities - especially those with less education and those who, for all the reasons above, do not like to give too many details about their private life. Misunderstandings about information threaten trust and the alliance before any therapeutic relationship can be established.

OTHER THREATS TO THE ALLIANCE

Many cultures have less individualistic and less technical communities than those familiar to traditional CBT practitioners. The idea of individual 'therapy' may be unfamiliar, unhelpful or, worse, perceived as self-indulgent. In the West, formal religion may be in decline; but across cultures, spirituality and religion have huge cultural significance and must be addressed in the transcultural CBT relationship (Watts, 2011). Equally alien may be the notion of an equal working partnership.

Instead, practitioners are seen as experts giving advice, educating those in distress, from a position of superior knowledge (Hall et al., 2013). Other barriers lead to high levels of non-attenders from other cultures – refugees may fail to engage at all. Trauma-focused CBT, for example, presents as fearful, complex, time-consuming and may be seen as untrustworthy (d'Ardenne, 2013).

Therapist: We need to talk about what happened to you in prison and make some sense of those terrible events.

Client: I just want to forget what happened, not be reminded!

Therapist: But you can't forget it now, even though you don't talk, can you?

Client: No ... but you will make it worse. How can you understand my life?

Therapist: I know I would find it very scary. But everything we discuss will be with you in control, and I promise you will not have more bad dreams if you talk about prison.

Client: And how do I know I can trust you? It feels more like torture.

Therapist: We work together. Just like we have always done. You set the pace, and I will follow you. OK?

Client: OK, we'll try it once, but if it doesn't work, will you see me anyway?

Therapist: Of course!

Therapist tips

- Consider the use of a relative/friend/advocate/spiritual leader to attend assessment.
- Establish with the client secrecy and confidentiality and who has a right to know. Write these down.
- Practice contact protocols; for no-shows, does he have enough money to keep his phone charged?
- Is he unable to say that he finds treatment unhelpful?

OTHER BARRIERS

Your client's progress on homework is not being maintained. The client has not been able to keep any diary, or he complains that he is being made to do too much work. Is his life chaotic? How reliable is public transport or his car? Does that make him vulnerable to cancellation?

Is he obliged to present himself to the police, the judiciary, landlord etc at short notice? Did he understand the significance of record keeping at the start? Does he have difficulty with numerical scales – might a visual analogue be easier? Does he have another idea about time-keeping/records/dates? Not all cultures place as much emphasis on these as we do.

Case example. Honour and shame

You have a client with depression who, during a CBT session, discloses that his wife was raped during civil conflict and that he has contemplated an honour killing – so great is his shame. His wife lives in Pakistan. You have no other evidence to suggest that she is at risk – but the values of the client leave you feeling unsafe or uncertain about the continued relationship.

Therapist tips

- Discuss with supervisor.
- What do you understand about honour killings?
- Are there other options open to your client?
- How much of your own values do you not share with your other clients, and how, if at all, does this threaten the therapeutic relationship? Discuss with your supervisor!

Case example

You are a Turkish CBT clinician who is feeling out of your depth with your client group – many of whom are ethnically Kurdish. You receive these referrals because your service is unaware of the ethnic differences and historical struggle of the Kurds and because they observe (correctly) that you are all able to communicate in Turkish. Your manager pleads with you to set aside your problems – as most of the clients 'don't seem to mind.' That is not your experience – clients appear anxious and overly polite when they see your name and work out your ethnic origins. You try to reassure your clients but remain unconvinced.

Similar threats can arise in any CBT relationship setting, but the complexity of cultural distance requires the clinician to take further, more proactive steps to anticipate and prevent further deterioration. Educating those who manage services is a good start, particularly at referral, and continues throughout the relationship until, and after, discharge.

ENDING THERAPY

Ending therapy starts with good beginnings. The idea of a time-limited professional relationship with specific outcomes planned in advance needs to be reiterated throughout the process - whatever the cultural background of the client. But the meaning of it - e.g. you are not in a friendship - may be different for a client from a world where allegiances and alliances are based on tribal or familial connections. The preparation of a progress or discharge letter and the sharing of this with the client is part of a good ending. The client contributes to this process and is invited to draw on resources in his life that will support and reinforce new ways of thinking and behaving. Follow-up sessions will be planned – as will methods of recovery should anything begin to deteriorate.

The process of working through threats becomes a model for CBT itself. The capacity to think through the consequences of a problem and to consider other ways of thinking about them provide the client and therapist with a rich resource for other areas of distress. The additional effort the therapist makes to tackle these issues provides the client with evidence of trust and commitment and is a good example of resilience in the face of adversity. The CBT relationship is used to process the feelings of loss and separation suffered by all clients – but aggravated by echoes of other losses, rejections and alienation. CBT practitioners are able to use the relationship to make these associations and help their clients find a constructive way of dealing with losses and transition. D'Ardenne and Mahtani (1999) propose a model of inviting the client to set a timetable of reduced contact in the relationship and increased pick up of other resources at the end of treatment – especially advocacy, liaison and community resources. *Relapse* is identified as a risk to the relationship, and planning for this is part of the end of therapy. *Saying goodbye*, a process that begins long before the end of treatment, does not mean that clients have resolved all their problems; but it does mean they are better resourced to face their difficulties than when they first began CBT. Similarly, friendships and social contact are ethical issues that have greater complexity in transcultural settings.

Case example

Client: Now that we have finished, I'd like to invite you for tea with my family to show my appreciation for all you have done.

Practitioner: Thank you! But we have already talked about the importance of my remaining separate from your personal life.

Client: So you won't come?

Practitioner: Sadly, no. But I know how much you have worked on your community's Carnival this month and would love to come and share some time with you there.

Client: Great!

Therapist tips

- Keep clarifying boundaries.
- Reaffirm client's cultural achievements and share where possible.
- Use the Carnival to learn more about the community you serve.

SUPERVISION AND TRAINING

Transcultural supervision and training is a lifetime commitment, whether it is the relationship or the adjustments made to the CBT. What is the cultural distance between you, your trainer and supervisor? Can racism and cultural prejudice be safely shared? Lago and Thompson (1997) propose a triadic model of counsellor, client and supervisor in differing transcultural permutations where supervisors in transcultural therapy require knowledge of the process of cultural and racial identities, the cultural norms of the communities being counselled, the nature of conflicts between black and white people and, most of all, a willingness to address anxieties in situations where racial or cultural identities are present in the therapy relationship. Other requirements may include using community advocates for additional supervision and training. Also, do your regular interpreters have access to training or supervision?

CHAPTER SUMMARY

This chapter argues that anti-racist policies, social inclusion, User and Human rights movements provide a compass by which to improve CBT engagement, trust and outcome. Barriers exist for practitioners who believe they do not have cultural competence, as well as their organisations, and these beliefs can be acknowledged, challenged and changed. The CBT relationship can benefit all, regardless of ethnic background, colour, language, religion, gender orientation or ability.

FURTHER READING

Bhugra D and Bhui K (2007) *A Textbook of Cultural Psychiatry.* Cambridge University Press. A good introduction to culture and mental health.

d'Ardenne P (2013) *Counselling Transcultural Settings; Priorities for a Restless World.* London: Sage. A practical text for all practitioners in global settings.

Lago C (ed) (2011) *The Handbook of Transcultural Counselling and Psychotherapy.* Maidenhead: Open University Press. Still the best text in the field.

REFERENCES

Bhui K and Bhugra D (2007) Ethnic inequalities and cultural capability framework in mental healthcare. In: Bhugra D and Bhui K (eds) *A Handbook of Cultural Psychiatry.* Cambridge: Cambridge University Press, pp. 81–90.

d'Ardenne P (2013) *Counselling in Transcultural Settings; Priorities for a Restless World.* London: Sage.

d'Ardenne P and Farmer E (2009) Using Interpreters in Trauma Therapy. In: Grey N (ed) *A Casebook of Cognitive Therapy for Traumatic Stress Reactions.* London: Routledge, ch. 18, pp. 283–300.

d'Ardenne P and Mahtani A (1999) *Transcultural Counselling in Action.* 2nd ed. London: Sage.

d'Ardenne P, Robjant K, Kasujja R, Nsereko J and Hunter E (2013) Culturally Tailored Training in Trauma-Focussed Cognitive Behaviour Therapy for Uganda. *African Journal of Traumatic Stress 3*(1): 7–12.

d'Ardenne P, Ruaro L, Cestari L, Wakhoury W and Priebe S (2007) Does interpreter-mediated CBT with traumatized refugee people work? A Comparison of patient outcomes in East London. *Behavioural and Cognitive Psychotherapy 35*: 293–301.

Dudgeon P and Kelly K (2014) Contextual Factors for Research on Psychological Therapies for Aboriginal Australians. *Australian Psychologist 49*: 8–12.

Fernando S (2010) *Mental Health, Race and Culture*. 3rd ed. Basingstoke: Palgrave.

Graham J, Sorensen S and Hayes-Skelton S (2013) Enhancing the cultural sensitivity of cognitive behavioural interventions for anxiety in diverse populations, *The Behavior Therapist 36*(5): 101–108.

Hall J, d'Ardenne P, Nsereko, J, Kasuija R, Bailey D, and Mpango R (2013) Mental Health practitioners' reflections on psychological work in trauma focussed cognitive behaviour therapy for Uganda, *African Journal of Traumatic Stress 3*: 65–70.

Hays PA and Iwamasa GY (eds) (2006) *Culturally Responsive Cognitive Behavioural Therapy Assessment, Practice, and Supervision*. Washington, DC: American Psychological Association.

Janelle S, Kelleigh R, Rotunmah D, Budden W and Beale D (2014) Can CBT be effective for Aboriginal Australians? Perspectives of Aboriginal practitioners trained in CBT. *Australian Psychologist 49*(1): 1–7.

Lago C (ed) (2011) *The Handbook of Transcultural Counselling and Psychotherapy*. Maidenhead: Open University Press.

Lago C and Thompson J (1997) The triangle with curved sides: sensitivity to issues of race and culture in supervision. In: Shipton G (ed) *Supervision of Psychotherapy and Counselling: Making a Place to Think*. Buckingham: Open University Press, pp. 119–130.

Mahtani A (2003) The right of refugees clients to an appropriate and ethical psychological service. *International Journal of Human Rights 7*: 40–57.

Mailloux S (2004) Ethics and Interpreters; Are you practising ethically? *Journal of Psychological Practice 10*: 37–44.

Patel V, Boyce N, Collins PY, Saxena S and Horton R (2001) *A Renewed Agenda for Global Mental Health*, London School of Hygiene and Tropical Medicine. UK *Lancet*. 2011 Oct 22; *378*(9801): 1441-2. doi: 10.1016/S0140-6736(11)61385-8. Epub 2011 Oct 16.

Robjant K and Fazel M (2010) The Emerging Evidence for Narrative Exposure Therapy; A Review. *Clinical Psychology Review 30*: 1030–1039.

Silove D (2011) The psychosocial effects of torture, mass human rights violations and refugee trauma; toward an integrated conceptual framework. *Lancet 378*: 1441–1442.

Tribe R and Morrissey J (2004) Good practice issues in working with interpreters in mental health. *Intervention 2*: 129–142.

Truax C and Carkhuff R (1967) *Towards Effective Psychotherapy and Counselling*. New Brunswick: Aldine Transactions.

Walcraft J and Bryant M (2003) *The Mental Health Service User Movement in England; Policy Paper 2*, London: Sainsbury Centre for Mental Health.

Watts F (2011) Reflections on psychology and religion. *The Psychologist 24*(4): 268–269.

PART IV

THE THERAPEUTIC RELATIONSHIP AND DIFFERENT MODES OF DELIVERY

17

CBT DELIVERED IN GROUPS

GRAEME WHITFIELD AND MICHAEL SCOTT

CHAPTER OVERVIEW

Group CBT (GCBT) has attracted far less research than the individual therapy. In common with all CBT, it is assumed that GCBT has a beneficial effect in two major ways: firstly, through the *content* of the sessions - mainly relating to the specific model for the disorder/difficulty being treated and the techniques which flow from that model - and, secondly, by *process* or *non-specific factors* such as the quality of the relationships within the group and the extent to which each attendee is motivated. The concept and term *group processes* go back over half a century to influential work in non-CBT models of group therapies (Foulkes and Anthony, 1965).

Despite an early acknowledgement in CBT of the potential importance of a strong collaborative relationship between client and therapist (Beck et al., 1979), there is still debate about how important these so-called process factors are as predictors of outcome (see De Rubeis et al., 2005 and earlier chapters of this book). This lack of clarity applies even more to GCBT. We particularly need answers to questions such as 'who can benefit from group therapy' and 'what types of therapist factors predict good outcomes?' Bordin (1979) suggested that the *working alliance* in therapy refers to the three areas of the *tasks* and *goals* of therapy and the emotional *bond* between therapist and client. Chapter 2 discusses this in relation to individual CBT, but it is likely to apply to groups, but in a more complicated way - it's not just two people in the room, so the alliance will apply to the relationship between each client and the therapist(s) as well as between each of the clients. The following chapter describes the background to the concept of working alliances in GCBT, and then goes on to describe the factors that affect engagement and wider factors which can influence relationships within groups. Some are obvious - for example, if clients do not feel emotionally safe in the group, then engagement will not happen. Other influences are more subtle, such as the extent to which the client believes other group members share common experiences: group members may not work together effectively if they perceive little commonality. The term most often used to refer to the collaboration between group members and therapist(s) is: *group cohesion*.

EARLY INFLUENCE OF GROUP PSYCHOTHERAPY AND OF YALOM

Group psychotherapy has its origins in psychodynamic/analytic models, which view the therapeutic relationship between client and therapist as the major 'vehicle of change.' This is in sharp contrast, therefore, to CBT, which has traditionally focused on disorder-specific models and the techniques that flow from them as the way in which disorder is maintained (Bieling et al., 2006). A major part of the philosophy of the CBT model is education - i.e. an ethos of *explicitly* imparting knowledge. This lends itself very well to the GCBT format, which in many ways, is akin to a classroom. A particularly influential set of proposed mechanisms of change in traditional psychodynamic-based group psychotherapy have been Yalom's so-called *'curative factors,'* which include concepts such as 'universality' and 'imitative behaviours' and 'imparting information,' which appear particularly relevant to CBT group work (Yalom, 1995).

ENGAGEMENT IN GCBT

It is the experience of both authors that many clients who are assessed for CBT are disappointed or apprehensive when offered a place in a group. Studies have shown that the number of clients who actively refuse CBT treatment in group format is high (e.g. 38% for an OCD group approach, O'Connor et al., 2005). The group modality therefore needs careful marketing, which can only be done when there is a full understanding of an individual's particular reservations about participation.

The obstacles to engagement in a group (and therefore to the formation of therapeutic alliances and group cohesion) are many and varied; often, it is a perception that the group will either not adequately treat their condition or that the group will, in some way, be intrusive or unhelpful. Some have an image in their mind (presumably from the media) of a group of patients sitting in a circle sharing their deepest emotions and failings.

The problems are not just with getting individuals to attend a group but also with getting them to continue attending. Clients may drop out if they do not feel heard or believe the sessions will not make a real world difference.

A number of suggestions have been made to try to enhance attendance. For example, Scott (2011) suggests that group sessions may need to be supplemented by individual sessions, both prior to the session as an informal welcome and in between group sessions to encourage motivation, deal with co-morbid conditions and attend to individualised formulations. Continued attendance at any group, no matter what the model, may also be helped by being clear from the outset about the *function of the group* and presenting basic group rules on issues such as confidentiality (establishing agreement on Bordin's goals and tasks).

GCBT is a particularly potent means of helping clients feel connected to others. Whilst the therapist relationship is important in individual CBT, for example, to ensure difficult homework tasks are complied with, the therapeutic enterprise takes place in a somewhat separate universe from the cut and thrust of normal social interactions. The group is a closer approximation to the real world. As Paul Gilbert reminds us: 'humans are an exquisitely social species, who from the first moments of conception, and then throughout life, are physiologically influenced and regulated via social relationships' (Gilbert, 2007: 106), thus making a group therapeutic intervention very germane.

Case example

Chetan attended a CBT group for social phobia. A major part of the work of the group was to explore the safety behaviours which the group members used to (in their minds) prevent unwelcome attention being placed upon them and to prevent them appearing odd. He had been bullied in school about his weight and told that he was a 'monster.' He was now in his late 20s and was conscious in social situations that others seemed to not want to talk to him – he assumed that this was because they believed he appeared threatening to them and monstrous. Chetan was surprised by the genuine interest and warmth exhibited by the other seven group members (all of whom had social phobia) and the two CBT therapists who led the group. They appeared to be genuinely surprised that he viewed himself as 'monstrous' and even 'scary.' Chetan trusted and respected the group members – they did not appear to be lying. He found out in community surveys that, whilst people identified him as overweight, they did not view him as monstrous or scary or as someone that they would avoid. The group members did point out to Chetan that he almost always avoided eye contact and that this may put people off engaging him in conversation. He practiced speaking in the group without averting eye contact and then experimented doing the same outside of the group as homework. He realised that the group's suggestion was probably correct, and he consciously stopped averting gaze in social situations. The positive effects of this increased his confidence and, over time, his social phobia dissipated.

As in the preceding case study, it is the quality of the therapeutic relationships with both the therapist, as teacher, and with other group members which is pivotal. Chetan's efforts to look after himself were fed back as understandable; that is, his cognitions and behaviours were normalised and validated, but he was also encouraged to try out new behaviours. Change can occur not only through effortful cognitive processing (cognitive restructuring) but also by seeing other group members as role models, adopting their thinking and behaviour. Observation of group members undertaking behavioural experiments or exposure tasks within the session can make it more likely that other group members will attempt to do the same (Lewinsohn and Clarke, 1999). They learn from others that undertaking a task or changing a viewpoint can have positive outcomes (vicarious learning). Furthermore, the general support and encouragement of the other group members, which are a product of group cohesion (White and Freeman, 2000), encourage participants to engage in tasks that they may otherwise have avoided. Positive outcomes are likely to be reinforced as a result of praise from the therapist and other group members (positive reinforcement) after completing tasks both within the session and between sessions (Lewinsohn and Clarke, 1999; Morrison, 2001).

A group provides a 'safe' environment where members feel secure in suggesting solutions for each other. In doing so, they can practice problem solving skills and gain a sense of mastery (White and Freeman, 2000). As yet, it is not clear what the most important mechanisms of change are; however, there are early indications that symptomatic change and quality of life improvement after GCBT may not be due to strategies designed to change client's cognitions (Oei et al., 2014).

INFLUENCES ON THE WORKING ALLIANCE IN GCBT

NUMBER OF THERAPISTS AND THEIR RELATIONSHIP

Some therapists work well together and complement each other and others don't. Some therapists can use their interaction to maximise effect, i.e. they can *synchronise* (Scott, 2011). Having more than one therapist can often help each keep on track - having a co-therapist can have some of the qualities of live supervision. They need to help each other to keep the *structure* of the group sessions intact: an ability to keep to a predefined structure is linked with better outcome (e.g. Bright et al., 1999, Shaw et al., 1999) - see 'Therapist tip' on the importance of structure.

Therapist tip

Structure, Structure, Structure ...

In GCBT, it is easy, faced with a group of individuals in a room, to get side-tracked by an interesting topic. For this reason, we need the 'scaffolding' of a pre-planned structure to keep us reasonably on-track. There will always be discussions which seem constructive and reasonably relevant to the task at hand that we want to allow to progress. Likewise, for the sake of group cohesion, where a group needs to share experiences, we might want to allow that to continue for a while. However, sooner or later we need to come back to the agenda or else we lose valuable time and necessary tasks are crowded out or rushed, impairing effectiveness. Ways to reduce the chances of this happening include always pre-planning the agenda of the session (together with an approximate idea of how long each task might take) and then writing that agenda on a white board at the beginning of the session that everyone can see. In common with 1:1 CBT, therapists need to be practiced at bringing the session back to the required task at hand. Live supervision methods, such as having your supervisor sit in a session to observe or having a session recorded for supervision purposes (with other group members' consent), can also help.

Having one therapist more actively focused on presenting the content of the session, with the other taking a more observational role, allows dynamics and processes to be noticed more easily. The observing therapist may more readily notice an attendee dominating the group or quiet group members not being included. They need to keep tuned-in to their own subjective feelings and to be able to use their responses to understand what is happening for other individuals in the room (Katzow and Safran, 2007). However, there need not be a rigid division of labour between the two therapists: the important task is that they 'dance' together.

As with individually delivered CBT, it is important to keep the group's emotional atmosphere or *group climate* at the right level, protecting some group members from undue criticism. The atmosphere of the group is important to allow the attendee to learn from the model and from others present. We need to distil group norms; for example, asking does a *group culture* prevail where the attendees feel safe to disclose personal information without fear of humiliation, i.e. is the *'climate'* non-threatening? (Johnson et al., 2005). Also, we need to question: is there an assumption that homework is an essential part of the process and that, therefore, the attendees really will complete tasks in between sessions?

The relationships within the group (therapist to group member and between the group members) must therefore be as *collaborative, empathic* and as *non-threatening* as possible (Johnson et al., 2005, White and Freeman, 2000). Unhelpful sub-groups/cliques can form which could interfere with the group's cohesion and future ability to achieve tasks together. The number of the therapists is important in other ways. Sometimes attendees of the group get distressed and need to leave the room, and it can be helpful to allow one of the therapists to attend. The remaining therapist can continue with the group, thus preventing too much disruption.

GROUP MEMBERS' SIMILARITY

Group members need to be part of the same story, engaged in gradually re-authoring their narrative. Diagnosis-specific groups are a way of ensuring the same story. Comments made by one group member to another are sometimes considered more seriously than those made by the therapist(s) - perhaps because they have more similarities, or perhaps because they are in some way seen as more impartial. In general, there has to be a certain degree of *commonality* between the group attendees to allow the group to function. Group members who can identify with the experiences and struggles of other group members are more likely to feel understood and have ownership of the model and group. This sense of commonality may be due to common illnesses, similar experiences, area of residence, social status etc. Without this sense of *commonality*, therapeutic group members may not develop a sense of *'belongingness'* (Lewin, 1951), i.e. of belonging to, and wanting to invest in, the group (Johnson et al., 2005). The therapists in any group need to foster this sense of commonality and belonging. Ways that therapists have done this in group psychotherapy have been to consciously use the pronouns 'we and us,' rather than 'I and me' (Foulkes and Anthony, 1965: 149), to try to foster a sense of *'teamwork'* (Bion, 1961: 52) and to encourage a *group culture* that promotes every attendee as equal (Bion, 1961: 57). Group members presenting with widely different conditions and problems can interfere with this sense of commonality and the degree to which group members feel they believe the group can help them (see Yalom's 'instillation of hope'). So-called *'trans-diagnostic groups,'* composed of attendees with differing underlying problems, e.g. mood and anxiety problems, have generally been shown to be less effective (Oei and Boschen, 2009).

THE CONDITION BEING TREATED

It is the experience of the authors that, to some extent, the successful group treatment of different conditions relies on different aspects of the therapeutic relationships.

For example, the treatment of OCD is often exposure-based and may be less dependent on an examination of the client's underlying core beliefs and assumptions than can be the case for depression, low self-esteem and personality disorder. However, OCD is a difficult disorder to remedy, requiring determination on the client's part and the motivation that comes from the encouragement of other group members. Therefore, the emphasis and mechanism of change, as well as general effectiveness, may vary in CBT groups by the condition being treated.

GROUP SIZE

In general, group-based CBT attempts to incorporate the key characteristics of individually delivered CBT. The therapist encourages a culture which supports the different group members to feel comfortable to gently question each other and to investigate and challenge behaviour patterns and cognitions. In this way, they are acting as *de facto* therapists to each other (Heimberg et al., 1993). However, the ability to have interactions between group members, to have individualised formulations and to be able to set and check individualised homework tasks will all be compromised as the group size increases, fundamentally changing the quality of the therapeutic relationship (both between group members and between therapist(s) and group members) (Whitfield, 2010). Much larger groups, even if they are run on CBT principles, become more of an information-imparting psychoeducational format rather than an interactive group. The psychoeducational group does have benefits – it can reach so many more people at once (e.g. see White et al., 1992). But it loses the qualities of a smaller CBT group, where the more intimate setting allows participants to learn from each other. For a summary of the differences between large group 'psychoeducational format' and traditional small group CBT, see Whitfield (2010).

An alternative format is to mix elements of small and large groups and also individual sessions together into the client's course of treatment. For example, some services now have educational introductory large groups which impart information to clients before they subsequently split up into their smaller treatment groups or 1:1 treatment. Scott (2011) describes the importance of mixing GCBT with 1:1 CBT sessions which focus on individual formulations and co-morbidities. This allows the group sessions to focus on the topics which the majority of members have in common. The same author also describes how enhancing motivation and troubleshooting can be achieved through these adjunctive individual sessions as well as informal welcoming gatherings, both before each session starts and sometimes in the form of a break-time during the session. Therapists can come under pressure from managers to run a group with just one therapist. This apparent cost-saving can dilute therapeutic effectiveness.

GROUP DURATION

In general, the longer the group continues for, the more likely that some group members can become quite dependent on the group for support and validation. Many CBT groups in the UK traditionally last between about 10–15 sessions. The exception to this may be longer term follow-up groups. This is a complex and difficult area, where health systems often emphasise the value of the concept of 'support' whereas clinicians often place more emphasis on skill and behavioural change. Indeed, excessive perceived support from the therapist in CBT groups for depression may result in worse outcomes (Oei and Browne, 2006).

INCLUDING 'LESS SUITABLE' GROUP MEMBERS

This factor can influence all three of Bordin's (1979) aspects of working alliance or the total sum of those alliances within the group: the *group cohesion*. Some people struggle to use the cognitive-behavioural model in any format. In general, people who are able to identify and articulate cognitions and emotions and who are then able to share them in a focused, non-defensive manner are those likely to benefit the most from CBT (Renaud et al., 2014). Also, those who try CBT but who do not accept their own 'responsibility for change' are significantly more likely to drop out of therapy compared to those who do accept this responsibility (Myhr et al., 2013). A common discussion point (which potentially connects with both of these findings) is whether clients with coexisting personality disorders should be included in groups for people suffering with mental illness such as depression. Personality disorder predisposes to the development of psychological problems such as depression and anxiety so that this question frequently arises. Scott (2011) discusses this with reference to CBT groups (see the next section). High levels of avoidance may, for example, have a negative impact on the group cohesion, as well as limiting agreement on targets and goals. If tasks are not completed by one group member, other group members may also fail to complete tasks. Also, people with narcissistic personality disorders and those likely to engage in severe self-harming and who are dependent on substances are more likely to be frankly disruptive to the group (Scott, 2011).

Case example

James had been referred for CBT for depression but it was also acknowledged that he had been severely traumatised by childhood sexual abuse, followed by workplace bullying two years previously. The intention had been to teach James CBT techniques, such as activity scheduling, in the group and then to offer 1:1 trauma-focused CBT after the group (hoping that his mood would have improved enough to allow the 1:1 work to progress in a smoother and safer manner). Within the first two sessions of the CBT group, James felt that a couple of the other group members were "looking down their noses" at him and he actually left the third session after 30 minutes, slamming the door behind him. He had gone home. During the next session, James sat quietly but appeared angry and surly. A few of the group members approached the two therapists at the end of the session to say that they had been upset for much of the preceding week, imagining that James could have done "something silly" such as kill himself. It was noted that the group was quiet and people appeared to be repeatedly glancing across the room to check out how James was. By the end of that

(Continued)

(Continued)

session, James seemed to be engaging better and when he was asked if he wanted to speak about his exit the week before – he declined. He did say that he felt better and was not a risk to himself. The following week, the issue of bullying was an item from another group member, and again, James exited the group mid-session and slammed the door. It was clear to the therapists that, although James' behaviour could be understood in terms of his background, it was unhelpful and disruptive to group cohesion, and indeed to the mental state of other group members. It was decided that the issue should not be left to the next group session, so James was invited to attend a meeting between him and one of the therapists, who further enquired about his behaviour and again checked risk. It became clear to the therapist that James had very abrupt changes in mood and that he had previously been given a diagnosis of borderline personality disorder (BPD). This had not been picked up at the initial assessment for CBT. The therapist explained to James that the current group environment was not likely to be beneficial to him, and James was referred through to another service offering group-work for BPD. Informing a group member that they should not remain in a group is difficult; however, when therapists avoid tackling issues such as a client's destructive behaviour, then damage to the working alliances in the group is the likely outcome. Overall, group cohesion will suffer, leading to inferior patient outcomes in the rest of the CBT group. These issues must therefore be tackled by therapists, no matter how daunting the prospect.

ENSURING THAT THE TRANSACTIONS IN A GROUP ARE A VEHICLE FOR MEANINGFUL CHANGE

It is perfectly possible to run a group as if the latter is an end in itself, with group cohesion as the primary target – in essence, a support group – but this would not be a CBT group. GCBT can be focused on the whole spectrum of a client's difficulties; most typically, clients attend who are suffering from two or more disorders. At first glance, it is not obvious how one would accommodate a client found to be suffering from, say, depression, panic disorder and having an avoidant personality disorder in a CBT group. A way forward is to: (a) decide with the client which disorder is most impeding their functioning and invite them to attend a group with this focus, (b) address the additional but subsidiary disorder primarily in concurrent individual sessions and (c) assess the relevance of any personality disorder with regards to the group.

The nature of any personality disorder has a great relevance to possible inclusion of a client in a group. Clients with an 'anxious' personality disorder (avoidant, dependent and obsessive-compulsive) can derive a benefit from a group modality that they are less likely to get from individual CBT. For example, the key feature of avoidant personality disorder is a belief, since at least early adulthood, that others are going to be critical and demeaning; this can lead to depression as the individual covers up mistakes, leading to precisely the criticism from others that they fear when the mistakes are discovered. In addition, the person with an avoidant personality disorder avoids informal gatherings because they fear others might discover that they are really 'an imposter,' deserving of rebuke. Often, clinicians and clients are unaware that it is the personality disorder that is driving the depression and that addressing the depression alone is likely to prove fruitless. Whilst the person with an avoidant personality disorder is likely to be particularly averse to joining a group, it can be explained that attending a depression group is the perfect opportunity to learn experientially that others (with any luck) are unlikely to be critical or demeaning. Clients with pronounced 'dramatic' personality disorders (borderline, narcissistic, antisocial and histrionic) would not be included in any group for depression or an anxiety disorder as they are likely to be too disruptive, but CBT groups have been run specifically for clients with a borderline personality disorder. Finally, clients with a pronounced 'odd' personality disorder (paranoid personality disorder, schizoid personality disorder, schizotypal personality disorder) are likely to be so extreme in their withdrawal there is virtually no chance of their considering entering a group.

The General Group Therapeutic Skills Rating Scale (GGTRS) is a nine item scale (Scott, 2011) for the group leader and co-leader to help ensure that they have been relating appropriately to group members and have been harnessing the power of the group to effect change. Box 17.1 shows an example item from the scale in relation to 'Additional Disorders;' items are rated 0–6.

Other items on the Scale relate to review of homework/agenda, relevance, adaptation, inclusion, magnifying support and minimising criticism, utilising group members as role models, therapist presentation skills and addressing group issues.

Box 17.1 The scoring of the 'Additional Disorders' Subscale of the General Group Therapeutic Skills Rating Scale (GGTRS)

'Additional Disorders'

Score of 0: Therapist either did not acknowledge a group member's expression of difficulties with a disorder that was not the prime focus of the group or spent such time on these concerns that other members were losing focus, e.g. chatting amongst themselves.

Score of 2: Therapist acknowledged a group member's additional difficulty but without signposting a direction from which appropriate help might come, e.g. an individual session, or tried unsuccessfully to address the additional difficulty but showed a lack of competence in this area.

Score of 4: Therapist managed group members' expressions of additional concerns and was mostly able to offer succinct advice and reassure that these difficulties could be addressed.

Score of 6: Therapist managed to address all group members' expressions of additional problems and suggest appropriate options for their resolution without losing focus on the main teaching for the session.

Use of the GGTRS presupposes that a client has been reliably assessed. Without an evidence-based initial overall assessment, assessing competence in managing group processes is meaningless. The first step in assessing a client's full story is screening clients for all the common mental disorders. This can be achieved using the First Step Questionnaire (or the interview format of the Questionnaire, The 7 Minute Interview) (Scott, 2011) and complementing this with the administration of a screen for personality disorders [Standardised Assessment of Personality – Abbreviated Scale (SAPAS)], reproduced in Scott (2011). The SAPAS is an eight item screen with 'yes' or 'no' responses, a score of four or more indicates probable personality disorder, but only if the person is already known to be suffering from a recognised psychiatric disorder on the basis of a standardised reliable diagnostic interview. Detailed inquiry then has to be made as to which personality disorder is present using the DSM criteria (American Psychiatric Association, 2013). The screening items in Scott's First Step Questionnaire have, for the most part, been demonstrated to have adequate reliability – see Scott (2009).

CHAPTER SUMMARY

Reviews of the literature point to approximately 30% of the outcome of individual CBT being due to so-called 'common factors' (which mainly comprise the therapeutic alliance) (Norcross, 2002). One might expect a similar impact in GCBT, but this is mainly hypothesis as the requisite studies have not yet led to definitive conclusions – recent studies have thrown up unexpected, but interesting, results that may allow us to further tease out the role of therapeutic relationships within GCBT. Norton and Kazantzis (2016) found that scores of working alliance and of group cohesion did predict client outcomes but at different points in the trajectory of transdiagnostic CBT groups for anxiety. Group cohesion seemed to be more important as a predictor of client outcome (anxiety levels) in the later sessions, whereas working alliance consistently predicted outcome throughout the course of therapy. Söchting et al. (2016), in a study of outcomes in GCBT for depression, found that the degree to which the group members viewed their treatment as 'credible' was unrelated to the working alliance. Similarly, it is not yet known whether scores of group leaders on the GGTRS (Scott, 2011) will predict outcome.

In this chapter, we have outlined a number of concepts that describe the therapeutic relationship in groups. Unfortunately, these constructs to some extent overlap. For example, a group that has great 'cohesion' is also likely to have a good 'group climate' and vice versa (Johnson et al., 2005). We have outlined factors, such as the inclusion of different diagnostic problems and group size, which appear in clinical practice to influence working alliances in groups, by extension the group cohesion and, by extension to that, the overall functioning of those CBT groups.

FURTHER READING

For a description of the rating scales (such as the GGTRS) used in GCBT, the impact of personality factors on suitability for GCBT and the delivery of GCBT for different disorders we suggest:

Scott MJ (2011) *Simply Effective Group Cognitive Behaviour Therapy: A Practitioner's Guide.* London: Routledge. *The appendices are freely available at: cbtwatch.com and clicking the Resources icon.*

For an overview of different formats of GCBT we suggest:

Whitfield G (2010) Group cognitive behavioural therapy for anxiety and depression. *Advances in Psychiatric Treatment* 16: 219–227.

REFERENCES

American Psychiatric Association (2013) *Diagnostic and Statistical Manual of Mental Disorders DSM-5.* Arlington, VA: American Psychiatric Press.

Beck J, Rush J, Shaw B and Emery G (1979) *Cognitive Therapy of Depression.* New York: Guilford Press.

Bieling PJ, McCabe RE and Antony MM (2006) *Cognitive-behavioral therapy in groups.* Guilford Press.

Bion WR (1961) *Experiences in Groups.* Routledge: London.

Bordin ES (1979) The generalizability of the psychoanalytic concept of the working alliance. *Psychotherapy: Theory, Research, Practice 16*: 252–260.

Bright J, Neimeyer R and Baker K (1999) Professional and paraprofessional group treatments for depression: a comparison of cognitive-behavioral and mutual support interventions. *Journal of Consulting and Clinical Psychology 67*: 491–501.

De Rubeis R, Brotman M and Gibbons C (2005) A conceptual and methodological analysis of the nonspecifics argument. *Clinical Psychology: Science and Practice 12*(2): 174–183.

Foulkes SH and Anthony EJ (1965) *Group Psychotherapy: The Psychoanalytic Approach.* 2nd ed. London: Maresfield Library.

Gilbert P (2007) Evolving minds and compassion in the therapeutic relationship. In: Gilbert P and Leahy R (eds) *The Therapeutic Relationship in the Cognitive Behavioral Therapies.* New York: Routledge, ch. 6.

Heimberg R, Salzman D, Holt C and Blendell KA (1993) Cognitive-behavioural group treatment for social phobia: Effectiveness at five-year follow-up. *Cognitive Therapy and Research 17*: 325–339.

Johnson J, Burlingame G, Olsen D, Davies R and Gleave R (2005) Group climate, cohesion, alliance, and empathy in group psychotherapy: Multilevel structural equation models. *Journal of Counselling Psychology 52*: 310–321.

Katzow AW and Safran JD (2007) Recognising and resolving ruptures in the therapeutic alliance. In: Gilbert P and Leahy R (eds) *The Therapeutic Relationship in the Cognitive Behavioral Therapies*, New York: Routledge, ch. 5.

Lewin K (1951) *Field Theory in Social Science.* Cartright D (ed). New York: Harper Brothers.

Lewinsohn P and Clarke G (1999) Psychosocial treatments for adolescent depression. *Clinical Psychology Review 19*: 329–342.

Myhr G, Jennifer JR, Marie S, Vicki T, Dominique B, Fatima K, Kia F and Gilbert P (2013) Assessing suitability for short-term cognitive-behavioral therapy in out-patients with psychosis: a comparison with depressed and anxious out-patients. *Journal of Psychiatric Practice 19*: 29–41.

Morrison N (2001) Group Cognitive Therapy: Treatment of choice or sub-optimal option? *Behavioural and Cognitive Psychotherapy 29*: 311–332.

Norcross J (2002) *Psychotherapy Relationships That Work: Therapist Contributions and Responsiveness to Patients.* Oxford: Oxford University Press.

Norton PJ and Kazantzis N (2016) Dynamic relationships of therapeutic alliance and group cohesion in transdiagnostic group CBT for anxiety disorders. *Journal of Consulting and Clinical Psychology 84*: 146–155.

O'Connor K, Freeston MH, Gareau D, Careau Y, Dufour MJ, Aadema F and Todorov C (2005) Group versus individual treatment in obsessions without compulsions. *Clinical Psychology and Psychotherapy 12*: 87–96.

Oei T and Boschen M (2009) Clinical effectiveness of a cognitive behavioural group treatment program for anxiety disorders: a benchmark study. *Journal of Anxiety Disorders, 23*: 950–957.

Oei T and Browne A (2006) Components of group processes: have they contributed to the outcome of mood and anxiety disorder patients in a group cognitive-behaviour therapy program? *American Journal of Psychotherapy 60*: 53–70.

Oei T, McAlinden N and Cruwys T (2014) Exploring mechanisms of change: The relationships between cognitions, symptoms, and quality of life over the course of group cognitive-behaviour therapy. *Journal of Affective Disorders 168*: 72–77.

Renaud J, Russell JJ and Myhr G (2014) Predicting who benefits most from cognitive-behavioral therapy for anxiety and depression. *Journal of Clinical Psychology*; *70*(10): 924–932.

Scott MJ (2009) *Simply Effective Cognitive Behaviour Therapy: A Practitioner's Guide*. London: Routledge.

Scott MJ (2011) *Simply Effective Group Cognitive Behaviour Therapy: A Practitioner's Guide*. London: Routledge.

Shaw B, Elkin I, Yamagughi J, Olmsted M, Vallis T, Dobson K, Lowery A, Sotsky S, Watkins J and Imber S (1999) Therapist competence ratings in relation to clinical outcome in cognitive therapy of depression. *Journal of Consulting and Clinical Psychology 67*: 837–846.

Söchting I, Tsai M and Ogrodniczuk JS (2016) Patient's perceptions of treatment credibility and their relation to the outcome of Group CBT for depression. *Archives of Psychiatry and Psychotherapy 4*: 7–15.

White JR and Freeman A (eds) (2000) *Cognitive-behavioral Group Therapy for Specific Problems and Populations*. American Psychological Association.

White J, Keenan M and Brooks N (1992) Stress control: A controlled comparative investigation of large group therapy for generalized anxiety disorder. *Behavioural Psychotherapy 20*: 97–114.

Whitfield G (2010) Group cognitive behavioural therapy for anxiety and depression. *Advances in Psychiatric Treatment 16*: 219–227.

Yalom I (1995) *The Theory and Practice of Group Psychotherapy*. 4th ed. New York: Basic Books.

18

COUPLE THERAPY

MARION CUDDY

CHAPTER OVERVIEW

Cognitive behavioural couple therapy (CBCT) poses particular challenges for the therapeutic alliance. Partners who seek help for their relationship often come with different perspectives on their difficulties, as well as different goals for therapy. The therapist must form a bond both with the couple and with each partner individually, and problems can arise in any of these alliances.

This chapter outlines how the therapeutic alliance can be conceptualised within the framework of CBCT. Factors affecting engagement in couple therapy are discussed. Common difficulties in the alliance and ways of predicting, preventing and working with alliance ruptures are described.

OVERVIEW OF THE MODEL

Within the broader framework of behavioural couple therapies, a number of ways of conceptualising relationship functioning have been proposed (e.g. Doss et al., 2013; Epstein and Baucom, 2002). Models need to consider individual aspects of each partner and differences between them, how they interact as a couple and the influence of the wider context in which they live on the relationship.

One simple and effective way of formulating a couple's difficulties is through the use of the 'figure-eight' diagram (Grant, 2011) presented in Figure 18.1. This model, which is essentially the interaction between two Beckian cognitive conceptualisations, illustrates the interplay between the partners' cognitions, emotions and behaviours. During a difficult interaction, Partner A's behaviour is interpreted by Partner B in a manner that activates his/her underlying beliefs, giving rise to a host of cognitive, emotional, physical and behavioural responses, which are then noted, interpreted and responded to by Partner A, in a process not dissimilar to that described between therapist and patient in the cognitive interpersonal cycle in Chapter 3.

Each partner's 'appraisal' of the other's behaviour is influenced by factors which include context, beliefs about themselves and others, degree of *relational schematic processing* (the extent to which each interprets the other's behaviour as being to do with them) and is vulnerable to the same cognitive biases that are often the focus of CBT interventions. Couples can also develop patterns of responding behaviourally to each other that contribute to a pervasive negative atmosphere in the relationship. It can be useful to distinguish between *primary distress*, which arises from one or both partners' needs not being met in the relationship, and *secondary distress*, which results from their maladaptive attempts to meet those needs.

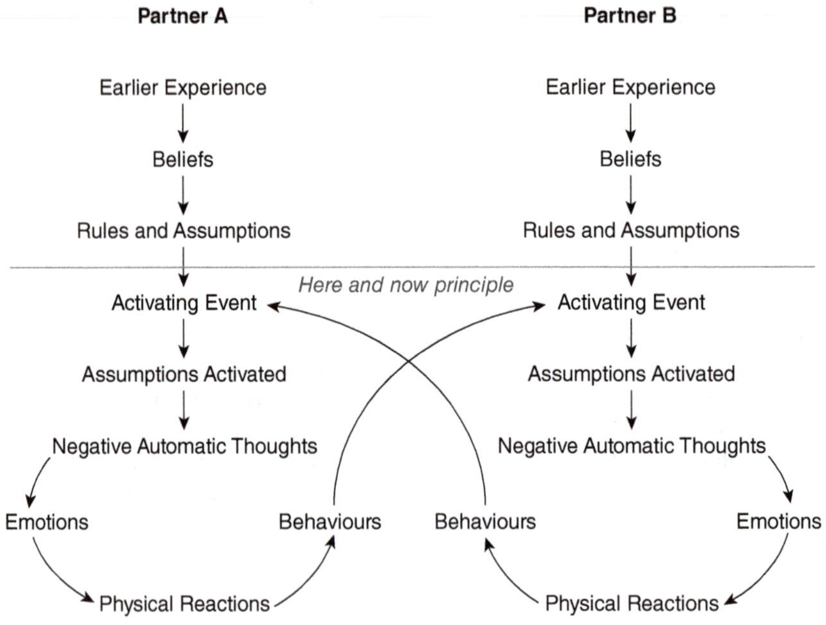

Figure 18.1 Cognitive behavioural interaction of the couple (Grant, 2011)

> Rita and James are in their late thirties. They have been together for 8 years and have a young daughter Clara. They describe a gradual deterioration in their relationship since they became parents. Rita complains that James is distant and unsupportive; she believes she has been left with most of the responsibility for parenting and running the household, even though she still works. For his part, James reports feeling constantly criticised at home. He does his best to help Rita, but has a stressful job and works long hours. He has a history of depression and finds the conflict in their relationship very difficult to deal with. They have very little support, as Rita's family live in Spain, whereas James is an only child and his parents are elderly.

The difficulties faced by Rita and James are typical of those of couples entering therapy. A number of cognitive, behavioural, emotional and contextual factors are likely to contribute to their distress. They may have individual differences in domains such as values and needs, emotional reactivity or coping style. They are describing a *demand–withdraw* pattern of interaction (Christensen and Heavey, 1990), in which Rita seeks closeness and support from James and feels distressed by what she perceives as his lack of engagement in the relationship. She reacts by increasing her demands, and James responds to this by withdrawing further. This demand–withdraw pattern is a secondary source of distress in the relationship; Rita's primary distress is due to her unmet need for closeness and intimacy in the relationship, whilst for James, the source of primary distress is not feeling valued or appreciated by Rita.

Cognitive processes such as attentional biases often play a role in maintaining and exacerbating relationship distress, with negative aspects of the relationship becoming more salient while positive ones go unnoticed (Baucom and Epstein, 1990; Beck, 1988). Rita and James may be making negative attributions about each other's behaviour, unlike people in happy relationships who tend to give their partner the 'benefit of the doubt.' For example, if James comes home later than expected, Rita may well attribute this to James not caring about her plans, rather than thinking he must have been delayed by an emergency at work.

James and Rita's different cultural backgrounds and family of origin experiences will have shaped their relationship assumptions, expectations and standards. Rita came from a poor but close-knit family, whereas James' parents led quite separate lives. The partners may have quite different expectations of married life, as well as rules or standards for what their relationship *should* be like.

Finally, contextual factors need to be taken into account, such as the transition to parenthood, external stressors, James' low mood and any strengths or sources of support available to the couple.

Typically, the initial focus of CBCT is on reducing the negative interpersonal behaviours contributing to secondary distress, so that the unmet needs causing primary distress can be identified and addressed. The couple may be helped to develop more constructive ways of interacting, through interventions such as guided behaviour change and communication skills training. During this process, unhelpful or extreme cognitions may become apparent and the couple will be helped to identify and address these. A range of cognitive behavioural interventions may be used to work on these and other difficulties, such as James' mood or the partners' difficulty expressing/containing emotions. Some couples face problems that cannot be resolved or needs that cannot be met, and these couples may need to work towards acceptance of these 'irreconcilable differences' (Jacobson and Christensen, 1996).

A number of studies have found strong positive associations between the quality of the therapeutic relationship and outcome in couple therapy (e.g. Davis et al., 2012). The therapeutic alliance in CBCT can be complex. The therapist needs to relate to each partner individually as well as forming an alliance with them as a couple. The partners themselves also need to have a good working alliance for therapy to succeed. This 'expanded' therapeutic alliance (Sprenkle et al., 2009) creates additional opportunities for ruptures to occur. Many couples enter therapy with a poor *collaborative set* (i.e. the shared view that they are both responsible for the relationship difficulties and both need to change to address these; Jacobson and Christensen, 1996). The therapist may want to start by addressing the partners' hostile or destructive pattern of interaction (secondary distress), whilst the couple would prefer to work on their lack of emotional connection (primary distress). Or, the therapist can find one partner's behaviour unpleasant and empathise more with the other, leading to a 'split' in the alliance.

Bordin's conceptualisation of the therapeutic alliance (Horvarth, 1994), described in Chapter 2, is very relevant to CBCT. In many couples seeking therapy, the partners have a different perspective on their relationship and what needs to change, or differ in their level of commitment to the relationship. These differences can make it hard to agree the goals and tasks of the therapy, and thus jeopardise treatment outcome (e.g. Norcross and Wampold, 2011) by preventing the therapist and clients from engaging in *active shared work*. Furthermore, for the therapist, expressing empathy and validating each partner's concerns without alienating the other can be a highly nuanced process when they hold such differing views.

If the couple's own alliance is poor, the goals and tasks of therapy may be directly related to addressing this. For example, integrative behavioural couple therapists would initially focus on promoting *acceptance* if a couple's collaborative set is poor, as change-oriented interventions are unlikely to succeed if the partners are unable to collaborate, accommodate, or compromise (Jacobson and Christensen, 1996). In this context, acceptance involves promoting empathy, letting go of the struggle to change the other person (empathic joining), and/or externalising the problems rather than seeing them as a flaw in the partner (unified detachment).

ENGAGING THE CLIENTS

Couple therapy is a demanding process - it may involve making difficult behavioural changes, disclosing thoughts and feelings that make one feel vulnerable and learning to accept a partner's imperfections. The therapeutic alliance is key to engagement in therapy, and in order for Rita and James to trust their therapist, Mark, and start to negotiate goals and tasks, a number of things must happen. The therapist must establish his credibility, by demonstrating a good understanding of relationships and of their specific concerns as well as the skills to competently take them through a process to address these. It is necessary to establish an atmosphere of safety, where each partner feels able to explore different ways of relating to the other. Mark needs to work collaboratively and flexibly with the couple, becoming more or less structured or directive as needed. The main focus should be on the couple, not on treating each partner individually.

Numerous factors can affect therapist credibility in the eyes of a couple, including age, gender, interpersonal style, cultural factors and level of clinical experience. The process of forming a therapeutic alliance varies from one couple to the next, and the therapist may need to adapt language and methods of engagement. For example, couples vary in how they respond to warmth, humour or level of therapist directiveness. The potential significance of cultural differences should not be underestimated; these should be explored in a sensitive manner, with the therapist seeking to understand the cultural influences on each partner and their impact on the relationship and the therapeutic alliance.

Instilling hope is an important part of engagement. In distressed couples, individuals have a tendency to attribute relationship difficulties to negative qualities in their partner (e.g. Bradbury and Fincham, 1990). This attributional style can make it difficult to take personal responsibility for making changes in the relationship.

Reflective question

Mark, the therapist, is also a new father, with a busy and stressful job. How might this affect his therapeutic alliance with Rita and James?

Reframing the difficulties in a more contextual and less blaming manner can therefore help each partner to identify their contribution to them and commit to making individual changes (Sprenkle et al., 2009), improving their collaborative set.

A comprehensive assessment process may assist engagement in therapy. Offering both conjoint and individual assessment appointments can facilitate the development of the 'expanded' therapeutic alliance, and use of observational methods and self-report questionnaires to support the process can help identify important individual and contextual factors that might otherwise be missed.

Evidence suggests that even brief interventions that are limited to assessment, formulation, feedback and goal setting can improve relationship satisfaction (Cordova et al., 2014). These processes may help by promoting collaboration, enabling the partners and therapist to develop a shared understanding of the relationship and its difficulties. This can help the couple to recognise their strengths and alter their perspective on their problems in a way that gives them hope and enhances commitment to therapy (Halford et al., 2016).

Therapist tips

At the start of therapy:

1. Invest in the assessment process and develop a shared formulation with the couple.
2. Differentiate primary and secondary sources of distress.
3. Instil hope and motivation by helping the couple to view their difficulties in a more contextual, less blaming way.
4. Work towards both acceptance and change, and make this explicit.
5. Be flexible in your approach and be prepared to be more directive, particularly if the couple's discussions escalate, or the opposite, if one or both partners seem disengaged.
6. Be aware of, and sensitive to, cultural influences on the relationship, both at a broad level and also more 'locally,' e.g. family traditions.

PREDICTING AND PREVENTING THREATS TO THE THERAPEUTIC ALLIANCE

Problems in any aspect of the therapeutic alliance can arise over the course of treatment, even if therapy gets off to a good start. There are a number of things a therapist can do to monitor the alliance and reduce the risk of difficulties occurring.

AGREE A THERAPY CONTRACT

Some therapists present couples with a written contract outlining the roles and responsibilities of each person at the start of therapy. Socialising the couple early on to the idea that the *relationship* is the client, and that each partner must try to consider the other's perspective, take responsibility for their own behaviour and make an effort to change things for the better, conveys the expectation that each participant will take an active role in therapy. Furthermore, such conversations also offer a good opportunity to discuss ground rules and boundaries.

MONITOR PROGRESS

Actively monitoring the therapy alliance as well as progress in treatment can help the therapist identify and respond to warning signs that all is not well (Sprenkle et al., 2009). A recent study found that lack of improvement on a measure of relationship functioning mid-way through therapy was predictive of poor outcome in a substantial proportion of couples (Halford et al., 2012). These authors suggest that monitoring progress in therapy in order to identify couples who are 'off-track' could enhance outcome by flagging difficulties early on. Feedback could mediate outcome through a number of mechanisms: by refocusing the clients or therapist on the key tasks of therapy, by influencing other factors such as the therapy alliance or by prompting a change of direction in the therapy itself.

Although methods have been developed specifically for the purpose of tracking the expected progress trajectory in couple therapy (e.g. Pinsof et al., 2009), these can be complex and time consuming, and most therapists will find methods traditionally used in CBT more practical. Eliciting verbal feedback regularly (e.g. *what are you taking away from our session today?*), observation methods, regular review of measures of individual and relationship functioning, and alliance rating scales all provide useful information, which can be discussed during therapy sessions so that obstacles to improvement can be identified and addressed.

Reflective question

Think about a couple you are working with. What sources of feedback, both formal and informal, could you use to monitor the alliance and progress in therapy, and how would you introduce these to your clients?

ADDRESSING EMOTIONS

Individuals vary greatly in their experience and expression of emotions. Some appear not to be very emotionally reactive; taken to the extreme, this can make them seem aloof or disconnected. Others have difficulty regulating or containing their emotions, and this can create difficulties in therapy sessions as well as in the relationship. Unhelpful or extreme beliefs about emotional experience and expression can also be problematic for couples and for therapy (e.g. Epstein and Baucom, 2002). In Rita and James' relationship, Rita was more comfortable displaying her emotions than James, but her level of emotional arousal sometimes escalated beyond what was constructive, and their therapist had to take quite a directive stance in order to help her contain her feelings. Over the course of therapy, it also became apparent that James held some unhelpful beliefs about emotional expression (e.g. *showing your feelings is a sign of weakness*), which needed to be addressed.

'BALANCING' THE ALLIANCE

The therapeutic alliance can be compromised if the therapist finds himself 'taking sides' with one partner. This can happen when difficulties presented by a couple activate one's own individual or relational schemas; for example, if one partner behaves in a way that the therapist sees as objectionable. Reflecting on questions such as '*what is the function of partner A's behaviour?*' and '*how is this relationship working for each partner?*' can help the therapist to look beyond the observable behaviour at underlying needs and motives. Understanding what is driving a person's behaviour can make it easier to feel empathy towards them, particularly when the behaviour is negative. Supervision can also be used helpfully to reflect on the impact of one's own beliefs and values on the therapeutic alliance.

Sometimes one partner is more dominant in sessions than the other, making it hard for the quieter partner to participate actively. As well as seeking to understand this pattern of behaviour, in these circumstances the therapist may need to take a more directive role in balancing the session. It may be useful to be explicit about this at the start of therapy:

> *Therapist*: It is my job to make sure you both get a chance to express your concerns and that therapy is fair and balanced. I will ask you not to interrupt the other person when he/she is talking, even if you don't agree with what they are saying. I will make sure you have a chance to express your view too, but it is really important to let them finish. There may be sessions where it feels like we are focusing more on one person's concerns – if this happens, I will make sure we prioritise the other person the following week. I'll be checking in with you regularly about how you think therapy is going, so please tell me if you don't think the balance is right.

WORKING WITH THREATS TO THE ALLIANCE

The therapeutic alliance is dynamic and evolves over the course of therapy. Ruptures can occur with both partners as a couple, as a 'split' in the therapeutic alliance or as problems in the couple's own working alliance. Common difficulties include, but are not limited to:

- Disagreement about the goals for therapy.
- Lack of commitment to therapy, or to the relationship.
- Lack of progress.
- One partner being more dominant than the other during sessions.
- The therapist feeling more empathic towards one partner.
- The therapist's own relationship standards compromising his/her objectivity.
- Difficulty preventing the couple's interaction from escalating and becoming destructive during sessions.
- Defensiveness or avoidance of emotional expression.

After several weeks where Rita and James had not been able to complete their homework, the couple and their therapist were feeling quite demoralised. From the therapist's point of view, the homework task (to practice communication skills) was based on a shared formulation, was directly linked to the couple's goals for therapy (to improve communication and feel more connected) and had been clearly agreed with both partners. Potential obstacles to carrying out the homework had been discussed and addressed. Why were they unable to do it?

Threats to the therapeutic alliance can be addressed using standard cognitive behavioural interventions for relational difficulties. They can therefore have a 'silver lining' in CBCT, in that they give the therapist the opportunity to model the attitudes and behaviours he is encouraging the couple to adopt. The first step in addressing alliance ruptures is to clarify the issue through the use of questioning and feedback. Here, the therapist can model good expressive and listening skills and support the partners in using these.

Therapist: It seems like you're getting a bit stuck with practicing your communication skills outside the session. A lot of things can make it difficult to do homework. I'd like to understand what is going on for each of you, because how we move forward depends on what is making it hard for each of you to have those conversations. Let's start with you James – what are some of the things that get in the way for you?

Here, the therapist approaches the issue in a clear and non-blaming way. He provides a rationale for exploring underlying difficulties and invites each partner to give feedback:

James: Well, we've been really busy this week between work and looking after Clara and there hasn't been much opportunity to practice.

Therapist: I see. I know you both have hectic schedules and I can imagine the difficulty finding time and energy to fit something extra in. Were there any times though when you were both together on your own, for example, when your daughter was in bed?

James: Yeah, I guess so, but there's still a lot to do even then.

Therapist: Yes, I'm sure that's the case – you don't have much 'down' time. But, during these times, did you think about the homework task at all, and if so, do you remember what went through your mind, or how it felt?

James: Well, you know, things are always so tense between us so it feels really hard. And, at the moment, I have so much on at work. The last thing I want to do is get into a discussion that's going to lead to an argument ...

Here, James starts by attributing the homework difficulties to factors external to the relationship, but careful questioning and validation by the therapist helps to elicit some negative expectations about the task, which have contributed to his avoidance.

The next step is to develop a shared formulation of the problem, in which the therapist should acknowledge his own role and responsibility if appropriate:

Therapist: So, Rita, if I understand correctly, you tried on several occasions to start a conversation with James, and you felt disappointed and frustrated when he didn't want to talk. And James, you felt really stressed and didn't want to add to that by starting a conversation you thought would lead to an argument. Is that right?

James: Yeah.

Rita: Yes, we couldn't even get started ...

Therapist: One thing that maybe I didn't make clear enough was that the task was to practice talking about neutral or positive topics, things that don't matter and are not likely to lead to an argument. That's because, first of all, I want you to get good at using the communication guidelines before we start talking about trickier issues. It sounds like one of the things that got you stuck James was that you were expecting the conversation to get difficult. Perhaps I could have suggested some topics for you to discuss, and I can certainly do that going forward. Do you think this would help?

With this couple, there seems to be a split in the alliance, with Rita insisting that she is on board with the task whereas James is less committed to it. Split alliances can be particularly challenging. On the one hand, the therapist needs to maintain the alliance with the engaged client, and a change of direction or tactic in therapy may well threaten this. On the other hand, the couple is unlikely to make progress if both partners are not fully involved in the process. The therapist therefore needs to respond in a manner that supports the efforts of one partner whilst at the same time trying to find ways to help the other partner to engage.

Therapist: What I'd like to do is take a close look at what actually happened between you those times when Rita tried to start a conversation. Sometimes, when communication is difficult, both partners have really good intentions but there seems to be a 'black hole' between what one person means to say and what the other understands, and then things don't go well. I'm wondering if something like this happened to you. Rita, can you remember one of these occasions when you tried to start a conversation? What were you both doing, and can you remember what you said to James to start the conversation?

Further questioning regarding Rita and James' experience of the interaction revealed that their demand-withdraw pattern was playing out, with Rita's attempts to initiate a discussion being perceived as aggressive by James, and his natural response of withdrawal increasing Rita's frustration.

Once the therapist and couple have clarified and developed a shared understanding of the difficulties, they can work together to identify possible solutions. Rita and James identified their main priorities as being able to move forward with their communication practice in a way that felt less aversive to James and that did not leave Rita feeling the responsibility for initiating the homework task was left to her. The couple and their therapist identified two strategies that would help them to work towards these aims.

ADDRESSING THEIR PATTERN OF INTERACTION

To help Rita to express her needs in a way that James experienced as less threatening and help James to remain engaged in an interaction even when he felt anxious. This was done in a graded way, starting with rehearsal during sessions:

> *Therapist*: What I'd like for us to do now is to practice, so that you find a way of starting a conversation that works for both of you. This might feel a little awkward, at least to start with. James, for you it is going to mean staying in a conversation even if you are feeling anxious, and Rita, your job is going to be to help James to stay engaged by making it feel as comfortable as possible for him, and that might mean changing how you respond to him. Let's have a go, and then you can give each other some feedback, and I will make some suggestions too. So, let's pretend that you're at home, and it is the time you had agreed to do the homework. Who is going to start this time?

Being explicit that partners will take turns at initiating the conversation will help them to share responsibility for this, which was one of Rita's priorities. The therapist then observes the couple's communication, elicits feedback from each partner, where appropriate explores alternative ways of approaching the issue with both partners and rehearses these new behaviours. The therapist may also 'coach' the couple, using psychoeducation, feedback about their individual expressive and receptive communication skills and modelling alternative ways of interacting. The couple can then practice this new way of interacting outside of therapy sessions.

MAKING HOMEWORK TASKS MORE STRUCTURED TO START WITH

To make it easier for each partner to know what is expected and when.

Therapist: So, you have agreed that on Thursday evening, after your daughter has gone to bed, you will have a sharing thoughts and feelings conversation about your favourite TV show at the moment. James will start the conversation, and you will each spend about five minutes in the speaker role, while your partner uses the listener guidelines to listen actively. Afterwards, you will spend a few minutes individually thinking about what went well and what you need to work on, and we will talk about this in our next session.

Increasing the structure in homework tasks can be useful to 'set the ball rolling' when motivation or perceived ability to change is low. Of course, this can feel somewhat artificial and constraining, and there is a risk that the couple will attribute improvements to following 'rules' and structure rather than to their own efforts. Once the couple have had some success with homework tasks, their efforts should start to become naturally reinforcing and the level of structure can be reduced.

Like any other intervention, strategies put in place to address alliance ruptures should be evaluated. Knowing that the plan will be reviewed after a certain time makes it easier for individuals to commit to trying it out, and the therapist needs to check whether the intervention has been successful. Furthermore, as the alliance can change over the course of therapy, new situations may arise which may require further attention. Therefore, the therapist and clients need to agree on a plan to monitor and review their chosen solution and its impact on the alliance and progress towards their goals.

Therapist tips

Addressing difficulties in the therapy alliance:

1. Monitor the alliance and progress in therapy to predict and prevent difficulties.
2. When problems occur, clarify the issue from both partners' perspective and consider own role.
3. Develop a shared understanding of what is happening.
4. Explore possible solutions collaboratively.
5. Agree how chosen solution(s) will be implemented and evaluated.

ENDING THERAPY

Couples often voice concerns about ending therapy. These concerns are not unwarranted; long-term follow-up studies have noted deterioration in a significant proportion of couples after the end of therapy (e.g. Christensen et al., 2010).

Couples can be reluctant to end therapy for a number of reasons. Some cite fears that they have not made enough progress, others that their motivation to attend to their relationship might wane without the supportive framework of therapy. Ending can be particularly difficult for couples whose relationship has not improved, who leave therapy still experiencing significant levels of distress.

The therapist can do a number of things to prepare a couple for ending:

- Discuss each partner's concerns about ending well in advance.
- Explicitly encourage the couple to use their own working alliance to address relationship issues and give them more responsibility for this as the end of therapy approaches.

- Ensure that a good therapy blueprint has been developed, which addresses both partner's concerns about ending and clearly states how each will contribute, both individually and as a couple, to maintaining and consolidating treatment gains.
- Normalise setbacks and fluctuation in relationship satisfaction, and ensure the blueprint contains a plan for dealing with these.
- Emphasise the need to work towards acceptance for 'unsolvable problems' and that this can take time.
- If the couple has made little or no progress, validate their feelings of disappointment and frustration and work with them to develop an understanding of what got in the way, both for them as a couple and for the partners individually, and what they could do going forward to address this.

Therapy cannot help all distressed couples to improve their relationship, and indeed, some couples might be better off apart. For these couples, helping them to become aware of this and to take steps towards separation could actually be a good clinical outcome (Halford, 2001).

CHAPTER SUMMARY

In this chapter, the case example of Rita and James was used to illustrate the expanded therapy alliance in CBCT. Ways of developing and monitoring the therapeutic relationship and predicting threats to it were described. The use of CBCT interventions to clarify and address difficulties in the therapeutic alliance was illustrated, and some suggestions were made to promote a good ending in couple therapy.

FURTHER READING

Epstein N and Baucom DH (2002) *Enhanced Cognitive-behavioral Therapy for Couples: A Contextual Approach*. Washington, DC: American Psychological Association. *A 'bible' for CBCT practitioners, with in-depth descriptions of the interventions outlined in this chapter.*

Jacobson NS and Christensen A (1996) *Acceptance and Change in Couple Therapy: A Therapist's Guide to Transforming Relationships*. New York: Norton. *An integrative behavioural couple therapy manual, focusing on both acceptance and change.*

REFERENCES

Baucom D and Epstein N (1990) *Cognitive-behavioral Marital Therapy*. New York: Bruner/Mazel.

Beck AT (1988) *Love is Never Enough: How Couples can Overcome Misunderstandings, Resolve Conflicts, and Solve Relationship Problems Through Cognitive Therapy*. New York: Harper & Row.

Bradbury TN and Fincham FD (1990) Attributions in marriage: Review and critique. *Psychological Bulletin 107*(1): 3–33.

Christensen A and Heavey C (1990) Gender and social structure in the demand/withdraw pattern of marital conflict. *Journal of Personality and Social Psychology 59*(1): 73–81.

Christensen A, Atkins D, Baucom BR and Yi J (2010) Couple and individual adjustment for 5 years following a randomized clinical trial comparing traditional versus integrative behavioral couple therapy. *Journal of Consulting and Clinical Psychology 78*: 225–235.

Cordova JV, Flemming CJE, Morrill MI, Hawrilenko M, Sollenberger S, Harp AG, et al. (2014) The marriage checkup: A randomized controlled trial of annual relationship health check-ups. *Journal of Consulting and Clinical Psychology 82*: 592–604.

Davis SD, Lebow JL and Sprenkle DH (2012) Common factors of change in couple therapy. *Behavior Therapy 43*(1): 36–48.

Doss BD, Benson L, Georgia E and Christensen A (2013) Translation of Integrative Behavioral Couple Therapy to a web based intervention. *Family Processes 52*(1): 139–153.

Epstein N and Baucom DH (2002) Enhanced cognitive-behavioral therapy for couples: A contextual approach. Washington, DC: American Psychological Association.

Grant L (2011) *Conceptualisation of Couples in Therapy*. In: BABCP 39th Annual Conference. Guilford: University of Surrey.

Halford WK (2001) *Brief Couple Therapy: Helping Partners to Help Themselves*. New York, NY: Guilford Press.

Halford WK, Hayes S, Christensen A, Lambert M, Baucom DH and Atkins D (2012) Towards making progress feedback an effective common factor in couple therapy. *Behavior Therapy 43*(1): 49–60.

Halford WK, Pepping C and Petch J (2016) The gap between couple therapy research efficacy and practice effectiveness. *Journal of Marital and Family Therapy 42*(1): 32–44.

Horvath AO (ed) (1994) *Empirical Validation of Bordin's Pantheoretical Model of the Alliance: The Working Alliance Inventory Perspective*. Oxford: Wiley.

Jacobson NS and Christensen A (1996) *Acceptance and Change in Couple Therapy: A Therapist's Guide to Transforming Relationships*. New York: Norton.

Norcross JC and Wampold BE (2011) Evidence based therapy relationships: Research conclusions and clinical practices. *Psychotherapy 48*(1): 98–102.

Pinsof WM, Zinbarg RE, LeBow J, Knobloch-Fedders LM, Durbin E, Chambers A, Latta T, et al. (2009) Laying the foundation for progress research in family, couple and individual therapy: The development and psychometric features of the initial Systemic Therapy Inventory of Change. *Psychotherapy Research 19*: 143–156.

Sprenkle DH, Davis SD and LeBow J (2009) *Common factors in couple and family therapy: The overlooked foundation for effective practice*. New York: Guilford Press.

19

SUPERVISION AND THE THERAPEUTIC RELATIONSHIP

STIRLING MOOREY AND SUZANNE BYRNE

CHAPTER OVERVIEW

There has been an assumption throughout this book that supervision is vital in helping therapists understand and manage challenges to the therapeutic relationship. This chapter looks at how the client–therapist relationship can be addressed in supervision and how to work with issues such as therapy interfering beliefs and 'transference' and 'countertransference.' Problems arising in the supervisory relationship will also be considered, together with the role of supervision of supervision.

SUPERVISION IN CBT

Few therapists would disagree that good clinical supervision is necessary for the safe and effective practice of CBT, but the evidence for the optimum supervision method is currently lacking (Watkins, 2014). While there is some research to suggest that supervision improves competence in therapists in training (e.g. Mannix et al., 2006), demonstrating that supervision improves outcome has proved more challenging (see Alfonsson et al., 2017 for a recent systematic review). It is not really surprising that it is hard to identify the effective ingredients of supervision given how difficult it is to disentangle the effective ingredients of therapy. CBT has the relatively circumscribed primary goal of symptom reduction, but supervision has a wider remit. Bordin (1983), for instance, identified eight goals of supervision: mastery of specific skills; enlarging one's understanding of clients; enlarging one's awareness of process issues; increasing awareness of self and impact on process; overcoming personal and intellectual obstacles towards learning and mastery; deepening one's understanding of concepts and theory; providing a stimulus to research and maintaining standards of service. Which of these goals is most important will vary depending on many contextual factors such as the supervisee's level of experience, the client group and the demands of the particular service. Supervision of a therapist in private practice will be very different from supervision of a therapist working in a busy health service setting like IAPT (Improving Access to Psychological Therapies). In the latter, the requirement to meet specific targets for outcomes and patient access inevitably shifts the balance away from in-depth consideration of professional development needs and leisurely reflective practice. Although there is, as yet, no truly evidence-based approach to supervision, there is a fairly well established consensus on the format and function of CBT supervision; this is summarised in Roth and Pilling's Supervision Competences Framework, commissioned by the Care Services Improvement Partnership (CSIP), Skills for Health and NHS Education for Scotland (Roth and Pilling, 2008 available on CORE website). Most supervisors will use a model of supervision based on the format of therapy itself. The rationale for this is that CBT is a problem-focused therapy in which the client learns self-management skills through a collaborative process of practice inside and outside the session with feedback from the therapist: similar methods may be used in supervision to aid the supervisee's development as a therapist. CBT supervision is therefore structured like therapy: agreed goals (learning objectives), an agreed session agenda, and summaries and feedback. The supervisee brings a specific supervision question and leaves with a collaboratively derived answer: this may involve a revised formulation, ideas on how to clarify the formulation, suggestions on the use of specific techniques or insights into the therapeutic relationship. Learning will be enhanced through guided discovery, role plays and reflection on recordings of therapy sessions. Various texts are available that outline this approach (e.g. Gordon, 2012; Liese et al., 1997; Lomax et al., 2005; Padesky, 1996). It is important, however, to recognise the areas where therapy and supervision are *different* (see, for instance, Newman, 1998) and to note the critique of this 'reflexive' model of supervision (Milne, 2008). Milne's contribution has been to remind us of the *educational* objective at the heart of much supervision. Kolb's cycle (Kolb, 1984) has been a significant influence on many CBT supervision models – the supervisee is helped to *reflect* on their practice, link this to their conceptualisation (*theoretical analysis)* and *plan* changes to their practice, which they then put into *action*. The cycle commences again with review and reflection on the effect of these changes. Vygotsky's 'zone of promixal development' (Vygotsky, 1978) and Bennett-Levy's (Bennett-Levy et al., 2015) model of self-reflective practice also inform this aspect of supervision. More detailed recent texts on CBT supervision include Corrie and Lane's excellent *CBT Supervision* (2015) and Milne and Reisers's newly developed *Manual for Evidence-Based Supervision*. This chapter will assume the supervisor is using the 'traditional' approach based on Padesky's (1996) chapter in the *Frontiers of Cognitive Therapy*.

TECHNICAL VERSUS RELATIONAL FOCUS IN SUPERVISION

Supervision is busy and the demands of case management often take precedence over discussion of the therapeutic relationship. This is not necessarily a fault in the supervisor since CBT is a problem-focused, not an interpersonal, therapy and, if there is evidence of good collaboration, the relationship does not need to be singled out for attention. When the supervisee brings a question concerning lack of progress in therapy, difficulties with a particular patient or an alliance rupture, it is wise to initially investigate them from a technical perspective before moving to an interpersonal one. The supervisor needs to check that the therapist has socialised the patient to the model, accurately conceptualised the presenting problems, explained the rationale for interventions, set appropriate and achievable tasks and properly reviewed the homework. Therapists may be frustrated by lack of progress and label patients as 'resistant' when in fact it is poor formulation or technique that has caused the problem (see Supervisor tip). When there are disagreements over the goals and tasks of therapy (Bordin, 1979), our advice would be to start at the technical level and then move on to examining the relationship if necessary.

Supervisor tip. An 'unmotivated patient'

A therapist mentioned in supervision that a patient with PTSD was cancelling appointments regularly and sighed and raised his eyes to the ceiling. When prompted, he said that the client 'is not motivated ... She's wasting mine and the service's time ... others on the waiting list could be seen'.

As a supervisor what would you do?

The supervisor encouraged the therapist to consider these cancellations in the context of the formulation:

'What do we know about PTSD and your client's circumstances?'

The client had been attacked by a group of youths on a Saturday afternoon when close to her home. She was stabbed and left unconscious.

The supervisor asked the therapist what had been discussed about the cancellations. The therapist had not raised the matter.

He subsequently called the patient to enquire why she was cancelling a lot of therapy appointments. It transpired that she was unable to leave her home when groups of children were gathered outside as this triggered intrusive memories. The client felt a lot of shame about what had happened and thought she should be able to get over it so didn't disclose this information to the therapist when she called to cancel her appointment.

Alliance ruptures can result from an incorrect formulation and treatment plan or from poor implementation of cognitive behavioural techniques. If this is the case, the focus should be on helping the therapist to revise their formulation and/or develop skills. Discussion of how to repair the alliance rupture then follows. The therapist may need to apologise to the patient if, for instance, they have set homework that was too difficult (e.g. asking a patient with panic and agoraphobia to visit the supermarket before they have done any behavioural experiments to test catastrophic fears), then revisit the formulation and agree a less challenging task.

WORKING WITH THERAPISTS' NEGATIVE RESPONSES TO PATIENTS

'Countertransference' is not a term that sits easily within CBT, coming as it does, from a very different theoretical tradition, but there is not a satisfactory alternative single word to describe this phenomenon of a therapist's negative reactions to a patient. In Chapter 3, a cognitive behavioural model for understanding transference and countertransference was introduced. Although it is possible to work on our own therapy-interfering beliefs using a reflective practice model (e.g. Bennett-Levy et al., 2015), there is no real substitute for exploring these thoughts, feelings and behaviours with a skilled supervisor. The categories defined in Chapter 3 (n.b. these are not mutually exclusive) are:

1. Personal countertransference - where the therapist's personal beliefs impinge on the therapy process.
2. Empathic countertransference - where empathy (or lack of empathy) with the client interferes with therapy.
3. Reciprocal countertransference - where the interaction between the interpersonal beliefs of therapist and client impede therapy.

PERSONAL COUNTERTRANSFERENCE (THERAPIST BELIEFS)

Personal countertransference refers to the thoughts and feelings a therapist brings to the session which are not directly invoked by the client (see Chapter 3). In CBT, this usually means therapy-interfering beliefs such as 'I must help all my patients all the time' or 'If my patient feels worse, it means I'm a bad therapist.' The focus in training on therapist self-reflection, e.g. identifying beliefs/schemas in relation to learning, scrutiny of skills deficits and reactions to patients, is the CBT equivalent of the personal therapy required in other schools of psychotherapy. It is helpful for therapists to consider their beliefs and interpersonal style using formats such as Young's Schema Questionnaire (available at schematherapy.com) or Leahy's list of therapist beliefs (Leahy, 2012). It can be helpful to advise novice therapists about some of these common therapist schemas, thus validating their experience and encouraging discussion. Supervisor self-disclosure can also be helpful:

> When I started to work in the specialist trauma service, I found the first few supervision sessions nerve-wracking. I was already quite experienced in CBT, being qualified for a few years, and had secured a senior role in the service. In my first supervision meeting, I felt very anxious about playing my first clip of therapy to my new supervisor who was an expert in PTSD. I worried he would think what I did was really poor and that he, and others, would wonder why they had employed me.

Therapist beliefs are usually only explored in CBT supervision in the context of therapy-interfering beliefs. Box 19.1 gives some tips on when this might be appropriate.

In practice, these beliefs often interact with the patients' beliefs in therapy, and therapist beliefs often present challenges to the supervisory relationship, so we will discuss them further under the headings of reciprocal countertransference and the supervisory alliance.

Box 19.1 Indications for addressing therapist beliefs

1. When beliefs get in the way of providing a key component of treatment, e.g. the therapist feels uneasy about reliving work for PTSD; 'If they revisit the trauma, I won't be able to deal with their distress.'
2. When repeated problems arise across patients, e.g. therapy sessions overrun; 'If a patient has something to say, it's important I let them say it and don't interrupt.'
3. When there are difficulties in the relationship with particular patients, e.g. patients with emotionally unstable personality; 'I must always be able to keep the session focused. We should stick to the agenda.'
4. When there are strong emotional reactions in the therapist, e.g. feeling sorry for an adolescent patient; 'She reminds me of my little sister.'

EMPATHIC COUNTERTRANSFERENCE (EMOTIONAL AND COGNITIVE EMPATHY)

In Chapter 1, we discussed some of the traps therapists can fall into by either empathising too much or too little. They can over-empathise with clients on an emotional level, and become hopeless through emotional contagion, but fail to fully understand the client's negative automatic thoughts (NATs). Or they may over-empathise cognitively and accept their client's negative views. When therapists are caught in this, they may not be able to see what is going on: supervision can give an alternative perspective. In Chapter 1, we met Joan, a 28-year-old single parent who had been depressed for a year following the ending of a relationship and treatment for breast cancer. Her therapist might feel hopeless and agree that, because Joan was facing abandonment, social isolation and the threat of recurrence, her situation was indeed hopeless. The supervisor could use various approaches:

1. Help the therapist map out the maintenance formulation and evaluate Joan's cognitive and behavioural reactions.
2. Explore and evaluate the therapist's hopeless negative thoughts.
3. Ask the therapist to role play Joan. Experiencing the supervisor modelling how to work with Joan's hopelessness might instill some hope and illustrate how Joan's negative emotions had become infectious.

Therapists may sometimes find it hard to empathise. If Joan's therapist was pushing behavioural activation very hard, this might be a result of failure to empathise due to emotional avoidance. The supervisor might ask more about how it felt to be with Joan, which might help the therapist recognise she was feeling cut off from her. Exploring this might reveal personal reasons for this avoidance (e.g. someone close to her suffering from cancer). The therapist might then need time to discuss these feelings and separate her thoughts and emotions about her relative from the situation with Joan. Narcissistic and antisocial patients and sexual offenders may seriously challenge our ability to empathise. Piers was a narcissistic entrepreneur who coped with his emptiness through drugs and sex and tended to denigrate his therapist and the therapy. Paul, his therapist, felt angry, defensive and repulsed by Piers' lifestyle. Recognising the vulnerability beneath Piers' compensatory strategies may help engender some empathy for Piers. Through guided discovery, the supervisor can enquire about Piers' childhood: where did his feelings of emptiness and self-hatred originate? How might he have felt as a child? Can we tell a story of how he learned to cope with vulnerability by acting in the way he does now? This may allow Paul to see that behind Piers' obnoxious behaviour is a vulnerable child.

RECIPROCAL COUNTERTRANSFERENCE (CLIENT–THERAPIST INTERACTIONS)

When the client's schemas meet the therapist's schemas, they either combine in a collaborative cycle or a toxic cycle of therapy-impeding interactions. Shared beliefs about working in partnership and taking responsibility for change help CBT progress smoothly. When the beliefs clash, as when a therapist with excessively high standards (you should always work hard in order to achieve) encounters an entitled client (I should get anything I want without effort), conflict occurs. The therapist works hard but resents the client for not working hard as well. If the entitled client met a therapist with self-sacrificing beliefs (I must always put others first), a collusive cycle is set up in which the therapist works harder and gives more while the client puts his feet up, sometimes literally! It can be difficult to recognise and extract oneself from these sorts of pernicious interactions. Supervision is invaluable in identifying and finding ways out of these traps. In Chapter 3, an example was given of how the Interpersonal Schema Worksheet (Moorey, 2013) can be used in supervision to help Piers' therapist manage his negative reactions to his client. We will review this from the perspective of the supervisor. Piers' sense of inadequacy had led him to develop protective strategies of self-agrandisement. Paul found it hard to empathise with him and became more strident and demanding, while Piers did less and less and put the therapist down. Paul expressed his exasperation in supervision, so the supervisor suggested he complete the worksheet as homework. Figure 19.1 shows the worksheet, as completed by the supervisee.

As we discussed in Chapter 3, Paul had a good understanding of *most* of what Piers was doing but was less clear about Piers' thoughts and beliefs. Listening to the recording of the therapy session in supervision, Paul picked up the critical tone of his voice and noticed silences during which he was actually thinking condemnatory thoughts. The supervisor observed that Piers was sometimes flattering the therapist. This had the effect of the therapist easing up on Piers for a little while. Supervision helped Paul see that he felt contemptuous of Piers but was also influenced by his flattery.

The new insights from supervision are presented in bold in Figure 19.2. The therapist recognised some moralistic standards he had not really thought about before, e.g. 'You must take responsibility for your actions. If you don't, you're contemptible.' The supervisor asked Paul to fill out some of the rules that might be driving Piers

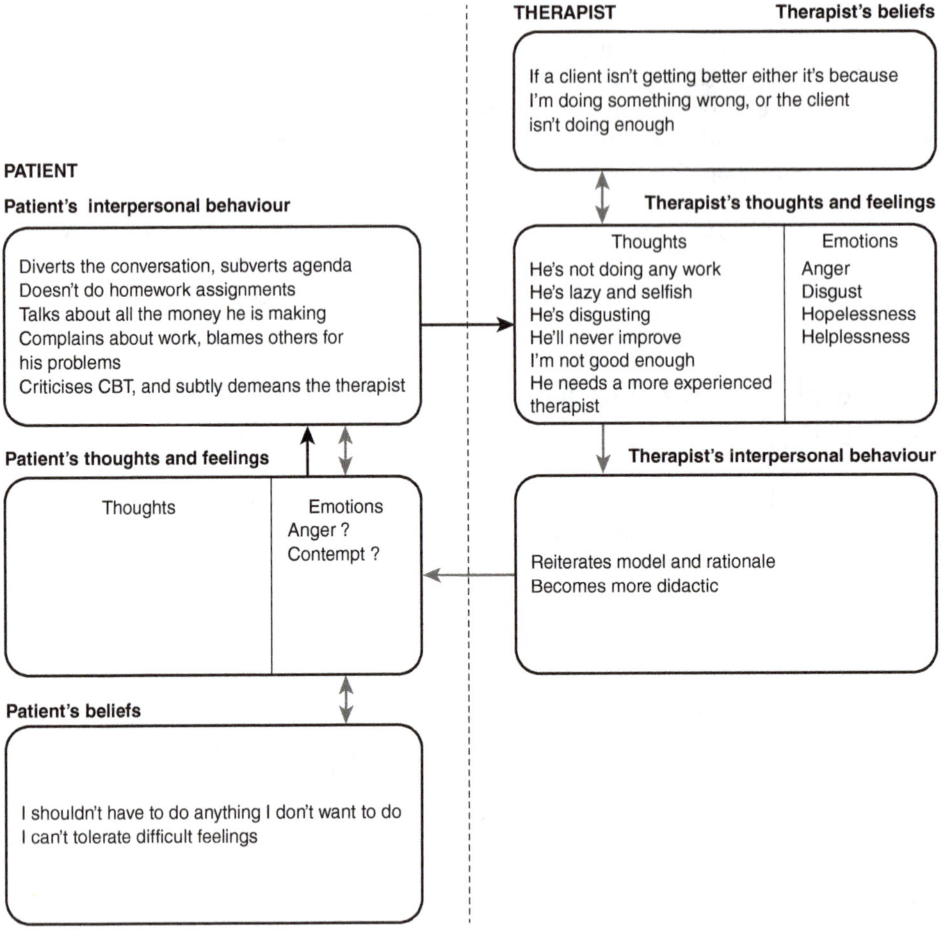

Figure 19.1 Piers' Interpersonal Schema Worksheet pre-supervision

therapy-interfering behaviours. Paul's feedback was that he now saw how his reactions were making him too directive and didactic in the session and that these were driven by punitive thoughts and feelings based on his judgements about Piers' behaviour. Paul found the idea that Piers' was attempting to gain some sense of self-worth through his behaviour helpful. Paul was more comfortable with maintenance conceptualisations, and the supervisor showed him how to construct a narrative of the client's life. To do this Paul needed to discover a little more about Piers' background. As he talked about being an only child who had been showered with material objects but no affection, and particularly when he spoke about going to boarding school at 7, Piers showed vulnerability for the first time. With the supervisor's help, Paul began to tell Piers' story: how he felt alone, unloved and worthless and the only things his family seemed to care about were material possessions and success. So he determined that this was what he wanted but it never satisfied him. He tried to distract himself with drugs and sex but these also were unsatisfactory, and he could not

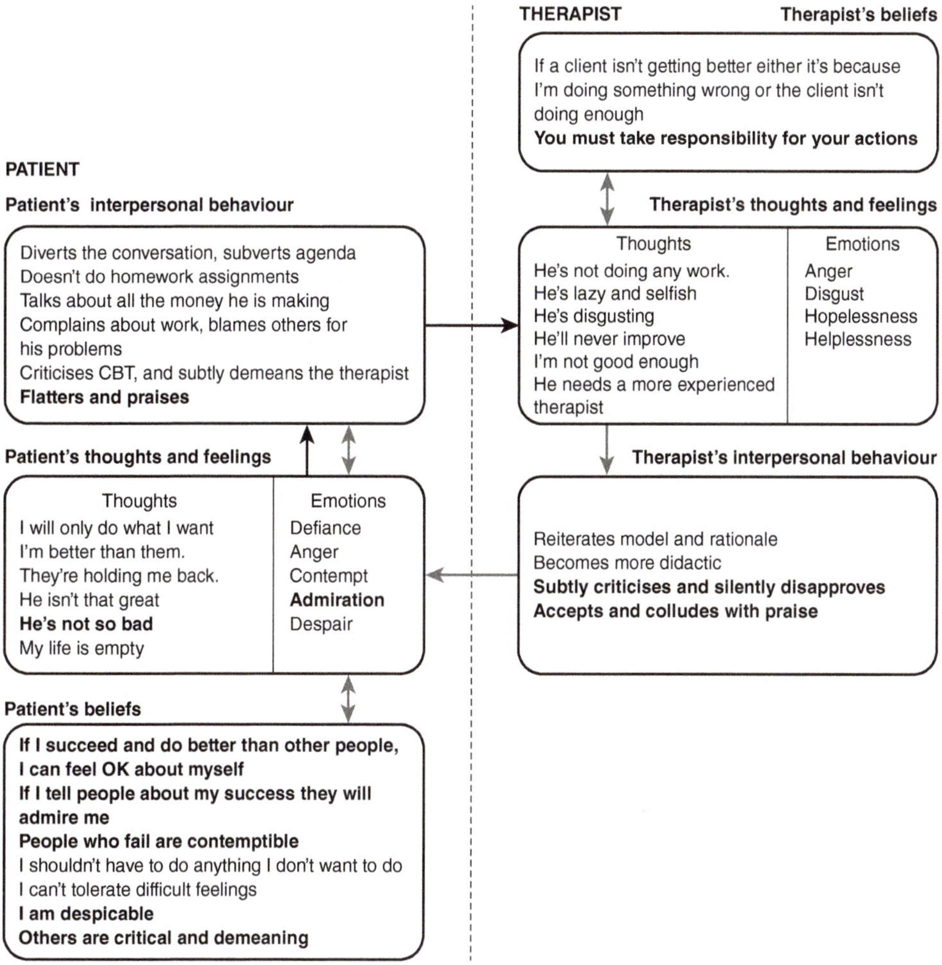

Figure 19.2 Piers' Interpersonal Schema Worksheet during supervision

escape from his core beliefs that he was despicable and that others would demean him if they saw who he really was. This narrative helped Paul see Piers in a new light and, over time, he was able to collaboratively share this hypothesised story, which helped them establish some degree of working partnership. The Interpersonal Schema Worksheet is a relatively unthreatening method to elicit therapist beliefs because it is framed in terms of the interaction: these are the beliefs that are activated when you work with this patient.

THE SUPERVISORY RELATIONSHIP

The relationship between supervisor and supervisee is built on mutual respect and, as in therapy, the core conditions of warmth, genuineness and empathy make up its foundations. The supervisee needs to feel safe enough to share his or her practice through recordings of sessions. This can be daunting for novice and experienced therapist alike. Establishing this supervisory bond is an important aspect of supervision alongside the goals (see above) and specific tasks (selecting supervision questions, preparing presentations of cases and observing practice: Bordin, 1983). A good supervisory alliance is associated with higher supervisee well-being, greater willingness to self-disclose during supervision, greater satisfaction with supervision and greater perceived effectiveness of supervision. A poor alliance, on the other hand, is associated with higher perceived stress, more burnout and more frequently perceived occurrences of negative supervision events (Watkins, 2014). However, as with research on the therapeutic alliance, the causal direction of these correlations is not clear. Fortunately, the interpersonal schemas of supervisors and supervisees generally allow for an adaptive complementary fit, though sometimes 'transferential' problems can crop up. In the final section, we discuss some of the common issues arising in the supervisory relationship. We are mainly concerned here with novice therapists. There is considerable overlap between these presentations and they can generally be subsumed under the themes of fear of negative evaluation and/or high standards and expectations.

AVOIDANCE

Exposing your practice to others for scrutiny is anxiety provoking. Supervisees find numerous ways to avoid: coming to sessions unprepared, avoiding discussion of cases that are not going well and failing to bring recordings of sessions. These problems can be reduced by establishing clear ground rules for supervision at the outset, including a supervision contract. The message that there should always be a clear supervision question and that recordings of sessions are essential sets the parameters. Anxiety about presentation of material can be allayed by the supervisor normalising the fearful thoughts and sharing his or her own experience of supervision as a trainee. Reminding supervisees that 80% of their practice is probably good but, to improve their proficiency as CBT therapists, they need to address the 20% where they want to develop skills. Asking therapists to bring examples of what went well, not just what went badly, can also be helpful. Identifying and rewarding good practice is an important component of giving feedback when listening to tapes or observing role plays. In a group setting, it is helpful to elicit NATs from all the supervisees at the beginning of supervision: the universality of the fears of negative evaluation helps to normalise the situation. It is important to be sure that the problem genuinely has its roots in avoidance. A disorganised trainee who brings vague supervision questions may be avoidant, or may lack time and task management skills. In one-to-one supervision, it is usually possible to address avoidance directly, to use Socratic questioning to identify the beliefs that might be generating anxiety and evaluate them together. This is not so easy in a group and supervisees may need to be seen individually to address the problem.

Later in the treatment of the PTSD case described in the Supervisor tip, the supervisor noticed the therapist was avoiding presenting and would offer to let others go first or say he had forgotten to bring the clip of therapy. It transpired that the therapist was not doing reliving. He had negative beliefs about causing distress: if the client was very upset, he would not be able to manage the affect. The supervisor suggested he watch a video of a reliving session and perhaps sit in on a session.

OVERT ANXIETY

Avoidance is the behavioural concomitant of anxiety. The avoidant supervisee may not show overt anxiety, but the anxious supervisee may be paralysed by it. The supervisor may be confronted by agitation, apologies and reassurance seeking. In individual supervision, this can be named and worked with directly by identifying the specific fears and evaluating them together. In group supervision, the approach may have to be less direct. An anxious supervisee's arousal can affect the whole group, so sometimes it may be helpful to begin the supervision with a brief mindfulness exercise to ground and calm the group. Utilising the group members to give the anxious trainee feedback can be helpful because they will usually do it in an inclusive manner, focusing on the positive points. Making any feedback specific can also help the supervisee to operationalise exactly what needs to be done, which may reduce worry.

RIGIDITY

Novice therapists want to know how to do therapy: the commonest supervision question is 'What do I do next?' The move away from generic cognitive conceptualisations to disorder specific models seems to have increased this need to find the correct protocol and 'do it right.' Trainees may have difficulty tolerating the messiness of real clients' lives and obsess about fitting the client's experience into the right boxes. This can be frustrating for the supervisor who needs to balance the simplicity of a taught model with the complexity of idiosyncratic case formulation.

A trainee therapist was working with a depressed client whose parents had been highly critical and undermining. The client's beliefs that she might be criticised if she did anything wrong made it hard for her to share her thoughts and feelings and do homework. The therapist's rigid approach to therapy played into this fear. The supervisor suggested the therapist might link the fear of criticism to her childhood experiences to demonstrate empathy and validate the client's feelings, but the therapist replied, 'We're only on session four. Isn't it too early to bring in the developmental conceptualisation?' He believed that it was necessary to complete a full developmental case conceptualisation diagram: anything less was not doing correct therapy. The supervisor demonstrated through role play how it was possible to simply reflect the patient's experience back to her without mapping her whole life story: 'Your parents were so critical of you that it's not surprising you're expecting to be told off at any point. Perhaps you developed a rule about being criticised if you made a mistake or even if you said anything? ... If you had to put that into words how would you express that rule?' The therapist saw that it was OK to bring in part of the longitudinal conceptualisation before the full picture was developed and shared.

PERFECTIONISM

Many of the examples above arise from high standards on the part of the therapist. Perfectionism can lead to rigidity, overt anxiety and avoidance in supervision. It can also present as challenges to the supervisory relationship in its own right. Training courses bring out these beliefs because the trainee is desperate to do well on ratings of their competency and focus on this at the expense of the client in front of them. The perfectionistic trainee may expect more of the supervisor and of themselves than either can deliver. Box 19.2 outlines some of the ways the supervisor may address perfectionism in the supervision setting.

Box 19.2 Helping the perfectionistic supervisee

1. Normalise the wish to do the best for the patient, and distinguish between realistic aspirations and unrealistic standards, e.g. 'I must get all my patients better.'
2. Share evidence that CBT therapists tend to have 'unrelenting standards' schemas.
3. Differentiate between 'perfect' and 'good enough' therapy. Technique may not always be the most important ingredient of successful therapy!
4. Use self-disclosure to demonstrate that even experienced therapists make mistakes.
5. Explicitly identify and evaluate perfectionistic beliefs.
6. In group supervision, use role play and discussion with group members to show that there is never one 'right' way to act in most therapy situations.
7. In individual and group supervision, listen to a recording of the session and stop it at key points to ask, 'What could we do next?', brainstorming all the possible routes the therapy could take.

SUPERVISION OF SUPERVISION

As can be seen, supervision is a complex activity: supervisors need to be able to respond in the moment and adapt their practice depending on what occurs in a supervision session. Because 'transferential' problems sometimes occur, it makes sense for supervisors to have support and space to reflect on their supervisory practice. Roth and Pilling (2008) discuss the benefits of having space for reflection on practice to foster the metacompetences of supervision. However, there is a paucity within the literature and lack of clarity from professional bodies about what this should entail (Milne, 2009). How supervisors receive support for their supervision practice will vary. Novice supervisors will often receive supervision from an experienced supervisor during their supervision training, but as supervisors become more experienced, supervisory supervision is often incorporated into clinical supervision. This might pose problems, for example, with clinical work often needing to be prioritised. Group supervision of supervision can be a useful format for experienced supervisors with a more collegial and consultative purpose. This can be facilitated by a senior supervisor or supervisors can facilitate the group themselves. Peer supervision groups run the risk of becoming cosy and colluding, and Borders (1991) recommends that groups explicitly address this with agreement for a balance between support and challenging interventions being a requirement. Whatever format supervision of supervision takes, there should be a structured approach with clear parameters being set, including playing recordings of supervision sessions. Supervisor beliefs might benefit from being explored, particularly when difficulties arise in the supervision relationship. The Interpersonal Schema Worksheet (Moorey, 2013) has been adapted for supervisors to complete: as with therapists, this is a non-threatening way to elicit supervisor beliefs that are potentially interfering with the process of supervision. The example shown in Figure 19.3 is that of a novice supervisor of the PTSD case discussed earlier. The supervisor became irritated with the supervisee in one of their meetings and took this to

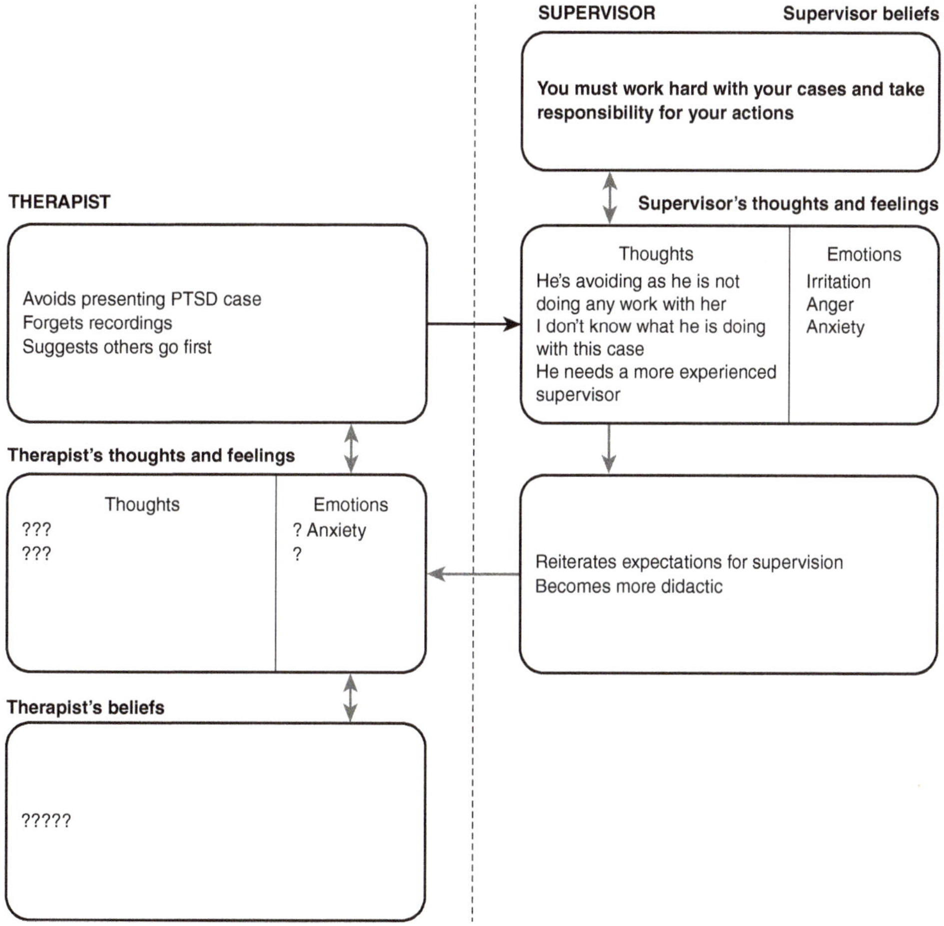

Figure 19.3 Supervisor's Interpersonal Schema Worksheet during supervision

supervisory supervision. By using the adapted Interpersonal Schema Worksheet, the supervisor was able to see that her own excessive standards were being activated and had impeded supervision, with her becoming didactic rather than enquiring (see Figure 19.3).

The supervisor could see this was most likely creating a harsher, punitive type of environment where the supervisee would not feel safe enough to discuss what was happening with this case. She was quickly able to formulate a plan for the next supervision session and, by being empathic and inquiring, created a safe space for the supervisee to discuss his anxiety about his ability to do reliving. With the help of supervision of supervision, the supervisor also decided to generate a new, more adaptive, belief which helped her transition from clinician to supervisor (see Figure 19.4).

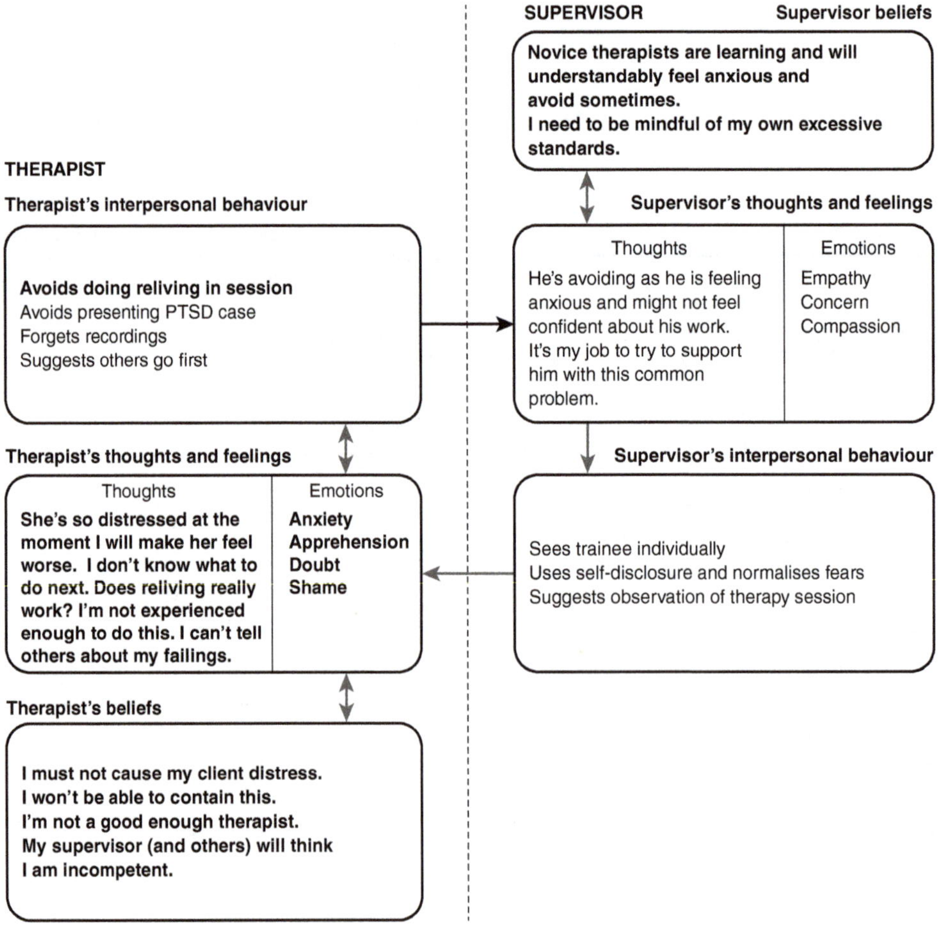

Figure 19.4 Supervisor's Interpersonal Schema Worksheet after supervision

CHAPTER SUMMARY

This chapter is inevitably a brief foray into the complex, challenging and rewarding subject of how the therapeutic relationship in CBT can be addressed in supervision. We have addressed it from the perspective of how supervision can help the supervisee understand their negative reactions to their patients. As such, it builds on the first three chapters of this book and looks at the same issues from the supervisor's perspective. In particular, we have taken the example of Piers and expanded on the interpersonal formulation in Chapter 3. In the second half of the chapter, we considered the supervisory relationship itself and have given some examples of commonly occurring challenges to effective supervision and some approaches to overcome them.

FURTHER READING

Corrie S and Lane DA (2015) CBT *Supervision*. London: Sage.

Padesky CA (1996) Developing cognitive therapist competency: Teaching and supervision models. In: Salkovskis PM (ed) Frontiers of Cognitive Therapy. New York: Guilford Press, pp. 266–292.

REFERENCES

Alfonsson S, Spännargård Å, Parling T, Andersson G and Lundgren T (2017) The effects of clinical supervision on supervisees and patients in cognitive-behavioral therapy: a study protocol for a systematic review. *Systematic Reviews 6*(1): 94.

Bennett-Levy J, Thwaites R, Haarhoff B and Perry H (2015) *Experiencing CBT from the Inside Out: A Self-Practice/Self-Reflection Workbook for Therapists*. New York: The Guilford Press.

Borders LD (1991) A systematic approach to peer group supervision. *Journal of Counselling & Development 69*: 248–252.

Bordin ES (1979) The generalizability of the psychoanalytic concept of the working alliance. *Psychotherapy: Theory, Research, Practice 16*: 252–260.

Bordin ES (1983) A working alliance model of supervision. *The Counseling Psychologist 11*: 35–42.

Corrie S and Lane DA (2015) *CBT Supervision*. London: Sage.

Gordon PK (2012) Ten steps to cognitive behavioural supervision. *The Cognitive Behaviour Therapist 5*(4): 71–82.

Kolb DA (1984) *Experiential Learning*. New Jersey: Prentice-Hall.

Leahy RL (2012) *Overcoming Resistance in Cognitive Therapy*. New York: Guilford Press.

Liese BS and Beck JS (1997) Cognitive therapy supervision. In: Watkins, CE Jr (ed) *Handbook of Psychotherapy Supervision*. Hoboken, NJ: John Wiley & Sons Inc, pp. 114–133.

Lomax JW, Andrews LB, Burruss JW and Moorey S (2005) Psychotherapy supervision. In: Gabbard GO, Beck JS and Holmes J (eds) *Oxford Textbook of Psychotherapy*. Oxford: Oxford University Press, pp. 495–506.

Mannix KA, Blackburn IM, Garland A, Gracie J, Moorey S, Reid B, Standard S and Scott J (2006) Effectiveness of brief training in cognitive behaviour therapy techniques for palliative care practitioners. *Palliative Medicine 20*(6): 579–584.

Milne D (2008) CBT Supervision: From Reflexivity to Specialization. *Behavioural and Cognitive Psychotherapy 36*: 779–786.

Milne DL (2009) *Evidence-Based Clinical Supervision: Principles and Practice*. Leicester: BPS Blackwell.

Milne DL and Reiser RP (2017) *A Manual for Evidence-Based CBT Supervision*. Chicester, West Sussex: John Wiley & Sons.

Moorey S (2013) The Interpersonal Cycle Worksheet. *Cognitive Connections*. Available at: http://www.cognitiveconnections.co.uk (accessed 22 May 2017).

Newman CF (1998) Therapeutic and Supervisory Relationships in CBT. *Journal of Cognitive Psychotherapy 12*: 95–108.

Padesky CA (1996) Developing cognitive therapist competency: Teaching and supervision models. In: Salkovskis PM (ed) *Frontiers of Cognitive Therapy*. New York: Guilford Press, pp. 266–292.

Roth AD and Pilling S (2008) *A competence framework for the supervision of psychological therapies*. Available at: http://www.ucl.ac.uk/pals/research/cehp/research-groups/core/competence-frameworks/Supervision_of_Psychological_Therapies (accessed 10 February 2018).

Vygotsky LS (1978) *Mind in Society: the development of higher psychological processes*. Cambridge, MA: Harvard University Press.

Watkins CE (2014) The supervisory alliance: A half century of theory, practice, and research in critical perspective. *American Journal of Psychotherapy 68*(1): 19–55.

INDEX

Page numbers in **bold** indicate tables and in *italic* indicate figures.